ROMANTICISM, RACE, AND
IMPERIAL CULTURE, 1780–1834

**Books are to be returned on or before
the last date below.**

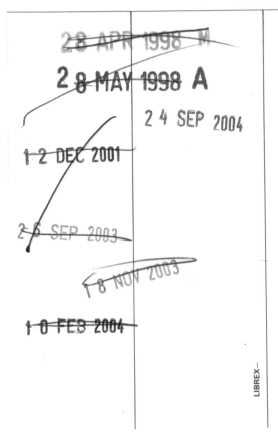

28 APR 1998 M

2 8 MAY 1998 A

2 4 SEP 2004

1 2 DEC 2001

2 6 SEP 2003

8 NOV 2003

1 0 FEB 2004

LIBREX—

Romanticism, Race, and Imperial Culture, 1780–1834

Edited by

ALAN RICHARDSON

AND SONIA HOFKOSH

INDIANA

UNIVERSITY

PRESS

Bloomington and
Indianapolis

The paper used in this publication meets the minimum
requirements of American National Standard for Information
Sciences—Permanence of Paper for Printed Library Materials,
ANSI Z39.48-1984.

Manufactured in the United States of America

Library of Congress Cataloging-in-Publication Data

Romanticism, race, and imperial culture, 1780–1834 / edited by Alan
Richardson and Sonia Hofkosh ; contributors, Laura Doyle . . . [et
al].

p.   cm.

Includes bibliographical references and index.

ISBN 0-253-33212-5 (cloth : alk. paper)

1. English literature—19th century—History and criticism.
2. Imperialism—Great Britain—History—19th century.   3. English
literature—18th century—History and criticism.   4. Imperialism—
Great Britain—History—18th century.   5. Romanticism—Great
Britain   6. Imperialism in literature.   7. Colonies in literature.
8. Race in literature.   I. Richardson, Alan, date.
II. Hofkosh, Sonia.   III. Doyle, Laura.

PR457.R6447   1996

820.9′358—dc20   95-48392

1   2   3   4   5   01   00   99   98   97   96

CONTENTS

III. Resituating Romanticism

ACKNOWLEDGMENTS

We wish to thank Robert Sloan, our editor at Indiana University Press, for his encouragement and advice as we began this project and for the confidence and support that made its completion possible. We also thank Cindy Ballard, Terry L. Cagle, and John Vollmer for their careful work on the production and editing of the volume. Our greatest single debt is to Marlon Ross for his painstaking and revelatory reading of the manuscript, a reading as generous as it was rigorous. Finally, we thank Deborah Blacker and Jonathon Hulbert for their support at every stage of our work together.

Alan Richardson
Sonia Hofkosh

ROMANTICISM, RACE, AND
IMPERIAL CULTURE, 1780–1834

Introduction

WORDSWORTH AND COLERIDGE'S avant-garde *Lyrical Ballads* of 1798 is rarely thought of in relation to European imperialism, despite the lines on the Spanish "discovery" and penetration of the Americas in "The Foster-Mother's Tale," the depictions of British colonial wars and their consequences in "The Female Vagrant" and "The Mad Mother," or the ethnographic exoticism of "The Complaint of a Forsaken Indian Woman." Opening the volume, "The Rime of the Ancyent Marinere" would have given its early readers a strong intimation of the collaboration's engagement with Britain's global ambitions and anxieties, telling (in the words of the "Argument") how a "Ship having passed the Line was driven by Storms to the cold Country towards the South Pole; and how from thence she made her course to the tropical Latitude of the Great Pacific Ocean; and of the strange things that befell."[1] With the voyages of Captains Byron and Cook—and also Bligh—still very much on the British public mind, the fortunes of the fleet under Nelson (which would in 1798 shatter Napoleon's Oriental ambitions at Aboukir) a daily concern, and continuing British domination of the transatlantic slave trade a festering barb in the national conscience, the trans-global drama of guilt and retribution that Coleridge sets in uncharted seas could hardly have failed to touch on public preoccupations with Britain's imperial destiny and fears that London might inexorably go the way of Rome. And yet few poems have been so relentlessly psychologized as "The Ancyent Marinere." Elaborated in terms of the artistic imagination, private psychological guilt, the col-

1

lective or personal unconscious, the slippage of the subject in language, or the dilemmas of literary interpretation, readings of the poem have hardly considered the Mariner *as* a mariner, nor has the tension between his outlandish ventures and his return to "his own Country" been correlated with the revision of "English" identity in the context of a growing maritime empire of far-flung islands, trading-posts, and stretches of coastline on five continents.[2]

Such gaps in the reception of one of Romanticism's echtcanonical poems are symptomatic of a larger absence in Romantic studies generally, an absence which the essays gathered in this volume seek to help outline and fill in. In contrast to the attention scholars in eighteenth-century and Victorian studies have paid to issues of imperialism and colonialism since the publication of Said's *Orientalism* in 1978, Romanticists have been slow to reconsider the field in specific relation to the growth of the second British empire, the slave trade, or the development of modern racist and imperialist ideologies, despite the unarguable relevance of these matters to British culture in the late eighteenth and early nineteenth centuries.[3] Such hesitancy may well reflect a long-standing (and itself "Romantic") emphasis within Romantic studies on the individual mind, and on the creative, questing, interiorizing imagination.[4] Ironically, this approach to Romanticism is exemplified by the very work that, in its attention to travel and exploration narratives, literary Orientalism and exoticism, popular and recondite works of geography and world history, might instead have stimulated a global approach to canonical British Romanticism long ago—J. L. Lowes's *The Road to Xanadu* (1927). But Lowes, while attesting to the range and intensity of Coleridge's reading on matters of imperial moment as well as exotic appeal, had set out to celebrate the sublime contraction of the "four quarters of the globe" into a freestanding work of imagination, a testament to the "imperially present" mind of the Romantic artist rather than the discursive presence of the Empire in the seemingly autonomous literary work.[5]

Lowes's precedent of exalting the synthetic imagination of the Romantic poet at the expense of considering the geopolitical implications of Oriental and other "alien" references and motifs remained long unchallenged, even by those few critics who kept the study of Romantic Orientalism current. While deeply critical of Lowes's "wrong-headed" associationist method, E. S. Shaffer's study of "Biblical Orientalism" in *"Kubla Khan" and the Fall of Jerusalem* (1975) nevertheless follows Lowes in celebrating Coleridge's "syncretist technique," his seeming power of rendering "all of Asia" present "in one spot."[6] In *India and the Romantic Imagination* (1987), John Drew similarly relies upon notions of "syncretism," and credits the "more imaginative" Romantic writers with a superior capacity for "absorbing and rendering coherent" the "influence from the Orient" made available by Sir William Jones and other Orientalist scholars.[7] Aijaz Ahmad has trenchantly diagnosed this "idea of the availability of all cultures of the world for consumption by an individual consciousness" as inseparable from the history of European colonialism: "one did not have to belong, one could simply float, effortlessly, through a supermarket of packaged and commodified cultures, ready to be consumed."[8] The persistence of such thinking (what might be termed the "Banana Republic" mentality) is also evident in Daniel Watkins's "social and historical" study of Byron's "Eastern tales," which argues that Byron "imagines whole societies" against a virtually blank "exotic" backdrop. This Romantic poet left his "social reality" behind, it seems, at some point west of Albania.[9]

As against such uncritical instrumentalization (when not wholesale erasure) of non-"Western" histories and cultures and the material and ideological relations that brought them within the ken of Romantic-era British writers, Marilyn Butler's matter-of-fact approach in an important series of recent essays is refreshing: "Whatever the East came afterwards to represent as an abstraction," she roundly declares, "in English culture in the Napoleonic war period it is also the site of a pragmatic contest among the nations for world power"; the "place of a poem's setting means what it says, and the time is always in some sense the present."[10] Butler contends that "Exotic Romanticism"—"those forays into the Third World which the academic consensus has long deemed marginal"—in fact grows out of a central Romantic concern with the "empires of the world and their imagined overthrow." Her work is consonant with the project of historians who have begun to detail how the late eighteenth- and early nineteenth-century construction of a British "nation" and of "British" identity was at once impelled by and defined against the "triumphs, profits, and Otherness represented by a massive overseas empire."[11] The half-century from 1780–1830, roughly corresponding with literary Romanticism as conventionally delimited, began in a mood of imperial crisis following the loss of the thirteen American colonies, the mismanagement of Bengal, and slave rebellions in the West Indies, but went on to witness the "massive expansion of British dominion, of techniques of governance and exploitation": by 1820 200 million people—over a quarter of the world population—would come under British domination.[12] During this period British rule over India was consolidated, Canada was aggressively developed, colonialism began in earnest in Australia, South Africa, Sierra Leone, Ceylon, and Java, and the Caribbean possessions (or "sugar islands") were augmented with the seizure of Trinidad and Tobago, St. Lucia, and British Guyana. These years were also marked by

a wrenching national debate over slavery, the abolition of British involvement in the slave trade (1807) and the ending of slavery in the
British colonies (1834), the development of imperialist and anti-imperialist ideologies on the part of British writers, and the emergence of
"modern racist categories."[13]

The considerable effect of these vast social and geopolitical developments upon Romantic-era British literature remains largely unana-
lyzed, despite longstanding associations between Romanticism and
literary exoticism, primitivism, and Orientalism.[14] Romanticists have
similarly failed to examine the widespread use in this period of many
written forms—from epic poetry to exploration narratives—in defining and justifying (when not decrying) the empire for a growing bourgeois public.[15] These are serious oversights. Many of the rhetorical
strategies, literary motifs, and cultural myths of modern colonialism
and racism took characteristic form during the years 1780–1834, and
scholars who can bring paradigms drawn from the study of colonial
discourse and post-colonial theory to bear on a wide range of Romantic-era texts are well positioned to begin filling in these gaps in the
history of British (imperial) culture. Further, at a time when definitions
of Romanticism and even its validity as a critical term have again been
called into question, analyses of how literature in this era is implicated
in nationalist, racist, and colonialist discourses should play a major and
productive role in the ongoing revaluation of the boundaries of British
"Romanticism."

That the imperialist enterprise may appear "obscurely derived and
motivated" in the Romantic era when compared with the "consistency
and density" of colonialist activity and discourse later in the nineteenth
century also impels this volume and the shifting emphases within Romantic studies which it represents and aims to extend.[16] Precisely because the discourses of race and colonialism were still in the process of
formation in the late eighteenth and early nineteenth centuries, anxieties are often more overt, contradictions and gaps more visible, and
distinct tendencies and competing ideologies have a rougher edge, not
yet codified and smoothed over as they will be at the height of the British empire later in the century. Sara Suleri, among others, has written
persuasively (in particular relation to Burke) about the incoherence,
terror, mutual vulnerability, and even (at times) mutual respect that
mark the cultural products of colonizer and colonized alike in what she
terms the "migrant moment" of colonial encounter.[17] British Romanticism itself—associated as it has been with the sublime, the exotic, and
the "primitive," and more recently implicated in the founding of an
"English" cultural identity and the grounding of a wishfully autonomous form of subjectivity, at once defensively isolated and yet aggres-

sively incorporative—may be interpreted as a response to the collective experience, ideological requirements, and deforming effects of imperialism.[18] Indeed, its long-overlooked interrelations with the British imperial enterprise may help account for some of the contradictions which have vexed attempts to define Romanticism as a critical term: it is associated at once with the local and the exotic, with a "blood and soil" mentality and with post-Enlightenment universalism, with selectively recovering a specific "English" or "Briton" identity and cultural past and with a global or "international" subject matter, with the domestic (or containing) and the sublime (or uncontainable). Much as historians have come to see the formation of "English" identity in this era as a function of the growth of the "British" empire, Romanticism may come to be seen as inseparably and dialectically related to the global culture of colonialism and empire building, and Romantic discourse as an artifact, in Mary Louise Pratt's formulation, of the "contact zones" between Europe and its "subordinated others."[19]

In critically addressing these issues in the essays that follow, the contributors to this volume make common cause with those few scholars—Butler, John Barrell, Nigel Leask, most prominently—working from within Romantic studies to disclose the long obscured interrelations of British Romanticism with British imperialism, as well as with those who, like Suleri, Gauri Viswanathan, and Javed Majeed, have brought critical methods and paradigms from colonial and post-colonial studies to bear on Romantic-era texts and practices without explicitly employing (or challenging) the categories of academic Romanticism. This is not to say, however, that our essayists constitute a unified argument or rely on a single shared methodology, nor that they fail to find room for revision and disagreement as well as grateful acknowledgment in grappling with the critical precedents set by the scholars just named. Like Barrell, Leask, or Majeed, they may locate "anxieties" in the literary construction of the exotic where earlier scholars found a lordly syncretism or leisurely escapism, but each demonstrates that there are as many ways to configure such anxieties (*"productive"* as well as disruptive in regard to the "imperial will")[20] as there are contributors to the volume. They might agree with Butler that "geographical considerations should be taken at face value" in the texts they address, but they are no less interested in the imaginary distortions and cultural reconstructions with which those same texts seek to tame, instrumentalize, or redirect the geopolitical desires their settings evoke.[21] Barrell's pioneering work on De Quincey provides a valuable model here, with its refusal to underestimate either the "primal and private" elements of De Quincey's oriental fantasies *or* the "fully social guilt" they equally serve to rationalize and displace at a time when "imperialist fantasies" became "all-pervasive in the national imagination." For Barrell, the exotic or colonial setting can figure simultaneously as a "blank screen" for the projection of whatever Europeans, "individually or collectively, wanted to displace or represent as other to themselves" and still remain "just what it appears to be," the locus of imperialist anxiety and guilt.[22]

Barrell's work is also exemplary in its emphasis (inspired in large part by the work of Homi Bhabha) on the "*hybrid*" character of colonialist identity and discourse, the colonialist writer's uneasy awareness that his or her relation with the colonial other is, "like that of an imperial power with its colonial 'dependencies,' " a relation of mutual interdependence "at best," which "can no longer be thought of in terms of a safe transaction between a self and an other."[23] Similarly, both Lisa Lowe and Suleri have challenged the binary or "alteritist" models derived from an insufficiently critical reading of Said's *Orientalism*; they underscore instead the "conditions of heterogeneity, multiplicity, and nonequivalence" marking colonialist discourses and practices, and the "productive disordering of binary dichotomies" which the colonial narrative may enact in giving form to the "anxiety of empire."[24] Said himself, with a nod to the critiques of Lowe and Suleri, has come to disavow the "binary oppositions dear to the nationalist and imperialist enterprise." His work now recognizes that, particularly in the wake of the imperialist era, "all cultures are involved in one another," "hybrid, heterogeneous, extraordinarily differentiated, and unmonolithic." Attending to the resistance—armed, cultural, and political—which "*always*" met the European imperialist in some form, Said exposes the opposition of an active and dominating West to a "supine or inert non-Western native" as itself a construct of the colonial project.[25]

The contributors to this volume similarly register the colonial or racial encounter as a two-way exchange marked not only by domination but also by subaltern resistance and mutual vulnerability, and they understand the cultural identity of the colonizer as no more unitary, stable, or immune to the effects of the encounter than that of the colonized. For example, Saree Makdisi's contrasting readings of *Childe Harold* and *Alastor* trace a broader discursive transition in the cultural processes of imperialism, suggesting that the shifting representations of the Orient in the early work of Byron and Shelley also indicate the re-invention of "Europe" itself. In her essay on Wordsworth, Alison Hickey locates the colonial encounter in that familiar Romantic territory, the imagination, but finds there that the resistance of the other subverts the imperial practice of subsuming difference into identity and displays the penetrability of the conceptual borders of self and of nation.

Among the oppositions which the following essays thus put into question is the fundamental one between center and periphery. In a variety of ways, these essays help substantiate Pratt's contention that "metropolitan culture" is not only received selectively and critically by (rather than seamlessly imposed upon) "subjugated peoples," but that, in cultural as well as geographical terms, the periphery defines the imperial metropolis no less than the metropolis seeks to delimit and control its peripheries, the ideology of the "civilizing mission" serving to blind the colonizer to the process of "transculturation from the colonies to the metropolis."[26] Gauri Viswanathan's *Masks of Conquest* sets an important precedent in this regard, showing in detail how such a seemingly central practice as the institutional study of a canon of literary works in English was anticipated and subtly informed by educational initiatives in the British colonies in India, which served as a "laboratory for testing educational ideas."[27] Whereas Pratt claims European Romanticism as itself a prime instance of "transculturation" from the (apparent) margins to the imperial center, Viswanathan suggests how the development of a vernacular "Literature" along with institutions for its dissemination—so intricately bound up with high Romantic ideology (exemplified, for instance, in Coleridge's "clerisy")—is itself steeped in a colonial context.[28] Moira Ferguson's essay in this collection specifies such inter-saturation in her discussion of the educational program Hannah Kilham devised for England and West Africa "in partial response to the ravages of slavery and the enforced linguistic heterogeneity of Sierra Leone" (chapter 5). Rejecting "standard eurocentric views of Africans," Kilham's dictionary "defines Englishness in African terms."

This opposition of center and periphery is also challenged by the essays gathered here in their collective reevaluation of what is central or canonical to British Romanticism and what is incidental, marginal, or "minor." Laura Doyle's examination of the racial dimension of the sublime aesthetics informing Romanticism and Anne Mellor's analysis of the portrayals of slavery in the plays of Joanna Baillie and Maria Edgeworth, for example, in their different ways implicitly revise Mary Jacobus's forceful argument that Wordsworth's *Prelude* is "exemplary" of "high Romantic discourse" in its necessary "historical repression" of the British slave trade. However true of *The Prelude*, such an argument relies both on a particular account of Wordsworth's career that prioritizes that poem, long unpublished, over such public poems as the sonnets to Clarkson, to Toussaint L'Ouverture, and "September 1, 1802" ("The Banished Negroes"), and on a version of the Romantic canon that effectively ignores the anti-slavery verses of Coleridge, Southey, Blake, Byron, and Shelley, as well as the abolitionist poetry, highly visible and valued in its time, of such contemporaries as Helen Maria

Williams, Anna Barbauld, Anne Yearsley, Hannah More, and James Montgomery.[29] Much as the newly historicized attention to literary Orientalism in the work of Butler, Leask, and Majeed has brought once celebrated writers such as Southey, Thomas Moore, and Sir William Jones back into critical view, Nancy Goslee's essay on Felicia Hemans's complex of racial stereotypes, Balachandra Rajan's discussion of novels by Elizabeth Hamilton and Sydney Owenson, and Alan Richardson's reading of Helen Maria Williams's epic, *Peru*, remind us that writers now neglected were at one time thought close to the "center," and that their engagement with questions of empire made no small part of their contemporary claim to cultural centrality. Indeed, one of the principal contributions this collection hopes to make is to demonstrate how these and other newly "recovered" women writers were by no means peripheral to the literary culture of their era, however marginal later reconstructions of a Romantic canon have rendered their voices.

The work represented in this volume similarly refuses to be bound by a post-Romantic construction of the literary or its hierarchy of genres, variously approaching such "extra-literary" modes as exploration narrative, political philosophy, abolitionist tract, and slave autobiography with the same attention to image, form, and rhetoric that is accorded to the novel and to lyric and narrative poetic texts, which are in turn valued for their ideological and polemical complexities no less than for their strictly "literary" properties. Ashton Nichols's exegesis of Mungo Park's *Travels in the Interior Districts of Africa* elaborates the debt literary formulations (such as the Byronic hero) owe to the explorer's quasi-anthropological prototype. Joseph Lew's inclusive style of reading *The Giaour* engages fragments of Colonel Welsh's *Military Reminiscences*, William Ward's ethnographic *History, Literature, and Mythology of the Hindoos*, and Wilberforce's parliamentary address on suttee delivered to the House of Commons in 1813. In her consideration of *The Interesting Narrative of Olaudah Equiano*, Sonia Hofkosh finds Romanticism's motivating assumptions about value modeled in the language of political economy.

Claiming a new centrality for writers, movements, and genres long held marginal to Romantic studies, this collection aims to demonstrate how inextricably such mainstays of English Romantic tradition as the imagination, the sublime, the self-possessed individual, the notion of Englishness itself, are linked to the material and ideological operation of a burgeoning empire. In a range of local instances—textual and geographic—Romanticism is seen to be invested in the categories empire evolves and deploys, political categories that are often gendered as well as racially construed. As the essay by Deidre Lynch establishes in relation to Burke and to women's novels of the early nineteenth century, the articulation of a national idiom also emplots a sexual scenario. Rajani Sudan's discussion of Wollstonecraft likewise uncovers the maternal function in the construction of a discourse of national identity. Together, the essays gathered in this volume disclose some of the intersecting modalities of gender and race inscribed in the elaboration and empowerment of Romanticism *as* imperial culture. In pointing to such intersections, we are concerned to trace the beginnings of the cultural codes that will frame British hegemony through the nineteenth century even as we recognize the ways in which that hegemony is tested, resisted, and revised in its early, Romantic formulations.

As a collection, the volume is arranged to foster dialogue and debate among the various formulations thus elaborated by its contributors. Rajan's reading of the "double seduction" of the Englishwoman in the colonies, for example, offers an implicit critique of Ferguson's history of Hannah Kilham's educational mission in Sierra Leone. Ferguson's discussion itself supplements Nichols's account of Mungo Park's " 'objective' discourse" by highlighting the function of gender in the rhetoric of the travel narrative. Lew and Makdisi trace divergent trajectories for the conjunction of orientalism and poetic form. And embedded in the essays by Richardson and Hickey are opposing arguments about the status of romance as conservative or destabilizing in relation to epic ambition. The dissenting voices thus heard both within and among these discussions will, we hope, provoke further dialogue and contention on the array of concerns the following essays help to define and begin to address.

NOTES

1. William Wordsworth and Samuel Taylor Coleridge, *Lyrical Ballads 1798*, ed. W. J. B. Owen, 2nd ed. (Oxford: Oxford University Press, 1969), 7.

2. In a recently published book that helps rectify this relative silence in Coleridge studies, Patrick J. Keane similarly notes that "The Ancyent Marinere" "remains for virtually all its myriad readers utterly ahistorical," *Coleridge's Submerged Politics: The Ancient Mariner and Robinson Crusoe* (Columbia: University of Missouri Press, 1994), 2. Keane also acknowledges those few earlier studies, by William Empson, Malcolm Ware, and J. B. Ebbatson, that raised issues of imperial expansion and the slave trade in relation to Coleridge but, until quite recently, remained largely ignored by other scholars and critics.

3. Edward Said, *Orientalism* (New York: Vintage, 1979). For critical overviews of British imperial activity and of Britain's role in the slave trade, colonial slavery, and their eventual abolition, see C. A. Bayly, *Imperial Meridian: The British Empire and the World 1780–1830* (London: Longman, 1989) and Robin Blackburn, *The Overthrow of Colonial Slavery 1776–1848* (London: Verso, 1988).

4. See Jerome J. McGann, *The Romantic Ideology: A Critical Investigation* (Chicago: University of Chicago Press, 1983).

5. John Livingston Lowes, *The Road to Xanadu: A Study in the Ways of the Imagination* (Boston: Houghton Mifflin, 1927), 134, 413.

6. E. S. Shaffer, *"Kubla Khan" and the Fall of Jerusalem: The Mythological School in Biblical Criticism and Secular Literature 1770–1880* (Cambridge: Cambridge University Press, 1975), 138, 142, 165. "The poles converge and the Line shrinks to a point." Lowes writes in yet more grandiose terms: "Into the warp of the voyage—the great historic route of discovery and adventure from Magellan to Captain Cook—was woven a woof the threads of which were caught up from the four quarters of the globe" (*Road*, 134). Cf. Shaffer's comment on the "sense of the immediacy, accessibility, and disposibility of the whole of Asia" in the writings of Sir William Jones (117).

7. John Drew, *India and the Romantic Imagination* (Delhi: Oxford University Press, 1987), 232, 253, 236.

8. Aijaz Ahmad, *In Theory: Classes, Nations, Literatures* (London: Verso, 1992), 128.

9. Daniel P. Watkins, *Social Relations in Byron's Eastern Tales* (Rutherford: Associated University Presses, 1987), 34, 16–17.

10. Marilyn Butler, "The Orientalism of Byron's *Giaour*," *Byron and the Limits of Fiction*, ed. Bernard Beatty and Vincent Newey (Totowa, N.J.: Barnes and Noble, 1988), 78.

11. Marilyn Butler, "Repossessing the Past: The Case for an Open Literary History," *Rethinking Historicism: Critical Readings in Romantic History*, ed. Marjorie Levinson et al. (Oxford: Basil Blackwell, 1989), 80, 83. Cf. Linda Colley, "Britishness and Otherness: An Argument," *Journal of British Studies* 31 (1992): 309–29 and *Britons: Forging the Nation 1707–1807* (New Haven: Yale University Press, 1992).

12. P. J. Marshall, "Empire and Authority in the Later Eighteenth Century," *Journal of Imperial and Commonwealth History* 15 (1987): 105–22 and Bayly, *Imperial Meridian*, 3.

13. Mary Louise Pratt, *Imperial Eyes: Travel Writing and Transculturation* (London: Routledge, 1992), 45. For two studies bearing on the literary and cultural impact of slavery in Romantic-era Britain, which have (until quite recently) rarely been cited by Romanticists, see Wylie Sypher, *Guinea's Captive Kings: British Anti-Slavery Literature of the XVIIIth Century* (Chapel Hill: University of North Carolina Press, 1942) and Eva Beatrice Dykes, *The Negro in English Romantic Thought: A Study in Sympathy for the Oppressed* (Washington: Associated Press, 1942).

14. Raymond Schwab had in fact redefined Romanticism in terms of an "Oriental Renaissance" in his study of 1950, *The Oriental Renaissance: Europe's Rediscovery of India and the East 1680–1880*, trans. Gene Patterson-Black and Victor Reinking, foreword by Edward W. Said (New York: Columbia University Press, 1984), but this work was effectively ignored, as Said has pointed out, by "Anglo-American authorities" on Romanticism (vii). Another useful French contribution, similarly passed over by Anglo-American critics, is Collete Le Yaouanc, *L'Orient dans la Poesie anglaise de l'epoque romantique 1798–1824* (Paris: Champion, 1975).

15. "Neither imperialism nor colonialism is a simple act of accumulation and acquisition. Both are supported or perhaps even impelled by impressive cultural formations that include notions that certain territories and people *require* and beseech domination, as well as forms of knowledge affiliated with domination." Edward W. Said, *Culture and Imperialism* (New York: Knopf, 1993), 9.

16. Said, *Culture and Imperialism*, 10.

17. Sara Suleri, *The Rhetoric of English India* (Chicago: University of Chicago Press, 1992), 5.

18. These issues are usefully broached by David Simpson in *Romanticism, Nationalism, and the Revolt against Theory* (Chicago: University of Chicago Press, 1993).

19. Pratt, *Imperial Eyes*, 6, 137–38.

20. Nigel Leask, *British Romantic Writers and the East: Anxieties of Empire* (Cambridge: Cambridge University Press, 1992), 2–3; see also John Barrell, *The Infection of Thomas De Quincey: A Psychopathology of Imperialism* (New Haven: Yale University Press, 1991), 19–20 and Javed Majeed, *Ungoverned Imaginings: James Mill's* The History of British India *and Orientalism* (Oxford: Clarendon, 1992), 102.

21. Butler, "Orientalism," 78.

22. Barrell, *Infection*, 21, 8, 20. Cf. Leask's contention that the "anxieties and transports of Romanticism . . . are as much the product of geopolitics as metaphysics" (*British Romantic Writers*, 12).

23. Barrell, *Infection*, 18. See also Homi K. Bhabha, *The Location of Culture* (London: Routledge, 1994), 31–39.

24. Lisa Lowe, *Critical Terrains: French and British Orientalism* (Ithaca: Cornell University Press, 1991), 24 and Suleri, *Rhetoric*, 4.

25. Said, *Culture and Imperialism*, xii, xxiv–xxv.

26. Pratt, *Imperial Eyes*, 6.

27. Gauri Viswanathan, *Masks of Conquest: Literary Study and British Rule in India* (New York: Columbia University Press, 1989), 8.

28. Pratt, *Imperial Eyes*, 137–41.

29. Mary Jacobus, "Geometric Science and Romantic History: or Wordsworth, Newton, and the Slave-Trade," *Romanticism Writing and Difference: Essays on* The Prelude (Oxford: Clarendon, 1989), 69, 90. The importance of the anti-slavery movement for canonical Romantic writers (amply documented in the works by Sypher and Dykes cited above) is stressed by Patrick Brantlinger in *Rule of Darkness: British Literature and Imperialism, 1830–1914* (Cornell: Cornell University Press, 1988), 175; for Romantic-era women writers and the anti-slavery theme, see Moira Ferguson's groundbreaking *Subject to Others: British Women Writers and Colonial Slavery, 1670–1834* (London: Routledge, 1992).

PART I

Race, Gender, and the Romantic Construction of English National Identity

One

LAURA DOYLE

The Racial Sublime

ALTHOUGH BISHOP PERCY'S *Reliques of Ancient English Poetry* may seem by now only an antiquarian's text, in it lies a neglected key to the racial interiors of both Romanticism and Western imperialism. As most scholars have noted at least in passing, *Reliques* undoubtedly had "a profound effect" on Romantic writers. Wordsworth considered it formative of his "taste and nature tendencies," while in general "Wordsworth, Southey, and Coleridge vie[d] with each other in commending the *Reliques,* and in acknowledging poetical obligations to their collector."[1] Percy's collection of early English poetry initiates an era in which it would become merely the most cited of many such publications of "barbarian" poetry.

But what cultural nerve did these volumes touch? What determined the deep appeal of the poems' nature, warrior, and romance sensibilities? The common assumption is that this rude yet lyric ancient poetry provided an antidote to the rule-ridden practices of Augustan poets and critics. If, however, we turn a contemporary light on these volumes, and consider them in relation to canonical Romantic writers and late eighteenth-century English history, we discover something more important.

On closer look one discovers in Percy's collection the articulation of a new narrative of origins for English culture: a racial narrative. Together with an increasing number of similar works, *Reliques* helped to establish that the most venerable forms of English language and culture could be traced not only to models which invited imitation but

15

also to race ancestors who bequeathed and evolved particular practices. This retrieval of native ancient literature very likely contributed to that late eighteenth-century shift, traced by Michel Foucault, away from taxonomic or Platonic modes of thought and toward historical or narratival ones—and should prompt us to consider whether race provides the key principle here. More specifically and more certainly, the discursive framing of these volumes for the late eighteenth-century reader (such as in Percy's Prefaces) generated a racial discourse that would become crucial to English political and literary history. In addenda and prefaces these texts fostered a racial nativism that is not exactly nationalism, for as we will see they tell a history of ancient races unidentical with the history of nations. They articulate a domestic or intra-European racialism which contrasts distinct European races and argues claims of superiority.

It may seem odd that at the moment when England became an empire following the Seven Year's War and the defeat of France in various corners of the globe, the English literati apparently turned inward and became preoccupied with local races; but in fact this coincidence of events indicates that the mythology of locally-rooted races was crucial to the imagining of an imperial Englishness. Early Romantic, intra-European racial narratives gave ballast to the ship of empire on its voyage out. Bringing to light the history of what Hannah Arendt once called "race-thinking before racism," we see the folk weight underlying hegemonic racial ideology.[2]

The sublime serves as a pivotal idea in this steadying exchange between folk and imperial race mythologies. Theories of the sublime negotiate the turn in Western aesthetics from classicism to nativism to racialism—ultimately opening the way to mid-nineteenth-century pronouncements that "Race is everything: literature, science, art, in a word, civilization, depend on it" and that "human character, individual or national, is traceable solely to the race to which the individual or nations belongs."[3] Romantic poets and philosophers aligned themselves with the brooding, wild, once-conquered, "Gothic" races of their own lands and then, in an inversion or "subreption" itself figured as sublime, refashioned this savage figure into the imperial, metaphysical, civilized European, fit to conquer and uplift the savages of other lands. In this move, the racial sublime of Romanticism situates itself in the place where nature meets history (in race) and it colonizes that place discursively. As Sara Suleri has also suggested, theories of the sublime thus played their part in the convergence of the literary and the colonial projects.[4]

My aim here to isolate the racial elements of the sublime leaves me little time to treat two aspects of it I consider equally important.

Because I have elsewhere analyzed the interplay of racial and gender myths in Romanticism, and want to introduce new research bearing particularly on race, my gender critique remains implicit and subordinated in this essay.[5] Ideally one would read this piece together with the earlier one. I regret as well that my critical-historical aims require that I neglect attention to the philosophical issues raised by theories of the sublime, for the metaphysical questions at stake in it remain questions which the cultural critic should not ignore. What follows from the act of deconstructing traditional notions of sublimity is a challenge to imagine a reconfigured sublime metaphysics—or, if you will, a somalogics—as critics Patricia Yaeger and Barbara Freeman have begun to do.[6] The following critique of the sublime may clarify another dimension of its problematic politics and so open the way to further revisionary work.

SAXON SUBVERSION

The prehistory of the late eighteenth-century "Gothic" or "Anglo-Saxon revival" begins more than a century before Percy published his *Reliques,* in a context quite remote from poetic notions of the sublime. The earlier setting is on the contrary a religious, legal, and political one in the period of the English Reformation and Revolution. In mounting their opposition to the papacy and the throne, seventeenth-century dissidents recast the debate over property and rights as a discourse of *natural* inheritances, wherein the claims and laws of an indigenous race were said to preempt those of the conquering race. Anglo-Saxonism begins in earnest, in other words, with the myth of the "Norman Yoke" analyzed by historian Christopher Hill.[7]

In the revolutionary period, antiquarian volumes on Anglo-Saxon customs suddenly became powerful political tools. To argue their cases against James I and Charles I, Edward Coke and other lawyers made the *Archaionomia* (a compendium of Anglo-Saxon laws published in 1568), "one of the key books of the common law interpretation."[8] Likewise William Camden's *Remaines of a Greater Worke* (1605) and Richard Verstegan's *A Restitution of Decayed Intelligence* (1605) became fodder in the political and religious battles that transformed England in the seventeenth century, for they lent dissidents historical authority for pitting a "common" English Saxon heritage (understood to derive from the Germanic Goths) against the "noble" French-Norman claims to sovereignty. While earlier accounts of the Anglo-Saxons had stressed either their barbarian and heathen ways or their military weakness before the Normans, Camden celebrated their "warlike, victorious, stiffe, stowt, and rigorous" qualities which were "mellowed and mollified" over time until the Saxons became champions of the "glory of God," carrying

Christianity to the Continent in the eighth century. Verstegan likewise downplayed barbarism in the Saxons, emphasizing instead that they "buylded colleges and schooles for the encrease of learning." Verstegan additionally highlighted the poetic force of the English monosyllable and so anticipated later linguistic debates, expressing "Thankes . . . to God that he that conquered the land could not so conquer the language."[9] These works found their largest audience not in their own day but in the revolutionary decades that followed theirs.

Like the lawyers, religious radicals invoked the "Norman Yoke" in arguing that the beliefs, property, and manners of Anglo-Saxons constituted the true inheritance of England's "common people." The Diggers and the Levellers typically identified themselves with the conquered Anglo-Saxons and cursed that "outlandish Norman bastard" William the Conqueror who had introduced French-Norman language and laws by which "the poor miserable people" were "cheated, undone and destroyed."[10] They appealed to the king to refuse the legacy of this ignoble conquest. The famous Leveller pamphleteer Gerard Winstanley argued in his "Law of Freedom" letter to Oliver Cromwell that "When the Norman power had conquered our forefathers, he took the free use of our English ground from them" and furthermore that "all Kings from his time to Charles, were successors of that conquest, and all laws were made to confirm that conquest."[11] Unless Cromwell undertook more radical reform, Winstanley insisted, he would only be perpetuating this old Norman Yoke. No doubt this racialized political discourse gave special resonance to Sir Henry Holcroft's 1653 translation of Procupius's *History of the Warres of the Emperour Justinian*, with its proclamation that "No government . . . be conferr'd upon strangers in blood / but such only have the place, to whose race it did belong."[12] It is in this political context that the term Gothic, being the generic name for the northern German "nations" or "races" of which the Saxons were one, first came to signify all that is free, strong, and independent.[13]

In the wake of Marxism, we late moderns tend to forget that early modern Anglo-European usage frequently elided the racial and the class vocabularies. As Holcroft's passage suggests, to speak of a racial politics in these early centuries of modern English history is no anachronism. On the contrary, in the class structures of pre-modern European states, "dividing lines of race and class coincided [with] and deepened each other."[14] That is, the early aristocracies of Europe and England were defined by their blood or kin difference from those they ruled, since originally they were made up of the descendants of foreign warriors who had invaded and taken power—as with the Franks who conquered the Gauls in France and in England the French Normans who conquered the Germanic Anglo-Saxons (who had themselves conquered the Celts). Thus in France, after Charlemagne's Frankish army defeated the Gauls, the Prologue of Salic law styled the conquerors in racial terms, deeming the Franks an "Illustrious race, founded by God himself, strong in arms, steadfast in alliance, noble and sound in body."[15] By the sixteenth century, race commonly referred to a noble, ruling class—that which Sir Thomas Sackville describes in *The Mirror of Magistrates* (1563) as a "kinglie race" with "noble blood" and Shakespeare helps to mythologize as the idea of the "lawfull race" that governs (*Antony and Cleopatra* III xiii, 107).[16] It is this history that leads Hannah Arendt to characterize the political conflicts of early modern Europe as those of "a 'race' of aristocrats against a 'nation' of citizens."[17]

Given the particularly common yoking of the words "noble" and "race" (as evidenced as well in the OED's highlighting of this usage) seventeenth-century rehabilitations of the Saxons as an honorable *race* therefore have an edge: to lay claim to a historical racial lineage is in effect to lay claim to nobility, to a preserved history, to precedent, law, and custom—in a word, to culture. To adopt the term race was to use the master's tools against the master, a subversive emulation.[18] Although insistence on the virtues of the Saxons developed amidst a welter of conflicts and controversies in which race was not always the dominant term (over such topics as taxes and church corruption), nonetheless Saxon heritage emerged as a rallying point that could encourage and explain new alliances among secular and religious professionals (e.g. lawyers and ministers) as well as with merchants, peasants, and some nobles. Race, as taken over and developed by the merchant and working classes (though the former group increasingly appropriates this project for itself alone) operated to this degree as a revolutionary, consensus-building notion which would continue to provide ballast for and essentialize national identity until the twentieth century.

Far from being narrowly apolitical or merely a synonym for family, then, invocations of "race" were always broadly political; became more explicitly so in the seventeenth century; and finally in the later eighteenth, as we will see, folded directly and problematically into the hierarchies of modern racism (e.g. between African or Indian and European). To comprehend the dynamics and power not only of modern racial dualities but also of the aesthetic of the sublime as it prepares those dualities, we must stay attuned to the racial resonances that echo from these earlier periods.

Sublime Barbarians

By the early eighteenth century Saxonism waned as an openly political movement, having served its domestic political function of mythologizing the shift of power away from the king and toward Parliament and

the merchant classes. Instead, the mythology of a Saxon origin for English culture was quietly codified in the course of the eighteenth century. In a number of multi-volume histories of England, such as ones
by David Hume and Jonathan Swift, authors typically detailed the
Anglo-Saxon period, spoke of the "wholly German" manners and customs of that people, and celebrated their spirit of "fierce and bold liberty which gave rise to those mutual jealousies and animosities between
them and the Normans."[19] The only other significant eighteenth-century expression of the Saxon-Norman antagonism came in the form
of skirmishes over language, specifically the mission to safeguard
Anglo-Saxon English against the invasion of "gallicisms." Commentators warned that "If we thus naturalize foreign words and foreign subjects, our blood, our manners, and our language will soon be alike adulterated."[20] Most famously, Samuel Johnson undertook his Dictionary
project in part to stop this flow of foreign, particularly French, words
and to redirect English into its proper course. In his Preface he explains
that "Our language, for almost a century, has, by the concurrence of
many causes, been gradually departing from its original Teutonick
character, and deviating towards a Gallick structure and phraseology,
from which it ought to be our endeavor to recall it."[21]

Ironically, in announcing that "The whole Fabrick and scheme of
the English language is Gothick or Teutonick," Johnson fixes in place
one cornerstone of the developing literary edifice from which he otherwise dissociated himself. Gothic and early Romantic poetry would find
no place of honor in the Johnsonian scheme of values. His loyalties
were to higher, timeless, and universal "models," not vernacular, soil-
nurtured, organic "forms." Yet his praise of the Gothic structure of the
English language reflects his inheritance of this quietly integrated
Anglo-Saxon mythology which is implicitly at odds with his classical
values. This tension between loyalty to classical models and to English
traditions finds similar expression in Sir Joshua Reynolds's *Discourses on
Art.* The very occasion of his Discourses is the annual matriculation
ceremony of the Royal Academy of Art, an instition devoted to the
promotion of a national art, and he warns the students against suc-
cumbing to foreign influences. Nonetheless, he deplores any artistic
interest in "particular customs and habits" or in a "dry, Gothic, and
even insipid manner, which attends to the minute accidental discrimi-
nations of particular and individual objects." Only arts representing
"general nature" will "live forever." Arts representing "manners" will
die with those manners.[22]

But, as Reynolds perhaps sensed, the interest in "particular customs
and habits" was increasing, not diminishing, and the arts were feed-
ing and being fed by this interest. In the work of Oliver Goldsmith

we glimpse the late eighteenth-century convergence of discourses that made manners not merely a passing curiosity but a sacred vessel of history and culture—as well as a subject for cultured poetry. His poem "The Traveller, or a Prospect of Society" gives a catalogue of peoples and places, delineating the qualities of the "nobler race" of "the bleak Swiss," the easiness of "the naked Negro," and the "independent" nature of the "Britons." Reviewers praised exactly the concrete particularity of his portraits, so that, in the words of one, when we turn from one nation to the next we feel as if we are encountering "people almost of a different species!"[23] This comment carries a charge in light of the emerging debate over polygenism versus monogenism, or whether the different "races" were merely distinct "varieties" or were radically different species.[24] Goldsmith himself had participated in this discourse in his *History of the Earth*, in which he devotes a chapter to the "Varieties of the Human Race," mainly drawn from the work of the monogenist Buffon who had identified six human types. Meanwhile, in "The Deserted Village" Goldsmith documents, and so attempts to forestall, the displacement of exactly those ancient folk customs that give his national/racial portraits their force.

That Goldsmith wrote both poetic and scientific works is hardly surprising in an age when "disciplines" were not strictly distingished. What *is* noteworthy is the subject common to his two genres: race (or nationality, or what was also called manners).[25] Goldsmith represents an emergent pattern, of which Immanuel Kant provides another example. I will return to Kant later, but for now we can note that he wrote extensively on the sublime aesthetic *and* he was also known as a student of the "temperaments . . . and virtues . . . of national characters"—having his lectures on man collected into a book called *Anthropologie*.[26] Kant's and Goldsmith's convergence of interests marks the tip of a literary-cultural iceberg.

With the publication nearly simultaneously in the 1760s of several powerful texts, together with the triumphant ending of the Seven Year's War, the cultural weather in Britain changed dramatically. The glacial-like incursion of Saxonism that began in the 1660s suddenly in the 1760s appeared in all its mass and depth—showing in full the possibilities for cultural realignment that Goldsmith had begun to realize and the new British empire demanded. The timing was remarkable. In 1762 MacPherson's *Poems of Ossian* struck readers like a thunderbolt (to borrow a favorite sublime image) and as if by electrical magic that same year Richard Hurd published his *Letters on Chivalry and Romance*—a book that legitimated and even venerated such rude, "native" literary forms, deeming them as sublime as those of classical authors. The following year, Hugh Blair consecrated "Ossian" as *the* sublime poet in a dissertation which was thereafter appended to most eighteenth-century editions of *Ossian*. Months later Bishop Percy published his *Reliques of Ancient English Poetry* (1764).

With Hurd, Blair, and Percy, the sublime was turned irrevocably into a new path, one that led not only into haunted forests, bloody battles, goblins and ghosts, but also into a new Western imaginary of racial origins. As if waking from a powerful dream, English writers and readers grasped a rich political unconscious. The old texts had lain dormant but were now ripe for use in the reimagining of Englishness—a youthful, revolutionary yet noble, imperial Englishness with just the right blend of battle-fever, melancholic brooding, and metaphysical reflectivity. Here were materials for the making of a race myth that could figure forth the English as both humble and heroic, sensitive yet superior, an ancient, soil-rooted folk fit to become modern, global conquerors—and they appeared just in time to ease the national identity crisis which Linda Colley suggests characterizes this early imperial period.[27] Most important for scholars of race, we should understand the negative rhetoric of race generated by slavery and mercantilism as formed in a dialectic with this celebratory, sublime rhetoric of the conquered but re-emergent Anglo-Saxon folk race.

In Hurd, we see this mythology in early formation. Pitting the "Gothic" against the Greek in literature, Hurd apparently speaks within the framework of the old ancients vs. moderns literary debate. But he gives the English a new edge by characterizing them as steeped in ancient traditions of their own—"Gothic" traditions. He challenges those who express "perpetual ridicule" of the medieval romances and poetry by suggesting that these dark-age "barbarians have their own [philosophy]."[28] The feudal values of chivalry and military valor indicate a degree of "agreement between the [classical] heroic and the gothic manners" (IV, 27). In fact, "tho' the spirit, passion, rapin, and violence of the two sets of manners were equal, yet there was a dignity, a magnificence, a variety in the feudal, which the other [the Greek] wanted" (VI, 48). In this recast debate, two ancient cultures compete and the native one emerges as not only equal but superior.

Hurd tinges his discussion with racial overtones, invoking Tacitus (as most writers on the Gothic do) and remarking that the "foundation of this refined gallantry was laid in the antient [sic] manners of the German nations" (III, 19). As one of the "German nations" under the Saxons, England is not just a piece of land in Hurd's rhapsodic description, it is a land of quaint "villages" peopled with "Prodigies, Charms, and Enchantments" (VI, 54). It is the soil, birthplace, and legacy of "our forefathers" (VI, 54). It is "enchanted ground, my friend" (VI, 55). This charmed, rough land makes the English "bards . . . more sublime, more terrible, more alarming, than those of the classic fablers" (VI, 55). Enchanted land and inherited customs shape the character of the great English poets, an idea aligned with the developing racialism of contemporary anthropology and echoed as we will see by Wordsworth. Shakespeare's "terrible sublime"—"which not so much the energy of his genius, as the nature of his subject drew from him"—is "more poetical for being Gothic" (VI, 55). Like William Mitford and others who follow him, Hurd lionizes Milton and especially Shakespeare as appreciators and inheritors of the Gothic aesthetic, the true "native" poets of England. Although nurtured on the classical writers, "they both appear, when most inflamed, to have been more particularly rapt with the Gothic fables of chivalry" (VII, 56). For the latter have "by their nature and genius, the advantage of the [former] in producing the sublime" (VII, 60). The "Gothic language" itself "helped [them] to work up [their] tempests with such terror" (VI, 50).

Borrowing the methods of classical scholarship to give "Gothic" poets the advantage over classic, Hurd slyly accomplishes an early and influential articulation of the Saxon sublime. His is an incipient grafting of poetics to race. Hoyt Trowbridge's remark that Hurd plays a key role in "the rise of English literary history" and expresses the new "historical point of view" (Trowbridge, iv) suddenly provokes this question: Does the historical method partly depend for its scope and narrative momentum on an imaginary of race?

This speculative question arises more insistently when we turn to the polemical debates among the first champions of even younger native poets than Spenser or Shakespeare. In Percy, Blair, and MacPherson, the Gothic/Greek ceases to be the crucial opposition; instead, the European races are distinguishing among themselves and each claiming their poetry as most original, historical, and sublime.[29] In these internal polemics race gets worked up into a key term and yoked to a concept of the sublime that is increasingly metaphysical. Although the focus is on intra-British and European differences, this process of sorting differences eventually reveals itself as the consolidation of metaphysical identity according to race which will anchor the ship of empire at ports throughout the world.

Blair's dissertation on Ossian echoes Hurd's view that the islands of Britain and their conquering history encourage sublimity: "amidst the rude scenes of nature, amidst rocks and torrents and whirlwinds and battles, dwells the sublime."[30] Like Hurd, Blair favorably compares the sublimity of this "native" poet to Greek poets, especially Homer, and so far merely supplements the well-established debate over the virtues of the ancients vs. the moderns. But, in prominently contrasting the "Goths" with the Scottish Celtic peoples, to the advantage of the Celts, he also helps to initiate a newer discourse about the interrelations and relative virtues of European peoples. He considers the Scots, of whom Ossian is the bard, a Celtic tribe, and thus part of "a great and mighty people" who are "altogether distinct from the Goths and the Teutones."[31]

Blair's grouping of Scots and Brits with Celts and against Goths, while seemingly harmless to the twentieth-century reader, was highly controversial. For, first of all, not all readers felt comfortable with this close association of Scots and Irish (not surprising, given the increasing subjugation of the Irish). MacPherson himself felt compelled to dissociate the Highland Scottish people from the Irish (who had "pretensions to Ossian" as their poet) as well as from the Celtic Britons and the Saxons. In his Preface to *Ossian*, MacPherson depicts the Ossianic culture of the Highland Scots as a highly isolated one which resisted not only the incursions of the "Saxon race" (70) but also the mixing of the southern Scots and Celts so that the Highland Scots remained of "a different race from the rest of the Britons" (59). As a result, their "language is pure and original, and their manners are those of ancient and unmixed race of men" (59). It is this "most ancient" (74) of European nations and this "more pure" (75) language combined with the secluded "magnificence" of "mountains and hanging woods" (71) that gives rise to Ossian.

Few scholars honored Macpherson's sharp distinction between ancient Scots and Celts, but they participated in similar racial polemics over whose race is most sublime. Bishop Percy wrote some of the most impassioned and influential histories of literary-racial lineages. He engages openly in debate with other writers on race in Europe, as when he points out the "fundamental error" in M. Pelloutier's *History of the Celts*: like so many other unfortunate authors, Pelloutier overlooks "the radical distinction between the Gothic and the Celtic" and so instead of performing a "noble task" his book becomes a "perpetual source of mistake and confusion."[32] In his Prefaces to the *Reliques* and to M. Mallet's *Northern Antiquities*, Percy provides a careful account of the Gothic scalds—one that privileges them over and against the Celtic bards and thus stands diametrically opposed to Hugh Blair's account and at odds with MacPherson's.

In his dissertation on Ossian, not only had Blair associated the Irish and Scots but he had also slighted the Goths in the realm of poetry. Aiming, Blair says, "to discover whether the Gothic poetry has any resemblance to the Celtic or Gaelic," he attempts generosity toward the Goths: although known "for their ignorance of the liberal arts, yet they too, from the earliest times, had their poets and their songs" (92). In ostensibly neutral scholarly fashion, Blair (a professor of rhetoric at

Edinburgh) explains that these poets were called "Scalders" and presents a fragment from the work of the king and scalder Regner Lodbrog. After three full pages of Lodbrog's bloody battle imagery accented by the refrain "the whole ocean was one wound," Blair has prepared us to see that "When we turn from the poetry of Lodbrog [of the Goths] to that of Ossian [of the Celts], it is like passing from a savage desert into a fertile and cultivated country" (96). For in Ossian we find not only the "fire and enthusiasm of the most early times" but also "tenderness, and even delicacy of sentiment, greatly predominant over fierceness and barbarity" (96). He goes on to consider the evidence that, in general, the "Celtic tribes" were "addicted in so high a degree to poetry" that they preserved their traditions throughout many invasions and changes of government (98) and to claim that "The two great characteristics of Ossian's poetry are, [sic] tenderness and sublimity" (107).

Percy virtually reverses Blair's argument. He states unequivocally that the Celtic and Teutonic nations "were two races of men *ab origine* distinct" (Mallet 16) before detailing the backwardness of the Celts who "do not appear to have had that equal plan of liberty, which was the peculiar honor of all the Gothic tribes" (Mallet 10). But above all, as Blair had done for the Celts, Percy seeks to honor the Goths as the more poetical race. In *Reliques* he is content to comment that poets were admired by "all the first inhabitants of Europe, whether of Celtic or Gothic race; but by none more than by our Teutonic ancestors."[33] Several years later, in his Preface to Mallet's *Northern Antiquities*, Percy's contrast sharpens to the point where he considers the Celts to lack "so much as an alphabet of their own" (Mallet 14). "In this," he concludes, ironically echoing the language of Blair "the institutions of Odin and the Skalds was [sic] the very reverse. No barbarous people were so addicted to writing . . . no barbarous people ever held letters in higher reverence, ascribing the invention of them to their chief deity, and attributing to letters themselves supernatural virtues" (Mallet 14). In adopting a position opposite to Blair's, Percy creates a mirror image that reflects the same racialization of poetic genius and even speaks the same language of "addiction to poetry."

Within three decades after the publication of the *Reliques*, according to Carl Berkhout, "a 'myth' had developed in the English literary world."[34] Though Berkhout does not say it, this rapidly proliferating myth was racial and political as well as poetical. By the time William Mitford wrote his "Inquiry into the principles of Harmony in Language and of the Mechanism of Verse, Modern and Antient" (1804), he could speak of the different principles of "Harmony" experienced by "all the races of mankind in their respective languages" as a popular topic: "In our own country, especially of late years, publications, of which it is either the principal or an incidental topic, have been numerous."[35] Mitford builds on Hurd to determine the formal principles of "native" English poetry and to characterize the "energetic language of our early forefathers" (132), holding that "the form of the English language has hardly in any degree been derived from the French" (367), for despite the Norman-French invasion (both political and linguistic in his account) "the genius of the [Gothic] Anglo-Saxon pronunciation at length prevailed" (142). Mitford's unorthodox notion that accentual rather than syllabic verse was native to the British isles fostered the prosodic aspect of the Romantic poetic revolution, so that in the following years "trisyllabic substitution bursts into full bloom in the works of Southey, Coleridge, 'Monk' Lewis, Sir Walter Scott, and John Leyden."[36] His theory also helps to confirm a place for Robert Burns, who openly deviates from the syllabic models on the defense that "there is a certain irregularity" in the old Scotch songs, "a degree of wild irregularity" (Fussell 145).

That Mitford's accentual theory is considered by Paul Fussell and others to be highly influential in the history of modern English prosody again prompts us to consider the ways racial myths and literary theories impel one another. Mitford himself hints that this racialized linguistic and literary history puts wind in the sails of the imperial venture in his closing praise of English as the language that has "spred [sic] in all quarters of the globe" (429). He admonishes his readers: "This speech it becomes us to cherish and preserve; to know its merits, that we may know how to ward it against injury" (430).

THE SUBLIME TURN, THE RACIAL PIVOT:
KANT, BURKE, AND WORDSWORTH

Now we can begin to discover an underlying racial logic in the apparently paradoxical fact that, as Donald Pease notes, "despite all the revolutionary rhetoric invested in the term, the sublime has . . . always served conservative purposes."[37] I suggest, however, that it is not so much a matter of revolutionary appearance versus conservative essence as of a pivotal and strategic doubleness. The domestic racial discourse on which modern early Romantic theories of the sublime drew had originally done power-wresting work for the Puritans and mercantilists; but at the end of the eighteenth century, with the entrenchment of the Protestant middle class (self-styled as a race), that discourse had to begin its power-conserving work.

The Romantic sublime is importantly constituted, in other words, by its function to transform a revolutionary racial discourse into a hegemonic one. Times were a-changing since the day when "Pride in one's

Saxon ancestry was important . . . for urging one's fellows either to discover the origins of the true church or to cast off the Norman yoke."[38] The late eighteenth-century attention to the sublime marks a climax of this middle- and educated-class revolutionary discourse—and serves as its pivot into an imperial racial project. Hereafter the Anglo-Saxon race is not only rightful but also poetic, metaphysical, sublime, and *herein* superior to all others, as reflected for instance in Sir Richard Burton's insistence, typical for the later nineteenth century, that the "stagnation of mind" in the "lower races" marked them as "inferior to the active-minded and objective . . . Europeans."[39] Intranational, Anglo-European polemics over the "original" poetic race set the stage for these claims.

We see this turn from a domestic, originally revolutionary rhetoric to a global, conservative ideology achieved most obviously in Kant's early writing on the sublime. Although not known in English until later, it is remarkable that Kant's *Observations on the Feeling of the Beautiful and Sublime* (1763), appears at nearly the same moment as Percy, Blair, and Hurd's texts and like them measures sublimity in relation to national and racial differences. Kant sets out to distinguish among two kinds of "finer feeling," the beautiful and the sublime, both of which include "thought" and "intellectual excellences" and "presuppose a sensitivity of soul."[40] In his third chapter Kant explicitly genders these qualities, speaking of the "fair sex" as susceptible to the beautiful and the "noble sex" as attuned to the sublime. Such gendering of the sublime has various repercussions, as others have analyzed, but for my purposes it is sufficient to note that it strengthens the racial and national distinctions he goes on to make.[41] In his fourth chapter, "Of National Characteristics, so far as they depend on the Distinct Feelings of the Beautiful and Sublime," Kant implicitly genders nations and races, revitalizing an old practice that would become scientifically codified by the end of the nineteenth century.

Directing our attention to "the mental characters of peoples," he explains that the Italian and the French prefer the beautiful, the German, English, and Spanish the sublime (implicitly masculine and superior). Following these broad generalizations, he spends several pages making finer distinctions, such as that the Italian show a modified sensitivity to the sublime, but the (feminine) French demonstrate none. He furthermore considers various kinds of sublime feeling as they affect national attitudes toward honor, love, and religion. In short, he gives extended attention to a nationalist sublime in a period when nationality was mingled rhetorically with notions of class, ancestry, and race. His correspondence of beautiful and sublime feelings with the character types of the sanguine, choleric, melancholic, and phlegmatic (63), which had themselves been traditionally used to stereotype nations as well as individuals, further reflects the essentializing impulse of his nationalist typology of the sublime.

One of the most telling details of Kant's essay, however, is his manipulation of the word "noble" ("edel" in German). Noble has historical racial associations insofar as the aristocracies of Europe had long been considered noble races, as mentioned earlier. That is, the word noble was the racially-inflected word for the aristocracy. Significantly in Kant's description, first of all, apprehension of the sublime in nature constitutes an ennobling experience, so much so that he sometimes uses "the noble" as a synonym for "the sublime." He repeatedly emphasizes that the sublime finds its best expression in the "simple and noble" (48; also see 98, 104, 106). Kant hereby removes the word noble from its traditional aristocratic terrain and instead positions it in the natural, "simple," and emotional worlds where apparently all (men) can have access to it.

Given the cultural, specifically racial, associations of the word noble, Kant's use of it is important: for as he defines it the sublime is accessible to peasant, citizen, and aristocrat alike. He proposes that youth must be taught an appreciation of the beautiful and the sublime so as to "elevate the moral feeling in the breast of every young world-citizen to a lively sensitivity" (115). In effect, apprehension of the sublime could make nobles of citizens. (This move, and the whole recovery of barbarian poetry, clearly recalls the eighteenth-century idea of the noble savage, though unfortunately it is beyond the scope of this essay to explore this rich connection.) The discourse of the ennobling sublime thus emerges as a race-transgressive or usurptive discourse, in that it appropriates the aristocratic vocabulary of nobility for the common citizen. Kant's championing of a noble citizenry is not exactly the same as the English championing of a folk identity except insofar as it shares the project of universalizing the noble so as to claim its virtues for the middle and lower classes.

But while this articulation of access to an ennobling sublime operates as a revolutionary move in this sense, it simultaneously opens the way to a new imperial mythology that ranks races, especially "civilized" over "savage," according to their differential sensitivity to the sublime. Herein does Kant initiate the use of the sublime as a pivot for the turn from domestic to global-imperial race distinctions. In the second half of chapter 4 Kant turns his attention from nation-specific sublime perceptions among a noble-ized citizenry to the "Oriental" and the "savage races," which distinguish themselves by their relative indifference to the sublime and the beautiful alike (111, 112). While he considers the Arab to have a taste for the sublime and therefore to be "the noblest man in the Orient," unfortunately this taste "degenerates very much into the adventurous" (109). The Persians are the frivolous "French of Asia," while both the Asian-Indian and the Chinese show appreciation only of the "grotesque" (109–10). Most starkly, the "savage races" of America and Africa "show few traces of a mental character disposed to the finer feelings" (112). The Negroes of Africa in particular "have by nature no feeling that rises above trifling" and indeed "Not a single one was ever found who presented anything great in art or science or any other praiseworthy quality" (111).

So here we have the sublime turn that is a racial turn: the broad extension of the "noble" to the natural and the emotional gets delimited in a second phase to the rational and the European (especially the masculine "Gothic" European of England, Germany, and Spain). That dynamical introjection, by reason, of the power of an awesome alien nature which Kant deemed a "subreption" replays itself here as the dynamical reversal of the values of feeling and reason so as to subdue the power of an alien racial other. A revolutionary, potentially widely disruptive racialization of history gets violently contained and transmuted within a hierarchical economy of "mental character" and reason over "finer feeling"—a containment Kant undertook more systematically in *The Critique of Judgement*. In the latter, although references to "the savage" and the Iroquois appear only in passing, Kant expands upon the notion that "preparatory culture" is "requisite for the judgement upon the sublime."[42] The sublime "pleases immediately by reason of its opposition to the interest of sense" (*Critique* 118) and because it "employ[s] itself upon ideas involving higher finality" (*Critique* 92). In this later work Kant need not specify a racial framework; it is encoded in his emphasis on "preparatory culture" as it would have been understood in the culture at large in the opposition between reason and sense.

In Edmund Burke's early essay *A Philosophical Enquiry into the Origin of our Ideas of the Sublime and the Beautiful* (1757), he fails to delimit the sublime along racial lines.[43] His descriptions of the terror induced by blackness and in one striking instance by a mulatto woman in the eyes of a young child (144–45) do anticipate the kind of intersection between the sublime and race ultimately expressed in, say, Conrad's *Heart of Darkness*. Yet what is less commented upon[44] and yet equally important, is the way he manages the rhetoric of savagery we have seen yoked to the sublime. Burke draws neither national nor racial boundaries around ancestral energy. Innovatively grounding it in human physiology, Burke discovers equal manifestations of sublimity in the "ancient heathen temple" of Stonehenge (*Enquiry* 77), the sacred forests of the Druids (*Enquiry* 59), and the "barbarous temples of the

Americans" (*Enquiry* 59). Sublimity is thus evidence of identity among originary cultures rather than a measure of their difference. At the same time his examples follow the contemporary practice of locating the origins of the sublime in "savage" races.

Turning from the *Enquiry* to his *Reflections on the Revolution in France*, however, we find an impulse to contain the savage sublime, accompanied by Burke's controversial shift in political allegiances. In the *Enquiry*, Burke had described the sublime as a spectacle in which "modifications of power" are staged and negotiated (*Enquiry* 64). Within the gaze of the witness, astonishing displays of sublime might (which are often, in Burke's examples, political as well as natural, as Suleri has emphasized) are contained and thus modified. For Burke in this early text, savages of all nations capably confront and modify awesome power as reflected in their awesome or brooding temples. But this universalism provides the principle for the perceptual process which in *Reflections* becomes the historical one of preserving and refining, or modifying, ancient "savage" customs. The savage gaze is turned on the savage, "his" modifications themselves become modified. This appropriation provides the basis for Burke's argument that the French Revolution could have, and should have, proceeded as the English one had.

That is, in *Reflections* Burke himself achieves a sublime modification by transmuting the violent and radical practices of the common English revolutionaries into a politics of reason and a vocabulary of noble inheritance. Burke explains that the French revolutionaries should have "derived your claims from a more early race of ancestors" as the English revolutionaries did. Instead of representing themselves as "a gang of Maroon slaves, suddenly broke loose from the house of bondage," the revolutionaries should have "resolved to resume your ancient privileges."[45] Disruption becomes resumption in this modified account so that a conquered race is no longer an unruly, debased race; on the contrary, as the English had discovered, they could be rendered more sublime, more "noble" than the triumphant invaders. Pursuing his own sublime alchemy of race and rights, to borrow Patricia Williams's apt phrase, Burke goes on to point out that if the French had difficulty finding their own Magna Charta or "discerning the obliterated constitution of your ancestors," they might have "looked to your neighbors, who had kept alive the ancient principles and models of the old common law of Europe" (*Reflections* 123).

Burke's transmutation of savage temple into constitutional state marks a crucial moment of recuperation in Anglo-European culture, or a historical sublimation, as Hayden White might analyze it,[46] a kind of oedipal narrative writ large wherein the common-law son becomes the noble conqueror-father of whom he had stood in terrified awe.

In effect, Burke synthesizes seventeenth century with late eighteenth century Anglo-Saxonism, making the English the true European race which preserves "the spirit of freedom . . . tempered with awful gravity" and ennobled by "pedigree and illustrating ancestors" (*Reflections* 121)—that is, the sublime, lawful race of Europe. For Burke, it is by recovery of such ancestry that "our liberty becomes a noble freedom" (*Reflections* 121). The French revolutionaries—who did indeed invoke their own racial mythologies of themselves as conquered Gauls throwing off a Frankish yoke[47]—missed the opportunity to make "noble" their racial heritage—mistakenly inspired instead, as Burke hints, by the "Maroon slaves" of America or Toussaint L'Ouverture of St. Domingo (*Reflections* 123).

If Burke's sublime turn is dramatically rhetorical, Wordsworth's is quietly lyrical. We might indeed supplement Keats's comment that Wordsworth created an "egotistical sublime" by tracing the internalized racial politics of that ego. For Wordsworth's sublime ego does not simply radiate out into the cosmos; it first gathers energy by humbly appropriating to itself, as the voice of a nation, the voices of the "folk" who work the soil. Wordsworth transforms folk manners and the objects "to which they are attached" into the materials of racialized nationhood, but he does so in an imagery that naturalizes the process so successfully as to make it invisible.

As mentioned, Wordsworth himself names the *Reliques* along with Cowper and Burns as "powerfully" influential on his "taste and nature tendencies." He goes on to hold up these salutary native influences as "a warning to youthful Poets" so that they might resist "the inundation of foreign literature, from which our own is at present suffering so much."[48] Clearly a nationalist nativism is integral to Wordsworth's sublime poetic, which he eventually builds up into the image of the "Poet of Imagination" who is at once noble conqueror and humble shepherd. But in addition, Wordsworth's nationalist poetic partakes of the emergent racialism of the day. In the same letter, Wordsworth calls especially on Burns to exemplify his idea that poetry should treat "manners connected with the permanent objects of nature and partaking of the simplicity of those objects." "In Burns," he continues, "you find manners everywhere," which is why Burns is "energetic, solemn, and sublime in sentiment."[49]

You find "manners everywhere" in Wordsworth as well, and these manners are naturalized, or rendered as "native growths," especially through a rhetoric of trees and soil, an imagery Martin Bernal has linked to racial paradigms.[50] In the Preface to the *Lyrical Ballads*, Wordsworth explains that he has chosen characters from "humble and rustic" life as his subject because "in that condition, the essential passions of the heart find a better soil in which they can find their maturity, are less under restraint and speak a plainer and more emphatic language."[51] Elsewhere he essentializes this fusion of laborer and soil even further, suggesting that the laborer is "in his person attached, by stronger roots, to the soil of which he is the growth" (*Prose* 230). Similarly, in his public letter protesting the extension of train lines into the lake district, Wordsworth tells of a "magnificent tree" on one of the properties threatened by the railway. When advised to fell the tree for profit, the yeoman who owns it exclaims "Fell it . . . I would rather fall on my knees and worship it" (*Prose* 76). Wordsworth hopes that his reader will enter into the "strength of the feeling" and remarks that the "attachment which many of the yeomanry feel to their small inheritances can scarcely be over-rated" (*Prose* 76). The tree symbolizes the yeoman's attachment to his inheritance and to the soil of which it, and he (and Wordsworth's poetry), are the "growth."

These soil and tree metaphors for the laborer take on more than local metaphorical significance in the light of the emerging science of national or racial "character." The predominant, lay-scientific explanation for racial difference in this period was still the climatic theory— i.e., that racial features were shaped, or birthed, by the soil and climate of a country. Wordsworth expresses his endorsement of this theory in answer to John Wilson's inquiry about "the influence of natural objects in forming the character of nations." Wordsworth explains that insofar as the terrain and flora and fauna of a country "must have been not the nourishers merely but the fathers of [the People's] passions, they will make themselves felt powerfully in forming the character of the people, so as to produce a uniformity or national character" (*Prose* 309). As I have elsewhere discussed, especially in regard to Wordsworth's essay on "The Convention of Cintra," the gendered language of nourishment and fathers helps to further naturalize this essentialist account of nations wherein the land nurtures "peoples" as well as plants. Clearly Wordsworth's project is to voice these soil-rooted, nation-specific "passions."

As in contemporary theories of the sublime (most notably Kant's "Aesthetic of the Sublime" in *The Critique of Judgement*), reason serves to regulate Wordsworth's sublime modification of power, his transfer of nativized energy from peasant to poet. In the Preface to the *Lyrical Ballads*, although Wordsworth throws poetic tradition to the winds and embraces his humble, naturalized subjects, he carefully "measures" his embrace. That is, he literally measures his relation to his subject through meter, which is, as he acknowledges, the one traditional poetic feature he retains. Since, as Wordsworth explains, in a poetry of "manly" passion and language, "there is some danger that the excitement may be carried beyond its proper bounds," he uses meter for the purpose of "tempering and restraining the passion" (*Prose* 296). By such an enclosure of passion within meter, Wordsworth trusts that "a dissimilitude will be produced altogether sufficient for the gratification of a rational mind" (*Prose* 287). This dissimilitude between passion and restraint carries out exactly the contemporary idea of the sublime, in which the sublime provides (in Kant's words) a "negative pleasure" because it puts a "momentary check" on the "vital forces" (*Critique* 91). Not surprisingly, then, we find on second look that the oft-quoted phrase from Wordsworth's Preface that "good poetry is the spontaneous overflow of powerful feeling" receives immediate qualification in the same sentence: "though this be true, Poems to which any value can be attached were never produced . . . but by a man who . . . had also thought long and deeply. For our continued influxes of feeling are modified and directed by our thoughts" (*Prose* 283). Insofar as long and deep thought are the prerogatives of the leisured, empire-enriched classes, Wordsworth subordinates the soil-bound "passion" of the yeoman to the leisured man's prerogative of thought. He immerses the supposedly "manly" laborer in an inchoate "flux" of "feeling" which gets "directed" or "modified" by the poet.

Wordsworth achieves his ultimate subsumption of a sublime racial inheritance into the figure of a reasoning masculine poet in his identification of the visionary poet with "Hannibal among the Alps" or, in other words, with the conqueror figure. In *The Contours of Masculine Desire*, Marlon Ross documents the widespread presence of a "conquering" trope in English Romantic poetry.[52] He brilliantly teases out the gender politics of the visionary conqueror poet, a politics in which a femininized materiality is "colonized" and put in the service of a masculinized will to poetic power over feminine materiality. As Ross shows, much Romantic poetry deifies the thinker-poet whose visions transform and conquer the world, as when Byron speaks of the poetic soul which "preys upon high adventure" and harbors a "lust to shine or rule" (*Childe Harold's Pilgrimage*, Canto 3, stanzas 42–43). Wordsworth imagines the visionary poet as "Hannibal among the Alps" whose poetic subjects "change in their constitution from [his] touch" (*Prose* 383). Nineteenth-century readers echo this conqueror-poet myth, as in the case of a critic who in 1818 identified Scott, Wordsworth, and Byron as the "three great master-spirits of our own day . . . who may indeed be said to rule, each by a legitimate sovereignty, over separate and powerful provinces in the kingdom of the Mind."[53]

I suggest that this trope of conquering came readily to hand within the racial discourse that Bishop Percy and others revived and made literary. Wordsworth argues in his Supplementary Essay in 1815 that the poet who aims to "[widen] the sphere of human sensibility" (*Prose* 410), must undertake the "breaking of the bonds of custom" (*Prose* 408). Meanwhile, like the conqueror, the poet practices "the application of powers to objects on which they had not been exercised, or the employment of them in such a manner as to produce effects hitherto unknown" (*Prose* 410). This Romantic adoption of a conqueror self-image partakes of the contemporary mythology wherein the subjugated native race becomes the new visionary and noble race. Wordsworth most reveals the agenda of conquest which the national and the poetic project have in common when he asks, in reference to the expanding and transforming effects of a poetry of "Imagination": "what is all this but an advance, or a conquest, made by the soul of the poet?" (*Prose* 410).

Race and gender operate together in this conqueror self-image. Wordsworth's later poems that feature conqueror-shepherd figures fully play out a drama in which an avenging conqueror who combines a humble, feminine, soil-inspired sensibility with a noble, masculine, warring spirit returns from "homefelt pleasures" to vindicate his "race." In "Song at the Feast of Brougham Castle upon the restoration of Lord Clifford, the Shepherd, to the Estates and Honours of His Ancestors," the shepherd Clifford enacts revenge on the past injustice done to his "Race."[54] One day recompense "on the blood of Clifford calls."

> Happy day, and mighty hour,
> When our Shepherd, in his power,
> Mailed and horsed, with lance and sword,
> To his ancestors restored
> Like a re-appearing Star,
> Like a glory from afar,
> First shall head the flock of war! (*Poems*, I, 730)

This shepherd "Avenger" succeeds in part because his cause is the cause of the soil itself: "Earth helped him with the cry of blood":

> Loud voice the Land has uttered forth,
> We loudest in the faithful north:
> Our fields rejoice, our mountains ring,
> Our streams proclaim a welcoming. (*Poems*, I, 727)

After his bloody battle, sanctioned by the maternal earth, Clifford returns to a gentle life in earth's embrace where "the Shepherd-lord was honoured more and more" (*Poems*, I, 730). Similarly in "Character of the Happy Warrior," we meet a warrior "whose master-bias leans / To homefelt pleasures and to gentle scenes" and yet "if he be called upon to face / Some awful moment" in war, he is "happy as a lover" (*Poems*, I, 661).

Out of such materials Wordsworth formulates his late myth of the poet who—via immersion in and subsumption of a racialized nature—transforms warring impulses into a reasoned poetry. In "The Recluse," it becomes clear that Wordsworth's picture of the warrior as a man who harbors a nature-sensitive sensibility enables him to cast the nature-sensitive poet as a man who harbors, without contradiction, the soul of a warrior—and thus quietly carries on the conqueror legacy. At the end of "The Recluse," the poet recalls himself as an "innocent Little-one" who, in addition to his "tender moods," very much felt "Motions of savage instinct." "Deep pools, tall trees, black chasms and dizzy crags, / And tottering towers" were all challenges that "urged" the child-poet to "daring feat[s]" (*Poems*, I, 716). These "savage" impulses remain alive in the adult. In a passage which recalls G. W. F. Hegel's account of a primordial battle for subjectivity (itself later racialized by Hegel) in any meeting between two self-conscious individuals who "prove themselves and each other through a life-and-death struggle,"[55] the Recluse poet writes that "to this hour I cannot read a tale of two Vessels matched in deadly fight / And fighting to the death, but I am pleased / More than a wise man ought to be. I wish / Fret, burn, and struggle, and in soul am there" (*Poems*, I, 716). Wordsworth here narrates the archetypal sublime scene, the barbarian confrontation with raw power, that encounter which for the modern poet provokes thoughts of a "higher finality."

And, indeed, as the savage child-poet enters (cultural) adulthood, "Reason" transforms his thirst for battle into a quest for truth; and so the sublime turn comes, in Wordsworth's poetry, to provide a narrative structure for the racialized imperial self. The voice of reason assures the poet not to fear "a want of aspirations" or "foes / To wrestle with, and victory to complete . . . the undaunted quest" for these shall survive "though changed in their office." The poet thus bids "farewell to the warrior's schemes." Instead, his "Voice shall speak" "On Man, on Nature, and on Human Life / Musing in Solitude" (*Poems*, I, 717). "The Recluse" narrates the poet's transformation from weapon-wielding race conqueror to word-wielding race visionary. He heralds the arrival of what Burke in his *Reflections* deems "this new-conquering empire of light and reason" and what Michel Foucault later clarified as the invasive intentions of reason's discourse.

The critic who named Wordsworth one of the "great master-spirits" of the day probably did not intend a pun. Yet the mastery Wordsworth achieved and articulated was indeed double, both intensely personal and deeply cultural, at once revolutionary and hegemonic. Wordsworth, Kant, Burke, and other Romantic-era writers alchemize the sublime to create an imperial folk-subject. Their work ultimately precipitates a wealth of Victorian literary and cultural projects, as wide-ranging and yet equally rooted in race as Thomas Carlyle's *Sartor Resartus*, Ernest Renan's "The Poetry of the Celtic Races," Thomas Hardy's sublime portrait of the race-burdened Tess Durbyfield, and Francis Galton's founding of the science of eugenics on his research into "geniuses" of the English race. The Romantic writers' poetry and legacy, their transformation of the materials gathered by Percy, Burns, Mitford, Hurd, Blair, and MacPherson, recall for us the subtle turns by which literary practices make imperial histories.

NOTES

1. Richard C. Payne, "The Rediscovery of Old English Poetry in the English Literary Tradition," in Carl T. Berkhout and Milton Gatch, eds., *Anglo-Saxon Scholarship: The First Three Centuries* (Boston: G. K. Hall, 1982), 153. Quoted in *Robert Burns: The Critical Heritage*, ed. Donald A. Low (Boston: Routledge, 1974), 163. Thomas Percy, *Reliques of Ancient English Poetry*, ed. James Nichol (Edinburgh: James Nisbet, 1858), vol. I, Editor's Introduction, x.

2. Hannah Arendt, *The Origins of Totalitarianism* (New York: Harcourt Brace Jovanovich, 1948, 1979), 158.

3. Robert Knox, *The Races of Men* (Philadelphia: Lea and Blanchard, 1850), 3.

4. Sara Suleri, *The Rhetoric of English India* (Chicago: University of Chicago Press, 1992). See especially Chapter 2, "Edmund Burke and the Indian Sublime." Also valuable for understanding the structural relationship between imperialism and English literature is Gauri Viswanathan, *Masks of Conquest: Literary Study and British Rule* (New York: Columbia University Press, 1989).

5. See *Bordering on the Body: The Racial Matrix of Modern Fiction and Culture* (New York: Oxford, 1994), Chapter 2.

6. See for example Patricia Yaeger, "Toward a Female Sublime" in *Gender and Theory*, ed., Linda Kauffman (New York: Basil Blackwell, 1989), 191–212; and " 'The Language of Blood': Toward a Maternal Sublime," *Genre* XXV (Spring 1992), 5–24; and Barbara Claire Freeman, *The Feminine Sublime: Gender and Excess in Women's Fiction* (Berkeley: University of California Press, 1995).

7. Christopher Hill, "The Norman Yoke," in *Puritanism and Revolution* (New York: Schocken, 1958, 1964) and discussions throughout his work. See *Collected Essays*, vols. I and II (Amherst: University of Massachusetts, 1985–86).

8. J. G. A. Pocock, *The Ancient Constitution and the Feudal Law* (Cambridge: Cambridge University Press, 1957), 36. See the discussion in Michael Murphy, "Antiquary to Academic" in Berkhout, 5.

9. Quoted in Sandra A. Glass, "The Saxonist's Influence on Seventeenth-Century English Literature" in Berkhout, 91–92, 99.

10. See Christopher Hill, *Puritanism and Revolution*, 69.

11. Gerard Winstanley, *The Law of Freedom in a Platform*, ed. Max Radin (Sutro, CA: California State Library, 1939), 22–23.

12. Holcroft, trans. (London: Humphrey Moseley, 1653), 7.

13. Murphy in Berkhout, 7.

14. V. G. Kiernan, *Lords of Humankind: Black Man, Yellow Man, and White Man in an Age of Empire* (Boston: Little, Brown, 1969), 229.

15. Quoted in Leon Poliakov, *The Aryan Myth: A History of Racist and Nationalist Ideas in Europe*, trans. Edmund Howard (London: Chatto Heinemann, 1974), 22.

16. Thomas Sackville of Dorset, "The Complaint of Henry, Duke of Buckingham" in *The Mirror for Magistrates*, ed. Marguerite Hearsey (New Haven: Yale University Press, 1936 [Orig. 1563]), 61.

17. Arendt, 161.

18. For an analysis of more modern instances of this subversive emulation, see the very useful essay by Nancy Leys Stepan and Sander Gilman, "Appropriating the Idioms of Science" in Dominick La Capra, ed., *The Bounds of Race: Perspectives on Hegemony and Resistance* (Ithaca: Cornell University Press, 1991), 72–103.

19. David Hume, *The History of England from the Invasion of Julius Caesar* (London, 1762), vol. I, 141.

20. Quoted in Susie I. Tucker, *Protean Shape: A Study in Eighteenth-Century Vocabulary and Usage* (London: Athlone Press, 1967), 38.

21. Samuel Johnson, Preface, *Dictionary of the English Language* (New York: AMS Press, 1967).

22. Sir Joshua Reynolds, *Discourses on Art* appended to Longinus, *On the Sublime*, trans. Benedict Einarson (Chicago: Packard, 1945), 147, 95.

23. Quoted in Goldsmith: *The Critical Heritage*, ed. G. S. Rousseau (Boston: Routledge and Kegan Paul, 1974), 42.

24. See Nancy Leys Stepan, *The Idea of Race in Science* (Hamden, CT: Archon, 1982).

25. As I have noted elsewhere, the terms race and nation have been crisscrossed and conflated in various ways since the 18th century. See *Bordering on the Body*, Chapter 1. In the texts I discuss here, race is the more inclusive category, so that one race may populate several nations, as when Thomas Percy speaks of the "nations of the Gothic race," *Reliques*, 217.

26. See the editor's introduction to Immanuel Kant, *Anthropology, from a pragmatic point of view*, trans. and with an introduction by Mary T. Gregor (The Hague: Nijhoff, 1974).

27. See Linda Colley, *Britons: Forging the Nation, 1707–1837* (New Haven: Yale University Press, 1992), especially 102–105.

28. Richard Hurd, *Letters on Chivalry and Romance*, ed. Hoyt Trowbridge (Los Angeles: William Andrews Clark Memorial Library, 1963), publication No. 101–102 [orig. 1762], Letter I, 2. All further references will appear in the text with a Roman numeral letter number followed by the page number.

29. One is reminded of Basil Davidson's argument that competition among European nations impelled the slave market and the colonization of Africa. As he shows, Europeans fought one another on African land or water more than they fought any African peoples. African leaders gained

market power according to their ability to play European diplomats and generals against each other. See *The African Slave Trade* (Boston: Little, Brown, 1980).

30. Cited in Samuel Monk, *The Sublime: A Study of Critical Theories in Eighteenth-Century England* (Ann Arbor: University of Michigan, 1960 [1935]), 68. All further citations appear in the text.

31. *The Poetical Works of Ossian*, trans. James MacPherson and including "A Preliminary Discourse and Dissertation on the Era and Poems of Ossian" (Boston: Crosby and Nichols, 1863), 96. All further citations from both Blair and MacPherson's Preface appear in the text.

32. M. Mallet, *Northern Antiquities; or, an Historical Account of the Manners, Customs, Religion and Laws, Maritime Expeditions and Discoveries, Language and Literature, of the Ancient Scandinavians. With Incidental Notices Respecting our Saxon Ancestors*. Trans. Bishop Percy (London: Henry G. Bohn, 1847 [1770]), 19. All further citations appear in the text as Mallet.

33. Bishop Thomas Percy, ed., *Reliques of Ancient English Poetry, Volume I* (London: James Nisbet, 1858 [1765]), xxxi. All further citations appear in the text as *Reliques*.

34. Berkhout, 153.

35. William Mitford (London: T. Cadell and W. Davies, 1804), 1. All further citations appear in the text.

36. Paul Fussell, Jr., *Theory of Prosody in Eighteenth-Century England* (New London: Connecticut College, 1954), 146. All further citations appear in the text.

37. Donald Pease, "Sublime Politics," *Boundary* 2 (Spring/Fall 1984): 275.

38. Glass in Berkhout, 93.

39. Cited in Patrick Brantlinger, *Rule of Darkness: British Literature and Imperialism, 1830–1914* (Ithaca: Cornell University Press, 1988), 183.

40. Immanuel Kant, *Observations on the Feeling of the Beautiful and Sublime*, trans. John T. Goldthwait (Berkeley: University of California, 1991 [1961]), 46. All further citations appear in the text.

41. On gender and the sublime, see especially Freeman (cited above).

42. Immanuel Kant, *The Critique of Judgement*, trans. James Meredith (New York: Oxford, 1966), 112, 93, 115. All further references to this volume appear in the text as *Critique*.

43. Edmund Burke, *A Philosophical Enquiry into the Origin of our Ideas of the Sublime and Beautiful*, ed. J. T. Boulton (London: Routledge and Kegan Paul, 1958). All references to this volume appear in the text as *Enquiry*.

44. Suleri comments on this example (43–44), as does W. J. T. Mitchell in *Iconology: Image, Text, Ideology* (Chicago: University of Chicago Press, 1986), 131.

45. Edmund Burke, *Reflections on the Revolution in France and on the Proceedings of Certain Societies in London relative to that Event*, ed. Conor Cruise O'Brien (New York: Penguin, 1982 [orig. 1790]), 123. All further citations appear in the text as *Reflections*.

46. See Hayden White, "The Politics of Historical Interpretation: Discipline and De-Sublimation," *Critical Inquiry*, 9 (September 1982), 113–38.

47. See Poliakov, 24–26.

48. Low, 163.

49. Low, 131.

50. Martin Bernal, *Black Athena: The Afroasiatic Roots of Classical Civilization*, I (New Brunswick: Rutgers University Press, 1987), 205. For fuller discussion of this imagery in Wordsworth, see Doyle, *Bordering on the Body*, Chapter 2.

51. William Wordsworth, *Selected Prose*, ed. John O. Hayden (New York: Penguin, 1988), 282. All further citations appear in the text as *Prose*.

52. Marlon Ross, *The Contours of Masculine Desire and the Rise of Women's Poetry* (New York: Oxford, 1989).

53. Cited in Ross, 53.

54. William Wordsworth, *Poems, Volume I*, ed. John O. Hayden (New York: Penguin, 1977), 51. All further citations appear in the text.

55. G. W. F. Hegel, *Phenomenology of Spirit*, trans. A. V. Miller (New York: Oxford University Press, 1979), 113.

Two

DEIDRE LYNCH

Domesticating Fictions and Nationalizing Women: Edmund Burke, Property, and the Reproduction of Englishness

I could not perceive the propriety of a man's liking two
women at the same time, or a woman's having a platonic
attachment for half a dozen lovers; and I owned that I did not
wish divorce could be as easily obtained in England as in France.
All which proved that I have never been out of England—a great
misfortune! I dare say it will soon be discovered that women as well
as madeira cannot be good for any thing till they have crossed the line.

—Maria Edgeworth
Leonora [1805]: an admonitory report on the latest fashions from France

She is perceived as more of an outside agitator
than even an inside saboteur—a foreign female . . .

—Patricia J. Williams,
"Bewitched: The Demonization of Hillary Clinton" [1993]

IN THE COURSE of the French Revolution, Seamus Deane explains, "England created a series of images of France which then produced countervailing images of England." As a participant in this process, Edmund Burke contributed to a formation of English nationalism with remarkable staying power: while writing against France, Burke extolled the political wisdom that inspired Englishmen to give "our frame of polity the image of a relation in blood" and to adopt "our fundamental laws into the bosom of our family affections."[1] At intermittent conjunctures since the era when Jacobins undertook a universal crusade for liberty and when Antijacobins like Burke championed insular wisdom, the symbolism of Englishness has emphasized the familiar, familial pleasures of life at home. Indeed, English nationalism's project of identity formation has frequently operated by reminding citizens that they all have mothers.

This political project, which Burke's francophobic writings of the 1790s outlined in a preliminary way, correlates political obedience with a loving filial submissiveness. It identifies state authority with the "pleasing illusions" that domesticity fosters, and that a man subscribes to whenever he "subdue[s] [his] pride and power" and sits himself down at his tea-table or fireside (*Reflections*, 171). To dismiss the rational republic that was being constructed by Jacobin France, Burke lauded the superior attractions of a *mother*-country that would be loved because it was "lovely" (*Reflections*, 172). With the matrocentric inflection that Burke gave it, this statecraft aimed at no more than what comes naturally to speakers of English: to homogenize the private and public meanings carried in the words "home" and "domestic," to make home life underwrite the authority of administrative institutions like the Home Office, and to make mothering the very type of domestic policy.

Political scientist Cynthia Enloe has observed that nationalism, more so than other ideologies, has space in its vision for real as well as symbolic women, since no nation can survive without children being born and nurtured. Historian Linda Colley has shown how Burke's female contemporaries found routes to public activism while, stitching flannel garments for British troops and raising statues to Wellington, they enlisted in small units of patriotism at home.[2] Nonetheless, the rapidity with which an American "first lady" has become a "foreign female" should signal to us just how precarious the position of nationalized women can be. In *Reflections on the Revolution in France* [1790], Burke famously portrayed Queen Marie Antoinette as a lovely mother in distress—and mourned because "ten thousand swords [did not leap] from their scabbards" in the royal parent's defense (170). Yet Burke also alluded to female fertility with horror. "Revolution harpies of France" are even now, he warned in *A Letter to a Noble Lord* [1797], "both mothers and daughters," "adulterously lay[ing] their eggs in the nest of every neighbouring state."[3] What is horrible about those harpies is what they do to the distinctions that underpin personal and national identities. Their adultery contests the fictions of paternity that tell men who they are: their migratory maternity mixes up and menaces the system of differences through which nations identify their selves.

In an age of growing demographic and pronatalist consciousness, when state policies first dictate the medical surveillance of pregnancy and administration of child-rearing, Burke envisions monster mothers— home(land)-wrecking mothers—of this sort with some regularity. And doing so, Burke also points despite himself to the contingent politics of reproduction. He points to how motherhood is a social category, subject to constant contest.

Nonetheless, few commentators look beyond Burke's self-portrait— where the patriot is imaged as ladies' man—and acknowledge the instabilities in his view of the ladies. Commentators who do look this far harmonize two very different views of female generativity into a single structure of meaning when they manage that ambivalence by spreading it over the consecutive stages of an oedipal narrative.[4] One can easily read the conjunction of harpies and lovely mothers in this way. One can chart a history in which generation after generation of sons accede to patrimony. In such a history, as we know, the menace to masculine identity and self-ownership exercised by the phallic mother at last gives way (because the pre-oedipal *is* merely a phase) to the serene passivity proper to the mother/wife, object of desire and exchange, who secures men's relations for them. My aim in highlighting the de-territorialization of mothers that Burke's excurses into the grotesque evoke, and that Burke's heritage-based idea of the nation in fact demands, is different from this. Rather than detecting in Burke's francophobia this boy's own story about property-owning selves, I hope in this essay to frame the intertwining of mother-love and matrophobia in Burke's texts in a way that contests rather than assumes Romantic-era inventions of motherhood and nation.

Noting Burke's allusions to an un-homey or anti-national maternity can prompt us to recognize women on the outside of the oedipal economy's confines. It can prompt us to recognize Romantic-era narratives of desire and generation that are not organized by the principle of the nation-state—and so provoke us into attending more carefully to the paradoxes of that nationalist identity-discourse that was, in the final analysis, a by-product of imperial confrontations, an idiom adapted to that chaotic moment when English prosperity depended as never before on expropriating the resources of far-flung colonies and on dominating international trade. My hope in this essay, then, is to combine an attention to the gender-specific dislocations that have constituted English *Romanticism,* with a rethinking of *Englishness* that would take its cue from Sara Suleri's argument about the unsettling intimacies that arise under the aegis of Empire, intimacies that mean that English nationalism (as much as Indian post-coloniality) is "vexed by its formulation in other worlds."[5] Reconsidering how Burke articulates national existence with women's reproduction of the species can provoke us into rethinking the readiness with which we assimilate women's cultural labors to the labor of the nation's self-production, and to the domestic in multiple senses of that term.

As I shall argue in the first section, women embody the Romantic

nation, and at the same time they stand to one side of the inter-generational transmission of property and (what amounts to the same thing
for Burke) of nationality. This instability in women's place compromises Burke's exposition of Englishness as a "family settlement"—and
his exposition of patriotism as the offspring of those "natural impulses"
that sustain a network of kin relations (*Reflections*, 120). This suggests
a way to read Burke's alarmist allusions to a migratory maternity and,
in a related set of tropes, to the mutations that "English" and "French,"
and "metropolitan" and "colonial," manufactures and meanings undergo in the course of cross-channel or trans-imperial commercial traffic. The sometime M.P. for the port of Bristol, representative for a community of slave-traders and merchant-adventurers, often deploys these
tropes. He often evokes (with Maria Edgeworth) occult associations between women and well-traveled bottles of madeira, and obsesses over
the diversions and decontextualizations of objects that are a conspicuous feature of international relations of production and expropriation.
(Burke obsesses, that is, over exactly those commercial entanglements
that English merchants created when they "improved" their madeira
by dispatching the cargoes on trans-equatorial circuits from Madeira,
to the East Indies, and only then to England).[6] With tropes like these,
I shall argue, Burke's texts half-acknowledge that "relations" are subject to rewriting. Burke's texts hint that those confined meanings of
"relation" that a filial patriot might wish to promote—ideas of consanguinity and connections made inside mothers' bodies—might well be
derivative of another meaning, something like the unrestricted, denatured sense that "relation" is assigned in the *Anti-Oedipus*, where a relation is "a report or an account, an inscription within the over-all process of inscription."[7]

   As Homi Bhabha maintains, a nation is not sustained solely by the
pedagogy that tells us who we all are—that inscribes us with, in Burke's
parlance, the "stamp of our forefathers" (*Reflections*, 181). A nation
depends, in addition, on a different modality of narrative, the performativity whereby its everydayness and ongoingness are signified. This
performativity requires women and men to be authors of their own
utterances and actions.[8] It allows them the power to re-inscribe—rewrite—relations. As exercised by women of the Romantic period, such
authorship produced plots that disarticulated "mother" and "country."
The Burkean themes of migrant maternity, disinheritance, and sexual
improprieties of multinational proportions preoccupied a significant
strand of early-nineteenth-century women's fiction. In the brief, concluding section to my essay, I hope to illustrate that point as I sketch
the denaturing of national codes of place, belonging, and body politics
that features prominently in an "English" novel authored by Frances

Burney, in an "Anglo-Irish" novel authored by Lady Morgan, and in a "French" novel, a disorienting staging of both English domesticity and Napoleonic family values, authored by Germaine de Staël.

In disassembling the nation's structures of reproduction and transmission, these three women writers acquired a certain notoriety; they did not, however, secure themselves places within either Romanticism or the alternative canons engendered by feminist revisions. Their marginality is in part the consequence of the way Burke's nationalism has been harnessed to the pedagogic projects of the nation-state. For the Victorian architects of English studies Burke's Antijacobin writings were touchstone texts. Bracketing Edmund Burke's Irish birth and Catholic associations, celebrating him instead as a card-carrying defender of the national interest, figures like David Masson and Henry Morley of London University and Edward Dowden of the University of Dublin made texts like *Reflections on the Revolution* and *A Letter to a Noble Lord* crucial components of the state's educational apparatus. Burke was, for example, one of three authors studied in the inaugural 1867 session of London University's English section. Late-nineteenth-century aspirants to the baccalaureate in English expected to sit examinations on Burke's style. Masson, Morley, and Dowden made Burke's capacity for seeing "the life of society in [a] rich, concrete . . . way" and his horror of the Jacobins' zeal for universal truths into *the* reference-points for a project of canon-formation that insisted upon the bond between "poetry and patriotism of the best sort." When, accordingly, one reads in Dowden of Edmund Burke's devotion to family life, of how Burke was able to conceive the "majesty" of a nation's life because he knew "the beauty of his own daily life," one witnesses the institution of a Romantic imagination that ever since has domesticated all it regarded.[9]

The order of verisimilitude created as those English professors set out the terms for Englishness relegated the women's narratives with which I am concerned to inaudibility. At those times when "the theme of identity saturates the discursive field, drowning out other social and cultural possibilities," women writers' narratives, especially, have had to be "domestic."[10] The studies that have set the terms for female authors' inclusion within Romanticism too often perpetuate those idioms of consanguinity and filiation—tested and true modes of naturalizing social hierarchy—that underwrite notions of "mother countries" and underwrite the protocols of literary legitimacy.[11] (To turn from William to his sister, Dorothy, or to redefine Romanticism by privileging scenes of Englishwomen and men's job-sharing—like those *Frankenstein* images in its portrayal of the DeLaceys' cottage economy—is still to conceptualize the cultural terrain in the circumscribed terms of the nation and the family affair.)[12] The fact that Romanticism continues to wield this domesticating power motivates my return to the digressions and figurative excesses that disorganize Burke's formative articulation of the national idiom. For when Burke evokes moments of disintegration in the nation's family romance, he opens the space for other, denatured relations.

Like domestic fictions, Burke's Antijacobin writings recount love stories. He hymns a love of country that is itself bred by mother-love. When Burke applauds the English constitution because it adopts laws "into the bosom of our family affections," he reveals a state that strives not to contain, as in earlier political theories, but to harness and to incite the citizen's passions (*Reflections*, 140). "To be attached to the subdivision," Burke writes in the *Reflections*, "to love the little platoon we belong to in society, is the first principle . . . of public affections. It is the first link in the series" (136).

In granting priority to the political subject's affective life, Burke at once presupposes and advances an epochal sexualization and oedipalization of domestic space. According to Foucault, the sexological sciences and confessional apparatus that arose in the late eighteenth century made that system of relations we now call "the family" into an "obligatory locus of affects, feelings, love": within "the family," "sexuality ha[d] its privileged point of development [and was] incestuous from the start." The emphatic heterosexuality of Burke's *Enquiry into the Sublime and the Beautiful*—where the son's yearning for his beautiful mother and terror of his sublime father constitute the very bases of aesthetic judgment—operates to similar effect.[13] The clutter of "armorial portraits," "monumental inscriptions," "records, evidences, and titles" that makes the *Reflections* into something of a cabinet of antiquities could be viewed, to be sure, as the trappings of an *ancien régime* apparatus of power, one focused on maintaining a system of family alliances (*Reflections*, 121). That should not distract us, however, from how, in his eagerness to make the political subject *feel*, to invigilate the citizen's sensibilities, Burke also contributes to that newer device of power, "the deployment of sexuality." Burke's political anxieties extend, after all, as far as the "cold relation," a target for family therapy in so far as his incapacity for sentiment prohibits him from becoming a "zealous citizen" (*Reflections*, 315). This means that the lovely and loved nation-state Burke idealizes when he writes against the French Republic conforms to the profile of Foucault's "modern governmentality": such a state governs by means of a knowledge that constitutes collectivities, according to the slogan that to govern means to populate, *and* it governs by means of that sexual saturation of the family that renders kinship a matrix of individualization.[14]

Patriotism intersects with that individualization via a new conception of the time of the nation and of the self, one that Michael Warner connects to the heterosexual order when he describes "repro-narrativity"—"a relation to self that finds its proper temporality and fulfillment in generational transmission." By linking the nation to the oedipal household, Burke presents the state as the primary means for effecting the continuation of the species, as the very image of the historical. His aim is to persuade the English to envision the nation, as he himself does in a much-anthologized draft of a 1782 speech, not "as an idea of . . . individual momentary aggregation, but . . . an idea of continuity, which extends in time as well as in numbers and in space."[15] To live in a nation is for Burke a happy condition because it means participating in "a partnership between those who are living, . . . who are dead, and . . . who are to be born" (*Reflections*, 195). This higher form of parental narcissism ensures that "the dust and powder of individuality [will not] at length [be] dispersed to the winds" (*Reflections*, 193).

In "Fear of a Queer Planet," Warner interrogates the presuppositions lending glamour to this "partnership." He shows how the institution of a paradigmatically reproductive sexuality has falsely equated heterosexual sex with *the* route to self-transcendence and social reproduction (as if the population would not continue to "sustain itself even if every coupling were random as to gender"). At the same time, Warner suggests, this "repronormativity" has also mediated the imperatives of a capitalist growth economy. Ruth Perry, in a similar vein, identifies in the growing demographic consciousness emerging in England during the Seven Years' War ("when more people were needed to . . . sail the ships, defend the seas, and populate the colonies") a "heady new belief in the . . . manipulation of natural forces for greater productivity." She associates that instrumentality not only with the eighteenth century's empire-building, capitalizing of agriculture, and industrializing of manufactures, but also with contemporary rearrangements in the psychological constellation of the family.[16]

What Burke's paean to partnership between those who are living, dead, and yet to be born should bring home to us is that his status in political theory as a redoubtable ideologue of tradition rests (as C. B. Macpherson noted) on his defense of a *capitalist* tradition specifically.[17] Tradition can (in Blackstone's *Commentaries* for instance) denote a transfer of property; and it is tradition in just this narrowed sense of heritage that inspires Burke's Antijacobin writings. Thus, as Mary Wollstonecraft observed, one of the few rights of man that Burke will acknowledge is man's right to perpetuate property in his family. That one can do this with property is, Burke proposes, one of the most "interesting circumstances belonging to it" (*Reflections*, 140), and he uses "interesting" here in two senses, according to a usage, becoming obsolete in the 1790s, that made interesting objects those to which persons had legal title, and also in the modern sense denoting that which appeals to persons' emotions and which makes them feel.[18]

Burke's feeling exposition of the importance of being English draws directly on the juridical framework that underpins a growth economy and that allows property to become productive and imperially self-expanding. Furthermore, Burke conceives of English liberty, and the Englishman's nationality, *as* objects of property, articles to which some have title and others do not. "It has been the uniform policy of our constitution to claim and assert our liberties, as an *entailed inheritance* derived to us from our forefathers, and to be transmitted to our posterity" (*Reflections*, 119).

Entails—legal devices used to keep estates within family-lines and prevent their liquidation—register the paradoxical way in which Anglo-American property law vests rights and power in property or in the fact of ownership, rather than in the owner. Tolerating some vagueness or precariousness in the connection between owners and their properties, property law has customarily deemed the state to have a greater interest in assuring against failures of continuity and of perpetuity, than in making property definitively personal. Judith Roof makes this aspect of property law central to her study of the parallels that link present-day abortion statutes to the fair-use provisions of copyright laws. She argues that the property rationale organizing the regulation of reproductions (of photocopies and progeny) can be discerned both in case law's concentration on the "work of authorship," rather than the author, and in its concentration on the fetus and the pregnancy, rather than the mother. As Roof explains, the law's privileging of perpetuity undermines the legal visibility of women. In so far as the copyrightability of a work can be purchased, the author recedes as a protected legal personage behind the owner (publisher). And, in the same way, the attaching of rights to the fetal "work" undoes the biological link between pregnant woman and fetus, replacing it with "a property-engendered uncertainty . . . that works to wrest control of reproductive processes from the mother to the state (father)."[19] The very property principles that Antijacobins defend through the 1790s effectually make mothers and authors into non-owners, classifying them as those who through making copies exert control over material belonging to another, a control that is not legally sanctioned and that must be legally delimited.

The analogy between English liberties and an entailed inheritance does useful work in Burke's discourse, providing, it would seem, the perfect device for imaging and reinforcing national distinctness and unity as well as national perpetuity. By definition, an entailed property stays within the family. There it fortifies the boundaries that separate insiders from outsiders. However, if we think hard about the paradoxes of the property principles from which entails derive, and if we think hard about this analogy between entails and statutory limitations on abortion, we will be able to discern something odd about the logic of Burke's narration of the nation. The moment at which the woman disappears from the family—recedes into legal invisibility—is also the moment when the idea of the nation that Burke applies to his indubitably commercial state reveals itself as self-cancelling. When Burke defines Englishness as "locked fast as in a . . . family settlement, grasped as in a kind of mortmain forever" (*Reflections*, 120), a property rationale overrides Burke's concern that the state be sutured by "natural impulses," and it supersedes even those feelings regularly enlisted to legitimate capitalist accumulation. In the tradition of possessive individualism issuing from Locke's *Treatise on Government*, what could seem more *un*natural than being prohibited from doing what one wishes either with one's property or with the products of one's body?

What is revealed, then, when one makes gender central to one's hermeneutic, is that the image of the entail does more than capture the nation's self-identity. It also makes visible a breakdown in the discursive and libidinal mechanisms that states set in place for mediating between citizens' formative attachments and their patriotism, between the home and the homeland. For in deploying this trope for national-belonging, Burke ceases to privilege that particular narrative about "natural impulses" which centers on the reciprocal affection between mother and child, a prime image in Western culture for an ethic of mutual care. Women are transported here from the center of a nationalizing system of affect to the system's margins: this is a de-territorialization of maternity at which Burke actively connives. "The 'motherland' of male nationalists," Anne McClintock observes, "may . . . not signify 'home' and 'source' to women": "*gender* difference between women and men serves to symbolically define the limits of *national* difference and power between *men*. Excluded from direct action as national citizens, women are subsumed symbolically into the national body politic as its boundary and metaphoric limit."[20] When Burke construes Englishness as patrimony—when he delineates history as the transmission of economic value and nationality from father to son—he disinherits women.

Burkean statecraft empowers the male citizen so that, like Freud's narcissist, he is "the mortal vehicle of a[n] . . . immortal substance."

But within this scheme female identity is bereft of the stability that proprietorship customarily provides in Enlightenment theories of political individuality, where possession of an estate is "personality-sustaining."[21] For this reason perhaps, because women's self-possession is by law tenuous, Burke is repulsed by women's assertions of "their" political citizenship. When he describes the October Women's March on Versailles or women's presence in the public space of the National Assembly, when he encounters women who actively claim a direct relation to national agency, Burke sees prostitution, and he re-sees the nation as a marketplace. At such moments, female fertility represents to Burke the power to derail the generational transmission of economic value and to demolish the sexual economy of patriotism. Burke's first *Letter on a Regicide Peace* [1796] reserves its most vituperative rhetoric for the Frenchwoman who appeared before the National Assembly in 1792 to request the repeal of civil incapacities on illegitimate children. The Jacobins, Burke sneers, call her a "mother without being a wife." He calls her a "prostitute." (In fact the woman was most likely a spokesperson for the populationist policies of the Republic's Comité de Mendacité: the committee had advocated that repeal as a means of multiplying that useful human resource, "the enfants de la patrie.")[22] The passion that propels Burke in this passage is the same that incites him when he presents the difference between a French revolution and its English forerunner as the difference between a "nursery of future revolutions" and a "parent of settlement" (*Reflections*, 112), or when he describes the Jacobin Republic as a breeding woman who gives birth to "an abundant litter of constitutions" ("Second Letter," 305). Burke is incited to matrophobia by a runaway female sexuality, a disorder that simultaneously over-produces babies and fails to replicate the politico-economic order. Linda Zerilli comes to similar conclusions when (quoting the *First Letter on a Regicide Peace*) she analyzes Burke's opposition to the National Assembly's establishment of civil marriage and its relaxing of divorce laws:

> the symbolic figure of the "frenzied" mother or woman that haunts Burke's rhetorical universe represents an inverted social world . . . in which reproduction outside of marriage destroys property and all other forms of male self-representation by destroying the legal fiction of paternity. For "when the matrimonial connection is brought into so degraded a state of concubinage," the common prostitute and the conventional wife are not only the same in law . . . ; they are engaged in a similar occupation: that of producing children without fathers.[23]

The channel-crossing "Citoyenne" whom Burke envisions in his fourth *Letter on a Regicide Peace*—she who is "spouse of the twenty-first husband, he the husband of the thirty-first wife" and who is nonetheless welcomed by deluded Englishwomen into "the rank of honourable matrons"—is his caricature of the numerous Frenchwomen who, through broaching the question of divorce to the National Assembly, also manifested their new sense of national belonging ("Fourth Letter," 113). (Two-thirds of the divorces declared in Lyon and Rouen between 1792, when the Assembly reformed marriage laws, and 1803 were initiated by the wives.)[24]

Burke's habit of accusing political women of licentiousness has been notorious since Wollstonecraft defended Parisians as industrious mothers and said, glossing her adversary's purple passage on "the furies of hell": "probably you mean women who gained a livelihood by selling vegetables or fish" (*Vindication*, 30). Wollstonecraft's identification of the women would, however, do little to assuage Burke's fears. Costermongers would remind Burke of "constitution-mongers" (*Reflections*, 304). And the "usual emblematic burden" of costermongers, as Catherine Gallagher notes, is to bring to view the unnaturalness and unremitting mobility of an expanding money economy.[25] They make Burke see all those aspects of the market that make it hard for a patriot to describe an Englishness that is inalienably England's. In transforming the single mother who has the temerity to speak to the National Assembly into "a prostitute," Burke exacerbates these difficulties. He compounds the error committed by this "unnatural mother" of a natural child as he makes it the outcome of her participation in commercial exchange. As Zerilli notes, the profligate reproductive powers exercised by *sans-culottes* women look to Burke too much like another Jacobin menace to the meaning of property, that form of unauthorized copying which multiplies paper money. Burke's alarm over the menace that women's fertility can pose to exactly those property principles that women's bodies, functioning properly as copy machines, are meant to ensure, was reprised, notably, when the *Antijacobin Review* gossiped about "the dreadful number of abortions" on the Jacobinical Continent.[26]

The moments when Burke finds it difficult to activate the trope of a passive maternity that underwrites the nation are often moments when he is obliged to think about the reproduction of cultural and economic value in terms that resist containment within a national framework. The model for the transmission of nationality and value that Burke takes from inherited property is shadowed by another model, that of trade. For Burke, the problem that costermongers, constitution-mongers, or the *Reflections'* "smugglers" of "adulterated metaphysics" (187) pose, is that they remind us that property does not always stay at home, but goes elsewhere. And to think about the long-distance journeys of commodities (even innocuous commodities like the vegetables and fish

Wollstonecraft puts into the Parisiennes' hands) is to think in a way that severs the connection between persons and things and undermines the concept of "perpetual ownership" Burke invokes to settle national identity. In a capitalist order, *any* property, to count as property, must be alienable. It must survive the process of being removed from its original owner.[27] Burke's problem is, then, his inability to ignore the violations of the personal intrinsic to the idea of property.[28] His political theory aims to use possessions and household belongings (our "gallery of portraits" [*Reflections*, 121]) to stabilize the nation's self-relation, but Burke's tropes dwell on the alienation of property and on the unmooring of identity that is inherent to exchange.

That Burke is intent on an exposition of Englishness makes matters worse. For Romantic political economy, the prosperity of the nation-state was to begin at home (much as, for Burke, public affection was to begin with the "little platoon"). As Wordsworth put it in a "Sonnet Dedicated to National Independence and Liberty," not from "fleets and armies and external wealth: / But from *within* proceeds a Nation's health." But, as a commercial, empire-building nation, England could perpetuate its identity only when it weakened the borders defining the place of its insiders, as it absorbed the alien resources beckoning from outside.[29] England "existed out of itself as much as in."[30] At repeated moments in her *Letters from France* [1790], the Girondist-sympathizer Helen Maria Williams takes stock of the English patriot's conflicted attitude toward the global commerce that both supports the nation and compromises its self-identity. In Englishmen's cherished emblem of their expansionist energies and their constitutional talents as navigators, Williams finds a symbol for the Jacobinism that Englishmen feared. She compares the new Jacobin politics, with its universalizing cast, to "a modern ship of discovery," which, "sailing sublimely over the untracked ocean, unites those together whom nature seemed for ever to have separated, and throws a line of connexion across the divided world." And, lamenting her countrymen's hostility toward France's new constitution, castigating the *Reflections on the Revolution* in particular, Williams writes: "I cannot but suspect that, while the fair and honourable traders of our commercial country act with the most liberal spirit in their ordinary dealings with other nations, they wish to make a monopoly of liberty, and are angry that France should claim a share of that precious property; by which, however, she may surely be enriched, without our being impoverished."[31]

There is another reason for labelling Burke a monopolist. He would like to present commercial instability (and the form of reproductive crisis represented by the "fraudulent circulation and depreciated paper" of a credit economy [*Reflections*, 136]) as problems monopolized by the French. However, allusions to cross-channel traffic pepper the *Letters on a Regicide Peace* and the *Reflections on the Revolution*; Burke finds it hard to deny the complicities that unite the two economies. Thus, in a passage that disputes the French Jacobins' claim to be no more than imitators of England's constitutional-monarchists, Burke casts revolutionary ideas as pre-eminently portable, smuggle-able properties: "we ought not, on either side of the water, to suffer ourselves to be imposed upon by the counterfeit wares which some persons, by a double fraud, export to you in illicit bottoms, as raw commodities of British growth though wholly alien to our soil, in order afterwards to smuggle them back again into this country, manufactured after the newest Paris fashion" (*Reflections*, 110). In a 1791 speech on the Quebec Act, which had as its flimsy pretext the supposition that Parliament might provide a Jacobin constitution to the recently conquered and French-speaking colony of Quebec, Burke envisioned similar dangerous liaisons. The lines of connection he conjures up undo the differences not just, in this case, between England and France, but also between the metropolis and England's ("French") colonies, and—thanks to brokering purveyed by the Marsellais—between the Orient, source of England's raw cotton, and the Occident: "Ought this example to induce us to send to our colonies a cargo of the rights of man? As soon send them a bale of infected cotton from Marseilles."[32]

In passages of this kind Burke negates the question of a cargo's place of origin in order to follow commodities around. The mobility of property he foregrounds blurs the line between identity and difference by which a nation postulates its self. Burke all but acknowledges here that the English "customs"—the habitual practices, common law, "second nature"—that his Antijacobin texts revere fail to operate as "customs" in the second sense of the term—as economic barriers that might stop traffic at the frontier and secure the differences between the outside and the inside of the body politic.[33]

Around the turn of the nineteenth century, a new gender-coding made the commercial "world of moving objects" into a feminine space, and installed economic man as conquering hero in the place of that comparatively feminized eighteenth-century creature, the financier-speculator wrestling with his appetites and fantasies.[34] Trading with its entanglements could be unequivocally separated off from possessing, consumption from production, once these interdependent functions were re-viewed through the polarizing framework provided by nineteenth-century ways of thinking gender. As Sally Shuttleworth has shown, nineteenth-century medicine's concern with regulating the female uterine economy contributed to that gender-coding. When medicine began to predict physiological and moral catastrophes for women if the circulation of their blood was impeded, if their bodies did not flow, men were offered a displaced resolution to anxieties about self-possession that had been exacerbated by the new conditions of the industrial labor market. Men were exempted from the unsteady oscillations of the body, and the uncertain flux of social circulation that was figured through those oscillations. Thus reassured, they could believe themselves to be "the living incarnations of the rational individualists and self-made men of economic theory." If Burke in the 1790s anticipated this gendered polarization of exchanging and possessing, he could also look backward for an association of women, luxury, and trade imbalances that operated to a similar reassuring effect. At moments, his Antijacobinism seems to reprise a genre of political insult that flourished at the time of the Seven Years' War, and that involved abusing rival politicians for the cross-border shopping their women did. A standard way to humiliate the Jacobite or francophile politician was to show him a picture of his mistress arriving at Dover with portmanteaus full of "French cloaths, laces, and trinkets."[35]

In some respects, Burke seems to mobilize these strategies of scapegoating: for in his abuse of the Jacobins he goes out of his way to evoke what was already seen as a feminized and sexualized terrain, associated with women readers and writers. He evokes Romantic culture's prime image of disorderly women and consuming passions when he describes the English Constitutional Society, his first target in the *Reflections*, as, at base, a circulating library—"intended, for the circulation, at the expence of the members, of many books, which few others would be at the expence of buying" (*Reflections*, 86). Likewise, again summoning the image-repertory that connected women and circulation, Burke repeatedly locates the origins of the French menace in correspondence—in letters that cross and recross the English Channel. Letters are a problem for Burke's statecraft of propertied patriotism because by their nature they involve an impropriety that troubles ascriptive ties—that troubles the system of self-representation that is property. For whose property *is* a letter, its recipient's or its author's? Burke's complaint is that the English Jacobins have opened up a correspondence with strangers (e.g., *Reflections*, 88; "Fourth Letter," 106). And, like the improper letter-writing that tempts the novelistic heroines of his era, such correspondence can only lead to criminal conversation.

Burke's writings on the Revolution are, however, themselves epistolary: *Reflections* is conceived of as a letter sent to a young man in Paris, and Burke's own contribution to cross-channel traffic.[36] The feminization implicit in Burke's self-indulgence "in the freedom of epistolary intercourse" is generally explicated with reference to his appropriation of a terrain of feminine sensibility—Wollstonecraft remarked, "Even . . .

ladies, sir, may . . . retail in theatrical attitudes . . . your sentimental exclamations" (*Reflections*, 92; *Vindication*, 8). But Burke also perforce
aligns himself with women when, as in his extended metaphor about
the fraud presenting "counterfeit wares" as commodities of British
growth, he places himself on both sides of the Channel at once. When
he finds himself, as he says, "on either side of the water," when he follows deracinated commodities and missives around, Burke enacts the
transnational mobility of his Revolution harpies.

I have described Burke's nationalist discourse as presenting a double
image of maternity—first, a mother whose lovely image guarantees the
nation's cohesion and whose womb is an "awful family trust," and, second, a mother whose procreative powers cannot be assimilated to the
construction of a family history or to the formation of a Mother country, a woman whose fertility imperils the inheritance of national belonging. As I have suggested, Burke finds thinking about this second
sort of mother useful for acknowledging, and also for distancing himself from, that "extra-territoriality" which is the "true genetic code of
Britishness."[37] She helps him adjust to the hard economic fact that his
nation-state cannot easily be envisioned as an awesome partnership between the living, dead, and unborn. Given the continuing hegemony
of imperial commerce and international banking over domestic industrial production, what makes England English is still much closer to
what Burke described with disdain as a "partnership agreement in a
trade of pepper and coffee, callico or tobacco" (*Reflections*, 194).

But just as Burke at some points in his prose cannot tell what side
of the channel he is on, it can be difficult to tell these two mothers
apart. A woman disappears in the *Reflections on the Revolution* in a passage immediately preceding this reference to the "pepper and coffee"
of the English import-export trade. In this passage, the Jacobins' failure
to revere political tradition makes Burke think of "those children of
their country who are prompt rashly to hack that aged parent in pieces,
and put him into the kettle of magicians, in hopes that . . . they may
regenerate the paternal constitution and renovate their father's life"
(194). Burke is here reworking Medea's story in Ovid's *Metamorphoses*.
Infanticide and patricide—women's destruction of patriarchal lines—
make that story famous: Medea kills her sons and tricks the daughters
of Pelias into killing their father. However, the section of the narrative
that seems to have attracted Burke pivots on how Jason, having conveyed Medea from her "barbarian" land to Greece, having converted
displacement into domestication according to the classic pattern of the
civilizing mission, asks his new wife to prove her love by saving his father, Aeson, from old age. Burke edits out the substance of his allusion
and, uncharacteristically, the gender-identity of the patricide. Perhaps,

one might surmise, Ovid's tale of a daughter-in-law who is exiled by marriage and who no longer counts as "a child of her country" may resemble too closely the romance that Burke relates in the *Reflections* when he tells of how in 1701 the architects of the Act of Settlement "searched in strange lands for a foreign princess . . . in order that the monarchy might preserve an unbroken unity through all ages" (109). Medea's tale could easily be the story of Princess Sophia, the Electress of Hanover—just as it could be the story of any of the queens (Caroline, Charlotte) who succeeded thereafter to the post of first lady of the land.

Such domestications of "foreign females," I have argued, were crucial to Romantic Englishness: in some measure English state formation was a matter of administrating child-bearing women as national, nation-preserving resources. For Burke, England's community identity depends, at a time of Jacobin viciousness more than ever, on an acculturation process involving the reproduction of examples of good manners. How better to form such good habits than at one's mother's knee—in the presence of beauty, which is, according to Burke's *Enquiry*, a site where men are governed by the passion for repetition and for imitation? Suggestively, Tom Paine in *The Rights of Man* ascribed Burke's political and rhetorical eccentricities to his having missed out on such a formative acculturation. In the course of a larger argument about England's want of a written constitution, Paine diagnosed Burke's genius as likewise lacking "a constitution. It is a genius at random and not a genius constituted."[38] Burke offers a plan for ensuring the continuity of the Englishman's distinctive patrimony, a theory of a nationalized femininity that might guarantee the patriarchal self-same. But, as the radical John Thelwall wryly observed, Burke's Antijacobinism had the effect of "making more democrats" in the 1790s than any text by Burke's adversaries. The diverse analogies "at random," the ungovernable metaphoric transformations, and (as James Mackintosh put it in his reply to the *Reflections*) the "undisciplined rabble of arguments" that distinguish Burkean discourse might still draw out those contradictions that nationalism's identity politics would disavow.[39]

However, in order to argue that there is something *valuable* about the way Burke's flights into figurative language link disorientation, dispossession, and women, I shall have to choose my terms carefully. The embarrassment that many now feel in the face of earlier feminisms' claim that "sisterhood is global" is testimony to how conditions of exile or statelessness lend themselves easily to romanticizing, and in too many senses of that term. The domestic politics mandated by nationalism—the policing of desire and sexuality that a nationalist statecraft entails—may well look like reasons for rejecting out of hand the terms

on which women have been included in the nation. But a feminist refusal to give hostages to the state's project of trans-generational stability must deal with the fact that, in practice, nationality is not merely
basic to claims that states make on individuals, but also basic to those
claims that individuals make, and *want* to make, on states.

Indeed, one way that we might use the moments of disintegration
in Burke's exposition of nation-ness is to remind ourselves that "the
history of women" comprises in many instances the trans-national histories of political and economic refugees, stateless denizens of those
"unimaginable communities" that are the frequent legacy of colonial
encounters.[40] The ambivalence that informs these histories of displacement and shelter-seeking, and the intricate calibrations of outside and
inside and here and there which that ambivalence necessitates, would
be lost to feminist critique if we either merely reiterated, or merely contested, the associative chain linking woman to home and to homeland.
Within current neocolonialist arrangements of the global economy, for
instance, the primary source of foreign currency for the Philippines
and Sri Lanka are the Philippine and Sinhalese women who labor
abroad as domestic servants, child care workers, or nurses. Their enforced expatriation was anticipated in Victorian England by the hundreds of thousands of Irish maidservants—Burke's countrywomen—
whose fate during the heyday of English domesticity was to be both
strangers within the home and laborers charged with the reproductive
preoccupations of home-making.[41] Remembering these women's status
as *international* actors can enhance current literary-feminist projects
of recovering the desires and antagonisms that made the "domestic
sphere" a hybrid and hybridizing location at the very time when it also
functioned as the retreat where the *paterfamilias* would recover his self-
possession.

Burke's bizarre conjunction of domestic fictions and of nightmares
about insurrectionary journeys taken by commodities and mobile
mothers reappeared recently. In the spring of 1992, when the European Community's Maastricht Treaty was up for ratification, Irish
voters confronted a conflict between the treaty's human rights codes
and the pronatalist regulation of reproduction that is written into Ireland's post-colonial constitution. Using the tool-kit that a national constitution provides to adjudicate between the claims of the "us" and of
the "them" had become tricky, because, not long before the plebiscite,
an Irish girl of fourteen, raped by a friend's father, had been prevented by federal injunction from traveling to England for an abortion.
Burke's ambivalence was reinscribed in the double image of Irish
womanhood that the media conjured up as they speculated on the
precedent that injunction set. The scenario the media envisioned was

one in which all women leaving Ireland would have to submit to a pregnancy test at the border-crossing, airport, or ferry terminal—even, it was said, women going to England for a bit of shopping. What has changed for Irishwomen in an age of globalization and Common Markets is that they're no longer apt to fall under suspicion because of goods they might smuggle inside the country, no longer incriminated by an association with contraband tea or lace. They fall under suspicion now because of fetuses they might smuggle out.[42]

When critics for the newly influential periodicals of the Romantic era wanted to teach certain women writers a lesson, they too relied on references to unnatural mothers and promiscuous female traders. In suggestive mixed metaphors, John Wilson Croker, reviewer for the *Quarterly* and avowed disciple of Burke, lambasted the novelist Lady Morgan as a "commercial bagman," who had, with the aid of her "man-midwife" husband, carted the "embryo manuscript" of her latest publication across Europe, only to see the work drop at last "all but stillborn from the press." Croker also (so the *Dictionary of National Biography* maintains) floated the malicious report that Morgan's anti-domestic itinerancy began when her mother gave birth to her aboard the Dublin packet, midway across the Irish Sea. This is of a piece with Croker's now notorious trashing of Frances Burney's last novel, *The Wanderer*. Burney's heroine is for Croker "a most [implausibly] moveable person," who "flies to London, about London, and from London." Burney too is for Croker a disgustingly gadabout woman, and he all but accuses her of treason because she mentions in *The Wanderer* the peace and good government she enjoyed as an internee in Napoleonic France.[43]

The geopolitical anxieties couched in this preoccupation with women on boats, on foot, and in carriages become evident when we realize that the reviewers' frequent allusions to the "Sapphos of the day" were also allusions to stateless women. Through new translations of the chronicle of Greek history carved into the Parian marble, Sappho the abandoned woman had, in the Revolutionary era, become Sappho the political exile. The result was, for patriots preoccupied with émigrés and foreign agents, a redoubling of the sexual threat that "Sapphos"—women who "cast aside at once the fetters of custom and the bonds of virtue"— posed to the patrilineal transmission of property and nationality.[44] That nemesis of national uniqueness, Burke's matriarchal community of harpies, seems to hover over the portrait of monstrous miscegenation that the *Anti-Jacobin* sketches when it reviews de Staël's *Corinne* (in some measure, a re-creation of Sappho's narrative of romantic catastrophe and exile) and complains that a heroine who unites "Italian and French voluptuousness with English virtue" represents a "physical impossibility." Burke's sneers at the "gipsey jargon" of the rights of man ("First Letter," 205) are reiterated when the *Quarterly* suggests that the language of Lady Morgan's texts is not English, but "terms picked up in all countries," and when the *Anti-Jacobin* avers that Morgan writes as if "our language" were not "sufficiently copious" for her "high-flown delineat[ions] of ideal sensations."[45] Worry over the fate of their mother tongue comes naturally to reviewers whenever they consider that the "inbred sentiments" which Burke made central to the nation's upkeep might be bred out of the national subject.

Because of the obsessive degree of concreteness such curmudgeonliness entails, reading the reviewers' tirades is like reading Burke, and is useful in the same way that registering Burke's rhetorical excesses can be. Burke's statecraft says one thing; his tropes say another. Likewise, in legislating the terms on which women's writings will be valued, the reviewers constantly remind us of the geopolitical stakes of an axiomatics that operates most successfully when those exigencies elude representation. Once we have read their abuse of mobile women, the reviewers' accolades for the "well-conducted" female novel that "confines imagination within due bounds" begins to read like the act of denying the woman's text a passport.[46]

In this respect, then, even as it helped to banish their writings from the canon, the reviewers' abuse contributes to what I take to be the common project of many Romantic-era women writers—one I shall trace by considering Morgan's *Woman, or, Ida of Athens* [1809], and, more extensively, de Staël's *Corinne, or Italy* [1807] and Burney's *The Wanderer* [1814]. That project involves divesting the reader of the fixed viewpoint that allows her to be sure about what belongs to home and what belongs elsewhere. Written in the aftermath of the Code Napoleon of 1804 and the copycat legislation other states enacted to bring their conditions for national belonging into line with those of France, the novels each interrogate the decree that a woman's nationality should follow her husband's and that her "citizenship in the nation [should be] mediated by the marriage relation within the family."[47] Each novelist calls attention to the normally muted narrative about the intergenerational transmission of patronym and property that sustains the narration of the nation, and that underlies her own reiteration of the nation's home truths. I am grouping the three texts together for an additional reason. The lines of transnational influence and translation (often in this era, women's work) that connect Lady Morgan to de Staël, and connect de Staël to Burney, should in themselves caution us against automatically classing women's works as the domestic products of distinct national traditions.[48]

A novelist like Burney not only conforms with the precepts laid down for "domestic fiction," when, for instance, she writes in the Preface to *The Wanderer* (a dedicatory epistle to her father) that the special task of the novel is to transmit "knowledge of the world" in a form that enables "juvenile credulity" to stay safely at home.[49] At a time when various Traitorous Correspondence and Alien Bills made exports and imports suspect, Burney also calls attention to the amphibious capitalism sustaining this domestic space. She characterizes *The Wanderer* not just as her tribute of filial love, not just as a prophylactic, home-saving device, but also as an object on a transnational commercial circuit that, she writes, "has already twice traversed the ocean in manuscript" and been vetted "at the Custom-house on either—alas!—hostile shore" (4).

Extending the rubric of novelist of disorientation to de Staël and Morgan will seem strange to those who know them as shrewd exploiters of the feminized matrix of patriotism and as developers of the genre of the national tale.[50] As they promote the cause of distinct, local cultures, both de Staël (writing for, and so in a sense imagining into existence, an Italy that was simultaneously being assimilated to Napoleon's imperial regime) and Morgan (writing in succession for Ireland, Greece, India, and Belgium) draw upon the idiom of civic allegory that throughout the nineteenth century produced postage-stamps and recruiting posters imaging Mariannes, Britannias, and Mother Irelands: beautifully generic national symbols capable of swaying whole populations to put on Burke's "soft collar of social esteem" (*Reflections*, 170).[51] Yet the assertion about the locality of identity that is made by the national tales' characterization, the assertion that the heroine is one with the nation, is counteracted by the narratives' peculiar way of reminding us that a real woman has two parents and that her allegiances are divided. Their heroines are by and large irredeemably hybrid. The equation between Ida and Athens, or between Corinne and Italy, that Morgan's and de Stael's titles foreground sits oddly with the circumstances of each heroine's birth and fate.

Ida is the daughter of an English mother and a Greek father; she is also for a moment (in a dystopic parody of the allegory of transcultural union that concludes Morgan's earlier *Wild Irish Girl*) bride to the Turkish governor of Greece. The disdar-aga's sudden death (on their wedding night) and the ensuing political unrest in Athens propel Ida across Europe and then to England. Ida's story concludes with her (re-)marriage to an exiled Greek nationalist who has turned to soldiering for Catherine the Great, presumably in the belief that Russian foreign policies will advance the cause of Greek independence. Similar hybridity and displacements organize de Staël's novel, even though, from the opening scene of her coronation at the Capitol, it invites us to view Corinne *as* Italy. De Staël does more than put her heroine on stage in this scene: in watching the Romans watching their muse ("an admirable product of our climate and our arts, an offspring of the past, prophet of the future"), we also witness a people experiencing its unity, as the Romans rapturously behold "their common bond."[52] (Corinne incites precisely that rallying together of the nation that Burke envisioned when he thought about the ten thousand swords leaping to the French queen's defense.) In her celebrated improvisations, Corinne is inspired by the voice of tradition. She speaks in the authentic accents of the *vox populi*. She is, at the same time, an Englishman's daughter, who, following the death of her Roman mother, has been raised in Yorkshire by her father's second wife. When, midway through her narrative, she leaves Italy in the hope of reunion with the lover who has abandoned her, an Englishman who happens to encounter Corinne assumes she is a compatriot, observing " 'You know very well that foreigners can never pronounce our language without an accent' " (*Corinne*, 380).

By contrast, the English of Frances Burney's heroine is accented (*Wanderer*, 643). This Wanderer *is* English no matter whether one traces her descent by her maternal or paternal bloodlines, yet well into its fifth volume her narrative still casts doubt on what that claim on the nation-state might mean. The offspring of a clandestine marriage that crossed class lines, Juliet Granville is raised in exile in a French convent: that surrogacy arrangement suits her father even better after, following Juliet's mother's death, he marries an Englishwoman of his own class and starts a second family. At the start of the French Revolution the father dies, having secured some part of his estate to his eldest child, but without ever having publicly acknowledged her existence or legitimacy. The onset of the Terror and a chain of circumstances that sees her blackmailed into marriage with an agent of Robespierre force Juliet to leave France and seek refuge in England—only to find herself harassed by threats of deportation, and "a helpless foreigner" in her "native country" (*Wanderer*, 210). Every move of this moveable person is thwarted by the cross-channel alliance formed between the Jacobin husband who wants her property and the English aristocrat—a distant relation—who wants to preserve his and his wards' property against her claims.

When she first arrives in England, Juliet believes that to traverse the Channel is to leave behind French slavery and enjoy English "liberty" (*Wanderer*, 751). The remainder of Burney's narrative confounds this schematic spatialization of political choices and, with it, the order of national differences. The blackface Juliet assumes for her crossing (a choice of disguise unmotivated by the demands of the plot) may be this heroine's private emblem for the translation in her condition: in the

aftermath of the Mansfield Judgment of 1772, the air of England was—
if only proverbially—too pure to be inhaled by slaves. Read in conjunction with the policies that preserved *Frenchness* from the miscegenating
intimacies of Empire—the *code noir* that in 1685 prohibited marriages
between French colonists and blacks; Napoleon's 1802 expulsion of
blacks from France following slave rebellions in the Caribbean colonies—Juliet's blackface accrues different meanings.[53] It becomes less a
costume to be shed at the happy conclusion of her narrative and so less
a prop to negotiations between England and France, home and away,
self and other; it becomes, instead, the narrative's sign for the contingency of national belonging. Her appearance as a "tawny Hottentot"
(*Wanderer*, 12)—coupled with the fact that Juliet contributes to Burke's
anxieties about cross-channel correspondence and traffic, smuggles
into England a letter addressed to a French émigré, and herself enters
the country under the auspices of a French pilot whose cargo is ordi-
narily contraband laces and cambricks—means that this heroine's "domestic virtues" seem beside the point, at least until her wedding and
installation in a home bring down Burney's curtain.

   In an argument that seeks to distinguish between the anti-imperial
project of a national liberation movement and the national*ism* that is a
hegemonic concept within the Irish nation-state, David Lloyd discrimi-
nates between two usages of feminine figures within Irish politics. Lloyd
proposes that a crucial difference of social dynamic distinguishes the
cultural nationalism organized around that iconic figure of her mother
country, Kathleen ni Houlihan, from the agrarian insurgencies, like
those of the Whiteboys or the Defenders, that organized themselves
around local female figures like Molly Maguire or Queen Sive:

> If the organizational structure of the Whiteboys can be seen as occupy-
> ing the metonymic axis of contiguity, nationalism and the state occupy
> the metaphoric axis, seeking to educe a moment of identity out of the
> disparate populations and individuals that constitute the people. . . .
> Whereas in the rhetoric of nineteenth-century nationalism, Kathleen
> operates as a symbol, literally calling upon good nationalists to subordi-
> nate their private interests to the greater will of the nation, Sive can be
> instantiated momentarily by any of the oppressed, transforming the in-
> dividual into an allegory of collective distress. The latter process re-
> quires a rhetoric of solidarity, but not necessarily of identification.[54]

Lloyd's distinction can help us to question how the novelists deploy
feminine civic allegory. More important, it can help us to understand
how it is that a book like *The Wanderer* seems to veer erratically between,
on the one hand, chronicling native English pluck and, on the other

hand, romancing an exotic, insurrectionary, diasporic subject, between reiterating and resisting the pedagogic relations nation-states use to tell us who we are. Juliet, "la sage petite Anglaise," really does strike us as a "female Robinson Crusoe" (*Wanderer*, 644; 873)—since she refuses to go native in English social circles too corrupted by luxury to tolerate a real domestic woman. Simultaneously, through her association with the slaves of the Revolutionary-era Caribbean, Juliet embodies a theorem about women's exilic condition, which not only sits awkwardly with her narrative's dynamic of repatriation, but which also appropriates the histories of women of color and displaces the specific reasons why an Afro-Carib subject might emblematize a mutinous and diasporic consciousness.[55] The sub-genre that Burney, Morgan and de Staël represent is preoccupied with *both* the enclosure and the crossing of geopolitical boundaries, with both that defining domestic affair, the reproduction of mothering, and the conditions of dispossession and bastardry that arise when desire takes women abroad.[56] Their sub-genre tries to offer a view of those non-national forms of social allegiance that Lloyd evokes, but it does so, with bewildering results sometimes, from a vantage point that necessarily lies inside the nation. This may be a vantage point from which one can image extra-territoriality or fantasize a "travelling theory" only by exploiting the figurative resources provided by the nation's empire-building—by evoking the histories of the Empire's moveable goods or of the Empire's equally deracinated and commodified peoples.

Granting paradigmatic status to Burke's tale of ruffians who take the king's place in the queen's bedchamber, Ronald Paulson maintains that the plot Europe used to explain the French Revolution was the oedipal story—hence, a romance about sons' succession to their patrimony and about the inter-generational transmission of men's property-rights in women. Paulson overlooks how the plot elaborated by Romantic-era women plays ex-tradition against the patrilineal mechanisms of tradition. Exploiting the narrative possibilities opened up by the warfare as well as by the legal reforms of the Revolutionary era, their plot turns on displacements—and on what we might well read as instances of divorce, surrogate mothering, and artificial seminations.[57] Their heroine's lack of a patronym—and her habit of contracting marriages (like the Wanderer's or Ida's) that don't really count as such—disorder family plots. In order to elude her pursuers the Wanderer refuses to use any name, true or false. When her identity is discovered, she proves to be both Julie Granville (in French) and Juliet Granville (in English), and so in one sense of the term to possess no identity at all. We never learn her married name—and the lacuna underscores how this contraband subject scrambles the terms by which the English law sorts out female identities; it underscores how, in the aftermath of the Republic's divorce decree, the married woman in France was a different sort of legal subject from the married woman in England.[58]

De Staël's Corinne is self-named: she adopts the name of a writer of classical Greece (an associate of Sappho) and seemingly takes herself out of the category of patriarchal property, after her stepmother, learning that she intends to return to Italy, forbids her the patronym. Even so, a father's will, and an almost verbatim re-presentation of Burke's narration of the nation, are the cause of Corinne's final victimization. Prompted by a letter from home in which his father tries to call him back to "local attachments," a letter which he receives only after his father's death, Corinne's English lover, Lord Nelvil, sacrifices Corinne to the demands of a dynastic, procreative plot. Nelvil's object is to conserve what his father calls, in the Burkean tones he manages to utter from beyond the grave, "that sense of nationality, those prejudices . . . that bind us together and make of our nation one body" (*Corinne*, 330). Yet the "natural" feelings, attachments and erotic energies that are nurtured in the family so as to "bind us together" produce by the close of the novel an unnatural effect very different from what Nelvil's father or Burke may have anticipated. Lucile, the woman who has become Lady Nelvil in Corinne's stead, is also the English half-sister to whom Corinne had been "a second mother." During her pregnancy, Lucile is "absorbed with memories of her sister" (*Corinne*, 386). The consequence is a daughter, Juliette, who is born with an Italian's dark hair and eyes, who resembles Corinne closely, and her parents not at all. The novel concludes with Juliette's Italian lessons, tutelage Corinne gives her from her deathbed. Artificial semination—the consequence of an irregularly conducted confinement and an improper exercise of an unconfined imagination—underwrites a fantasy of a trans-nation, in which Italy and England overlap to form a space for feminine solidarities and feminist identifications. De Staël manages to locate reproduction outside nature and outside the confines of the nation-state: in the movements of a woman's imagination, in the circulation of languages among women.

"Even in books, I like a confined locality." With that praise of Jane Austen's exposition of Englishness, Mary Russell Mitford opens in 1820 the series of sketches that became *Our Village*. For Mitford, Austen inaugurated a mode of fiction that allowed heroines and readers to stay at home in "a country village," "quite sure . . . of becoming intimate with every spot and every person it contains," and quite safe from "be[ing] whirled half over Europe at the chariot-wheels of a hero." In 1820 the reviewer of the *New Monthly Magazine* wrote in similar terms of the relief readers would take in resigning Lady Morgan's books and taking up Austen's. Such a turn was a repatriation, to, at the same time, England's green and pleasant land and a maternal bosom: "we turn from the dazzling brilliancy of Lady Morgan's works to repose on the soft green of Miss Austen's sweet and unambitious creations."[59]

By the time figures like Dowden and Morley set up the first departments of "English" in the mid-nineteenth century, that concept of idyllic domesticity could serve as the ground of self-evidence that connected Dowden's praise of Burke's ability to "see the life of society in [a] rich, concrete . . . way" to Morley's account of how "Miss Austen," "like Wordsworth[,] . . . sought to show the charm that lies under the common things about us."[60] This sanctioned reading of Jane Austen's villages—as resting-places that can function within the institution of Romanticism as adjuncts to Wordsworthian spots-of-time—has shaped the conditions under which other women have found admission to the canon. At the same time it has helped to repatriate Romantic-era writing and helped English departments to ignore that canon's "formulation in other worlds."

To read Austen or Mitford or Edmund Burke's filiopietistic love stories, as various modes of effecting the hegemony of the national remains something of a formalist gesture, unless we *also* enquire into those narratives that, from the perspective of the identity-discourses of the nation, never came to seem self-evident or truthful.[61] Perhaps a challenge feminist literary history should now take up is to see women's domestic fiction not solely (as Nancy Armstrong would have it) as an intervention into class politics that secured the dominance of a specific class sexuality, but also as an intervention that contested other ways of conceptualizing the locality of identity—that contested now unimaginable communities that drew differently and disorientingly on the cultural flows of Empire. As the recent intensification of nation-states' policies of compulsory maternity reminds us, as recent immiphobic discourses with their images of "foreign females' " profligate maternity should remind us too, some women have had reason to doubt domestic fictions' assertion that a woman's place is in the nation.

NOTES

1. Deane, *The French Revolution and Enlightenment in England, 1789–1832* (Cambridge: Harvard University Press, 1988), 3; Burke, *Reflections on the Revolution in France*, ed. Conor Cruise O'Brien (Harmondsworth: Penguin, 1968), 140. Subsequent references are to *Reflections* and appear in the text.

2. Enloe, *Bananas, Beaches, and Bases: Making Feminist Sense of International Politics* (Berkeley: University of California Press, 1990), 61; Colley, *Britons: Forging the Nation* (New Haven: Yale University Press, 1992), 254–61.

3. *Letter to a Noble Lord*, in R. B. McDowell, ed., *Writings and Speeches of Edmund Burke*, vol. 9 (Oxford: Clarendon, 1991), 156.

4. See, e.g., Linda M. G. Zerilli's "Text/Woman as Spectacle: Edmund Burke's 'French Revolution,' " *Eighteenth Century: Theory and Interpretation* 33 (1992): 47–72. Zerilli's discussion has been helpful and heartening for me. We both set out to supplement a narrow critical focus on Burke's chivalry and to examine how Burke reacts when women, as political actors, refuse to be associated with the traits of submission that are central to his gendered coding of social crisis. Still, I depart from Zerilli significantly: to posit a pre-oedipal mother is still (to quote Zerilli quoting Neil Hertz) to bring terror "back home to the father" (53), and in my view a psychoanalytic reading of the crises of procreative certainty dramatized in Antijacobinism reinstates exactly the discursive categories that Romantic culture developed to cope with those crises. Psychoanalytic critics have generally been more successful than Burke at folding desire and procreation smoothly into social reproduction and at bracketing the junctures where biological and cultural transmission are disarticulated. Psychoanalytic criticism of Burke overlooks the nervousness his prose exhibits whenever he depicts the deterritorialization of production and of biological reproduction.

5. *The Rhetoric of English India* (Chicago: University of Chicago Press, 1992), 10. See also Marlon Ross, "Romancing the Nation-State: The Poetics of Romantic Nationalism," in Jonathan Arac and Harriet Ritvo, eds., *Macropolitics of Nineteenth-Century Literature* (Philadelphia: University of Pennsylvania Press, 1991), 63, to which I am indebted throughout this essay.

6. On these diversions and recontextualizations of goods, and the shared history of colonial entanglement unfolding through such transactions, see Nicholas Thomas, *Entangled Objects: Exchange, Material Culture, and Colonialism in the Pacific* (Cambridge: Harvard University Press, 1991).

7. Gilles Deleuze and Félix Guattari, *Anti-Oedipus*, vol. 1 of *Capitalism and Schizophrenia*, trans. Robert Hurley et al. (Minneapolis: University of Minnesota Press, 1983), 48.

8. "DissemiNation: Time, Narrative, and the Margins of the Modern Nation," in Homi Bhabha, ed., *Nation and Narration* (London: Routledge, 1990): 291–322; I am indebted to James Donald's use of this essay in the Introduction to *Sentimental Education: Schooling, Popular Culture, and the Regulation of Liberty* (London: Routledge, 1992), 2.

9. I quote Dowden, *The French Revolution and English Literature* (New York: Scribner's, 1901), 115, 110; and, on these educators' association of poetry and patriotism, Franklin Court's *Institutionalizing English Literature: The Culture and Politics of Literary Study* (Stanford: Stanford University Press, 1992), 146. An equation of English identity, inbred sentiments, and local attachments is also set out by the Victorian canon-makers in the many passages in which they recount how the first-generation Romantics set up housekeeping. Morley, for instance, devotes pages to details about Wordsworth's houses and how he afforded them (*Of English Literature in the Reign of Victoria* [Leipzig: Tauchnitz, 1881], 128–32).

10. David Lloyd, *Anomalous States: Irish Writing and the Post-Colonial Moment* (Durham, N.C.: Duke University Press, 1993), 152, 3.

11. In "Family Feuds: Gender, Nationalism, and the Family," Anne McClintock analyzes the imperial uses of familial thinking: "The metaphoric depiction of social hierarchy as natural and familial—the 'national family', the global 'family of nations', the colony as a 'family of black children ruled over by a white father'— . . . depended on the prior naturalizing of the social subordination of women and children within the domestic sphere. . . . [Furthermore,] since children 'naturally' progress into adults, projecting the family image on to national and imperial 'Progress' enabled what was often murderously violent change to be legitimized as the progressive unfolding of natural decree" (*Feminist Review* 44 [1993], 64). In a number of recent essays, Mary A. Favret makes a broadly analogous argument about how, since the Romantic era, the patterns of the family romance have constrained our thinking about cultural production (see, e.g., "Telling Tales about Genre: Poetry in the Romantic Novel," *Studies in the Novel* 26 [1994]: 153–72).

12. I owe this point to Lawrence Needham's "Constructing the Domestic/National Space in British Romantic Literature," paper delivered at the 1993 M.L.A. convention, Toronto.

13. *The History of Sexuality*, trans. Robert Hurley (New York: Vintage, 1980), 108.

14. In "The Subject and Power" (Afterword to Hubert Dreyfus and Paul Rabinow, *Michel Foucault: Beyond Structuralism and Hermeneutics* [Chicago: University of Chicago Press, 1985]), Foucault describes modern power as calibrating the techniques that individuate people—techniques for producing subjectivities—with the procedures that constitute collectivities—procedures aimed at controlling populations. The groundbreaking account of (white) women's relation to modern power is Nancy Armstrong's *Desire and Domestic Fiction: A Political History of the Novel* (New York: Oxford University Press, 1987). Drawing on Armstong, Zerilli notes how the domestic ideology of the middle classes informs the purple passages Burke devotes to Marie Antoinette in the *Reflections*: "Whereas queens were traditionally regal figures, whose lavish bodily display signified the power of the aristocracy, Burke's 'Marie Antoinette' is nothing but a domesticated vision" (68).

15. Warner, "Introduction: Fear of a Queer Planet," *Social Text* 29 (1991), 7; Burke, "Speech on a Motion for a Committee to Inquire into the State of the Representation of the Commons in Parliament," in *Writings and Speeches of Edmund Burke*, vol. 7 (London: Bickers, n.d.), 95.

16. Warner, "Queer Planet," 10; Perry, "Colonizing the Breast: Sexuality and Maternity in 18th-Century England," *Journal of the History of Sexuality* 2 (1991), 206.

17. Macpherson, *Burke* (New York: Hill and Wang, 1980), 61.

18. See Wollstonecraft, *A Vindication of the Rights of Men*, in Janet Todd and Marilyn Butler, eds., *The Works of Mary Wollstonecraft*, vol. 5 (London: Pickering, 1989), 22. Subsequent references are to *Vindication* and appear in the text. In his *Commentaries*, Blackstone is similarly enthusiastic about property's unleashing of affect: "there is nothing which so generally strikes the imagination, and engages the affections of mankind, as the right of property" (quoted in Teresa Michals, " 'That Sole and Despotic Dominion':

Slaves, Wives, and Game in Blackstone's *Commentaries*," *Eighteenth-Century Studies* 27 [1994], 213).

19. Roof, "The Ideology of Fair Use: Xeroxing and Reproductive Rights," *Hypatia* 7 (1992), 66. Roof admits that, on the surface, statutory treatments of human reproduction and copyright laws "seem to be the inverse of one another." "Reproductive laws such as abortion statutes attempt to arbitrate the potentially conflicting rights of mother and fetus, limiting the termination of reproduction. Copyright laws define the circumstances under which artistic works can be freely reproduced, limiting reproduction. However, tracing the parallels between abortion statutes and the 'fair use' provisions of copyright law reveals that they share the same underlying party in interest—the male (pro)creator—and shaping motive. Inducing laws treating both kinds of reproduction is the need to protect an investment by creating a certain link between an absent creator or owner and a creation or work where such bonds might otherwise not obviously exist" (64).

20. McClintock, "Family Feuds," 62.

21. "On Narcissism," in *A General Selection from the Works of Sigmund Freud*, ed. John Rickman (New York: Doubleday, 1957), 107; J. G. A. Pocock, "The Mobility of Property and the Rise of Eighteenth-Century Sociology," in Anthony Parel and Thomas Flanagan, eds., *Theories of Property* (Waterloo, Ontario: Wilfrid Laurier University Press, 1979), 111.

22. Burke, "Letters on a Regicide Peace," in R. B. McDowell, ed., *Writings and Speeches*, vol. 9, 243. Subsequent references are to "First Letter," "Second Letter," and so on, and appear in the text. On the "enfants de la patrie," see Olwen Hufton, *Women and the Limits of Citizenship in the French Revolution* (Toronto: University of Toronto Press, 1992), 63–64.

23. Zerilli, "Text/Woman as Spectacle," 63.

24. My information on divorce in the Republic comes from David Simpson, *Romanticism, Nationalism, and the Revolt against Theory* (Chicago: University of Chicago Press, 1993), 116.

25. Gallagher, "Response" to Neil Hertz's "Medusa's Head: Male Hysteria under Political Pressure," in Hertz, *The End of the Line: Essays on Psychoanalysis and the Sublime* (New York: Columbia University Press, 1985), 195.

26. Zerilli, "Text/Woman as Spectacle," 63; the *Antijacobin Review* is cited in Simpson, *Romanticism, Nationalism*, 101.

27. I draw here on the discussions of transient commodities and of alienated property in, respectively, Arjun Appadurai, "Introduction," in Appadurai, ed., *The Social Life of Things: Commodities in Cross-cultural Perspective* (Cambridge: Cambridge University Press, 1986), 24; and Frances Ferguson, "The Nuclear Sublime," *diacritics* 14 (1981), 6.

28. I owe this formulation to Sonia Hofkosh, "The Writer's Ravishment: Women and the Romantic Author—the Example of Byron," in Anne K. Mellor, ed., *Romanticism and Feminism* (Bloomington: Indiana University Press, 1988), 99.

29. I owe this formulation and citation from Wordsworth to Ross, "Romancing the Nation-State," 79.

30. Tom Nairn, *The Enchanted Glass: Britain and Its Monarchy* (London: Pan, 1988), 11.

31. *Letters from France* (Delmar, N.Y.: Scholars' Facsimiles and Reprints, 1975), vol. 1, 222, 68–69.

32. Burke's speech on the Quebec Act is cited in Conor Cruise O'Brien, *The Great Melody: A Thematic Biography of Edmund Burke* (Chicago: University of Chicago Press, 1992), 419.

33. See Tom Furniss's account of the difficulty Burke has in fixing an irrevocable distinction between England and France: *Edmund Burke's Aesthetic Ideology: Language, Gender and Political Economy in Revolution* (Cambridge: Cambridge University Press, 1993), 123, 235.

34. Pocock, "Mobility of Property," 153.

35. Sally Shuttleworth, "Female Circulation: Medical Discourse and Popular Advertising in the Mid-Victorian Era," in Mary Jacobus et al., eds., *Body/ Politics: Women and the Discourses of Science* (New York: Routledge, 1990), 54–55. For political insults tendered via references to women's shopping, see, e.g., *The North Briton* no. 83 (January 7, 1769).

36. As James K. Chandler points out, the epistle's vexed relation to the principle of property also makes it resemble paper currency. "Burke seems to be aware that his own 'speculations'—'reflections,' as he pointedly calls them—will also appear . . . as paper representations of England and of the French Revolution" ("Poetical Liberties: Burke's France and the 'Adequate Representation' of the English," in François Furet and Mona Ozouf, eds., *The French Revolution and the Creation of Modern Political Culture*, vol. 3 [Oxford: Pergamon, 1989], 48). On the dangers of epistolary exchange, see also Mary A. Favret, *Romantic Correspondence: Women, Politics, and the Fiction of Letters* (Cambridge: Cambridge University Press, 1993) and Nicola J. Watson, *Revolution and the Form of the British Novel, 1790–1825: Intercepted Letters, Interrupted Seductions* (Oxford: Clarendon, 1994).

37. Nairn, *Enchanted Glass*, 246.

38. Paine is cited in Chandler, "Poetical Liberties," 54.

39. I am indebted here to Furniss's account of how Burke's political adversaries turned his language to their advantage: *Burke's Aesthetic Ideology*, 136. Mackintosh's *Vindicae Gallicae* (1791) is cited in O'Brien, *Great Melody*, 414.

40. The phrase "unimaginable communities" is Suleri's in *Rhetoric of English India*, 4.

41. See chap. 8 of Enloe, *Bananas, Beaches, and Bases.*

42. I owe this point to Julia Miller's Ph.D. dissertation-in-progress, "The Women's Troubles: Domestic Terror and Political Violence in Nineteenth- and Twentieth-Century Irish Literature."

43. Croker, Rev. of *Italy* by Lady Morgan, *Quarterly Review* 25 (1821), 530; Croker, Rev. of *The Wanderer* by Madame d'Arblay, *Quarterly Review* 11 (1814), 128. On Burke's influence on the reviewers, see Deane, *French Revolution and Enlightenment*, chaps. 1 and 2.

44. I quote "On the Female Literature of the Present Age," *New Monthly Magazine* 13 (1820), 271; on Sappho's transformation into a figure for the political exile, see Joan DeJean, *Fictions of Sappho, 1546–1937* (Chicago: University of Chicago Press, 1989), 158–66.

45. Rev. of *Corinne, or Italy* by Madame de Staël, *Anti-Jacobin Review* 32 (April 1809), 456; Croker, Rev. of *Woman, or Ida of Athens* by Miss Owenson (Lady Morgan), *Quarterly Review* 1 (1809), 52; Rev. of *Woman, or Ida of Athens* by Miss Owenson, *Anti-Jacobin Review* 32 (March 1809), 366. Even the Edinburgh reviewer's account of de Staël's *Delphine*—a text composed, of course, in French—finds an occasion to connect the female-authored novel's assault on family values with the adulteration of English. Jeering at the Scotticisms of de Staël's translator, Sydney Smith writes, "The bookseller has employed one of our countrymen . . . who appears to have been very *lately caught.* The contrast between the passionate exclamations of Madame de Staël, and the barbarous vulgarities of poor Sawney, produces a mighty ludicrous effect. . . . We doubt if Grub-Street ever imported from Dundasia a worse translator" (*Edinburgh Review* 2 [1803], 174–75). On the gendered associations that link the figure of the adulteress (a heroine like Delphine), to the unfaithful translator, and to the faithlessness of international politics, see Lori Chamberlain, "Gender and the Metaphorics of Translation," *Signs* 13 (1988): 454–72.

46. Rev. of *Tales of the Heart* by Amelia Opie, *Gold's London Magazine* 2 (1820), cited in Ina Ferris, *The Achievement of Literary Authority: Gender, History, and the Waverley Novels* (Ithaca, N.Y.: Cornell University Press, 1991), 54.

47. McClintock, "Family Feuds," 65.

48. See April Alliston, "The Value of a Literary Legacy: Retracing the Transmission of Value through Female Lines," *Yale Journal of Criticism* 4 (1990), 125, n. 22.

49. Frances Burney, *The Wanderer; or, Female Difficulties*, ed. Margaret Doody et al. (Oxford: World's Classics, 1991), 7. Subsequent references are to *Wanderer* and appear in the text.

50. The ur-plot of the national tale is, to cite Katie Trumpener's helpful account, one in which an English character travels to the British periphery, "which he or she expects will be devoid of any culture at all. Instead, under the tutelage of a new, native friend, he or she will come to appreciate its cultural plenitude. . . . Each book ends with the traveller's marriage to his or her native guide in a wedding which allegorically unites English and Celtic 'national characters' " ("National Character, Nationalist Plots: National Tale and Historical Novel in the Age of Waverley," *ELH* 60 [1993], 697). The textbook form of this plot is laid out in Morgan's 1806 *The Wild Irish Girl* (London: Pandora, 1986), in which the heroine, Glorvina, attracts the Englishman whom she will eventually wed because she offers him the opportunity to study the "pure national, natural character of an Irishwoman" (56). This narrative of union was, as Trumpener notes, versatile enough not only to be employed by other inhabitants of Britain's Celtic margins (Scott rewrote it in *Waverley*), but also to be taken up by the creole administrators of overseas colonies as a means to reconcile the mandates of Empire with their ambivalent allegiances to the cultural particularities of the peripheries. At the same time, however, that her plot becomes a resource for others, and a prime literary means by which diverse nationalisms were dialectically generated out of colonialisms, in subsequent novels Morgan herself seems—perhaps having learned from *Corinne*—to reject this folkloristic model of national character as (in Trumpener's words [698]) "a synecdoche of an

unchanging cultural space." Instead, in the later work national types like Glorvina are outnumbered by hybrid heroines (e.g., the eponymous heroine of *Florence Macarthy* [1818] and Beauvoin O'Flaherty of *The O'Briens and the O'Flahertys* [1827], who are, respectively, as Spanish and Italian as they are Irish).

51. As Naomi Schor notes, in an essay on how post-Revolutionary French novelists deployed this iconography, "the nineteenth-century heroine . . . is always inhabited by the uncanny shadow of the state whose very laws serve to silence and oppress her" (in Sara Melzer and Leslie W. Rabine, eds., *Rebel Daughters: Women and the French Revolution* [New York: Oxford University Press, 1992], 139).

52. Madame (Anne Louise Germaine) de Staël, *Corinne, or Italy*, trans. and ed. Avriel H. Goldberger (New Brunswick, N.J.: Rutgers University Press, 1987), 25. Subsequent references are to *Corinne* and appear in the text.

53. On the Mansfield Judgment, see Michals, " 'That Sole and Despotic Dominion,' " especially 204–206. Juliet's choice of disguise also invites us to align her with the Afro-Carib rebels—the Maroons of Jamaica or followers of Toussaint in Haiti—who figure prominently in Antijacobin nightmares about post-Revolutionary social chaos, nightmares elaborated at length in Burke's Speech on the Quebec Act.

54. *Anomalous States*, 147.

55. Compare Susan Meyer's "Colonialism and the Figurative Strategy of *Jane Eyre*," in Arac and Ritvo, eds., *Macropolitics of Nineteenth-Century Literature*, 159–83.

56. Compare Alliston, "Value of a Literary Legacy," 125, n. 20.

57. Paulson, *Representations of Revolution (1789–1820)* (New Haven: Yale University Press, 1983), 8, 61. I am inspired here by Mary A. Favret's recent account of *Frankenstein* ("A Woman Writes the Fiction of Science: The Body in *Frankenstein*," *Genders* 14 [1992]: 50–65) and by her insistence on locating motherhood within a domain created by technologies of gender rather than by Romantic notions of organic nature.

58. Thus, Mr. Scrope, a minor character who acts as a mouthpiece for Britons' francophobic hysteria, expresses alarm at reports that a Jacobin's "wife and daughter belong to any man who has a taste for them" (*Wanderer*, 79). Croker's distorted plot-summary of *The Wanderer* is informed by a similar hysteria. He describes conventional complications in the romantic subplot of *The Wanderer* as pivoting on a "common lover," and appears unable to decide which is worse, that the agent of Robespierre has the temerity to claim an Englishwoman as a wife, or that this Englishwoman "divorces her Revolutionary spouse." Such a divorce would, as I have indicated, have been in the minds of even those readers calmer than Croker, but Burney never explicitly mentions that narrative possibility. Instead, while rescuing the marriage plot for her novel, she hedges her bets: she implies that the ceremony of marriage was illegitimate in the first place *and* arranges for the Jacobin husband to be executed in France for treason.

59. Mitford, *Our Village*, ed. Ernest Rhys (London: Walter Scott, n.d.), 2; "Female Literature of the Present Age," *New Monthly Magazine*, 637. I owe the latter reference to Ferris, *Achievement of Literary Authority*, 48.

60. Dowden, *French Revolution and English Literature*, 115; Morley, *English Literature in the Reign of Victoria*, 112.

61. Here I follow Lloyd's Introduction to *Anomalous States*, 5.

A brief version of this essay appeared in *The Wordsworth Circle* 25 (1994); I am grateful to the editor, Marilyn Gaull, for permission to reprint it here in altered form. Financial support that helped with my research costs came from the Victor Johnson fund of the English Department, SUNY at Buffalo. For other kinds of assistance, I would like to thank the participants in my fall 1991 and fall 1993 graduate seminars, as well as Mary Favret, Ina Ferris, Shaun Irlam, Tom Keirstead, Katie Trumpener, and Nicola Watson.

Three

RAJANI SUDAN

Mothering and National Identity in the Works of Mary Wollstonecraft

UPON THE "maternal bosom the minds of nations repose; their manners, prejudices, and virtues,—in a word, the civilization of the human
race all depend upon maternal influence" writes Louis Aimé Martin in
1840. Margaret Homans opens her chapter on maternity and authorship with this particular quote as a way of introducing the ways in which
women in early Victorian England engaged in cultural production
by embracing motherhood as a vocation, as well as by participating in
signifying practices that may be read as simultaneously reproductive
and literary.[1] It seems, however, that propped up against the notion of
motherhood—naturalized and sustained, as it were, by the accommo-
dating breast—is the concept of "nation." This relation in itself is nothing new; Rousseau expostulates at length on the "civilizing" presence
of the woman of sensibility in *Emile* seventy years or so before Martin's
The Education of Mothers of Families. What seems a more absorbing issue
is the way in which ideologies of nation and of motherhood continue
to be reproduced in close connection to one another, both in eigh-
teenth- and nineteenth-century formulations about women's identities
and in more contemporary feminist theories about identity politics.

The 1790s proved to be a highly vexed period for Britain, especially
in the context of the revolution in France and an emerging politics
of the Enlightenment. During this period, the construction of subjectivity in relation to *national* affiliation provided a foundation upon
which notions of a universalizeable manhood were being invented, notions Martin disseminates later in the nineteenth century. The problem

72

this subjectivity posed to women, however, was qualitatively different; in most of western Europe and North America, women were "formally excluded from exercising political rights, and in England and Wales the restrictions on them were harsher in some respects than elsewhere." Even if a renewed emphasis on functional differences between men and women such as of the sort that Rousseau proposed in *Emile* helped stay the potential threat the enfranchisement of women posed to upwardly mobile British men, however, events like the Taunton March in Somerset in June 1814, and, more critically, the Duchess of Devonshire's political campaigns for her son in 1784, indicated that middle-class women's roles may be shifting, perhaps *because* of the violent retaliations they precipitated.[2] Mary Wollstonecraft's revolutionary feminist manifesto, *A Vindication of the Rights of Woman*, then, was hardly produced in a political vacuum.

Donna Landry's assessment of the *Vindication*'s cultural impact as an "impure idealization," however, suggests that the "radical" moves made toward enfranchising women were vastly overrated, even if there seemed to be some ideological space for the woman patriot. She points out that "[n]ot even the revolutionary potential of British social movements of the 1780s and 1790s could be said to represent an historical rupture, and the revolutionary potential of these years was itself ruthlessly suppressed by arms as well as the persuasive arts."[3] Reading Wollstonecraft in this context might cause us to re-evaluate our assumptions about historical representations of the feminine. On the one hand Wollstonecraft is engaged in an ideological maneuver around questions of identity, and, in some cases, it may be argued that she is constructing a foundation upon which to base the political subjecthood of women. It may, however, also be crucial to take into account the structural continuities of ideological underpinnings—of nationalism, imperialism, xenophobia, political identity—informing constructions and reconstructions of identity. The deep ambivalences that writers like Ann Yearsley and Hannah More expressed toward Wollstonecraft's bourgeois radicalism, as Donna Landry has pointed out, may also suggest other disturbing social and cultural ideological continuums that ensured for British women "different sorts of accommodations to the revolution in France" even if "accommodate themselves they did."[4]

One might usefully turn to recent formulations about identity to help uncover some of the problematic positions facing the construction of a place for "women" in the context of citizenry and nationhood at the close of the eighteenth century. Judith Butler, for example, suggests in *Gender Trouble* that the foundationalist reasoning of identity politics tends to assume that "identity must first be in place in order for political interests to be elaborated, and, subsequently, political action to be taken."[5] Preconceived formations of identity have dominated many of the ways in which we have addressed questions about national and cultural identity, especially in relation to authorship. Such foundationalist assumptions about national and cultural identity perform the task of constructing a privileged and valorized space for authorship without necessarily accounting for the powerful ideologies underwriting these assumptions.

Taking into account the problems foundationalist assumptions about national identities pose, scholars like Benedict Anderson have formulated models of nationalism that demonstrate the ways in which it is ideologically constructed as an "imagined community." Assumptions about nationality that get naturalized as a transcendent entity, complete with biological characteristics are, in fact, produced by ideologies of "community."[6] Preconceived formations of identity have also dominated many of the ways in which we have thought about "women": how we have recovered women's texts, women's voices, women's work, and women's various negotiations with being agents, resistant subjects, objects, figures, representations, and victims. The invocation of a feminist "we," according to a scholar like Butler, "denies the internal complexity and indeterminacy of the term and constitutes itself only through the exclusion of some part of the constituency that it simultaneously seeks to represent."[7]

Are there ways in which the questions of foundationalism vis-à-vis identity may be asked of Wollstonecraft's representations of "women" in her corpus? What sort of relationships between investigations into her political and historical contexts and more postmodern interrogations of identity might be usefully uncovered? My interest here is to reassess the ways in which Wollstonecraft establishes a ground for representing "women" with these questions in mind. I am particularly concerned with the reproduction of national subjectivity in the context of a female "vocation" of mothering; and what a "vocation" would imply for women in Britain, uncitizened and disenfranchised, whose position in English culture was increasingly dependent on a "natural" identification with motherhood. Specifically, I want to investigate the ideologies that produce certain popular conjectures about identities: the notion that "women" are inevitably linked to mothering, whether or not they actually perform this function, and the idea that nationality is something everyone can "have."

In the case of Mary Wollstonecraft, we must bear in mind Gayatri Spivak's contention that it "should not be possible to read nineteenth-century British fiction without remembering that imperialism . . . was a crucial part of the cultural representation of England to the English," despite attempts of her contemporaries to label her as French and antipatriotic.[8] Eighteenth- and nineteenth-century British literature is pre-occupied with maintaining a discrete sense of self as culturally English and imperially British.[9] These formations of national and imperial identity within Britain often seem to depend on representations of the foreign and the feminine: such constructs employ the language of xenophobia and gynophobia in a system of othering that creates the foreign body in order to cast it out.[10] What happens, however, when we turn to the question of women's authorship during the romantic period? Are the same foundationalist assumptions about national identity in place or do women's texts represent moments of resistance to the dominant ideologies that produce "Great Britain" as a source of imperial subjectivity? What happens when we consider Mary Wollstonecraft's political exhortations in particular with attention to motherhood and nationhood? Does the fact that she "pay[s] particular attention to those in the middle class, because they appear to be the most natural state" pose problems to audiences, historical and contemporary, and suggest the fact that interlocking discourses or race, class, gender, sexuality, and nationality may not be equally articulated?

"FACT"

Mary Wollstonecraft stands as an emblem of feminist thought in a newly constructed canon of feminist representation. As a writer concerned with female equality, Wollstonecraft centered her agenda on the rejection of sensibility, a rejection which has engaged the attention of scholars like Marilyn Butler, Mary Jacobus, and Mary Poovey, who have problematized this notion. Some of the implicit issues of nationalism in her work, however, have remained relatively untouched. Most recently, the focus on Wollstonecraft has shifted to other questions about identity, and scholars such as Moira Ferguson have connected Wollstonecraft's work for women in England with crucial metaphors of enslavement and the discourse of colonialism. Donna Landry's work has established even more crucially the connections between class, race, and sexuality, in the context of an emerging discourse of nationalism. I would like to propose a different reading of the presence of colonialist language in Wollstonecraft's work. If we turn to the histories of dominant ideologies and examine how they inform cultural production, how are we to read—and problematize—the "radical" departure from eighteenth-century notions of "women" in Wollstonecraft's writing?[11] Long regarded as a feminist thinker who scrutinized the conditions of women's lives more critically than previous writers, and often heralded as one of the "first feminists," Wollstonecraft's writings pose peculiar problems for a materialist analysis of her corpus. If she has been recovered and reclaimed as speaking about women's oppression, and if she has been

co-opted by an undifferentiated feminism to perform the very necessary work of making women's voices heard and women's work recognized, is there a way in which the counter-narrative of dominant ideologies is also articulated in her writing? What happens when we apply
the same investigation of ideologies of nationalism and imperialism, of
xenophobia and political identity, that materialist feminists have conducted within their own field to the overtly feminist work of Wollstonecraft? For example, there are disturbing differences between sentiment
and its representation that ventriloquize the insidiousness of such ideologies. These differences may suggest that one has to think through
the issues of women's oppression as an *articulation* of various interlocking discourses, particularly of maternity and nationalism.

The modern historian Linda Colley's treatment of eighteenth-century British patriotism might be helpful in uncovering some of the conflicting ideologies of national and gender identity operating in Wollstonecraft's texts. Colley discusses the relationship between the "welfare
of Great Britain"—a welfare that increasingly depends on both imperialist expansion and an enduring sense of national identification—
and the "cult of a prolific maternity" that was favored enthusiastically
by those who believed (before the 1800 census) that the population of
Great Britain was in decline, and by "those who simply wanted more
live births so that the nation might better compete in terms of cannon-
fodder with France."[12] Colley also goes on to spell out some of the anxieties about keeping this *British* maternity prolific, arguing that an increase in urbanization foregrounded, for moralists, an anxiety about
the impact on female manners and behavior; women might, writes
Colley in a moment of irony:

> come into contact with new and disreputable ideas. They might, like
> Sheridan's Lydia Languish, read unwholesome novels, or still worse,
> write them. . . . They might, free from the supervision of husbands and
> fathers, encounter men. They might cease to be virtuous.[13]

Embedded in this anxiety about female virtue is the fantasy of a capricious, fitful, inconstant, and therefore volatile female "nature" that
must be restrained and managed within the confines of *national* and
patriotic duty. As such, Colley suggests, the particular concern for fertility and maternity:

> increased along with the scale of European warfare, as witnessed by the
> spate of maternity hospitals established for the benefit of the poor in
> London and elsewhere. . . . Encouraging women to breed, urging the
> benefits of maternal breast-feeding over wet-nursing, rescuing found-
> lings and orphans, all of these causes became increasingly attractive to

British legislators, pundits and charitable bodies in the second half of the eighteenth century.[14]

Of course, maternity is a slippery category that functions differently in different political contexts. In the case Colley discusses, women's bodies and women's labor—specifically, women's capacity to produce offspring—are commodified in order to represent a physically palpable and morally healthy British "nation" and to regulate the feminine body. However, in other contexts maternity is the site of contamination and disease, and in some Romantic accounts, the maternal proliferation of (other) races is both horrific and threatening to the integrity of the English (male) individual.[15]

There seem to be ways in which Colley's accounts of ideologies of British maternity in relation to patriotism inform, ironically, Wollstonecraft's representational projects, especially the moral lessons about reading. In her *A Vindication of the Rights of Woman*, Wollstonecraft constructs an English woman by implication. She argues, among other things, for the intellectual autonomy of women, claiming that given a chance at an equal education, women would match men in achievement. Her analysis of the oppressed social conditions for women cuts across apparent hierarchies of class, although not, apparently, across lines of race and ethnicity. Even if she compares the plight of women as chattel to the plight of black slaves, these comparisons represent different forms of commodification: in the case of women, their cultural *difference* from black slaves is marked by the very fact of the analogy. She employs an amalgamation of Orientalist metaphors with which to compare the plight of English women. Wollstonecraft's indiscriminate references to Eastern alterity take shape as "Chinese bands" that torture the "limbs and faculties" of women, the "seraglio" that makes "necessary" the "art" of feigning a "sickly delicacy" for that Oriental "epicure" who "must have his palate tickled," her contention that "Mahometanism" produces the authoritative model for women's subordination, and all spell out the ways in which a prevailing imperialist ideology informs cultural representation, whether or not they are articulating the subject position of the socially marginalized.[16]

Wollstonecraft's Introduction describes her:

> profound conviction that the neglected education of my fellow-creatures is the grand source of misery I deplore; and that women, in particular, are rendered weak and wretched by a variety of concurring causes. . . . (7)

As with "flowers which are planted in too rich a soil," so a "false system of education" has reduced "the civilized women of the present century" to model themselves after "alluring mistresses than affectionate wives and rational mothers." Wollstonecraft concludes that "books of instruction, written by men of genius" enfeeble the women to whom they are addressed: in the "true style of Mahometanism, [women] are treated as a kind of subordinate beings [*sic*], and not as part of the human species." *We* may conclude that the implied danger in such acts of reading by "*civilized*" women is that they will be implicated in a dehumanizing Mahometan system.

She calls up the example of the differences between a man and a woman journeying, the former "in general, with the end in view" while the latter is in particular concerned with being a "figure on a new scene; when, to use an apt French turn of expression, she is going to produce a sensation." Sensationalism, sensibility, and the tendency for women to be creatures of sensation originate, according to Wollstonecraft, from "novels, music, poetry, and gallantry." Yet the opening lines of the *Vindication* juxtapose two different concepts of what it means to read that create opposing openings to her project. Directly before her invective against women's education and its enervating effects on their characters, Wollstonecraft writes:

> After considering the historic page, and viewing the living world with anxious solicitude, the melancholy emotions of sorrowful indignation have oppressed my spirits, and I have sighed when obliged to confess that either Nature has made a great difference between man and man, or that civilization which has hitherto taken place in the world has been very partial. (7)

Even while offering a logical and effective way to begin to overturn women's oppression, Wollstonecraft's opening sentence "seems to turn history into sentimental spectacle, and the author herself into its spectator rather than an agent of reformation," as Charlotte Sussman has pointed out. Such a fissure between two paradigms of reading—"the sentimental imperative to turn the world into an affecting page, and the empirical sense of texts as storehouses of information"—addresses the conflict of dominant ideologies in Wollstonecraft's project.[17] Wollstonecraft argues that women's characters are:

> thus formed in the mould of folly during the time they are acquiring accomplishments, the only improvement they are excited, by their station in society, to acquire. This overstretched sensibility naturally relaxes the other powers of the mind, and prevents intellect from attaining that sovereignty which it ought to attain to render a rational creature useful to others, and content with its own station.

It seems difficult *not* to compare her advice with that of the very eighteenth-century male writers against whom she argues: moralists who worry that middle-class wives and daughters might, like Sheridan's Lydia Languish, read "unwholesome novels" and therefore be contaminated by detrimental and unhealthy ideas (a sentiment that is not confined to the eighteenth century by any means).[18] What is also interesting about this conflict, however, is the fact that Wollstonecraft's prescription for a healthy diet of rigorous education, devoid of potentially enervating novels and French sensationalism, curiously and problematically parallels the eighteenth-century patriotic fervor to better the lots of British mothers for the good of a national whole.

Even more complicated, especially given the potentially xenophobic allusion to French sensation and to French women, is Wollstonecraft's admittedly vexed and problematically executed relation to Rousseau's representation of the physical, intellectual, emotional, and functional differences between men and women in his *Emile*.[19] Wollstonecraft's understanding of the capacity for Rousseau's arguments to eradicate the difference between public and private life that he is so careful to set up also ironically privileges his notion of separate spheres of activity for men and women. Her careful construction of the contributions of the family in *Vindication* announces this difference: "if children are to be educated to understand the principle of patriotism," she argues, "then their mother must be a patriot as well." Only if women are "to acquire a rational affection for their country," could they be useful in *their* sphere, the home.[20] Rousseauian ideals of femininity imagine them within the domesticated space, exercising a "gentle and improving sway over her husband," and influencing the next generation in a similarly indirect and subordinate manner, in which children would presumably ingest a national identity and sense of public-spirited duty along with their milk during a moment of patriotic breast-feeding. However conflicted Wollstonecraft's relationship to Rousseau may be in the *Vindication*—on the one hand she identifies the urgency for uncovering the ideologies that allocate women their social position and cultural definition (specified by Rousseau), on the other she repeats his exclusionary (male) practices that have defined women—it is also clear that she identifies with other dominant ideologies of patriotism, imperialism, and xenophobia in her representation.

"FICTION"

A Vindication of the Rights of Woman is a philosophical treatise that urges "civilized" English women to take political control of their place in culture. Of course, embedded within the term "civilized" is an established role for women, even if technically uncitizened, that capitalizes on differences produced and sustained by imperial culture. Do the same sorts of problematic representations of "women" and "mothers" as figures of national identity exist in Wollstonecraft's fictional works? What difference does fiction make? Anna Wilson suggests that many critics "treat the space of the psyche as if it were outside history."[21] The question Wilson asks that bears repeating is why novels and their language are politically suspect? Both of Wollstonecraft's novels, *Mary* and *Maria, or The Wrongs of Woman*, although in many ways entirely different projects, represent implicitly national identity values in the context of women's capacity for "mothering," even if these characters don't necessarily embody a monolithic account of Wollstonecraft's philosophy (even if one could represent Wollstonecraft's positions as such).

Turning to *Mary*, Wollstonecraft's first novel, we read a story about the representation of women that depends on formulations of nationalism, although we may also read a problematized relation to mothering. If *Mary* is, as Janet Todd has pointed out, a late work of sensibility and "an early effort at the creation of an alienated intellectual woman," a position that Wollstonecraft attempts to radically revise with her *Vindication* and her later novel *Maria*, it is worth noting the structural and ideological continuities informing all three of these works.[22] The advertisement to *Mary* claims that this novel will not be a delineation of either a "Clarissa" or a "Sophie"—both of which are masculine definitions of the feminine ideal—but rather will forge another kind of representation of the mind of a woman. Yet *Mary* is complicated by the problems of political, gender, sexual, and national identity that complicate Wollstonecraft's representation of women in other texts.

Although Mary is not a mother, and does to a certain extent practice alternative sexual and domestic arrangements, the itinerant position in which she finds herself is framed by mother-like activity. She is continually escaping from her husband, attempting to form alternative domestic arrangements with her friend Ann: an "extreme dislike took root in her mind; the sound of his name made her turn sick; but she forgot all, listening to Ann's cough, and supporting her languid frame. She would then catch her to her bosom with convulsive eagerness, as if to save her from sinking into an opening grave" (16). Here it seems quite clear that Mary, despite her transgression from the position of "wife," reassumes a maternal role as nurse to Ann. Even if her friendship to Ann "resemble[s] a passion," the potential for erotic involvement with her is rewritten as motherly solicitude. Replacing Ann's mother, Mary proves far more sympathetic than Ann's nurse "who was entirely engrossed by the desire of amusing her" (15). Mary takes care of her friend until her death, and then assumes other kinds of charitable rescue-work encouraged by eighteenth-century British culture to live up to the patriotic motto "increase of children a nation's strength."[23]

As if demonstrating the ways in which mothering is connected to dominant ideologies of nationalism and political identity, Mary and

Ann's alternative domestic household in Lisbon is destined to fail: after all, Ann dies abroad, and Mary is left alone to cope with her failure as a substitute mother. As the domestic coherence in un-English countries is suspect and prone to a sort of decay, so alternative familial arrangements along lines of gender seem to fall prey to the same propensity. On the Continent, Mary's wandering is ostensibly bleak—she is a lone woman among foreigners. Her wandering is placed against the rightful place of house and home she eventually finds back in England. Two women by themselves cannot constitute a coherent household, but need to be invested with the authority of the father, represented in this text not only by the sympathetic male, but also by the authority of religious and national identity. Even if Mary attempts to reinvent the roles of mother/daughter according to the rules of English domesticity, she must resort to the "affection" of her countryman to save her very life:

> Two days passed away without any particular conversation; Henry, trying to be indifferent . . . was more assiduous than ever . . . his spirits were calmly low . . . what was that world to him that Mary did not inhabit; she lived not for him. . . . He was mistaken; his affection was her only support; without this dear prop she had sunk into the grave of her lost—long-loved friend;—his attention snatched her from despair. Inscrutable are the ways of Heaven! (34)

This particular position is made all the more acute during a storm that occurs when she crosses the ocean to return to England:

> One of the sailors, happening to say to another, "that he believed the world was going to be at an end;" this observation led her into a new train of thoughts: some of Handel's sublime compositions occurred to her, and she sung them to the grand accompaniment. The Lord God Omnipotent reigned, and would reign for ever, and ever!—Why then did she fear the sorrows that were passing away, when she knew that He would bind up the brokenhearted, and receive those who came out of great tribulation. . . . The Lord Omnipotent will reign, and He will wipe the tearful eye, and support the trembling heart—yet a little while He hideth his face, and the dun shades of sorrow, and the thick clouds of folly separate us from our God; but when the glad dawn of an eternal day breaks, we shall know even as we are known. . . . After writing, serenely she delivered her soul into the hands of the Father of Spirits; and slept in peace. (37–38)

Mary considers *first* Handel and *then* Corinthians (I Corinthians 13:12) in this dense passage. If we consider the national institution Handel had become in Hanoverian England, the fact that the language of *The Messiah* transmitted the idea of Britain as Israel, and the veiled allusion to George II in the Hallelujah chorus, what enables and comforts Mary

is a reaffirmation of the continuity of her *national* identity rewritten—
and naturalized—as religious affiliation.[24]

Her ordained place is in England, even if she encounters a bewildering world once she reaches the shores of Great Britain. At first, Mary
attempts to minister to the needy multitudes. Horrified by the poverty
she sees in England, her recent alien wandering made all the more
poignant by the fact that she has returned to her native land, she supports and sustains a family: "She visited them every day, and procured
them every comfort; contrary to her expectation, the woman began
to recover . . . " (41). Yet Mary herself contracts the "fever," which has
made the woman ill in the first place, and which makes "alarming progress" because of her want of "a tender nurse" (41). It takes Henry to
procure for her a "natural" place in the domestic world—certainly her
experiments with formulating alternative domestic arrangements only
meet with complete failure. Henry, of course, has returned to England
because his "*native* air may work wonders, and besides, [his] *mother* is a
tender nurse" (45—italics mine). In the end, Mary's new position as
the adopted daughter of her would-be lover's mother (and not her husband, from whom she is permanently estranged) stabilizes her. Henry's
mother announces:

> I come to request you to spend not only this day, but a week or two
> with me.—Why should I conceal any thing from you? Last night my
> child made his mother his confident, and, in the anguish of his heart,
> requested me to be thy friend—when I shall be childless. . . . If I am to
> lose the support of my age, and again be a widow—may I call her
> "Child whom my Henry wishes me to adopt?" (50)

Such a realignment of the positions of mother and daughter, when
made according to the wishes of the masculine voice of authority, and
not by the transgressive wishes of the transient woman, have such a
rehabilitating effect that the novel ends with Mary engaged in relatively
happy and useful work: she establishes manufactories, throws her estate
into small farms, visits the sick, supports the old, and educates the
young, her "gleam of joy" being constituted primarily by the fact that
she is "hastening to that world *where there is neither marrying*, nor giving
in marriage" (53). On the one hand Wollstonecraft addresses the unnaturalness of the definition of women's positions as wives, mothers,
or daughters; on the other she uses that very definition as a solution
for Mary's dilemmas.

Turning to *Maria*, Wollstonecraft's last and unfinished novel that
functions, in some ways, as an "answer to the sentimental but sexually
frightened *Mary* and in other ways as a continuation of *A Vindication of
the Rights of Woman*," we may also read the ambivalence with which Wollstonecraft articulates that part of the Rousseauian ideal that confers

political power on the woman, with the materiality of women's oppression.[25] *Maria* opens with alternating images of imprisonment and maternity: her sorrows, products of a torturing "maternal apprehension," seem to "be pictured on the walls of her prison, magnified by the state of mind in which they were viewed . . . " (61). Yet this compelling comparison between the alternating institutions of incarceration, domestic and otherwise, conflicts with the image of maternity on which Wollstonecraft focuses:

> Her infant's image was continually floating on Maria's sight, and the first smile of intelligence remembered, as none but a mother, an unhappy mother, can conceive. She heard her half speaking half cooing, and felt the little twinkling fingers on her burning bosom—a bosom bursting with the nutriment for which this cherished child might now be pining in vain. From a stranger she could indeed receive the maternal aliment, Maria was grieved at the thought—but who would watch her with a mother's tenderness, a mother's self-denial? (61)

Maria's imaginative recall of her daughter's image is bound up with her body: she *feels*, even as she *imagines*, the "twinkling fingers on her burning bosom," while the breast itself, uncomfortably full, is a reminder of the absence and loss of her child's material presence. The conflict between Maria's feeling and sensibility, and her intellectual acknowledgment of the ways in which she has been immured, collapses in this representation of motherhood. Maria's problem is that she has no place to fill; she is cut off from her motherhood, and yet the fact that the biological connection between mother and child is unquestioned, unproblematized—indeed, emphasized—literally leaving the woman with no place but a prison, ventriloquizes the oppressive dictates of eighteenth-century definitions of "women." One can also locate this fissure in the books Maria reads. Reading and feeling are especially conflicted:

> Earnestly as Maria endeavoured to soothe, by reading, the anguish of her wounded mind, her thoughts would often wander from the subject she was led to discuss, and tears of maternal tenderness obscured the reasoning page. She descanted on "the ills which flesh is heir to," with bitterness, when the recollection of her babe was revived by a tale of fictitious woe, that bore any resemblance to her own; and her imagination was continually employed, to conjure up and embody the various phantoms of misery, which folly and vice had let loose on the world. The loss of her babe was the tender string; against other cruel remembrances she laboured to steel her bosom. . . . (65)

One is reminded of the opening of *Vindication*, where sentimental and empirical imperatives war against each other. Here, the "reasoning page" gives way to Maria's unabashedly sentimental recollections of her baby. However, one also may read Maria's position as a *mother* as one that profoundly affects her position as a *reader*. Maria reads Dryden's *Fables*, Milton's *Paradise Lost*, and Rousseau's *Heloise*—books given to her by Henry Darnford—all of which she finds "a mine of treasure" (68). Here, the materiality of these books, figured by their potential as "treasure," produces the materiality of her baby's presence.

Upon reading the Dryden, Maria notices "some marginal notes" that are "written with force and taste" and contain "various observations on the present state of society and government, with a comparative view of the politics of Europe and America. These remarks were written with a degree of generous warmth, when alluding to the enslaved state of the labouring majority, perfectly in unison with Maria's mode of thinking" (68). The notes, of course, are Darnford's, and are a result of his travels in America, during which he concludes, among other things, that he is "heartily weary of the land of liberty and vulgar aristocracy," especially of American women, in whom he finds a "want of taste and ease . . . that renders them, in spite of their roses and lilies, far inferior to our European charmers" (75–76). The metaphors of enslavement, produced by colonialist discourse and employed on the behalf of class (by Darnford) and of gender and class (by Maria), turn into the language of incarceration for Maria. While the use of the terms of colonial slavery certainly corresponds with her own situation, as she self-consciously recognizes, in the end she returns to Rousseau's ideas of femininity, domesticity, and maternity. After the disppointment of not seeing Darnford that evening—who at this point represents the possibility of illicit love—and feeling "the disappointment more severely than she was willing to believe, she flew to Rousseau, as her only refuge from the idea of [Darnford] . . . (71)." Rather than providing a moment of empowerment generated by engaging with the "reasoning page," the act of reading puts Maria in an infantilized position, recalling the way in which reading only calls up the presence of her baby. Maria's eager perusal of Dryden's *Fables*, Milton's *Paradise Lost*, and Rousseau's *Heloise* then simultaneously offers her an intellectual freedom and a corporeal prison.

Wollstonecraft's ambivalence about Maria's position is also represented by the novel's conclusion; bereft of the "true" benefits of motherhood, unable to assume any clear social identity because she is deprived of the privilege of breast-feeding, Maria's daughter is doomed to die. In the memoir Maria writes to her daughter, she makes an allusion to the "extraordinary partiality" her own mother had for her eldest brother, the only child her mother had suckled, while Maria herself has a "great affection" for the nurse who has suckled her. We can read this maternal narrative as a displaced narrative of breast-feeding.[26] Like the ways in which the act of reading conjures up images of her baby, so the writing of the memoir similarly invokes an image of motherly solicitude—her "many observations" which "flow from [her] heart, which only a mother—a mother schooled in misery, could make" (94). Yet because of the way in which biological connections to motherhood are privileged, this narrative cannot restore the mother's function: Maria's daughter dies.

In this memoir Maria writes:

> As my mind grew calmer, the visions of Italy again returned with their former glow of colouring; and I resolved on quitting the kingdom for a time, in search of the cheerfulness, that naturally results from a change of scene, unless we carry the barbed arrow with us, and only see what we feel. (133)

Maria's "barbed arrow" may be read as the barb of an oppressive national, political, and cultural identity; in Maria's case anatomy *is* destiny. Having torn herself free from the confines of her existence as a "woman," relinquishing her marital ties, she is also forced to leave behind her natural and cultural progeny: "I had thought of *remaining in England, till I weaned my child,* but . . . I had soon reason to wish to hasten my departure" (134—italics mine). As a result, her improperly nourished child dies, and the escape to what would have been the Italian haven from cultural oppression turns into the prison of the English madhouse:

> My God, with what a light heart did I set out for Dover!—It was not my country, but my cares I was leaving behind. . . . I was already in the snare—I never reached the packet—I never saw thee more. . . . All I know is that [the maid] must have quitted the chaise, shameless wretch! and taken (from my breast) my babe with her. How could a creature in a female form see me caress thee, and steal thee from my arms! I must stop, stop to repress a mother's anguish; lest, in bitterness of soul, I imprecate the wrath of heaven on this tiger, who tore my only comfort from me. (134)

This invective is complicated by many issues that come together to problematize the position of mother as an essential, transcendent, biological phenomenon. Even if her life in England is oppressive, she cannot abandon her "country," but, rather, rewrites her escape abroad as one from her "cares." Mothering and national identity come together in Maria's denunciation of the maid, who becomes a "tiger": a monstrous, and, most importantly, exotic, non-British—specifically non-English—"creature" onto whom Maria scapegoats her failed maternity. Paradoxically, she is, in a manner of speaking, forever confined to the country that has invented her "madness," England, as Wollstonecraft dies—in a horrible irony, from complications of childbirth—before she can resolve the various conclusions to Maria's history.

In many ways, the problems Wollstonecraft articulates of the 1790s are ones that face women and feminists in the 1990s. Her work may be read as an attempt at establishing a foundation on which to build a political subjecthood of women, and then exploring various ways in which women could subvert those roles: their positions as national subjects as well as their "vocations" as mothers. Taking into account Homi Bhabha's theory of "hybridity," however, as the primary culturally specific effect of colonialism, Wollstonecraft's allusions to colonialist discourse assume a different meaning.

> If the effect of colonial power is seen to be the *production* of hybridisation rather than the hegemonic command of colonialist authority or the silent repression of native traditions, then an important change of perspective occurs. It reveals the ambivalence at the source of traditional discourses on authority and enables a form of subversion, founded on that uncertainty, that turns the discursive conditions of dominance into the grounds of intervention.[27]

Wollstonecraft's call to arms in *Vindication* and her representational models of feminine alterity in *Maria* and even *Mary*, suggest to readers a form of political resistance. Yet if we consider the notion of subversive mimicry in relation to Wollstonecraft's corpus in a different way, "an important change of perspective occurs." May one subvert a visibly politicized discourse to uncover disturbing alliances with other hegemonic discursive models of nationality, race, xenophobia, and imperialism? Postmodern readings of identities problematize and politicize their status in authorship. Wollstonecraft criticism has focused by and large on her position as feminist, her concerns with sensibility and mothering, but important changes of perspective may need to start with a reconsideration of those very problems not as privileged, unproblematic categories but as formulations that need to be debated.

The argument for thinking through a politics of identity that doesn't depend on foundationalist reasoning but, rather, works through other interlocking discourses of dominant ideologies uncovers the problematic position of "motherhood" as implicitly bound up with other questions of identity. The model of reading provided by constructionist thinking and materialist feminism enables us to examine the various social and cultural formations that invest identities with authority. The importance of rethinking essentialist terms, especially in the interests of feminist investigation, is primarily political. Yet equally compelling are the ways in which essentialism may be deconstructed and analyzed for its deployment in various discourses. One needs to acknowledge the ways in which anti-essentialism "itself can become a reactionary position if it is allowed to freeze into an orthodoxy, to lose a sense of its own strategic deployments."[28] On the one hand, we see the usefulness—some might argue need—for mobilizing this aspect of women's work as an arena of women's power. On the other, as writers such as Mary Wollstonecraft have demonstrated, there are problems with relying too heavily on these models as a *telos* for feminist studies. Conducting such inquiry may lead us to questioning the status of motherhood and nationhood, literal and figural: are they free-standing stable identities or are they informed by dominant ideologies about nationalism, subject to shifting definitions, and often acting against parts of the very groups that invest them with authority?

NOTES

1. Margaret Homans, *Bearing the Word: Language and Female Experience in Nineteenth-Century Women's Writing* (Chicago: University of Chicago Press, 1989), 153.

2. Linda Colley, *Britons: Forging the Nation 1707–1837* (New Haven: Yale University Press, 1992), 238–50.

3. Donna Landry, *The Muses of Resistance: Laboring-Class Women's Poetry in Britain, 1739–1796* (Great Britain: Cambridge University Press, 1990), 254.

Landry notes Richard Polwhele's poem *The Unsex'd Females* as a crucial example of the ways in which Wollstonecraft's status as a pro-revolutionary, feminist, democratic writer is, in part, an invention of various men theatened by the possible enfranchisement of British women. Landry writes:

Wollstonecraft looms as a sinister spectre of radicalism within the text, a woman whose writing serves as a rallying cry for impressionable females shamed by her raillery into imitating her dangerous militancy. Polwhele hyperbolically turns Wollstonecraft's plea for women's rights into female tyranny, a sexual world turned upside down. (255)

4. Ibid., 254.

5. Judith Butler, *Gender Trouble: Feminism and the Subversion of Identity* (New York: Routledge, 1990), 142.

6. Benedict Anderson, *Imagined Communities: Reflections on the Origin and Spread of Nationalism* (London: Verso, 1983).

Benedict Anderson argues that the concept "nation" implies several things. First, it is *imagined* because each member of a nation "lives [in] the image of their communion" (nationalism invents nation), the imagined nation has clearly defined borders ("no nation imagines itself coterminous with mankind"), the nation is imagined as "sovereign" because "the concept was born in an age when Enlightenment and Revolution were destroying the legitimacy of divinely-ordained, hierarchical dynastic realm," and finally the nation is perceived as a *community* because "regardless of the actual inequality and exploitation that may prevail in each, the nation is always conceived as a deep, horizontal comradeship" (15–16).

7. Judith Butler, *Gender Trouble* 142.

8. Gayatri Spivak, "Three Women's Texts and a Critique of Imperialism," *"Race," Writing and Difference*, ed. Henry Louis Gates, Jr., (Chicago: University of Chicago Press, 1986), 262.

9. The terms "British" and "English" are problematic because they imply different things even though they are often used synonymously. If one considers the ways in which "Great Britain" was created—"England" appropriating Scotland and Wales in the Act of Union of 1707—then it seems as if its identity as a unified nation, representing to itself an equally unified subjectivity in various cultural productions, is invested with the same sorts of exclusionary practices as its imperialist relations to the rest of the world.

10. In a related study, I examine the formation of national and imperial identity through representations of otherness in English canonical texts from the late eighteenth and early nineteenth centuries. Although I address complications posed by issues of sexual difference in authorship, my contention is that representations of the English self are determined by the conjunction of the foreign and the feminine.

11. Even if the French Revolution dramatized for women on both sides of the channel the potential for other radical departures from established roles, Landry has pointed out that the notion of "revolutionary women" in Britain is a "contradiction in terms."

12. Linda Colley, *Britons*, 240.

13. Ibid., 241.

14. Ibid., 240.

15. I discuss the relationship between maternal proliferation and the unified subjectivity of the English male in "Englishness amuck: Addiction and Contamination in De Quincey's *Confessions*" (forthcoming *Genre*), and in "Foreign Bodies: Constructing Identity in Johnson's *London* and the *Life of Savage*" (*Criticism*, 32 1992:2).

16. Mary Wollstonecraft, *A Vindication of the Rights of Woman* (New York: W. W. Norton, 1988), 8–29.

Landry discusses the "Turkish prejudice" in Wollstonecraft, Hannah More, and Ann Yearsley as a "traditional figure of otherness within British culture," and, using Gayatri Spivak's formulations of different forms of otherness, persuasively argues that in the case of Hannah More, references to Eastern alterity performed the necessary task of consolidating "her audience's sense of cultural identity" precisely because it capitalized on a collective cultural imaginary about the "Orient."

17. From unpublished manuscript in author's possession. I am indebted to Charlotte Sussman for this point.

18. See Mary Poovey, *The Proper Lady and the Woman Writer* (Chicago: University of Chicago Press, 1984).

19. See Mary Jacobus, *Romanticism, Writing and Difference: Essays on The Prelude* (New York: Oxford University Press, 1989) for a fuller account of Wollstonecraft's relation to Rousseau.

20. Linda Colley, *Britons*, 274.

21. Anna Wilson, "Mary Wollstonecraft and the Search for the Radical Woman," *Genders* 6 (1989):91.

22. See Janet Todd's introduction to Mary Wollstonecraft and Mary Shelley, *Mary, Maria, Matilda*, (Harmondsworth: Penguin, 1992), x–xiii.

All references to *Mary* and *Maria* will be made from this text and will be noted in parentheses.

23. Linda Colley, *Britons*, 240.

24. Ibid., 31–33.

Colley argues that "one of the most powerful transmitters of the idea of Britain as Israel" can be located in Handel's oratorios. She points out that Handel deliberately inserted comparisons between moments of British history and the exploits of the prophets and heroes in the Old Testament in order to establish the moral that Israel's violent and uncertain past could be recovered by the Protestant Hanoverian Dynasty:

> It was because he celebrated Britain in this glowing fashion that Handel became such a national institution. As the eighteenth century progressed, his oratorios were performed at Westminster Abbey, at cathedral concerts like the annual Three Choirs Festival at Worcester, Gloucester and Hereford, in northern dissenting chapels, in Welsh assembly rooms and in Scottish cities and towns eager to advertise their fashionability . . . the men and women . . . listening so intently were indeed engaged in an act of faith. Only what many of them were worshipping was Great Britain, and indirectly themselves. (33)

25. Todd, introduction to *Mary, Maria, Matilda*, xiii.

26. One needs to keep in mind the ways in which middle-class feminine identity was problematized by the convention of wet-nursing, especially vis-à-vis the new political identification of a vocation of motherhood for women. Nevertheless, I would still maintain that ideologies of class and race were often called up as justifications for such anxious solicitudes.

27. Homi K. Bhabha, "Signs Taken for Wonders: Questions of Ambivalence and Authority under a Tree outside New Delhi, May 1817," *"Race," Writing and Difference*, ed. Henry Louis Gates, Jr. (Chicago: University of Chicago Press, 1986), 173.

28. Donna Landry and Gerald Maclean, *Materialist Feminisms* (Oxford: Blackwell, 1993), 147.

PART II

Imperial Fictions:
Romantic Others,
Other Romantics

Four

ASHTON NICHOLS

Mumbo Jumbo:
Mungo Park and the
Rhetoric of Romantic Africa

EARLY IN HIS *Travels in the Interior Districts of Africa* (1799) the Scottish explorer Mungo Park recorded a West African ritual that helped to import a new phrase into the English language:

> I arrived at Kolor, a considerable town; near the entrance to which I observed, hanging upon a tree, a sort of masquerade habit, made of the bark of trees, which I was told on inquiry, belonged to *Mumbo Jumbo*. This is a strange bugbear, common to all Mandingo towns, and much employed by the Pagan natives in keeping their women in subjection; for as the Kafirs are not restricted in the number of their wives, every one marries as many as he can conveniently maintain; and as it frequently happens that the ladies disagree among themselves, family quarrels sometimes rise to such a height, that the authority of the husband can no longer preserve peace in his household. In such cases, the interposition of Mumbo Jumbo is called in, and is always decisive. (39–40)[1]

Park's own text is not unlike Mumbo Jumbo; his words are designed to resolve a dispute among Europeans about the direction of flow of the River Niger and the characteristics of the various peoples who inhabit the region. When Park goes on to describe the details of the Mumbo Jumbo ceremony, however, we see how an apparent resolution of disputes—textual or otherwise—can often lead to cultural confusion or outright violence:

> This strange minister of justice (who is supposed to be either the husband himself, or some person instructed by him), disguised in the dress that has been mentioned, and armed with the rod of public

93

authority, announces his coming (whenever his services are required)
by loud and dismal screams in the woods near the town. . . . It may easily be supposed that this exhibition is not much relished by the women;
for as the person in disguise is entirely unknown to them, every married female suspects, that the visit may possibly be intended for herself;
but they dare not refuse to appear when they are summoned; and the
ceremony commences with songs and dances, which continue till midnight, about which time Mumbo fixes on the offender. This unfortunate victim being thereupon immediately seized, is stripped naked, tied
to a post, and severely scourged with Mumbo's rod. (40)

I quote these passages at length because they serve so well to situate
our understanding of Mungo Park's own rhetoric. Park sets forth his
accounts of Africa as texts designed merely to resolve geographical and
historical disputes within his own society; in fact, his travelogues help
to shape a powerful Romantic discourse that offers Western ideological
assumptions in the guise of geographical objectivity, while also preparing the way for a more violent Victorian discourse of cross-cultural
domination.

Park was perhaps the prototypical pre-colonial explorer, deeply embedded in the rhetoric of his own culture, but willing to acknowledge
moments when he is confronted by a cultural "other" for whom he does
not always have effective metaphors or language. The results, in Park's
case, are texts that give credence to eighteenth-century assumptions
about humanity and nature, while at the same time granting powerful
verbal authority to the perceptive and rhetorical skills of the first-per-
son European observer. The more general Romantic construction of
Africa embodied a similar contradiction: here were descriptions of a
land of extraordinary natural beauty filled with untold resources and
a peaceful population—contrasted with images of an overgrown waste-
land inhabited by dangerous animals and savages who were a threat to
all forms of civilized life. Park's texts emerge between 1799 and 1815,
early in the modern construction of this contradictory myth, presenting a pre-Byronic explorer-hero who offers an image of Africa that
fulfills a variety of idealized Romantic assumptions, while at the same
time preparing the way for the dominating discourse of Victorian imperialism.

Such a critique of Park draws on recent work in the language of
empire and the complexities of culture and racial difference in texts
produced by European colonizers. Patrick Brantlinger notes that "portrayals of Africans between 1800 and the 1830s were often both more
positive and more open-minded than those of later years"; he thus
extends the period of "relative objectivity" previously described by
Katherine George and Winthrop D. Jordan.[2] Brantlinger notes a num-

ber of Romantic factors that contributed to "a golden age of accuracy and lack of prejudice in writing about Africa; among these were the satiric tradition of the noble savage, turned to effective popular use by Aphra Behn in *Oroonoko; or, the Royal Slave* (1688); and later by many abolitionists; the Enlightenment belief that all people should be treated equally under the law; the growth of the abolitionist movement; and the exploration of the Niger River by Mungo Park and others, starting in the late 1700s."[3] More recently Sara Suleri has described what she calls the "migrant moment of dislocation," which she sees as "far more formative, far more emplotting, than the subsequent acquisition of either postcolonial nation or colonial territory."[4] Mungo Park is, from this perspective, a pre-colonial contributor to this "objective" discourse about Africa, a dislocated traveler whose motives for exploration are not as clear-cut as a colonizer's; his attitude toward the country and its inhabitants is neither monolithic nor monologic. For all the scholarly attention to Victorian imperial texts, as well as more recent emphasis on the literature of travel and exploration, less commentary has been directed at specific examples of the Romanticization of Africa in the late 1700s and early 1800s.[5]

Park's texts shape a polyvalent discourse about Africa that at once sanctions a Romantic ideology (nature is redemptive, Africans share a common humanity with Europeans, the "state of nature" is benevolent—as are "noble savages"—primitives are childlike, women are superior to men), while also preparing the way for various Victorian forms of cultural imperialism (non-Christians are barbaric, African nature is so wild as to need taming, European knowledge is a form of power necessary to control unjust African forms of authority). Such a reading reminds us that an explorer like Park is an often-overlooked contributor to an emergent Romantic ideology in the 1790s, while at the same time suggesting that the discourse of exploration contributes in significant ways to the colonial "horrors" of the subsequent century. Scholars have typically thought of Romantic ideology in terms of the works of poets, novelists, and other writers of imaginative and philosophical texts, as well as the parallel discourses of painting, music, and the visual arts. To this group we should add a figure like Park (and numerous explorers, such as John Barrow, James Bruce, Richard Lander, John Steadman and others) whose cultural framework helped to produce a series of metaphors, points of view, and unquestioned assumptions that at once created and critiqued emerging ideologies— not only of Africa—but of a more broadly "Romantic" sensibility. If romanticism presents any single "ideology," then it is one with complex, and sometimes conflicting, sources and results.[6]

In this regard, as Mary Louise Pratt has noted, the travel narratives

of explorers are a particularly multivalent ideological site. "Partly because it has never been fully professionalized or 'disciplined,' travel
writing is one of the most polyphonous of genres . . . readers of these
books received nothing like a fixed set of differences that normalized
self and Other in fixed ways."[7] Precisely such polyphony is evident
throughout Park's texts. He is not trying to fulfill a set of generic or
readerly expectations, in part because his published accounts emerged
only when it became clear how interested the public was in the details
of his first journey, in part because his own motives for exploration
remained somewhat vague and imprecise. Park often describes himself
as though he is merely looking for "information." Pratt's extended analysis of Park, in *Imperial Eyes: Travel Writing and Transculturation*, sets out
to reveal how Park's "sentimentality both challenges and complements
the emergent authority of objectivist science."[8] She argues convincingly
that Park sets himself forward as a "sentimental hero" who is, at the
same time, the "non-hero of an anti-conquest"; based on his "innocence
and passivity" he constructs himself textually "as a non-interventionist
European presence" (78). As the product of such an apparently "transparent [and Romantic] eyeball," the tensions in Park's works actually
echo parallel tensions in British views of Britain in the period 1790–
1830.

Texts like Park's thus contribute to the cultural category of "Romanticism" to a greater extent than has been previously acknowledged.
Thomas de Zengotita connects what he calls "romantic refusion" with
the history of cultural anthropology.[9] But cultural anthropology begins
in the West precisely with pioneering incursions by the likes of Park
into parts of the world that had been hitherto incognito. De Zengotita
notes the romantic shift from a world conceived as the unified product
of a single "Maker," to a world conceived of on the basis of multiple
perceptions by single privileged individuals: the "tabula rasa invited
Enlightened man to remake himself out of raw (rude) materials in the
state of nature. The natural right of labor to its products undermined
the claims of the Newtonian Maker, and he was replaced as the pheno-
menological subject of the world by the self-regarding and self-govern-
ing self we so often take ourselves to be and live to serve" (76). The
individualized Romantic "seer" thus becomes a definer and arbiter of
culture. Park, like many of his exploratory counterparts from 1750–
1830, is just such a "seer." His words reveal, at least to his own society,
what the world *is* (from his new and privileged perspective), how humans behave in far-flung places (in new and unexpected ways), what
humans seem to share (common behavioral traits and emotions); in
short, he provides information that needs to be accommodated into
any modern understanding of human experience.

Park's texts are important examples of another Romantic tendency that Marianna Torgovnick has described as the act of self-projection via otherness: "For Euro-Americans, then, to study the primitive brings us always back to ourselves, which we reveal in the act of defining the Other."[10] Park's writings participate in that tendency of Western culture to define itself by opposition, positive or negative, to culturally generalized non-Western behavior: "Is the present too materialistic? Primitive life is not—it is a precapitalist utopia in which only use value, never exchange value prevails. Is the present sexually repressed? Not primitive life—primitives live life whole, without fear of the body. . . . Does the present see itself as righteously Christian? Then primitives become heathens, mired in false beliefs. . . . The primitive does what we ask it to do. Voiceless, it lets us speak for it" (8–9). In speaking for the Africa and Africans he encounters, Park is participating in the process Torgovnick describes. At a time when British, like European, self-definition had been destabilized in so many ways—political revolutions, social and economic restructuring, class anxiety—Park's Romanticized Africa, and the subsequent romanticization of Park's own life by Europeans, contributes in important ways to the creation of the discourse of the colonizing culture that would soon "dominate" the globe. In addition, as Dorothy Hammond and Alta Jablow have noted, British explorers particularly tended to project two forms of British self-image onto Africans: "In one, the Africans represent the pejorative negation of all the good traits of the British. In this set of images the African is lewd, savage, instinctual, thoughtless"; but the other projection is equally revealing: it "depicts a nostalgic view in which the Africans represent the former, now lost, values of the British. Here, the African is the 'noble savage'."[11] European culture between 1790 and 1815 had strong reasons for seeing itself poised between savage brutality and a "noble" past that was conceived of in terms of the image of a golden age.

In addition, the "exploratory impulse," as we might call it, motivated many Europeans, just as the revolutionary impulse had triggered nation-altering social actions in 1776 and 1789. This revolutionary spirit required that cultures change in order to remake themselves. The exploratory (geographical) impulse of the 1700s and 1800s rested on a similar, and equally revolutionary, assumption. The exploring culture (Europe) needed to *know* (the course of rivers, locations of mountains, customs of inhabitants) in order to *control* (open trade routes, establish settlements, extend influence). This impulse arose from and fostered a very Romantic conception: the same power that feels itself in touch with the vital and benevolent forces of life (creation, imagination, natural beauty, innocence, the immaterial) is likewise a power that can be invoked for domination, control, destruction, and absolutist forms of authority.

This exploratory impulse is clearly critiqued by Mary Shelley in

Frankenstein (1817). Robert Walton wants to "satiate" his "ardent curiosity with the sight of a part of the world never before visited" so that he can "confer on all mankind" an "inestimable benefit." Likewise, Victor Frankenstein wants to "pioneer a new way" and "explore unknown powers," but he soon acknowledges "how dangerous is the acquirement of knowledge," and he links the drive which led him to create life with a destructive force, without which "Greece would not have been enslaved; Caesar would have spared his country; America would have been discovered more gradually; and the empires of Mexico and Peru had not been destroyed."[12] We can call this force the creative imagination if we like; or, we can call it the Nietzschean "will to power." But whether this exploratory impulse is seen as positive or negative, it is often described in terms that link it with "the sublime." In fact, "the sublime" is important to Romanticism at least partly because the concept becomes a site of intersection between positive and beautiful aspects of this impulse and the fearfully uncontrolled elements of the same energy. Mere perceptual observation becomes a form of tyranny when it leads to subsequent cultural sanctions for control.[13] An explorer like Park says: I have observed these places; I have seen these people up close. I know what is there; I know what these people are like. The next step is, of course, much more suspect in light of the subsequent history of colonial expansion. Knowing what the explorers have told them, Europeans then claim to know what they should do. Knowing what the explorers have seen, Westerners suddenly claim to know how they should act toward these "other" people and these "other" places. One result of this new "knowledge" is empire.

Mungo Park arrived in Africa in 1795, intent on carrying out the mission of his London backers, Joseph Banks and the African Exploration Association. Three earlier African Association explorers had failed: Simon Lucas had turned back, John Ledyard had died before departing Cairo, and David Houghton had disappeared on a desert caravan.[14] As a result, Park's journey, in his own mind and the minds of his patrons, was colored from the first by contradictory senses of epic heroism and dangerous futility. At Pisania, the "kindly" and "hospitable" slave-trader (contradictions abound from the opening pages of the text) Dr. Laidley "equips" Park for his risky journey with a Mandingo interpreter named Demba, who had been promised his freedom in return for good service, and a former slave named Johnson who had been freed in Jamaica and returned to Africa by way of England. Park will "need" these faithful and knowledgeable natives if he is to pass through the unknown country unimpeded. Similarly, King Jatta of the Woolli warns of the life-threatening dangers awaiting any white man east of Medina: "He received me with a benevolent countenance, and tenderly entreated me to desist from my purpose of travelling into the interior; telling me, that Major Houghton had been killed in his route, and that if I followed his footsteps I should probably meet with his fate" (1799, 37). Park elegizes a dead European explorer as the only model for himself in this land, adding that cultural difference is a life-and-death matter in such circumstances: "[The king] said that I must not judge the people of the eastern country by those of the Woolli; that the latter were acquainted with white men, and respected them, whereas the people of the east had never seen a white man, and would certainly destroy me" (37).

The Africa Park describes in the early pages of his 1799 text is a land as plentiful as rural England, but often not as beautiful: "the country itself being an immense level, and very generally covered with woods, presents a tiresome and gloomy uniformity to the eye; but although nature has denied to the inhabitants the beauties of romantic landscapes, she has bestowed on them, with a liberal hand, the more important blessings of fertility and abundance" (9). The journey through this land begins in "sufferings," partly brought on by illness, but primarily the result of nonhuman nature: "the tedious hours during that gloomy season, when the rain falls in torrents; when suffocating heats oppress by day, and when the night is spent by the terrified traveller in listening to the croaking of frogs, (of which the numbers are beyond imagination,) the shrill cry of the jackall, and the deep howling of the hyaena; a dismal concert, interrupted only by the roar of such tremendous thunder as no person can form a conception of but those who have heard it" (9). Park's hyperbole—"torrents," "suffocating," "terrified," "beyond imagination," "tremendous," "no person"—in a single sentence reveals him intensifying his own experience, for whatever reasons: rhetorical flourish, economic gain, artistic license, or psychological revelation. His motives matter less to subsequent readers than our awareness that language in such cases is performing complicated ideological tasks.

The complex use of the pastoral as a generic category in exploration narratives has sufficient history to warrant a separate discussion. Images of a golden age, lost civilizations, bucolic harmony, and precivilized humanity were commonplace throughout the eighteenth century. Park's African pastoral, by contrast, is a somewhat simpler vision of a landscape in which the human inhabitants blend harmoniously because they place so few demands on their surroundings. Late in his first journey he reports: "we travelled with uncommon expedition, through a woody, but beautiful country, interspersed with a pleasing variety of hill and dale, and abounding with partridges, guinea-fowls, and deer,

until sun-set; when we arrived at a most romantic stream, called Co-
meissang" (330). Park's 1799 text is remarkable for its inclusivity, its
optimism, and its apparent liberalism about the possibilities of a universal human nature. The narrative draws on a whole series of eighteenth-century, often Rousseauistic, assumptions about the origins and
potential of human society.[15] An old woman who gives Park food, for
example, is the occasion for a meditation on the universal origins
of human hospitality. This woman, though a "poor untutored slave,"
nevertheless "without examining into my character or circumstances,
listened implicitly to the dictates of her own heart. Experience had
taught her that hunger was painful, and her own distresses made her
commiserate those of others" (70).

At Sego, the capital of Bambarra, the self-declared hero Park finally
gazes on the Niger for the first time, and he rapturously compares this
river with another famous waterway: "looking forwards I saw with
infinite pleasure the great object of my mission; the long sought for,
majestic Niger, glittering to the morning sun, as broad as the Thames
at Westminster, and flowing slowly *to the eastward*" (1799, 194).[16] Within
a page Park is describing the same spot in terms that stress the surprising grandeur of the African sight by way of comparison to European
expectations: "The view of this extensive city; the numerous canoes
upon the river; the crowded population, and the cultivated state of
the surrounding country, formed altogether a prospect of civilization
and magnificence, which I little expected to find in the bosom of Africa" (196).

The rhetoric of subsequent Victorian racist assumptions about Africa is almost absent from Park's log. His account, if anything, sets up
black Africans as the ethnographic equivalent of Europeans in regard
to almost all categories except "superstition." At Teesee, Park enjoyed
"conversing with the natives, who attended me every where with great
kindness and curiosity" (75). He attended "a sort of public entertain-
ment" near Doolinkeabo which "was conducted with more than common propriety," and at which food and drink were "distributed with
great liberality; and the women were admitted into the society" (193).
At Kamalia, a "friendly Negro" named Karfa "stretched out his hospitable hand" for Park's "relief"; this "benevolent landlord" nursed Park
through a severe illness, offering "kindness" and "simple manners"
(255). King Mansong is "prudent and liberal," even though he is curi-
ous about the motive for Park's mission: "He argued, probably, as my
guide argued; who, when he was told, that I had come from a great
distance, and through many dangers, to behold the Joliba river [Niger],
naturally inquired, if there were no rivers in my own country, and
whether one river was not like another" (200). When it comes time to

generalize, Park is no less complimentary about African moral thinking and daily behavior: "There are many instances of free men voluntarily surrendering up their liberty to save [slaves'] lives" (295).

Park's attitude toward Moslems, and Moors, is the exception to his more frequent charity and optimism about Africa and Africans. His hostility is consistent with the sorts of demonization of the Moslem world noted by Edward Said: "For Europe, Islam was a lasting trauma. Until the end of the seventeenth century the 'Ottoman peril' lurked alongside Europe to represent for the whole of Christian civilization a constant danger."[17] Park's Moors parallel other excessive Romantic accounts of the East: Southey's *Thabala the Destroyer* (1801) and *The Curse of Kehama* (1810), Thomas Moore's *Lalla Rookh* (1817), Shelley's "Zeinab and Kathema" (1810) and *The Revolt of Islam* 1817, Tennyson's "Timbuctoo" (1829).[18] Roger Sales notes, by comparison, that when Byron "went to Jannina in 1809, he saw plenty of examples of Ali Pasha's sadistic cruelty. His radicalism did not prevent him from admiring this stylish dictator."[19]

But Park's vitriolic account of the Moslem influence in Africa is also based on more immediately local tensions among Moslems, Christians, and pagan animists along the southern border of the great Sahara. Most of the area traversed by Park on his first journey was contested or politically unstable throughout this period. Attendants of Ali, autocratic ruler of nomadic Ludamar, counted Park's toes and fingers, inspected his white skin to see if he was human, and offered him pork to see if he would eat it. In his generalized and anthropological description of these Moors, Park abandons all pretense to objectivity in favor of a rabid anti-Moslem bias: "I fancied that I discovered in the features of most of them, a disposition toward cruelty, and low cunning; and I could never contemplate their physiognomy, without feeling sensible uneasiness. From the staring wildness of their eyes, a stranger would immediately set them down as a nation of lunatics. The treachery and malevolence of their character, are manifested in their plundering excursions against the Negro villages" (158–59).

Byron may have been just a boy when Park arrived at the mouth of the Gambia, but from the earliest pages of Park's narrative, the explorer presents himself in a series of postures that will come to be identified with the Byronic pose before the end of the next decade. Park is sophisticated in his dealing with local potentates, heroic in his posturing during dangerous circumstances, fatalistic in his confrontations with the possibility of his own death, and always supremely gracious in his dealings with women. These parallels remind us of the extent to which Byron's supposed uniqueness was itself derived from preexisting cultural positioning: the legendary Don Juan, Goethe's young

Werther, Casanova (1725–98), and Beau Brummel (1778–1840), among others.[20] Park also had in common with Byron the success of his first volume. *Travels in the Interior Districts of Africa* appeared in April 1799. The first printing of 1,500 copies went initially to 400 subscribers and then proceeded to sell out before the end of the month. Two additional editions were issued in 1799, a fourth in 1800, a sixth by 1810. French and German translations appeared in 1799 and 1800 respectively; the first American edition in 1800, another in 1803. Illustrated editions of Park's travels fostered the heroic—and titillating—pose of the explorer by including drawings of the white man emerging naked from his bath in the heart of the continent—drying himself indiscreetly with a piece of cloth—or reclining in a tent full of women attendants.[21]

Park's attitudes toward African women are among the most interesting and culturally significant of his observations. Hammond and Jablow cite him as perhaps the first European to single out "African women for particular notice or extended discussions."[22] By the end of his first expedition Park claims, "I do not recollect a single instance of hard-heartedness towards me in the women. In all my wanderings and wretchedness, I found them to be uniformly kind and compassionate" (263). At Shrilla, Park is overcome "with joy at so unexpected a deliverance" when a woman prepares him "a tolerable meal" and offers "a little corn" for his horse, after he has been rebuffed by the local head-man (181). Beyond Sego, a "worthy benefactress" performs "rites of hospitality" that once again leave Park filled with gratitude (198). Even when he is splashed with a bride's urine ("a nuptial benediction from the bride's own person") as part of a marriage ritual, Park offers kindness and solicitation: "I wiped my face and sent my acknowledgements to the lady" (136).

His attitude toward females is not always praiseworthy, however. Early in his journey he encounters one group of women who are dressed in "a thin French gauze" that is "well calculated to display the shape of their persons." The "manners of these females, however, did not correspond with their dress; for they were rude and troublesome in the highest degree; they surrounded me in numbers, begging for amber, beads, &c.; and were so vehement in their solicitations, that I found it impossible to resist them. They tore my cloak, cut the buttons from my boy's clothes, and were proceeding to other outrages, when I mounted my horse and rode off, followed for half a mile by a body of these harpies" (50). Even in this case, however, Park's attitude results from specific circumstances, not a general misogyny.

Perhaps Park's most famous encounter with women occurred while he was a virtual prisoner of the Moorish prince Ali at Benowm. A delegation makes their way into Park's hut, and he admits that he cannot evaluate their motives: "whether from the instigation of others, or impelled by their own ungovernable curiosity, or merely out of frolic, I cannot affirm" (132). This group of women has come to inspect the body of the prisoner: "the object of their visit was to ascertain, by actual inspection, whether the rite of circumcision extended to the Nazarenes, (Christians) as well as to the followers of Mahomet" (132). Park responds as any Romantic hero would: "I observed to them, that it was not customary in my country to give ocular demonstration in such cases, before so many beautiful women; but that if all of them would retire, except the young lady to whom I pointed, (selecting the youngest and handsomest), I would satisfy her curiosity" (132). The women depart without pleading their suit further, including the chosen inspector, who nevertheless sent Park "some meal and milk" for his supper.

But if Park was often charitable toward Africans, he could also be extremely judgmental. Mandingo "notions of geography" are "puerile," and their egocentrism is described by Park as though it is uniquely xenophobic among humans: "of all countries in the world their own appears to them as the best, and their own people as the happiest; and they pity the fate of other nations, who have been placed by Providence in less fertile and less fortunate districts" (272–73). His tone can often deprecate ("Some of the religious opinions of the Negroes, though blended with the weakest credulity and superstition, are not unworthy attention" [*sic*], (273), and he can then go on to describe the cultural authority of tradition as though it is, once again, somehow unique to Africans: "If they are asked, for what reason then do they offer up a prayer on the appearance of the new moon; the answer is, that custom has made it necessary: they do it, because their fathers did it before them. Such is the blindness of unassisted nature!" (273). Park's own view of nationalistic xenophobia (and patriarchal custom) seems strangely skewed by comments such as these. The Britain of 1799 was itself increasingly unclear as to whether it was "the best," or its people "the happiest." In a similar way, eighteenth-century Europeans were worrying whether customs should be continued solely "because their fathers did it before them."

Park's writings are technically precolonial, and for that reason they employ metaphors that will only be fully exploited later by overtly colonial texts: primitivism, paganism, savagery, and darkness. Park has little to say about cannibalism, but his one comment does relate to recent analysis of the discourse of cannibalism in significant ways. In Park's text the issue arises in the discussion of a long conflict between the Bambarra tribe and the inhabitants of the adjoining district, the Maniana. "West of Baedoo," Park reports, "is Maniana; the inhabitants of which, according to the best information I was able to collect, are

cruel and ferocious; carrying their resentment towards their enemies
so far as never to give quarter; and even to indulge themselves with
unnatural and disgusting banquets of human flesh" (217). Park immediately goes on to explain the source and potential limitations of this
information: "I am well aware that the accounts which the Negroes give
of their enemies, ought to be received with great caution; but I have
heard the same account in so many different kingdoms, and from such
a variety of people, whose veracity I had no occasion to suspect, that I
am disposed to allow it some degree of credit" (217). This evidence
based on independent reportage, however, is then countered by a detail
that undermines the same claims: "The inhabitants of Bambarra, in the
course of a long and bloody war, must have had frequent opportunities of satisfying themselves as to the fact: and if the report had been
entirely without foundation, I cannot conceive why the term *Ma dum-
mulo* (man eaters), should be applied exclusively to the inhabitants of
Maniana" (217). But the king of Bambarra, as we have just been told,
has been unable to subdue these ferocious people. As Park had suggested earlier in his own paragraph, there may be all sorts of reasons
to describe your enemy in dehumanizing ways, particularly in the case
of an enemy you are still trying to subdue or dominate. Much the same
logic may explain many Western tales of cannibalism from 1500–1900.

As Gananath Obeyesekere has recently observed in an account of
the James Cook voyages of 1779, cannibalism entered the discourse of
Westerners in part because of Westerners themselves.[23] On this view,
British and European explorers often brought a fear of being eaten
by "primitives" with them on their voyages, projected that fear onto
"Others" who may or may not have ever practiced cannibalism in any
form, and then reported whatever version of cannibalistic practice
seemed most appropriate to the rhetorical task at hand: we are scared
of these people, we must subdue these people, these people are not
like other humans, these people are not human. In many such cases,
the European discourse of dominance allowed for the attribution of
cultural practices for which there was, in most instances, no physical
evidence. Park comments on this precise phenomenon in his own experience. He interviews a group of slaves who express concern on this
subject: "They were all very inquisitive; but they viewed me at first with
looks of horror, and repeatedly asked if my countrymen were cannibals.
. . . A deeply rooted idea, that the whites purchase Negroes for the purpose of devouring them, or of selling them to others, that they may be
devoured hereafter, naturally makes the slaves contemplate a journey
towards the Coast with great terror" (319).

One culmination of Park's pre-colonial position occurs after a dramatic series of escapes, near escapes, and violent encounters with Afri-

cans. He has fled from Ali, been set upon by bandits, robbed, stripped, and all but left for dead: "After they were gone, I sat for some time, looking around me with amazement and terror. Which ever way I turned, nothing appeared but danger and difficulty. I saw myself in the midst of a vast wilderness, in the depth of the rainy season; naked and alone; surrounded by savage animals, and men still more savage. I was five hundred miles from the nearest European settlement. All these circumstances crowded at once on my recollection; and I confess that my spirits began to fail me. I considered my fate as certain, and that I had no alternative, but to lie down and perish" (243). Park is then saved neither by his European rationalism, nor by his Scottish common sense, nor by the might or wealth of his nation. Rather, he is preserved in the wilderness by a prototype of Wordsworth's daffodil: a Keatsian blossom, a Tennysonian flower, a botanical specimen, though not in a crannied wall: "At this moment, painful as my reflections were, the extraordinary beauty of a small moss, in fructification, irresistibly caught my eye. I mention this to shew from what trifling circumstances the mind will sometimes derive consolation; for though the whole plant was not larger than one of my fingers, I could not contemplate the delicate conformation of its roots, leaves, and capsula, without admiration" (244). The romantic poet is becoming the Victorian botanist; Park is rescued from cosmic despair by a moss.

We see a new tension arise when a pre-colonial explorer like Park imagines the colonial potential of Africa. At such a point, the conflicting strains of his rhetoric are clearly apparent. Concluding a passage on the natural riches and the human potential of the far-flung regions he has traversed, Park concludes: "It was not possible for me to behold the wonderful fertility of the soil, the vast herds of cattle, proper both for labour and food, and a variety of other circumstances favorable to colonization and agriculture; and reflect, withal, on the means which presented themselves of a vast inland navigation, without lamenting that a country, so abundantly gifted and favored by nature, should remain in its present savage and neglected state" (312). Here is the paradox of the romantic exploration narrative clearly stated. The land is rich but inaccessible and harsh; likewise, the people have promise but fall far short of their human potential: "Much more did I lament that a people of manners and dispositions so gentle and benevolent, should either be left as they now are, immersed in the gross and uncomfortable blindness of pagan superstition, or permitted to become converts to a system of bigotry and fanaticism" (312). The indigenous people may be "gentle and benevolent," but they are also in need of care and "development"; so says the Romantic voice of exploration that will soon become the economically and "spiritually" driven voice of Victorian empire.

The account of Park's fatal second journey, *Journal of a Mission to the Interior of Africa in the Year 1805*, is a very different sort of text from the 1799 *Travels*, in part because of its posthumous publication—complete with "other documents, official and private, relating to the same mission" and "an account of the life of Mr. Park"—but also because Park's own voice has become much more self-consciously anthropological, and therefore less personal.[24] The *Journal* is no longer the work of the "Surgeon" Park had described himself as being on the title page of his 1799 *Travels*; rather, the 1805 text records the self-conscious voice of a now-famous explorer, intent upon expanding his understanding of the region and solidifying his claim to scientific objectivity. Park now includes many more measurements of longitude and latitude, long lists of trade items with their respective values, as well as astronomical, economic, and geographic measurement. In this work we see the next step toward the rhetoric of empire; here are details that will allow subsequent colonists to make their way into a country that has previously been merely "described."

In 1805, Park's own lowest emotional state is presented as parallel to a moment in 1799, but the narrative has shrunk from several pages in the 1799 journal to a single sentence. Park is describing his feelings on the death of his brother-in-law, Alexander Anderson: "I shall only observe that no event which took place during the journey, ever threw the smallest gloom over my mind, till I laid Mr. Anderson in the grave. I then felt myself, as if left a second time lonely and friendless amidst the wilds of Africa" (279). By this time the "wilds" of Africa are already coming to be conceived of more in terms of commerce, trade routes, and natural resources and less as a natural and human space valuable in their own right, or as a source of general "information." At the same time, Park is still able to offer romanticized descriptions of landscape that conflate fact with fiction and natural wonders with the grandeur of human achievement: "June 24th.—Left Sullo, and travelled through a country beautiful beyond imagination, with all the possible diversities of rock, sometimes towering up like ruined castles, spires, pyramids, &c. We passed one place so like a ruined Gothic abbey, that we halted a little, before we could satisfy ourselves that the niches, windows, ruined staircase, &c. were all natural rock. A faithful description of this place would certainly be deemed a fiction" (191). This last quotation is a paradigmatic example of the rhetoric of Romantic Africa: perhaps there were people here who built the equivalent of a Gothic church; perhaps these natural objects are the ruins of a great civilization, perhaps no one will believe this account of these marvels. Or perhaps all of this speculation is merely a product of the mind of the privileged observer.

This last work by Park was assembled from notes brought out by one of the few surviving members of the expedition. Park himself perished, probably at falls on the Niger near Bussa, perhaps at the hands of irate locals—perhaps not. The fact that the *Journal* had been brought out of Africa while its author perished in the interior only added to the romance and mystique of both author and text. Park was reported to be alive in the interior well into the middle of the century. His death was the subject of speculation, gossip, innuendo, and artistic imagination.[25] He quickly became a prototype in the popular imagination of the romantic hero of African exploration. He died young, handsome, and famous, and he left a best-selling written record of his final exploits.

Public responses to both of Park's missions were widespread and long lasting. He was lionized while he lived and celebrated in story and song after his demise. Major Rennell, in his "Appendix" to the 1799 journey, described the explorer's achievements in no uncertain terms: the "journey of Mr. Park, into the Interior of Western Africa, has brought to our knowledge more important facts respecting its Geography (both *moral* and *physical*), than have been collected by any former traveller" (1799, a2). The most important facts credited by Rennell to Park were "the *course* of the *Niger*, and the history of the *Lotophagi*," since Park had described and illustrated lotus flowers and lotus-eating in extensive detail. By the time of the publication of the 1799 *Travels*, the Duchess of Devonshire had penned lyrics, and G. G. Ferrari had written a score, for the song sung to Park by cotton-spinning African women. The lyrics include a couplet that bears a striking metrical and rhetorical resemblance to the final lines of Wordsworth's "Solitary Reaper" (1802): the "White Man" must leave the safety of this village, "But ever in his heart will bear / Remembrance of the Negro's care."[26]

The advertisement for the 1803 New York edition of *Travels* describes Park in terms that elevate him over ancient geographers and modern explorers—"By Mr. Park's discoveries at length, the triumph of the antients over the moderns is complete" (iii)—because his observations confirm the opinions of Herodotus and Ptolemy.[27] By 1831 a volume entitled *Narrative of Discovery and Adventures in Africa* reveals the way Park entered history as an almost mythic figure: "Mr. Park was again on the Gambia; and on the 10th of June, 1797, reached Pisania, where he was received as one risen from the dead; for all the traders from the interior had believed and reported that, like Major Houghton, he was murdered by the Moors of Ludamar."[28] The "risen from the dead" metaphor is one that Park himself had used to describe this reception (358). Once he returned to Britain, the acclaim continued: "the report of his unexpected return, after making such splendid discoveries, kindled throughout the nation a higher enthusiasm than had perhaps been excited by the result of any former mission of the same nature" (*Narrative* 100).

Tensions evident in Park's account of Africa and Africans were apparent even in the earliest reviews of his work. The *Gentleman's Magazine*, within four months of the publication of the 1799 *Travels*, offered a positive interpretation of Park's view of Africans: "The Negroes of these districts are not to be considered as an uncivilized race; they have religion, established governments, laws, schools, commerce, manufactures, *wars!*". The *Annual Register*, by contrast, used a review of Park's text to offer up an antithetical view: in Park's Africa this reviewer saw "no consummate polity and pure religion; but forms of government, weak, imperfect or oppressive; the wildest fanaticism and the most debasing superstition."[29] That such contradictory responses could emerge so quickly is further evidence of the conflicted condition of Park's own rhetoric. At times he sounds as though he is glorifying the rustic simplicity of the life he finds around him in the interior. The people he meets are: "mild," "gentle," "cordial," "benevolent," "kind." At other moments he suggests that Africa and its people can only be effectively characterized in very different terms: "simple," "hostile," "cruel," "puerile," "bigotry," "fanaticism," "gross," "blindness."

The reception of Park's texts was also complicated by the status of the slave-trade debate between 1799 and 1830. Park's own attitude toward slavery has itself been the subject of much debate and dispute.[30] What seems clear throughout his texts is that Park is not specifically interested in the complexities of the slave-trade question, or at least is not willing to discuss such an interest in the context of his exploration narratives. He describes the torturous death of a female slave named Nealee from a series of repeated beatings with horror and sensitivity to her plight, but he does nothing to intervene. He reflects at numerous points on the contradictions inherent in human ownership of other humans, but he then goes on to describe numerous encounters between slaves and slave traders in dispassionate, objectifying terms. In the most often-quoted passage at the end of the 1799 chapter on slavers and slavery, he takes a position that is as ambivalent as it is carefully worded:

> How far it [slavery in Africa] is maintained and supported by the slave traffic, which, for two hundred years, the nations of Europe have carried on with the natives of the Coast, it is neither within my province, nor in my power, to explain. If my sentiments should be required concerning the effect which a discontinuance of that commerce would produce on the manners of the natives, I should have no hesitation in observing, that, in the present unenlightened state of their minds, my

opinion is, the effect would neither be so extensive or beneficial, as many wise and worthy persons fondly expect. (297–98)

This comment significantly includes no moral evaluation of the slave trade or of slavery; it simply claims that Park is not convinced that the abolition of the trade in humans would alter the way that Africans treat other Africans.

The present essay does not claim that Park's works are unique to, or uniquely revealing of, the rhetoric of Romantic Africa. Romantic studies would do well to consider other texts that would prove useful to our understanding of the role of exploration narratives in the construction of the cultural category we continue to call Romanticism: Francis Moore, *Travels into the Inland Parts of Africa*, London, 1738; W. Smith, *A New Voyage to Guinea*, London, 1744; J. Matthews, *A Voyage to the River Sierra Leone*, London 1788 [1966]; W. Patterson, *A Narrative of Four Journeys into the Country of the Hottentots and Caffraria*, London, 1789; Robert Norris, *Memoirs of the Reign of Bossa Ahadee, King of Dahomey*, London, 1789; Archibald Dalzel, *History of Dahomey*, London, 1793 [1967]; W. G. Browne, *Travels in Africa, Egypt and Syria from the Year 1792 to 1798*, London, 1799; J. Barrow, *An Account of Travels into the Interior of South Africa*, London, 1801; James Bruce, *Travels to Discover the Source of the Nile*, 2nd. ed., Edinburgh, 1805; F. Hornemann, "Journal," *Proceedings of the Association for Promoting the Discovery of the Interior Parts of Africa*, London, 1810 [1967]; H. Salt, *A Voyage to Abyssinia etc. in the Years 1809 and 1810*, London, 1814; R. Tully, *Narrative of a Ten Years' Residence at Tripoli in Africa*, London, 1816; J. L. Burckhardt, *Travels in Nubia*, London, 1819; T. E. Bowdich, *A Mission from Cape Coast Castle to Ashantee*, London, 1819; J. G. Jackson, *An Account of Timbuctoo and Hausa*, London, 1820; G. B. English, *A Narrative of the Expedition to Dongola and Sennaar*, London, 1822; J. Campbell, *Travels in South Africa . . . Being a Narrative of a Second Journey, 1820*, London, 1822; J. Adams, *Remarks on the Country Extending from the Cape Palmas to the River Congo*, London, 1823 [1968]; J. Dupuis, *Journal of a Residence in Ashantee*, London, 1824; Hugh Clapperton, *Journal of a Second Expedition into the Interior of Africa, and the Journal of Richard Lander*, London, 1829 [1966].[31] I include this long list of titles only to hint at the widespread discourse on Africa produced by non-Francophone observers before 1830; the textual construction of European "Africa" was as much a Romantic creation as it was a Victorian one.

By the time of Park's own "romantic" and mysterious disappearance in 1805, specifically British interest in African exploration was beginning to wane. Increased tension with France kept Britain, like most of continental Europe, preoccupied with the Napoleonic adventure, at least until the Battle of Waterloo. Although there were sporadic accounts of African travels and settlement, the next flurry of interest in African expansionism and exploration would await the 1830s. By then Victorian assumptions about Britain's relationship to the "subject" realms of the world was shaping a new, more powerful, and—from the hindsight that is history—more culturally destructive rhetoric. By mid-century, the discourse of Africa was not in the hands of apparently disinterested and polyphonous travelers and explorers any longer. It was moving slowly and irretrievably into the mouths and pens of those who sought specific cultural advantage from economic expansion and cultural domination. The brilliant light "glittering in the morning sun" on Mungo Park's Thames-like Niger yields inexorably over the nineteenth century to a more horrific vision of the Thames in flood, Joseph Conrad's "immense darkness" on the ebb tide above Gravesend.

NOTES

1. *Travels in the Interior Districts of Africa: Performed under the Direction and Patronage of the African Association, in the Years 1795, 1796, and 1797* (London: W. Bulmer, 1799) [New York: Arno Press and *New York Times*, 1971]. All my citations are to this edition unless otherwise specified. The OED cites Park as the second use of "Mumbo Jumbo" in English, attributing the first occurrence to Francis Moore, *Travels into the Inland Parts of Africa* (1738): "This is a thing invented by the Men to keep their Wives in Awe."

   I am grateful to my colleagues Bob Ness, Catherine Beaudry, and John Ransom for comments on parts of this essay.

2. Katherine George, "The Civilized West Looks at Primitive Africa, 1400–1800," *Isis* 49 (March 1958):62–72, and Winthrop D. Jordan in *White over Black: American Attitudes toward the Negro, 1550–1812* (Chapel Hill: University of North Carolina Press, 1986), 269–311.

3. "Victorians and Africans: The Genealogy of the Myth of the Dark Continent," *Critical Inquiry* 12 (Autumn 1985):166–203, 170, 173. See also Brantlinger's *Rule of Darkness: British Literature and Imperialism, 1830–1914* (Ithaca: Cornell University Press, 1988).

4. *The Rhetoric of English India* (Chicago: University of Chicago Press, 1992), 5.

5. Brantlinger notes that Blake, Southey, Wordsworth, Coleridge, Byron, and Shelley presented a unified Romantic front of antislavery lyrics (*Rule* 175). See also Eva Beatrice Dykes, *The Negro in English Romantic Thought* (Washington, D.C.: Associated Publishers, 1942) and Wylie Sypher, *Guinea's Captive Kings: British Anti-Slavery Literature of the Eighteenth Century* (Chapel Hill: University of North Carolina Press, 1942). Mary Louise Pratt argues that "Romanticism *consists*, among other things, of shifts in relations between Europe and other parts of the world," in *Imperial Eyes: Travel Writing and Transculturation* (London, Routledge, 1992), 138. See also Christopher Hibbert, *Africa Explored: Europeans in the Dark Continent* (New York: Penguin, 1984), Dorothy Hammond and Alta Jablow, *The Africa That*

Never Was: Four Centuries of British Writing about Africa (Prospect Heights, Illinois: Waveland, 1992) and Hammond and Jablow, *The Myth of Africa* (New York: Library of Social Science, 1977).

6. My emphasis critiques Jerome McGann's concept of "Romantic Ideology" by reminding us that there is no single Romantic "ideology"; there are only multiple Romantic "ideologies." Such a plurality makes problematic McGann's notion of "an uncritical absorption in Romanticism's own self-representations," see *The Romantic Ideology: A Critical Investigation* (Chicago: University of Chicago Press, 1983), 1.

7. "Scratches on the Face of the Country; or, What Mr. Barrow saw in the Land of the Bushmen," *Critical Inquiry* 12:1 (Autumn 1985):119–143, 141.

8. *Imperial Eyes*, 75.

9. "Speakers of Being: Romantic Refusions and Cultural Anthropology," in *Romantic Motives: Essays on Anthropological Sensibility*, ed. George W. Stocking, Jr. (Madison: University of Wisconsin Press, 1989), 76. De Zengotita cites Rousseau, Herder, Sapir, and Levi-Strauss as avatars of a uniquely Romantic view of human discourses and selfhood, each one a post-enlightenment speaker who "expresses and creates being" only "through utterance" (76).

10. *Gone Primitive: Savage Intellects, Modern Lives* (Chicago: University of Chicago Press, 1990), 11.

11. Hammond and Jablow, *Never Was*, 11.

12. *Frankenstein: or, the Modern Prometheus*, ed. Johanna M. Smith (Boston: St. Martin's, 1992), 26, 54–55, 57.

13. Pratt links Park to the term "anti-conquest," by which she means "the strategies of representation whereby European bourgeois subjects seek to secure their innocence in the same moment as they assert European hegemony"; she refers to the "main protagonist of the anti-conquest" as " 'seeing-man,' an admittedly unfriendly label for the European male subject of European landscape discourse—he whose imperial eyes passively look out and possess" (*Imperial Eyes* 7). My reading sees Park less inclined to "possess" by way of sight, and more inclined—perhaps like John Keats—to resolve a status, and class, anxiety partly by way of visual perception: "I see; therefore, I have power."

14. See Pratt (*Imperial Eyes* 71), Hibbert (53–56), and Kenneth Lupton, *Mungo Park: The African Traveller* (Oxford: Oxford University Press, 1979), 30–36. See also Frank McLynn, *Hearts of Darkness: The European Exploration of Africa* (New York: Carroll and Graf, 1992), 13–39.

15. As de Zengotita says, "a proto-Romantic cult of sensibility was as much a part of the Enlightenment as Newtonian abstraction . . . [Rousseau] envied the 'savage man' [*l'homme sauvage*] who 'lives within himself'; he pitied 'social man, always outside himself,' who 'can live only in the opinions of others' " (78).

16. Park is clearly not dealing in facts when he records such a moment. The Thames at Westminster in Park's day was much narrower than the Niger, as Park could plainly see. Accurate geographical information about sub-Saharan Africa was extremely hard to come by before the nineteenth century. John Ogilby recorded a seventeenth-century confusion that contributed to the need for Park's journey, in *Africa: Being an Accurate Description of*

the Regions of Egypt, Barbary, Lybia, and Billedulgerid, the land of Negroes, Guinee, Ethiopia, and the Abyssines (London: T. Johnson, 1670): "some hold Niger and Gambea to be one and the same River; and others will have it, that Niger is Rio Grande, or the Great River; both which opinions seem to have appearance of Truth, because the chiefest Geographers of this Age hold Gambea and Zenega to be two Branches of the Niger" (316).

17. *Orientalism* (New York: Random House, 1979), 59.

18. See, for example, George D. Bearce, *British Attitudes Towards India, 1784–1858* (Oxford: Oxford University Press, 1961), chap. 4, "Romantic India," 102–20.

19. See Roger Sales, *English Literature in History 1780–1830: Pastoral and Politics* (New York: St. Martin's, 1983), 219.

20. See, for example, Jerome Christensen, *Lord Byron's Strength: Romantic Writing and Commercial Society* (Baltimore: Johns Hopkins University Press, 1993), who links Beau Brummel to Byron: "The dandy's charm is, strictly speaking, inhuman" (160). Sanche de Gramont notes that in 1795 Park was "handsome in a romantic, wavy-haired, Byronic way. As he told one of his brothers, there was no doubt in his mind that he would 'acquire a greater name than any ever did,' " in *The Strong Brown God: The Story of the Niger River* (Boston: Houghton Mifflin, 1975), 72.

21. Several of these illustrations are reproduced in Timothy Severin, *The African Adventure: Four Hundred Years of Exploration in the "Dangerous Continent"* (New York: Dutton, 1973) 88–102.

22. Hammond and Jablow, *Never Was*, 70.

23. " 'British Cannibals': Contemplation of an Event in the Death and Resurrection of James Cook, Explorer," *Critical Inquiry* 18 (Summer 1992):630–54. Cannibalism has become a virtual feeding-ground for cultural critics in recent years. See, for example, A. W. Brian Simpson, *Cannibalism and the Common Law: The Story of the Tragic Last Voyage of 'Mignonette' and the Strange Legal Proceedings to Which it Gave Rise* (Chicago: University of Chicago Press, 1985) and *The Ethnography of Cannibalism*, ed. Paula Brown and Donald Tuzin (Washington, D.C.: Society for Psychological Anthropology, 1983). See also Peggy Reeves Sanday, *Divine Hunger: Cannibalism As a Cultural System* (London: Cambridge University Press, 1986) and W. Arens, *The Man-Eating Myth* (New York: Oxford University Press, 1979).

24. *The Journal of a Mission to the Interior of Africa, in the Year 1805*, 2nd. edition (London: John Murray, 1815). All my citations are to this edition, which also included "Isaaco's Journal," an account of the servant who returned to the Niger in 1810 to ascertain the fate of Park. This account was taken as confirming "the various reports of Mr. Park's death."

25. Speculation about Park's fate lasted well into the century. Lupton includes over a dozen accounts of Park's death or subsequent "sightings." Most accounts agreed that Park's party (only a handful had survived to this point) were wrecked (or ambushed) in the rapids at Bussa in early 1806. On 7 August 1824, however, Major Dixon Denham "heard a tale of a man with a white beard who was said to have lived three years at 'Gusgey on the Quolla', having no means to go on, and he died there" (Lupton 234).

26. This song is printed with its score as part of the frontispiece to the 1799 edition.

27. *Travels and Recent Discoveries in the Interior Districts of Africa, in the Years 1796 & '97* (New York: T. S. Arden, 1803).

28. *Narrative of Discovery and Adventure in Africa by Professors Jameson, James Wilson, and Hugh Murray* (New York: J. & J. Harper, 1831), 99.

29. *Gentleman's Magazine*, August 1799, 680–81; *Annual Register*, 1799, 489–90. See also Lupton, who notes that these reviews, remarkably, may have been produced by the same author, since they share an "identical opening paragraph" (112).

30. The slavery debate between 1780 and 1810 complicated all attempts to produce nonpropagandistic accounts of West Africa. See James Walvin, *England, Slaves, and Freedom, 1776–1838* (Jackson: University Press of Mississippi, 1986). See also Roger Anstey, *The Atlantic Slave Trade and British Abolition 1760–1810* (London: Macmillan, 1975) and Robin Blackburn, *The Overthrow of Colonial Slavery 1776–1848* (London: Verso, 1988).

31. Philip Curtin notes that "relative to their knowledge of the world in general, eighteenth-century Europeans knew more and cared more about Africa than they did at any later period up to the 1950s," in *The Image of Africa: British Ideas and Action 1780–1830* (Madison: University of Wisconsin Press, 1964), 9–10.

Five

MOIRA FERGUSON

Hannah Kilham: Gender, the Gambia, and the Politics of Language

How has my heart been affected in hearing of the conversations
of the interesting Garnon with the children, or rather her
attempt to communicate what they would willingly have replied
to, but for the affecting reason given, "Me no sabby (understand)
English." Could not a very small vocabulary be formed, by which
these children, though coming from various places, might learn
to convey their leading thoughts, and feelings and desires?
—Hannah Kilham, *Memoir*

HANNAH KILHAM JOURNEYED to West Africa three times between 1824
and 1832, when she died at sea, on her return to Sierra Leone from an
educational trip in Liberia. Intent on improving communications between Europeans and Africans through linguistic means, she devised
her educational program for England and West Africa in partial response to the ravages of slavery and the enforced linguistic heterogeneity of Sierra Leone. Her depiction of West Africa differed substan-
tially from that of her predecessors. Nominally, her involvement was
part of the colonial plan to teach Africans to read the Bible in the vernacular and acquaint Africans with grammar books and dictionaries.
But her program had wide implications for the greater autonomy of
the diverse African communities living there.

One of the African rulers at that time was "the Naimbana" who ruled
the Koya Kingdom and the Koya Temne people from 1775–1793. An
opponent of the slave trade, he required "important strangers" to report to his court at Robanna on their arrival, presumably to discuss the

reasons for their visit.[1] He signed the land treaty of secession with the British in 1788, and after his death in 1793 he was succeeded by Bai Farma II.

The double death of the Naimbana and his son dismayed British colonial administrators, since it threatened any hopes they cherished of transforming Sierra Leone into a slave-free territory. Debate on abolition in the British Parliament was then five years old. After serious setbacks to the bill's progress, due to the threats posed by the San Domingan and French revolutions, as well as fear of Jacobinism at home, it finally passed in 1807.[2]

In the meantime, the original Granville Town settlers, the black settlers known as Nova Scotians, and Jamaican maroons who had arrived at the behest of the British government, were in the process of establishing a workable community in Sierra Leone.[3] Concurrently in 1807, the African Institution was formed to promote trade, because the company was unwilling to abandon the land they had so painstakingly struggled to obtain from the Africans. The Abolition Bill fostered pro-slavery counterstrategies on the high seas that involved the enslavement of West Africans by British entrepreneurs who orchestrated illegal, clandestine sailings across the Middle Passage.[4] British officials responded to slave smuggling by establishing lookout ships and intercepting foreign slave ships. An official African policy under the auspices of the African Institution was in the making.[5]

A further British response was not long in coming. To facilitate their naval/maritime interceptions, a British vice-admiralty court was established in Freetown in 1807 to adjudicate the crimes, legally free the kidnapped Africans, and sell the ships as punishment. This court became the site for registering and resettling the illegally purchased slaves.[6] Between 1807 and 1815 naval captains received £191,000 in slave bounties by the Treasury. In 1816 2,545 recaptured slaves landed in Freetown.[7]

The court's main tasks, enunciated by its chief spokesman, Zachary Macaulay, was to suppress foreign slave trade and proselytize Western values. Macaulay was partly responsible for the vice-admiralty court being established at Sierra Leone and slave ships being returned there for "adjudication."[8] Since the British could see no way to return everyone to their home—as the government had managed to do with white Barbary coast captives—they "liberated" Africans on the spot. But the fact is that whites could not live in Sierra Leone and, in Sarah Lee's words, needed "other systems of mediation ... [African] men were educated purposely to enlighten their countrymen, whose complexities and constitutions were partially or wholly tinged with negro blood; and they by degrees carried the blessings of revealed religion into the heart of the continent."[9] In other words, the British government wanted and needed more Africans in the colony and no serious efforts were ever made to repatriate people captured from slave ships even if they lived nearby. Shortly after they landed, for example, officers of the Liberated Africans Department unceremoniously renamed slaves in the King's Yard according to their own European fancy. Dissolving the original identity of the "re-born" Africans was crucial to inculcating a new British value system based on Christian morality. Some examples of these new names are Kneebone, Alabaster, and Roman Augustus.

With their reassigned British names, the repatriated individuals were sent to settlement villages and invited to choose jobs. They could enlist in British regiments, join the navy, or be apprenticed in the colony. The Anglican Church Missionary Society (C.M.S.) established a Christian institution where freed children could be taught and trained for jobs as farmers, teachers, or missionaries.[10] Liberated children were sent to villages where the society's agents resided (28).

As a linguist, Hannah Kilham is innovative. For one thing, in that capacity she ventures much further in considering Africans as equals by granting explicit recognition to, rather than ignoring or ridiculing, African languages. She volunteered to go to Sierra Leone as a school missionary who could teach recaptured people from diverse African countries to read and write in their own languages. Furthermore, by means of her African-English pamphlets, Kilham enabled Africans and Europeans to communicate more easily; new self-constructions then came into play. By reversing the customary Eurocentric treatment of Liberated Africans—also known as recaptives—as malleable objects and addressing them as a community involved in education, Hannah Kilham affirms her concern with communication.

Unlike British officials in Sierra Leone, Kilham refused to acknowledge any linguistic binary system that consisted of a civilized language that was English and a barbaric language that was African. Her refusal to accept this equation constituted a challenge to the colonial paradigm and highlighted contradictions in the imperial enterprise.

Kilham's spiritual beliefs and her historical milieu fostered this desire to be a missionary, expressed in the resolutions passed at the second annual meeting of the African Institution. They provided:

> for the teaching of African languages to Europeans in Sierra Leone,
> and for the award of premiums on the produce exported from Africa. . . .
> Since Sierra Leone seemed to be the place in Africa where the efforts
> of the institution would be productive of the best results, correspon-
> dence was begun with persons living there. A commission of three was
> to be sent there to investigate conditions. A school was to be erected
> and the slave trade suppressed in this region.[11]

Kilham felt no compunction about her unorthodox orientation, happy to stand up for her principles, even within the Society of Friends. Nonetheless, she evades the question of how West Africans might respond to her decision to teach English in Sierra Leone, to anglicize, at least linguistically, African society.[12]

From 1816, when she expressed her desire to be a linguist, Hannah Kilham kept an extensive journal—mostly letters—in which she recorded her thoughts and experiences. They were included in memoirs published posthumously by her stepdaughter, Sarah Biller.[13] Primarily Hannah Kilham's correspondence, the memoirs also include a small amount of Biller's commentary. The particular selection of letters, however, collapses and somewhat distorts the timeframe in which Kilham wrote. For example, Biller places letters about the death of Richard Smith, who accompanied Hannah Kilham on her first visit, *before* Kilham's recital of how she received permission to go to Africa in the first place (170). Over half the correspondence is devoted to Kilham's three visits to Africa, where she hoped to teach linguistics and improve her knowledge of language:

> Prior to 1817 her journal show[s] the gradual growth in the mind of
> Hannah Kilham of that deep interest on behalf of the people of Africa,
> and more especially the children at Sierra Leone, which was attended
> with the conviction that it was an individual duty to devote herself to
> their improvement. (169)

Hannah Kilham also wrote several linguistic and historical reports about her African experiences. Her background explains those interests.

Hannah Spurr was born in 1774, the seventh child of civic-minded tradespeople in Sheffield. Her father was an Episcopalian, her mother, Hannah Brittlebank, a Yorkshirewoman sympathetic to John Wesley's teachings. After her mother died in 1786, Hannah Spurr raised her five brothers, with help from an older married sister who lived nearby. Following her father's death soon after her mother's, she was sent at the age of 14 to boarding school. Six years later, she joined the Wesleyan Methodists over the objections of family members and not long after joined the secession movement. In 1788 she married Alexander Kilham, founder of the secessionist Methodist New Connexion. An incessant preacher careless of his physical welfare, Alexander Kilham died eight months later: Hannah Kilham gave birth to a daughter, Mary, in April 1799, who died in an epidemic the next winter.[14]

Having opened a day school in Nottingham, a bereaved Hannah Kilham became acquainted with Quaker communities and took up membership in the Society of Friends in 1802. Rumor has it that she and her husband were interested in Quaker principles before his death.[15] Thereafter, she founded a branch of the Society for the Bettering of Conditions of the Poor, gaining a reputation as "indefatigable" for her efforts to alleviate poverty and suffering.

Through her friendship with Quaker William Allen, president of the African Institution, Hannah Kilham gradually felt a "sense of obligation to the future of the British colonial settlement at Sierra Leone."[16] Initiated by Allen, the African Institution was formed to implement the termination of the marine slave trade, to "civilize" Africa, and eradicate the now lucrative practice of smuggling slaves: "The association aimed also to further the sale of African products, to elevate the natives by means of education, and in general to show sympathy for them in every possible way."[17] The report of the committee to the general meeting states its Eurocentric purpose succinctly:

> to introduce the blessing of civilized society among a people sunk in ig-
> norance and barbarism, and occupying no less than a fourth part of
> the habitable globe, holds forth an object, the contemplation of which
> it is allowed, is sufficient to warm the coldest and fill the amplest mind.[18]

Hannah Kilham aimed to facilitate general communication because so few missionaries, compared to administrators, spoke English or any African languages. Several spoke German. For instructional purposes, she planned to use pamphlets she wrote in the United Kingdom that broke down African languages into component parts and placed the English equivalent alongside. By 1816 she wanted to implement her ideas more directly in Africa itself, to men, women, and children alike. At that point she was preoccupied with becoming not only a missionary but an educator who would transpose African languages into print.

Hannah Kilham's journal documents her efforts to visit Africa from 1816 until 1824, the date of her first journey. Since she had been an active Methodist-secessionist until 1802, she probably knew about earlier missionary ventures that progressed unevenly in this age of the "lexicographic revolution."[19] By the 1800s, for example, the Society for the Propagation of the Gospel was inactive in West Africa, while the Church Missionary Society (also Anglican) that began in 1799 dispatched missionaries in 1804. Seven years later, the Wesleyan-Methodist Missionary Society sent out missionaries for the first time.[20]

A prevalent sense of reform on the part of colonizers concerning Africans might also have influenced Kilham's decision to translate. Additionally, gender might have been an issue as a result of the involvement of many women in the huge antislavery petition. These drives resulted in approximately 1.5 million people out of a total population of 12 million signing petitions to be presented in Parliament. In one month alone, 700,000 signed eighty petitions.[21] In 1815 Wilberforce introduced a Parliamentary bill to abolish the slave trade.[22]

Nonetheless, several hurdles stood in Kilham's path. As a Quaker and pacifist, she deplored both the practice of illegally enslaving Africans and the Napoleonic wars, the effects of which could be felt on the West Coast of Africa.[23]

By the winter of 1819–20, Hannah Kilham was urging Friends to establish an informal committee that could publicize her concerns about Africa.[24] As the Committee for African Instruction, she pinned her hopes on it for several years (346). But the situation was left untended until the return to England in 1821 of the governor of Sierra Leone, Charles McCarthy, to receive a knighthood and the governor-generalship of British West Africa. Even so, the Quaker Yearly Meetings shied from initiating direct action in Africa. Finally, in 1821, the Society advertised Kilham's plan to visit, and asked for a companion(s) to accompany her; the Committee for African Instruction then pressed to have her request met.[25] Eventually an Anglican named Richard Smith agreed. A brother and sister named John and Ann Thomson and two Africans, Mahanadee, a Mandingo, and Sandanee, a Wolof, went too. Let me back up for a moment.

Around the time when Hannah Kilham was beginning her linguistic studies, other Europeans were also attempting communication with Africans.[26] "Exploration" of the West African interior in the 1790s provided the inspiration.[27] First, texts by the pioneer linguist of the Edinburgh Missionary Society, Henry Brunton, appeared in that decade. Among other items, he produced a reduction of the Soso language to a basic grammar and vocabulary—writing in Roman characters—an abridgment of the Bible and some of his own spiritual works.[28]

Second, Thomas Winterbottom, the botanist who had been present at Naimbana's death, had studied some Temne, Bullom, and Soso languages and appended his grammatical study to the two-volume treatise he wrote on Sierra Leone. It was obvious, too, that interpreters, and hence dictionaries, were sorely needed for negotiations with members of the African tribes in order for the British to be successful in their self-appointed role as imperial entrepreneurs.

Third, just before Hannah Kilham took up the challenge, Thomas Bowdich, an amateur naturalist and ethnographer and a writer for the company, had written *Travels in the Interior of Africa.*[29] His text included not only a vocabulary of English, Wolof, and Fula but also appended at the end some Serrere language translations.[30]

Given the groundwork already lain, Kilham's linguistic experiments were decidedly oppositional, since they were tied to political desire and her sense of injustice over the slave trade. For instance, part of what

Brunton discussed in his dialogues was Christian superiority and the fa-
tuity of the Soso religion.[31] In his preface about why he needs to write in
Soso, he calls it "a barbarous language [that] wants religious phrases."[32]
He goes on to state that "a great difficulty arises [for missionaries] from
the ignorance of barbarians. Mohammedanism is spreading fast in Africa. It is highly advisable to make vigorous efforts to destroy its spreading influence, while an opening is left."[33]

Yet that kind of commentary by Brunton did not deter Hannah Kilham. She had been able to begin her linguistic experiments because
of a fortunate discovery about the presence of West African sailors in
London. Almost coincidental with funds being raised by the Committee for African Instruction, these sailors arrived on the Thames from
the Gambian coast (112). In the winter of 1819–20, she hired two of
them to help her "in reducing the Jaloof or Wolof language" (132–33),
Sandanee, a Wolof, and Mahmadee, a Mande. Their board, lodging,
and manumission were paid for from committee funds. While learning
English and being educated in Tottenham, they assisted in transcribing
the Wolof language.

Concurrently, Kilham's efforts to study Mande and Wolof resulted
in two bilingual dictionaries that doubled as textbooks: in 1820 *Ta-Re
Wa-Lof, Ta-re boo Juk-à. First Lessons in Jaloff* (or Wolof) appeared anonymously.[34] By 1823 *African Lessons in Three Parts* appeared, followed in
1827 by *African Lessons, Mandingo and English*, and *African School Tracts*.
Consciously or not, Kilham's tracts were helping the formation of West
African nationalism and the "triumph of the vernacular."[35] More linguistic works followed, then Kilham's account of a visit to Sierra Leone,
and eventually her letters and the posthumous memoir. Kilham is at
pains not to specialize in any one African language. She takes into account the diverse languages spoken by the Liberated Africans and, to
begin with, attempts both translations and glosses in at least two languages, Wolof and Mande. Philip Curtin calls her work "the most systematic investigations of this period."[36]

With Quaker approval in hand, Hannah Kilham sailed for the settlement of Bathurst on St. Mary's Island at the mouth of the Gambia
River in 1824, accompanied by Sandingo and Mahmadee. In articulating her spiritual goals, she renders her opinion of Africans. Translating
African languages is a "natural" act and a prime duty; it bears the full
force of a divine privilege bestowed on whites. The assumption remains
that Africans cannot do things for themselves and any resentment on
the part of Africans is bypassed:

> Obedience, obedience, entire dedication, this is what I desire may be
> the pursuit of my life, without choosing my own path, or seeking to
> avoid what is difficult and opposed to my nature.

What I feel most desirable is the habit of daily mental self-denial, and the prevalence of that inward and outward order which must be the result of a constant attention to duty.[37]

But these spiritual goals with their implied attitudes toward indigenous people were not easy to implement since Kilham's missionary party arrived in a period of controversial, gubernatorial innovation.

Prior to Hannah Kilham's first visit to the Gambia and Sierra Leone, the evangelical, pro-monarchy governor, Charles McCarthy, was the force behind the reorganization of recaptive people in Sierra Leone into Christian communities, regardless of tribal origin. His administration had dramatically altered how Liberated Africans lived in Sierra Leone.[38]

The history of the colony up to that time bears directly on that nexus of events. From its beginning in the last quarter of the eighteenth century, British administrators had tried to instil an often evangelical Anglicanism into the colony's spiritual life. Conversion was the principal colonial mandate. But religion in Sierra Leone had remained a matter of some debate, especially after the arrival of the Nova Scotians. Affiliated with Dissenting churches, especially Methodist, the Nova Scotian community countered a British ruling class who underwrote the established church.[39] Zachary Macaulay had originally advised the Church Missionary Society to evangelize the Susu tribe, who inhabited land 100 miles north of the colony.[40]

The contestation over religion never ceased because religious uniformity was an important means whereby British officials hoped to control the population. Since the Nova Scotians spoke English, moreover, no form of linguistic control had ever been possible. With the Liberated Africans, the case was different. It was easier to influence the religious beliefs of communities who could communicate neither with the officials nor among one another. From a colonial vantage point, this difference was exploitable in many directions.

As a case in point, one Anglican governor after another had sought to convert and educate the Liberated Africans as a means of introducing civic order and enforcing European authority and control.[41] Concerned about 10,000 Liberated "heathen" Africans in early 1814, Governor Maxwell gave the Anglican Church Missionary Society fifteen to twenty acres for a schoolhouse. Maxwell was also concerned that the end of the Napoleonic wars and a resumption of the slave trade would increase the number of Liberated Africans.[42]

In addition, one of the Nova Scotian preachers, Reverend William Davies, became so intimate with Government House, i.e., Anglican officials, that he was excluded from the Nova Scotian chapel and subsequently turned his attention to the former slaves. Until that point, the

Nova Scotians had made scant effort to convert the "recaptured" slaves. Presumably, since the number of Liberated Africans only gradually grew, the Nova Scotians could not originally discern the still inchoate colonial plan for controlling the population and diminishing Nova Scotian power.[43] Soon Methodism and its chapels expanded within the so-called recaptive communities. Concurrently, the German missionary, Gustav Nyländer and his wife, instructed 150 regular scholars by 1810. But when the Methodists opened their school in 1812, Nyländer's pupils slowly disappeared. Nonetheless, he persisted in his missionary efforts with members of the (Sherbro) Bulom people on the Bullom shore.[44]

When McCarthy succeeded Maxwell as governor, he aimed for centralized control by refining his predecessor's plan for local government administration. McCarthy sought to reorganize Sierra Leone along religious and civil lines, with a particular stress on solidifying conversion in the peninsula. To that end, he gave 1,000 acres in the Freetown area to the Church Missionary Society to establish a central headquarters.[45] These donations of land for Anglican-colonial purposes affronted the Dissenter-based Nova Scotian population and indirectly created division between the black communities.

This state–church cooperation between the government and the Church Missionary Society continued uneasily for a while. The reluctance of English missionaries to come to Sierra Leone compounded the difficulties.[46] The area's notorious reputation as a white man's grave was based on mortality rates since the colony was founded; epidemiological research for the region's terrain was still in the early stages. These facts notwithstanding, at the start of McCarthy's administration in 1814 the Church Missionary Society had established schools where children could be taught scriptures and moral precepts. On the first Sunday after their liberation in Sierra Leone, recaptive people were obliged to attend church.

After Anglican missionary Edward Bickersteth reported to London in 1816 about the lax morals of the 6,500 people living outside Freetown, the Church Missionary Society agreed to begin education of the recaptive population in earnest.[47] In 1821 Parliament passed an act that placed all the regional forts commanded by the British and the new post at Bathurst on the Gambia under a single West African government stationed in Sierra Leone.[48] The Sierra Leone faction had politically come into its own again. Furthermore, in alliance with the African Association, the British government was vigorously sponsoring "exploration" of the African interior.[49] Put another way, the white colonial regime was drastically entrenching itself with a new black population, at the expense of the black loyalist population that had helped build the colony. This continued for McCarthy's eight-year tenure while Hannah Kilham was negotiating in London to visit the colony.

Systematically under McCarthy, any sharp division between church and state ceased to exist. At least temporarily, Sierra Leone had evolved into a network of nine parishes, virtually a religious state, though it was never legally formalized as such. McCarthy also organized an intense building program that dictated the shape of Freetown. One missionary went so far as to say of Governor McCarthy's obsession: "You know he is fond of buildings."[50] Increased British government funding contributed more to building construction than to basic human needs for clothes and rations. By 1819 Liberated Africans were existing on a minimal government subsistence diet: rice, palm oil, and salt.

Overall, these churches, schools, homes, hospital, and government buildings that McCarthy initiated created a new landscape on the West Coast. Sierra Leone entered a period of prosperity—gala affairs were the rage—where white men ruled the roost. Only five or six white European women lived in the colony at any given time in the early nineteenth century:

> The customs of the place . . . effectively preclude a white lady from accompanying her husband to the mansions of the unmarried man,
> where the coloured or black mistress might not show deference. Generally the mistress was quite an integral and apparently accepted member of the bachelor European's household in early Freetown.[51]

But cracks in the surface plastering began to show. By 1826 sixty-five of the seventy-nine Church Missionary Society missionaries, wives, and instructors who had come to work in Sierra Leone were dead. McCarthy himself had died in the Ashantee wars in 1824 just before Kilham arrived. Government funds dried up:[52] "responsibility for the development of Freetown and Sierra Leone society drifted increasingly into the hands of the Liberated Africans themselves."[53]

By 1832 African policy-makers pinpointed the Niger as Britain's new strategic focus of attention.[54] Peninsular personnel were to be reduced to a minimum; the heyday of church and state power was over. Unbeknownst to Hannah Kilham, she was one of the people who would help the transition toward independence from a deliberately evolving colonial policy over half a century.

HANNAH KILHAM'S FIRST VOYAGE

After numerous disappointments and false starts, Hannah Kilham set out in 1824 for Sierra Leone. When she arrived, she was unaware that the governor had died, that the colony and its funding were now in jeopardy and soon to be in turmoil. The governor had arranged for

Kilham's party to have a large house in Bathurst (now Banjul in the Gambia) on St. Mary's Island and, despite his death, these plans proceeded accordingly. Before she set out, Kilham was also unaware that the Committee for African Instruction intended a permanent settlement to be established at Bathurst, capable of expansion. Her desire had been to work in Sierra Leone, rather than to go further north with a settled population. This full-blown settlement—probably in the surrounding countryside with its indigenous population—was much more than Hannah Kilham had proposed or envisioned.[55] Having battled officials for almost a decade to work in Africa, Kilham was shocked at conditions in the Gambia:

> a small community confined almost entirely to the barren St. Mary's Island, only the Wesleyan Methodists, arriving in 1821, has preceded the Friends' mission party. [The Wesleyans established a mission up-river on Lemain Island, renamed MacCarthy Island in 1823.] The settled nature of most of the African population and the influence of Islam with its Koranic schools for boys altered the educational challenges from those Hannah had envisaged when thinking of Liberated African children. (163)

In her journals, Hannah Kilham scarcely acknowledges that her sponsors had "pulled a fast one." She expressed her thankfulness and emotionally expropriated the territory as her own "home" right away. Assuming the stance of a European who has come with goodwill to "civilize" the population, she keeps an open mind:

> I felt truly glad to tread the African shore, and was never, I think, more sensible of being at home at any place than now in this. The countenances of many of the natives whom we see about, appear interesting and intelligent, and bespeak a mental soil that would well repay a friendly and liberal cultivation.

Nonetheless, she understands the damage created by Eurocentric attitudes:

> I do not think that any full and sufficient trial has yet been given to a body of Africans, to enable Europeans to judge of the extent of their qualifications and ability for usefulness; and I cannot doubt from what is already seen and known, but that they are as susceptible of improvement as the people of other countries, had they fair and just measures afforded to them from other classes of mankind. (178–79)

This critical issue of intelligence—long a matter of debate among plantocrats and abolitionists—preoccupied Hannah Kilham. Presumably before her arrival, she had planned educational lessons according to conventional imperial beliefs about the intellectual inferiority of Africans. The Koranic schools, the palpable literacy and culture seemed to induce fissures in her colonial discourse. By and large, Europeans remained ignorant of the fact that

> libraries were assembled, and greatly prized. Books were written and published in manuscript copies; histories such as the *tarikhs* or Chronicles, written in Timbuktu, as well as a wide variety of works of secular or religious commentary, such as those by the famous Ahmed Baba (a few of which are in circulation to this day). According to a sixteenth-century report, the trade in books in the region was more profitable than any other.[56]

Kilham quickly disabused herself of conventional European tenets of faith and announced this change:

> The intelligent countenances of the children, both here and in the Gambia, and the degree of zeal which they evince in the manner of repeating their lessons, convince me, that they might be taught to good effect, and with as much facility as the English children, were proper methods of instruction pursued, and such as their state calls for. . . . Of the unfavourable traits in the dispositions of the mulattoes I have taken notice, and I may add, with regard to intelligence, we do not find the black girls at any degree behind the mulatto, or white children, so far as we have had opportunities to judge. (227, 241)

Once there in the Gambia, the party split up. Richard Smith and John Thomson journeyed with Mahmadee, the Mande speaker, to Bakau, two miles west of St. Mary's Island on the coast at Cape St. Mary, to prepare the land for agriculture.[57] Hannah Kilham, Ann Thomson, and Sahmadee remained in Birkow (Bathurst). The leader of that Moslem regime elicited conventional views from Kilham that strikingly contrast with other descriptions she tenders of Africans: the Alcaide's beliefs are clearly paramount in her evaluation. Kilham's distress about the Alcaide—the village leader who may or may not be the spokesman for matters of religion—probably stems from the fact that missionaries in the Gambia "as early as the 1820s . . . saw Islam as the greatest obstacle to the expansion of Christianity:"[58]

> He was sitting in the room with the Commandant; had a straw hat on his head; his whole appearance was uncouth, and expressive of listlessness and apathy. As I looked at him I could not but sigh to think, how very, very far remote these people are from a state of civilization— from that intelligent and Christian feeling, which is the result of right education and religious principle in our highly favoured country. (184)

She wants

> a school for children in the mornings, and another in the evenings for
> the king's-boys, (so called because British ships re-captured the kid-
> napped slaves). This was just what I could have desired—to have an
> opening for some usefulness toward the re-captured negroes, and to
> have a school for the Jaloff language. Sandanee may assist me in both,
> and, indeed, I wish him to be the ostensible person in both. (186)

Hannah Kilham was able to quickly implement her plan to educate
people in the Gambia because she had already tried to formulate her
linguistic principles in London. Linguistics had reached a stage of development where many known languages of the world were being
catalogued, a philological revolution that went hand-in-hand with burgeoning global nationalism.[59] Interest in West African languages had
especially arisen as early travelers like Brunton added to the existing
pool of vocabulary.

The improvement that Kilham envisioned was an important variant
on already existing experiments over language that linguistically reversed, in a sense, the colonizer-colonized relationship. Kilham's plan
was as follows: She aimed to reduce the vernacular or "native languages" to writing in order to render them a tool of communication, in
vernacular and in English, among the people. In other words, Kilham's
specific educational praxis principally involved composing linguistic
textbooks in African and English that promoted the vernacular. She
argued that one's own language must be the "interpreting medium" in
order to read and speak another. Otherwise, people learn the second
language as "words without meaning."[60] Through indigenous speakers,
she aimed to learn the African languages in question and then tran-
scribe them in a novel way. Thus Kilham collapsed the theory-praxis
dialectic and moved to implement use of the vernacular widely throughout the region. First, Kilham planned to compose an outline of the
main languages spoken by Liberated Africans to identify the dialects
of the different resident tribes—there were at least twenty-five. Then
in a multilingual book she would reduce them to written form.

In forming her orthography of Mande, Wolof, and Soso, Kilham applied three principles: first, she omitted any letter not sounded in the
word; second, she kept each consonant to one sound; and last, she
marked each vowel long or short. She also planned a small dictionary
of necessary and popular words. Another outline would prepare pupils
for a "better knowledge of English than they at present possess" (6); it
would certainly help the Liberated Africans who were receiving English
books with no translation. In an egalitarian spirit, she compares their
instruction to that of English children learning French—without the

aid of a translation book or dictionary. She mentions the added problem of the disjunction that exists between the "broken" English that non-natives speak compared to what they read in English. Kilham's consciousness about the problems British linguistic ethnocentrism had wrought is heightened. She states explicitly that because they grew up speaking English, the Nova Scotian children have a distinct advantage. Kilham's reading plan in the classroom was as follows:

> to read the vowels after me, in the first lesson, many times, until they seem to know them; then spell a few easy words, and read them after me; then, in the same way, to spell and read a few easy sentences; then spell the easiest words without the book. Then write, first the alphabet, and then words from their lessons, or from dictation. I believe that even two hours daily spent this way would advance a scholar very fast. Yesterday we had eight women pupils and sixteen girls. Several of the women had young children with them. (194)

This plan was so successful in its implementation of the Lancasterian system, that "several of the King's boys came to request . . . Jalof books, as they wished to teach all the people of this place who speak that language." She continues: "I gave to these and to others who followed, until twenty-two had been distributed" (198). Kilham, however, had some reservations about her ability:

> I can make myself understood by the Jaloofs in such phrases as seem most commonly in use; but am not familiar enough with the language to carry on a conversation, or to understand the particulars of their conversation, except when they speak in short phrases. (197)

Beyond this assessment of her capacity, Kilham always attends to the spiritual aspect of her work. She writes from "the position of the Christian subject" whose learning is underpinned by Christian tenets.[61] The topos of Christianity marks her translations, which become integral to the cultural milieu and practice of colonialism. But by being sanctioned to instruct along spiritual lines, Kilham can also claim a gendered authority simultaneously. These prescriptions work doubly: she maintains a religious dimension in her texts but she is permitted to publish.

One further issue that she addresses is so-called "broken" or pidgin English—the linguistic formation that springs up when people speak different languages.[62] Kilham objected to teaching Africans this hybrid. Living there and discussing the practice with friends made her realize how preposterous it was to teach simplistic as well as distorted forms of English to civilized Africans with complex languages of their own. She was influenced in this attitude by Joseph Klein, a chaplain, and his wife on the Isle de Los (just off Conakry, the capital of Guinea-Conakry), who were studying the Soso language in order to translate scriptures. She expresses her views forcefully in her journal:

> S. K. speaks against the practice of people amusing themselves with the broken English of Sierra Leone, instead of teaching the children to speak more correctly. "I believe there is great disadvantage in accustoming the Africans to such a limited vocabulary of words as this broken English furnishes, since by this they are prevented from acquiring such as are necessary for understanding what they read." (205)

She reaffirms this protest later, seeking to correct its popularity by introducing different textbook examples. At the same time, she mocks Eurocentric attitudes to Africans' speech:

> Might it not be of use to explain, in an easy lesson-book, a few of the phrases of broken English by correct, plain, intelligent phrases? There might, in some instances, be less amusement for Europeans, who like to hear anecdotes of the Africans in this style of expression; but on the other hand their intelligence would be cultivated, more real good might be done to them, and their advancement in useful knowledge would give more solid satisfaction, and much more variety of information might be conveyed than ever can be by this childish and fettering habit of adapting for them only a poor, barren, slang language. (221)

But despite attributing this practice to European ignorance about differences between British slaves and Africans, Kilham also reaffirms her conflictual stance on African intelligence and cultural position:

> In England, people see only a few of those who have been slaves, or mostly beggars, and too often judge from such specimens of the Africans in general. But, lacking as Africa is in regard to civilization and instruction, these are not what ought to be considered as a fair and just specimen of the people. . . . (221) It appears to me now more desirable than ever, that the system of teaching even the liberated Africans should, in the first instance, be through their own language. (213)

In letters written in February 1824 to William Allen, president of the African Institution and a member of the Committee on African Instruction, Hannah Kilham reported on these linguistic experiments. She also stressed how the consequences of illegal slavery were hindering her plans for education, since the people arrived in a severely debilitated state:[63]

> Oh! how do the abominations of the Slave-trade strike the heart, when we see how poor little emaciated creatures, little more than human skeletons, who, although they have been three months in the colony, and carefully nursed, have not reversed the effects of the inhuman bondage they have suffered in the slave-ships.

As Kilham planned her lessons, government officials were transforming the school system now that the Church Missionary Society was withdrawing— or rather being pushed out—from educational administration. In 1824 the government had taken over the CMS schools in the colony to provide a more "practical" education. She decided in 1825 to visit Sierra Leone to examine these new conditions for herself. Four months after McCarthy's death, she discovered that the colony was returning to a more secular educational base. Since missionary teachers would now be in even shorter supply, she reassessed her methodology:

> Hannah Kilham had visited schools in Freetown, and in every village, and her conclusions were radical and perceptive. It was perfectly clear to her . . . that it was folly to depend on British teachers—the turn-over was too appallingly high to make any continuity possible. All schools must be based on the system of mutual instruction, which had been the great discovery of Lancaster and Bell. (174)

This partly matched the effort of post-McCarthy governors to "keep the costs at a minimum."[64] Unwittingly, Kilham's dictionaries and attention to the vernacular also served to bond the repatriated Africans more securely: they transformed the knowledge into a proto-nationalist tool.

Most ironically, the new governmental, hands-off policy—"controlling, rather than determining or directing"—further served Liberated Africans in a positive way.[65] Although the bureaucratic plan was conceptualized differently, the net result of inspection rather than superintendence was to threaten the power of the British government:

> By the 1830's the policy of settlement by tribe had been accepted as a relatively inexpensive and efficient method to maintain stability in the villages. A manager of Regent [village] confirmed its continued use. By 1835 the government retained the newcomer on public works for the first three months in Sierra Leone. He was then sent to a village where he lived with "his country-people", and began to build his permanent hut. He retained his twopence per day government subsidy until his sixth month in the colony. The payment was usually turned over to the people with whom he resided during this period. They provided him with food and shelter in return. Even after the sixth month, however, his countrymen continued to "share their provisions" with the newly-located Africans.[66]

New capillaries of power based on the autonomy of the repatriated African residents were beginning to sustain themselves. Linguistic training was a fundamental stimulus. So was European refusal to risk death in aiding Africans so intensively. Things were beginning to shape up for the possibility of self-government in conjunction with a drive toward nationhood.

In addition to advocating linguistic flexibility, Kilham also favored agricultural development as part of a self-help program. Kilham saw the sense of useful trade practices that would help the community to run more profitably along economic lines. At some points, these ideas overlapped with official policy and the desires of commercial entrepreneurs:

> I wish the merchants were more engaged in promoting the civilization of the people. It can only be a mistaken and short-sighted estimate of things which can lead people to believe that promoting civilization can do injury. Were all Africa civilized, possessing substantial farmers and active merchants, there would yet be many things wanted from Europe which could not be manufactured in so hot a clime as this. (190)

On another occasion, she states that it might be "desirable to encourage Africans to trade for themselves, as well as to cultivate the soil, still pressing on them the importance of promoting school instruction" (242).[67] Furthermore, she ventures, Africans might want to instigate trade negotiations themselves to boost a self-supporting community and to offset the diffidence of British missionaries about coming to Sierra Leone:

> I cannot forbear to acknowledge that there is much in the climate that is trying to European constitutions, and am ready to think that Africa must and will be improved and civilized without many Europeans settling here, and that all we can do in England to promote their advancement in what is for their present and future good should be done. May it not, with this view, be desirable to encourage Africans to trade for themselves, as well as to cultivate the soil, still pressing on them the importance of promoting school instruction. (242)

Kilham cautions people about the need to establish priorities with (at least) merchants and missionaries:

> Whoever may come out in any society as Missionaries or teachers, whether here or at Sierra Leone . . . cannot be expected always to have at heart the good of the people, as a missionary or teacher ought to have. . . . Instead of the Missionaries bringing over the merchants to their views, the merchants rather bring the missionaries over to theirs, and induce them to conclude that little or nothing *can* be done for Africa. . . . How much do I wish that the people in Sierra Leone, and here also, may be led into a gentle, patient method of instructing Africans, in what they have to learn of domestic and mechanical labour. (247)

Basically, Kilham's spiritual goals invert colonists' ideas about desirable relations between trade and Christianity. In primarily focusing on education and Christianity, Kilham challenges a mercantile mentality. Her occasional positive references probably stem from her close friendship with William Allen, her Quaker supporter who inaugurated the African Institution that promoted trade as a primary concern.

Having returned to Gambia from Sierra Leone in March 1824, by May Kilham decided unexpectedly to return home and set sail in June. John Thomson died at sea, and by August Richard Smith, who had not traveled with them, was dead in the Gambia. The Gambian experiment, to all intents and purposes, died with him (187–88). These events irrevocably affected Hannah Kilham's future relations with the Committee for African Instruction.

Moreover, Kilham's observations on the Gambia experiment had alienated her from some Friends, who considered her partly responsible for its failure. Back in England, Kilham reported on her labors to the Society. Her remarks were published as *Report on a Recent Visit* (1824).[68] I want to elaborate briefly on this report to suggest how Kilham tried to represent her practices and construct Africa to her audience back home.

Since Kilham is reporting to the Committee for African Instruction, she concentrates on the group's accomplishments while commenting on drawbacks that she wants remedied. She opens with an overview of the Sierra Leone landscape that had been fundamentally transformed by Governor McCarthy's obsession with buildings. She admires the "handsome buildings" in Freetown that make it difficult to imagine how Europeans view life in Sierra Leone as an "unconquerable difficulty" (4). Then she provides a glimpse into the treatment of Liberated Africans immediately upon arrival. An older resident helps the newcomers build a (free) house with local material. The former slaves also receive clothing and a small subsistence for six months.

Insisting that Europeans bear a "duty toward Africa," Kilham believes in converting pagans and proselytizing western values (21):

> My mind has for years been impressed with a conviction, that our great duty toward Africa, is to strengthen the hands of the people, *to promote each other's good*; and, if we may be so permitted, to be instrumental in leading some to the acknowledgment of Christianity from experimental feeling, who may become humble instruments in the Divine hand of spreading the Truth and the love of it, and especially among the rising generation in Africa. It is the Africans themselves that must be the Travellers, and Instructors, and Improvers of Africa: let Europeans aid them with Christian kindness, as senior brethren would the younger and feebler members of their Father's family. (*Report on a Recent Visit*, 21–22)

Doubling as benevolent parents as well as models, Europeans, nonetheless, she contends, can only be auxiliaries. Her assertions flying in the face of British colonial desire to rule Sierra Leone, she compounds her unorthodoxy by expressing discomfort at the erratic state of official records. Whereas the superintendent's register in Freetown kept track of people, a notorious form of colonial control, by contrast in neighboring Leopold, where sickness and death frequently occurred without adequate reporting on health, no measures were taken to alter the situation (17).

Underdocumentation also hampers Hannah Kilham and like-minded people from being able to trace the whereabouts and conditions of children hired as apprentices:

> The breaking up of the schools of liberated African children some time ago, and their distribution as apprentices to such as would take them, is the more to be lamented, as there are not at present any means of collecting these children or ascertaining that they are well treated; some arrangement to bring them occasionally into view, is greatly wanted; some of the people who take them, after having paid ten shillings for an indenture, imagine that they have by this means purchased the children, and made them their own property. (*Report of a Recent Visit*, 17–18)

Kilham's contentions in this regard match those of Perronet Thompson who claimed that slavery in West Africa persisted throughout and despite the apprentice system.[69] She also addresses the thorny question of mortality that deters missionaries from coming to Sierra Leone. Having contracted fever and being aware of multiple deaths, Kilham knows that death could be imminent: "Life is I am aware to all uncertain," she stresses to the committee (*Report*, 20).

Kilham also points out the positive consequences of training Africans for skilled and unskilled jobs: agricultural schools, such as the one in Allen's Town, train African males as field laborers. Females, on the other hand, are directed toward schoolteaching and light industry (14).

On the question of education, Kilham waxes even more specific. Scholars in the Freetown schools are principally children of colonial American settlers—they were known as the "Nova Scotians"—as well as paid boarders. Admiring the children's capacity for quick learning, she enjoys their familiarity with scripture.

Plans are afoot, she happily asserts, to open schools run by Native Teachers in villages where none exist. London Quakers are helping to subsidize these ventures. Mindful of her influential audience, reinvoking the significance of high mortality rates and the precariousness of European life, she makes a plug here to return to Africa. Out of the twenty-six schools that are now established, twenty are taught and administered solely by Africans themselves—"Native Teachers" (pp. 11–12). Freetown schools for the village children and schools for the new "re-captives" are available. She describes Native Teachers as a "prompt and efficient help of the friends of Africa" (4).

In a footnote, Hannah Kilham underscores the presence of the church in secular affairs:

> Although the Village Schools, as part of the Liberated African department, are under the care and support of Government, the Church Missionary Society have still the charge of supplying them with books and other School apparatus. (8)

The introduction of an infant school system, she hints, still gives that alliance an early start. Kilham is keying her audience to the need for a systemic overhaul while quietly validating her own practices. The *Report*, however, does not seem to have greatly aided her efforts to return.

SECOND VOYAGE

In the first place, after Hannah Kilham's first visit to the African continent, administrators in Freetown came under heavy fire from the British Parliament; economic mismanagement and some embezzlement were major issues. The reorganization caused by this official critique encouraged a self-help system among Africans and a further, rather ironic, reluctance on the part of the Society of Friends to allow Hannah Kilham to return. Other factors played their part. From May 1825 until December 1830, there were four governors of Sierra Leone and seven acting-governors (one twice). Reversing Governor McCarthy's evangelical orientation, they returned to the old policy of settling recaptives by tribe. British colonial administration in Sierra Leone was disintegrating.

Nonetheless, Hannah Kilham had decided to visit again in a private capacity. She left London in November 1827 and arrived in Sierra Leone on 9 December. She left again on 20 February 1828. During this two-month stay, she worked in education.

In contrast to her first visit, however, she took time choosing a place to live that would fit her educational plans (326). Her goal was to grasp the educational system in Sierra Leone and the outlying villages and how she might adapt her linguistic program to people's needs. Her decision to stay with Mr. and Mrs. Thomas Weeks, CMS missionaries in Freetown, sharpens her already noted separation from the Society of Friends.

As a result, Kilham visited the major villages, including Wellington, where the Macfoys lived, Allen's Town, Leopold, Regent, and Gloucester. Her plan was to compose lists and categories of the leading words and numerals of the major languages spoken there by Liberated Africans. After compiling an outline, Kilham would reduce the languages to a simple written form. This would, she thought, help pupils to learn English more thoroughly and dispense with teaching in "broken" English, now a standard practice.

Kilham also preferred pupils not to read English until they could read in their own African languages. Learning two orthographies at once, she argued, made the process more difficult. She was happy to find male students in Freetown—the majority of whom turned out to be the children of Nova Scotians—attentive and intelligent (326).

In the outlying Liberated African villages, she noted the children in a poorer condition, especially when they had disembarked and been sent to their respective villages. She poignantly described the recaptives as "moving skeletons . . . [with] a feverish, ravenous appetite" (328). In spiritual terms, they struck her as "sheep without a shepherd" (373). With other missionaries, she started a school in Portuguese Town (formerly Pa Demba's Town) using Wesleyan teachers, a fact that would separate her further from the Society of Friends.[70] From 1824 to 1827 she had increased that division by speaking in favor of public worship, anathema to Quakers:

> It was dissatisfaction with outward forms of worship that had brought her to the Society of Friends; but Africa had shown her that this judgment could be too sweeping. "And it may also be right for me in some circumstances to sing with little children, in simplicity of heart, the acknowledgements of prayer and praise." (195)

These decisions explain Kilham's difficulty in procuring funding for the second voyage. The pamphlet about her experiences there indicate an even keener realization of the problems of multiple languages that were not all understood by communities living side by side. Her tracts were an effort to help alleviate the severe language barriers.[71]

Attitudes toward Indigenous Languages

Kilham's linguistic reformulations raise the question of colonial and imperial attitudes and policies toward the indigenous languages of the colonized people at the beginning of the nineteenth century. Contemporary attitudes toward colonized peoples and, logically, their languages are tellingly summed up in a conversation in the early 1790s between Henry Dalrymple, lately disappointed that he had not become governor of Sierra Leone, and Captain Philip Beaver. After Dalrymple glowingly describes to Beaver the island of Bulama, near the Sierra

Leone settlement, Beaver replies "Let us colonize it ourselves!" to which Dalrymple answers, "With all my heart."[72]

Together Dalrymple and Beaver decide what is the best way to expropriate the African continent. Their status as white Britishers entitles them—in their view—to this vantage point. That perspective reverberates in the writings of pioneer linguists.

Beginning with Henry Brunton—although his linguistic efforts were not concentrated in Sierra Leone, with its diverse linguistic population, but on the Soso languages—a silent assumption circulated about the inferiority of African languages. The organization of vocabularies into "reductions" of African languages (as if only a minimum vocabulary and grammar would suffice for a "simple" people) accompanied the constant privileging of English as the lingua franca.

A minister from the Church Missionary Society on the Bullom shore around 1810, Gustav Nyländer, continued this tradition in diverse ways by stressing rules of syntax and compiling endless vocabulary lists. Kilham redirects that orientation to privilege African languages, assuming first of all their large numbers, as well as their complex differential structures and vocabularies. Thus, it is not so much a difference in vocabulary words that governs Kilham's linguistic ventures, but a sense of what would be helpful to group together and be useful to the indigenous population in their day-to-day living.

Given that Hannah Kilham is dealing with populations of children who not only cannot read and write, but are speaking different languages, her task was challenging. Classroom lessons coupled with her texts enact an early staging of a relationship carefully interrogated in recent years by Ngugi Wa Thiong'o.[73]

At this early stage, the difference is that Hannah Kilham is *importing* English and rendering it one of the dominant languages while subscribing ideologically to the view that the vernacular must be privileged. As a colonizer in the final instance, Kilham is always situated in a conflictual position. But alongside her European linguist-contemporaries, Kilham's tracts could be used more as helpful handbooks; in that respect, they differed from offputting grammars and endless, decontextualized vocabulary lists. Perhaps her acquaintance early on with the two African males encouraged this orientation. The tracts had the advantage of being short, both in length and on cumbersome, Eurocentric rules. Her "schemes" for pronunciation take second place to efforts to encourage students to read in their own language and then translate into another. By downplaying rules that Europeans historically favor in their grammars, Kilham foregrounds the importance of African languages and puts them on a par with European languages. Given her time and circumstances, Kilham's tracts inevitably and silently include a Eurocentric orientation and design.[74] But even so, though the differences are subtle, Kilham linguistically underscores the concept of equivalence rather than reduction. In her own words, she aims to promote "a friendly and beneficial intercourse with the natives of the African continent." Put another way, Kilham is less abstract and technical, and more practical. She wants to offer lessons and texts to pupils that will facilitate communication in quotidian living.

THIRD VOYAGE

Three years elapsed before Hannah Kilham was able to leave for Africa again. Once she arrived, Kilham presented the governor with a copy of her pamphlet, *The Claims of West Africa to Christian Instruction through the Native Languages.*[75] In the pamphlet, Kilham explains why she opts to teach Africans English (or any other foreign language) in the vernacular. Impressed by her proposals, the governor consequently granted her permission to organize children newly arrived from slave ships and begin to teach them to read in the vernacular (371).

In *Claims*, Kilham argues conventionally to begin with: the colony was established out of "benevolent concern for the good of Africa, and as a place of reception for the unhappy victims" of slavery (1). Hence rescued children must be instructed as well as cared for; records must be kept. Specifically, Kilham fears for the undocumented and apprenticed children who are frequently re-enslaved: "Are we not the children of one Father?" (9). In an all-embracing spirit, she praises the Church Missionary Society, the British and Foreign Bible Society, and the Wesleyan Missionary Society for their collective practices.

She blames poor educational advancement in "using English lessons only, for children, to whom English is quite a foreign language" (4). How would an English child learn Latin without an English translation, she rhetorically inquires. Again she stresses the benefit of native agency because of the "relaxing effect of the climate on European constitutions" (7). Kilham ends with a short bibliography of works that Friends had recently printed; with due modesty, she does not mention that she wrote them. Then she recommends the system that she used, thanks the friends who supported her, and ends with a plea: she wants native Africans brought to England to be taught English and the art of translating, a home is to be established for that purpose, and a Provisional Committee set up to print potential texts. Contact names are appended for anyone interested in the project. Contending that missionaries should double as "farmers, spinners, weavers [and] joiners," Kilham proposes establishing links between vocational schools and missionary work (341–42). As part of her plan, she systematically visits the villages of the Liberated Africans, talking in favor of tract libraries (231).

The longer Kilham visits Africa, the more obvious the problems and the more urgency she feels. Post-abolition violations and their horrible effect on Africans were now well known.[76] Press reports made people aware that atrocities at the hands of slavery's entrepreneurs were continuing daily. Kilham continues to worry about the perennial problem she had identified as primary: rescued Africans hail from different African nations and can scarcely communicate once they arrive in Sierra Leone:

> How has my heart been affected in hearing of the conversations of the interesting Garnon with the children, or rather her *attempt* to communicate what they would willingly have replied to, but for the affecting reason given, "Me no sabby (understand) English." Could not a very small vocabulary be formed, by which these children, though coming from various places, might learn to convey their leading thoughts, and feelings and desires? (125–26)

She blames slavery for the miserable conditions of the "recaptured" Africans:

> A little girl I saw in the school this morning had lost one arm, and on enquiry of the cause, was told it was lost in the fight in recapturing a slave-ship, and that the slaves had often been much wounded, and some of them killed in these combats. . . . How would the Anti-Slavery Committee be stimulated could they but see the state in which some of the poor children even yet remain, after having been cared for several months since their rescue from the slaveship! (210, 222)

Having visited all the Liberated African villages inland from the River Sierra Leone and Freetown, Kilham set up quarters as the sole European in a mountain village named Charlotte. That village had been abandoned by the Church Missionary Society in favor of the large village of Bathurst after the Society's decision to give up the administration of schools. The dispersal of these recaptive pupils meant welcome new students for Hannah Kilham. She taught classes in Mande and English, using some picture lessons that she had printed in Wolof to use in Freetown. She stood by an educational approach that mixed gentleness, spirituality, and a Eurocentric vision of African culture:

> Hannah compared the Liberated African children to unripened fruit, sour and shrivelled, as if they had not been exposed to sufficient warmth and sunshine. She was a great believer in kindness and friendship eliciting a response where other methods failed, and an admirer of

the qualities which her own native sweetness drew out from Africans. (238–39)

Kilham's plan was so successful that later "several of the King's-boys [i.e. Liberated Africans] came to request I would give them books, as they wished to teach all the people of this place who speak that language." In Bathurst, she opened a book stall where twelve-page lesson sheets cost a halfpenny.

When twenty new children disembarked from slave ships, she compared the educational state of those who had learned no English with pidgin-speaking Liberated Africans. After an eight-day experiment with Yoruba girls who spoke no English, they knew their letters and numbers and could spell from pictures.

Understanding a permanent European educational settlement was unlikely to materialize, she enacts her plan for Africans helping other Africans with only this initial European intervention; dubbed the program of native agency, it still assumes that Europeans know best and must be the ones to set the plan in motion:

> It is the Africans themselves that must be the travellers and instructors and improvers of Africa. Let Europeans aid them with Christian kindness, as senior brothers and the younger and feebler members of their father's family; but let it be kept in mind, to which perpetual interruptions every purpose must be subject, that is made dependent upon European life on the African shores. (330)

Based on Kilham's knowledge of the English Lancasterian system that appoints monitors to instruct, the motto of the system—"Each one, teach one"—was firmly imprinted at the top of each page of the grammar. Nonetheless, her Christian ethnocentricity still elicits pity for the Africans—"for the bewildered and unChristian feelings of their minds." (444)

Kilham was further concerned about the situation in neighboring Liberia because she knew about thousands being legally transported there from America. Opposing the American Colonization Society, she praises a friend of the black abolitionist, Paul Cuffee, and decides to visit Monrovia, the capital of Liberia.[77] While there, she arranges for the children of distinguished families to be sent to England for education. She then set sail for Sierra Leone and died at sea in 1832.[78] A eulogy given by the Moravian poet-abolitionist, James Montgomery, identifies the colonial vantage point of Kilham's admirers:

> She has begun a work which has not only shown the way, but in some measure prepared it, for eventually and effectually civilizing and evangelizing the barbarous hordes on both sides of the Niger, whom the na-

tives of misnamed Christendom have been conspiring to plunder, en-
thral, and oppress by the most iniquitous traffic under heaven, for
three centuries past! . . . Prior to 1817 her journal show[s] the gradual
growth in the mind of Hannah Kilham of that deep interest on behalf
of the people of Africa, and more especially the children at Sierra
Leone, which was attended with the conviction that it was an individual
duty to devote herself to their improvement.[79]

The objective effect of Hannah Kilham's educational program was
to dissolve intra-national boundaries among Africans and make the
possibility of political unity more feasible. Hence Hannah Kilham's
work embedded, at one level, an anti-colonial dimension. Put another
way, she circulated an oppositional knowledge about the rights of Africans, even though her activities still aided the imperial goal to educate, "civilize," and Christianize Africans: "Her ideas for [using English
as a second language] and an African language were revolutionary
for her time."[80] In concert with her program to teach the vernacular,
Kilham firmly believed in a policy whereby indigenous people used
their own initiative in learning to translate. She tried to create a poly-
glot ex-slave intelligentsia, or at least she offered ways to bring that
social formation into being. Integral to this discourse that purports to
privilege Africans is a familiar assumption that Africans need Europeans to "get going" and know what is best. Kilham's textbooks featuring
basic grammar, orthography, reading and writing texts in the vernacular were made available for that purpose. As a result, Sierra Leone became a territory where people of various cultural origins, who spoke
complex languages, continually interacted. Liberated Africans participated much more fully in commerce and local politics.

Hannah Kilham's gaze, however, is still conflicted and often conventionally determined: not only are Africans configured as naturally inferior pagans, but "the Africans of the colony of Sierra Leone are acknowledged to be a docile, affectionate people, and easily governed. . . .
Africans have not been advanced in the scale of Christian society as
could be desired, and there has been in some things a state of depres-
sion not fully accounted for" (328, 343). In her daughter's words, she
wanted to "make known to a benighted people the unsearchable riches
of Christ" (366). Later she states:

Degraded as they are even here, as well as in their native districts, light,
and life, and love from the pure influence of the Redeemer's power,
and by the instrumentality which He shall mercifully appoint, will yet
be seen to prevail abundantly; both in this colony and in the many and
wide-spreading tribes of African people. We have strong hopes to see
them helped, whether they be looked upon as the last, and lowest, and
most oppressed of the human race, or whether the furtherest removed

in their native state from true Christianity and civilization. These plans
are each at times used against their instruction, yet they are so many
stimulants to the Christian duty of helping the weak and the sinful,
and following the lost sheep into the wilderness. (406)

How Africans might feel about territorial expropriation by the British, about having colonizers "teach" them the colonizer's language is a
moot point. Expatriates themselves, the Liberated Africans found the
colony as different as Europeans found it. Their anger at intervention
is read by Kilham as a plea for gentle missionaries:

> I am ready to believe there is not any people on the earth, toward
> whom the spirit of meekness and Christian patience is more necessary
> for their improvement than towards the Africans. In some of these
> people there is a frightful violence at times, uncontrollable resentment,
> and extreme obstinacy, which I do think cannot be effectually com-
> bated by anything so assimilated to its own nature as resentment, force,
> or a determination to exhibit power in punishing offenders. Such con-
> duct may indeed have a transitory effect, but it will not reach the cause,
> so as to prove a lasting remedy. (421–422)

As a linguist and educator, Hannah Kilham plays a different role
from the Sierra Leone administrators while cooperating with the diverse communities living there. But she does end up facilitating and
reinforcing colonial expansion. In particular, Hannah Kilham links up
the peninsula with the hinterland. Through her narrative and practice
of linguistics, she helps to unify the diverse communities. She understands that language can build "particular solidarities" that could eventually institute, from her perspective, a more democratic nation.[81] Her
work constitutes a critical part of the cultural vanguard that functions
within an ingrained paternalistic framework. Hannah Kilham views
God as a "beneficent Parent of all the families of the earth" and mimics
this attitude in her treatment of Africans. Within this framework, education and empire are inextricably related, a relationship worthy of Europeans because it benefits Africans. Much more to the point, however,
consciously or not Kilham's texts also narrate the possibility of nation.
In that connection, deliberate as well as unforeseen eruptions textually surface. First, Kilham makes it clear (given a certain rocky syntax) that she applauds self-determination and that its consequences are
not always controllable:

> Translations must be pursued, female education, and some more conso-
> nant system as to religious meetings, to take off, in some measure, from
> the dependence on foreign aid, should both, I believe, be regarded as
> among the duties owing to this interesting but suffering people. (344)

Second, Kilham embraces certain scientific principles that set matters on a new footing.[82] Her contentions assume an equivalence between African languages and English while privileging teaching and talking in the African language:

> I think, if I were among the natives, I should be more disposed to speak their language to them, when I could, than when there last year, and not to mind the objections of the Europeans against perpetuating this language, which they wish to supersede, if possible, in St. Mary's by the English. (260)

Thus in her discussion of African languages, Kilham tenders a tacit acknowledgement of a burgeoning political self-hood that could be potentially independent of other Europeans. At one level, she allows Africans a constructed linguistic self. In setting up words that equal one another—in a dictionary, say—she privileges African as much as English as an important referent. Put starkly, she defines Englishness in African terms.

Third, where originally she thought of Africans as the "poorest, lowest, weakest, and most neglected, and most oppressed of all the human race" (130, 139), she somewhat reformulates these views after her arrival. Thus she rejects standard Eurocentric views of Africans that assign Africans to less than human status:

> It is far too much the custom with Europeans in this colony to dwell on the faults and defects of the Africans around them, instead of affectionately, patiently, and steadily, as influenced by the love of Jesus, teaching day by day such as are ignorant, or out of the way, and praying in humility for heavenly help to bring them to a better mind. (400)

Despite the fact that her presence affirms British foreign policy, Kilham also exposes the predictable scenario in which merchants concentrated on profit. Kilham publicized the fact that Liberated Africans were being used as an exported/exploited colonial labor force: "Coercion was, indeed, used by the Crown administration of the colony (Sierra Leone) after 1808, though not for plantations. . . . Forced labour was made available to the earlier [white] settlers through a system of 'apprenticeship.' "[83] Both the African Institution and the African Committee were involved. The overt rationale of the pressure groups was definitely appealing: they wanted to stamp out violators of abolition. At the same time, they were intent on "the more general object of diffusing Western culture throughout Africa."[84] In a sideways critique of British colonialism, Kilham comments that "not enough is accomplished agriculturally" (469).

A gendered dimension exists too. She unites African women against a patriarchal praxis:

> it was their habit to fall down on their knees before their husbands, and thank them for their day's work. I cannot form a high estimate of this humiliation, as to its effect on the mind of either the woman or the man. (248)

Thus, although Hannah Kilham establishes acceptable colonial paradigms about Anglo-African relationships, she also undermines these very paradigms. First, she paves the way for political autonomy through her belief in self-help policies; second, she queries gendered roles; third, she democratizes education and aims at "mutual recognition."[85] She wants to teach children because all children (not just European children) are ready to learn:

> My mind has been drawn toward little children, in whom reason and reflection are just beginning to dawn, and I think we want some outward and attractive means of drawing the mind to devotional feeling. This, even in regard to little children, should have the pious and good for its agents, and such as act in it from the purest and most disinterested principles. As soon as the mind is capable of receiving heavenly truth, and how very early has the infant-school system proved that to be, children should, I think, be assembled occasionally to endeavour to seek the Spirit of prayer, and to be instructed in such Christian doctrines and precepts as their opening minds are prepared to receive. (320)

Lastly, through her polylingual dictionaries, Kilham enables the conceptualization of an African nation in the region that consists of multiple tribal communities, Nova Scotians, and Maroons. In that sense, her discourse was invariably oppositional because it provided a counternarrative to a colonial world view, to the civilizing mission.

NOTES

1. For the Naimbana, see Adeleye Ijagbemi, *Naimbana of Sierra Leone*, African Historical Biographies (London: Heinemann, 1976), 20.

2. Michael Craton, *Sinews of Empire: A Short History of British Slavery* (Garden City: Anchor, 1974).

3. Christopher Fyfe, *A History of Sierra Leone* (London: Oxford University Press, 1962), 104.

4. Craton, *Sinews*, 265.

5. Johnson U. J. Asiegbu, *Slavery and the Politics of Liberation, 1787–1861: A Study of Liberated African Emigration and British Anti-Slavery Policy* (London and Harlow: Longmans, Green, 1969), 23.

6. For carelessly undertaken registrations, see Richard Meyer-Heiselberg, "Research Report No. 1: Notes for Liberated Africans, Dept. in the Ar-

chives at Fourah Bay College, Freetown" (Upsala, 1967), quoted in Asiegbu, *Slavery*, 24.

7. For information, see Fyfe, *A History*, 114; Christopher Fyfe, *Sierra Leone Inheritance* (London: Oxford University Press, 1964), 131–32.

8. Philip D. Curtin, *The Image of Africa: British Ideas and Action, 1780– 1850* (Madison: University of Wisconsin Press, 1964), 157.

9. Mrs. R. Lee (formerly Mrs. T. Edward Bowdich), *The African Wanderers*, 362.

10. Fyfe, *A History*, 127.

11. There is no pretense here about the long history of British slave trade in Africa. For documentation, see particularly *The Foreign Slave Trade: A Brief Account of Its State of the Treaties Which Have Been Entered into, and of the Laws Enacted for Its Suppression, from the Date of the English Abolition Act to the Present Time*, vol. 1. (London: J. Hatchard, 1807, B. L. shelf mark 8157 c17), 163.

12. For a history of the West Coast of Africa that focuses on the indigenous people, see G. T. Stride and Caroline Ifeka, *Peoples and Empires of West Africa in History 1000–1800* (London: Nelson, 1971); Joe A.D. Alie, *A New History of Sierra Leone* (London: Macmillan, 1990); C. Magbaily Fyle, *The History of Sierra Leone* (London: Evans Brothers, 1981). See also Hannah Kilham, *Present State of the Colony of Sierra Leone, Being Extracts of Recent Letters from Hannah Kilham. Second Edition with Considerable Additions* (Lindfield: Printed at the Schools of Industry, C. Green, 1832). See further *Extracts from the Letters of Hannah Kilham Now at Sierra Leone* reprinted from *The Friends Magazine* (London: Edmund Fry, 1831). I thank the curator of Haverford College for this copy. Kilham's indirect encouragement of the colonial enterprise, especially in terms of language, is discussed in diverse contexts in: Gauri Viswanathan, *Masks of Conquest: Literary Study and British Rule in India* (New York: Columbia University Press, 1989). J. A. Mangan, "Images of Confident Control: Stereotypes in Imperial Discourse" in J. A. Mangan, ed. *The Imperial Curriculum: Racial Images and Education in the British Colonial Experience* (London and New York: Routledge, 1993), 6–22. In terms of attitudes then current that have important implications for the colonial situation in Africa, see Javed Majeed, *Ungoverned Imaginings: James Mill's History of British India and Orientalism*, Oxford English Monographs (Oxford: Clarendon Press, 1992), esp. chap. 5, "Susceptible Imaginations."

On language, see Robert Phillipson, *Linguistic Imperialism* (Oxford: Oxford University Press, 1992), esp. chap. 5, "A Colonial Linguistic Inheritance," 109–36; on Sierra Leone, see 115–16. See also E. Ashby, *Universities British, Indian, African: A Study in the Ecology of Higher Education* (Cambridge: Cambridge University Press, 1966). Although the emphasis is on the post-1880 period, for a specific study on an African situation (the only one, it seems) see Johannes Fabian, *Language and Colonial Power: The Appropriation of Swahili in the Former Belgian Congo 1880–1938*, African Studies Series 48 (Cambridge: Cambridge University Press, 1986; reprint, Berkeley: University of California Press, 1991), esp. chap. 5 on pidginization and the role of missionaries and missionary vocabularies.

13. Sarah Biller, *Hannah Kilham, Memoir of the Late Hannah Kilham; Chiefly Compiled from Her Journal, and Edited by Her Daughter-in-Law, Sarah Biller* (London: Darton and Harvey, 1837), 170, passim.

14. For information about Alexander Kilham and their marriage and child, see Mona Dickson, *The Powerful Bond. Hannah Kilham, 1774–1832* (London: Dennis Dobson, 1980), 24–51, passim.

15. Biller, *Memoir, Appendix, Notice of the Early Life of Hannah Kilham, Communicated by Her Sister,* 480; Clare Midgley, *Women Against Slavery: The British Campaigns 1780–1870* (London and New York: 1992), 54–55, 91, 163; Vron Ware, *Beyond the Pale: White Women, Racism and History* (London and New York: Verso, 1992), part II: "An Abhorrence of Slavery: Subjection and Subjectivity in Abolitionist Politics," 47–116.

16. Dickson, *The Powerful Bond,* 95.

17. Auguste Jorns, *The Quakers as Pioneers in Social Work,* trans. Thomas Kite Brown (New York: Macmillan, 1931), 223. See also Frank Klingford, *The Anti-Slavery Movement in England: A Study in English Humanitarianism* (New Haven: Yale University Press, 1926).

18. Charles H. Wesley, "The Neglected Period of Emancipation in Great Britain, 1807–1823," *Journal of Negro History,* vol. 17, April 1932:162.

19. Dickson, *The Powerful Bond,* 96. Note also Daniel Coker's vantage point on Sierra Leone in these years when he traveled there with over ninety Africans. *Journal of Daniel Coker, a Descendant of Africa, from the Time of Leaving New York in the Saint Elizabeth, Capt. Sebor. on a Voyage for Sherbro, in Africa. In the Company with Three Agents and About Ninety Persons of Color* (Baltimore: Edward J. Coale, in aid of the funds of the Maryland Auxiliary Colonization Society, 1820). In terms of the explosion of interest in philology, lexicology, grammar, and related matters, see Benedict Anderson, *Imagined Communities: Reflections on the Origin and Spread of Nationalism* (New York: Verso, 1983), 71ff; Hugh Seton-Watson, *Nations and States: An Enquiry into the Origins of Nations and the Politics of Nationalism* (Boulder, CO: Westview Press, 1977), 11, passim.

20. Dickson, *The Powerful Bond,* 164.

21. David Eltis and James Walvin, eds, *The Abolition of the Atlantic Slave Trade* (Madison: University of Wisconsin Press, 1981), 68.

22. Eltis and Walvin, *The Abolition of the Atlantic Slave Trade,* 168.

23. See Wesley, "The Neglected Period," and Philip D. Curtin, *The Image of Africa: British Ideas and Action, 1780–1850* (Madison: University of Wisconsin Press, 1964), 157, passim.

24. Dickson, *The Powerful Bond,* 111.

25. Dickson, *The Powerful Bond,* 126–28.

26. The relationship between imperialism and the "discovery" of language was nothing new. The institution of the English empire in India had precipitated Sir William Jones's study of Sanskrit in 1786. See Benedict Anderson, *Imagined Communities,* 70ff. See also Dickson, *The Powerful Bond,* 110.

27. Curtin, *The Image of Africa,* 220.

28. Henry Brunton, *A Grammar and Vocabulary of the Soosoo Language* (Edinburgh: J. Ritchi, 1802). See also Curtin, *The Image of Africa,* 220–21.

29. Curtin, *The Image of Africa,* 169.

30. G. Mollien, *Travels in the Interior of Africa,* ed. T. E. Bowdich, Conductor of the Mission to Ashantee (London: Henry Colburn, 1820). For a dis-

cussion of Wolof and Fula, see Westerman, Diedrich and M. A. Bryan, *The Languages of West Africa* (Folkestone, Dawsons of Pall Mall, 1970), 18–19. Serrere is a language, one of the West Atlantic languages, spoken in southern Senegal and Gambia, Westerman, 17–18.

31. Curtin, *The Image of Africa*, 220–21.

32. Brunton, *A Grammar and Vocabulary*, p. 111. See also *Allah ha Feë Sufuëk bè fe ra, Religious Instructions for the Susoos*, ed. J. Ritchie, 1801.

33. Brunton, *A Grammar and Vocabulary*, xvi–xxiv.

34. Anon [Hannah Kilham], *Ta-Re Wa-Loof, Ta-re book Juk-à: First Lesson in Jaloff* ([London] Tottenham: George Stockwell Coventry 1820). See Benedict Anderson, *Imagined Communities*, 71.

35. *African Lessons. Wolof and English. In Three Parts. Part First. Easy Lessons, and Narratives for Schools; Part Second. Examples in Grammar, Family Advices, Short Vocabulary; Part Third. Selections from the Holy Scriptures* (London: printed for a Committee of Friends for Promoting African Instruction, by William Phillips, George Yard, Lombard Street, 1823). For the national importance of these dictionaries, see Benedict Anderson, *Imagined Communities*, p. 73.

36. Curtin, *The Image of Africa*, 221.

37. Biller, *Memoir*, 177.

38. J. B. Webster and A. A. Boahen, with a contribution by H. O. Idowu, *History of West Africa: The Revolutionary Years—1815 to Independence* (New York: Praeger, 1970). John Peterson, *Province of Freedom*, 81–149. See also Christopher Fyfe, *Sierra Leone Inheritance* (London: Oxford University Press, 1964), 131–36.

39. J. B. Elliott, *The Lady Huntingdon's Connexion in Sierra Leone* (London: n.p. 1851), 14–15. See also Fyfe, *Sierra Leone Inheritance*, 119–20.

40. Peterson, *Province of Freedom*, 64.

41. Peterson, *Province of Freedom*, 67–70.

42. Hannah Kilham's own views of liberated Africans offer a different vantage point. See *Extracts from the Letters*, 8–11. Peterson, *Province of Freedom*, 71.

43. Alie, *A New History*, 64.

44. Biller, *Memoir*, 207, passim. See also Peterson, *Province of Freedom*, 64–66.

45. Peterson, *Province of Freedom*, 72.

46. Peterson, *Province of Freedom*, 36–40, p. 127.

47. Peterson, *Province of Freedom*, 73–77.

48. Curtin, *The Image of Africa*, 169. Charles McCarthy's governorship of Sierra Leone now included the Gold Coast forts. In an unprecedented government-missionary alliance, McCarthy used Bickersteth's report to establish Church Missionary Society religious representatives in a double role: as administrators as well as educators.

49. Curtin, *The Image of Africa*, 151. By 1831 the African Association had merged with the Royal Geographical Society.

50. Peterson, *Province of Freedom*, 83.

51. Peterson, *Province of Freedom*, 83.

52. Macbaily Fyle, *The History*, 72.

53. Peterson, *Province of Freedom*, 117.

54. In the mid-1820s, Sherbro Island and its coastal territory came under the protection of Sierra Leone during Governor Charles Turner's administration. That was soon reversed, with the British evacuating the Gold Coast in 1825. Richard and John Lander's *Journal* had clinched the downgrading of Sierra Leone when they charted the all-water route into the interior. Curtin, *The Image of Africa*, 171, 175. See also Fyfe *A History of Sierra Leone*, 156–59; Alie, *A New History*, 115. For the original source, see Richard and John Lander, *Journal of an Expedition to Explore the Course and Termination of the Niger; with a Narrative of a Voyage Down That River to Its Termination*, 3 vols. (London: J. Murray, 1832).

55. Biller, *Memoir*, 142.

56. Basil Davidson, *The Story of Africa* (Mitchell Beazley; based on the television series "Africa," co-production in association with Nigerian television authority), 99. For more information on the Gambia, Christianity, and Islam, see Lammin Sanneh, *West African Christianity: The Religious Impact* (London: C. Hurst, 1983), esp. 83–89; 140–44. For a general overview, see Peter B. Clarke, *West Africa and Islam: A Study of Religious Development from the 8th to the 20th Century* (London: Edward Arnold, 1982).

57. Dickson, *The Powerful Bond*, 154–55.

58. Peter B. Clarke, *West Africa and Christianity*, 44.

59. Curtin, *The Image of Africa*, 219, 220. Benedict Anderson, *Imagined Communities*, 77.

60. P. E. Hair, *Notes and Queries. For readers and writers, collectors and librarians*, ed. L. G. Black, D. Hewitt, and E. G. Stanley, New Series, vol. 31, no. 1 (March 1984):58–62, and esp. 60.

61. Mary Jean Corbett, "Feminine Authorship on Victorian Women Writers Autobiographies," *Women's Studies*, vol. 18, 1990, 19.

62. See John Holm, *Pidgins and Creoles*, vol. 1, 4–11, 13–24, 71–104, for a detailed discussion on the nature of pidgins and creoles, especially the Atlantic Creoles of the African Diaspora; and Suzanne Romaine, *Pidgin and Creole Languages* (London: Longman, 1988), 115.

63. Biller, *Memoir*, 320.

64. Peterson, *Province of Freedom*, 151. Note that Kilham watched the teaching practice of Thomas Macfoy, an African-Caribbean friend and manager of Wellington village. Kilham was also able to visit Reverend Nyländer and other schools administered according to Lancasterian principles.

65. Peterson, *Province of Freedom*, 158. Governor Campbell continued Governor Turner's policy of rendering the upkeep of liberated Africans less expensive and more productive. He adopted a plan that gave new arrivals threepence a day for the first six months. This new practice, he hoped, would stimulate the local economy. The British government was slowly returning to its former plan to try to develop Sierra Leone as an export and import base for trade purposes. But attempts to economize on expenses clashed with efforts to increase trade. Governors Denham and Campbell quarrelled over decreasing the number of children in school. Denham also improved the roads, moved produce to town markets and built new settlements. After both died of malaria, Governor Ludlam took over.

66. Peterson, *Province of Freedom,* 163.

67. Biller, *Memoir,* 194, 208. Paul Cuffee, *A Brief Account of the Settlement and Present Situation of the Colony of Sierra Leone in Africa* (New York: Samuel Wood, 1812).

68. Hannah Kilham, *Report on a Recent Visit to the Colony of Sierra Leone. To the Committee for African Instruction, and other Friends Concerned in Promoting Its Objects,* 3–24, signed Hannah Kilham, Tottenham 26/5/28 (London: William Phillips, 1828). All references will be to this edition.

69. L. G. Johnson, *Perronet Thompson,* 34, passim; *Report,* 17–18. For information by Hannah Kilham on abuses of the apprenticeship system, see *Extracts from the Letters,* 12–13.

70. Fyfe, *History of Sierra Leone,* 119.

71. See, for example, *Specimens of Some of the African Dialects.*

72. W. H. Smyth, *The Life and Services of Captain Philip Beaver, Late of His Majesty's Ship Nisus* (London: John Albemarle, 1829), 47–107.

73. See Gayatri Chakravorty Spivak, "How to read a 'culturally different' book" in Francis Barker et al., *Colonial Discourse/Postcolonial Theory* (Manchester: Manchester University Press, 1994), 126–50; and Ngugi Wa Thiong'o, *Decolonizing the Mind* (London, 1986).

74. Hannah Kilham's linguistic tracts draw from previous European grammars and vocabularies. The first were Reverend Mr. Brunton's tracts on the Soosoo [*sic*] language, printed and funded by the Society for Missions to Africa and the East. Thomas Winterbottom talks of these texts as "an event of no small importance," and goes on to enumerate them: "The books already printed in Soosoo are as follows, viz. 1. A Grammar and Vocabulary; 2. A Spelling-book and Church Catechism; 3. An easy First Catechism; 4. A Second Catechism; 5. An Historical Catechism; 6. Three dialogues on the Advantage of Letters, and Absurdity of the religious Notions of the Soosoos, and the comparative Value of the Christian and Mahommedan Religion; 7. Christian Instructions, being an Abridgment of the Scripture History and Doctrine" (218). Winterbottom also includes very long appendices of the vocabulary of the "Bullom" and "Timmanee" (Temne) and "Soosoo" languages (337–62). A second influence on Hannah Kilham was the *Grammar and Vocabulary of the Bullom Language,* by Rev. Gustavus Reinhold Nyländer (London: Ellerton and Henderson, 1814). Nyländer's text first addressed "letters and their powers," then various parts of speech that include conjugations. The third section, on syntax, contains a collection of Bullom phrases as well as the names of the months, several towns, and proper names. He ends with a vocabulary section, Bullom with English and then English with Bullom. Coming a decade or two after Brunton and Nyländer, Kilham opted for less dense syntactic description and a more accessible vocabulary in the form of brief narratives. Certainly both Brunton and Nyländer used helpful sentences, but Hannah Kilham seemed to raise usefulness and familiarity to a principle. In keeping with the European religious ethos, she also included short narratives about scriptures and referred to but did not centerstage the concept of a Christian God in her vocabulary charts. See also Hannah Kilham's *African Lessons.* In *Specimens of the African Languages,* she continued to put her ideas into practice, transposing

the numerals and leading words in twenty-five African languages into written script, with the English translation side by side.

75. *The Claims of West Africa to Christian Instruction through the Native Languages* (London: Harvey and Darton, 1830), 1. All references will be to this edition. Thomas Clarkson, *The Cries of Africa to the Inhabitants of Europe: or, A Survey of that Bloody Commerce Called the Slave Trade* (London: Harvey and Darton, ca. 1822). This text illustrates how the human cargo was packed on a slave ship.

76. For conditions that smuggled slaves endured, see Basil Davidson, *The Black Man's Burden: Africa and the Curse of the Nation-State* (London: James Currey, 1992), 23–26.

77. Biller, *Memoir*, 46.

Partarien expresses his conviction that friends would be received by the natives with confidence, and would succeed in their attempts to introduce improvement; but he believes they would find it requisite to trade as well as teach, in order to do all the good they would wish, in promoting industry, and furthering the great object of the general welfare of the people. . . . In our conversation on agriculture he mentioned that cotton is cultivated with great ease, and grows immediately after the rice-crops, on the same ground. Coffee and arrow-root grow wild here with little trouble. If the okra could be dried and exported as a vegetable soup, it might be of much value; and, in short, this country has not any lack in its powers of production, and only wants agricultural labourers of sincere good will to guide and instruct the Africans in their labours so as to supercede, by fair and judicious measures, all plea of necessity for selling each other. (194, 208)

See also Paul Cuffee, *A Brief Account of the Settlement.*

78. Biller, *Memoir, Appendix*, 482–83. Beyond her research in linguistics, Kilham was also involved in various social issues: for example, she comments on a woman who is whipped into carrying a huge stone on her head (384). On another occasion, she mentions cruelty to animals:

I am so sensibly reminded of the uncertainty of life that I must soon try to acquit myself of what I think a debt of duty, in writing to James Montgomery, on the subject of cruelty to animals, which I have seen partially brought forward in an infant-school hymn. (448)

79. Biller, *Memoir*, 482, 169.

80. Lammin Sanneh, *West African Christianity*, 66.

81. Benedict Anderson, *Imagined Communities*, 133.

82. Sara Mills, *Discourses of Difference. An analysis of Women's Travel Writing and Colonialism* (London: Routledge, 1992), 83.

83. Curtin, *The Image of Africa*, 128.

84. Curtin, *The Image of Africa*, 157.

85. Edward W. Said, "Orientalism Reconsidered," in F. Barker, ed., *Europe and Its Others*, vol. 1, Proceedings of the Essex Sociology of Literature Conference, 1984, July, University of Essex, Colchester, 19.

Six

BALACHANDRA RAJAN

Feminizing the Feminine: Early Women Writers on India

THIS ESSAY DEALS largely with two novels: Elizabeth Hamilton's *Translation of the Letters of a Hindu Rajah* and Lady Morgan's (Sydney Owenson's) *The Missionary*. Both novels were widely read in their time and are scarcely known in ours. Elizabeth Hamilton's novel is hard to find and commentary on it is strikingly scanty. *The Missionary*, kept alive till now by Shelley's commendation of it, was once far more celebrated than anything Shelley produced. Despite some revival of interest in Owenson it remains the least commented upon of her novels.

To write on these novels is not simply to search the margin in yet another of the incremental operations of scholarship. Recontextualization of these works restores their topicality and helps to explain why they mattered in their time. But recontextualization also retrieves a literary sophistication which would otherwise not be present in our reading of these novels. Their relationship to the discourse of imperialism is befittingly complex; but to savor that complexity we have to situate them with some care in relation to a quite brief time-span in the development of that discourse. Significantly, much of the writing of the Romantic era is in alignment with this time-frame and can be read as responding to its possibilities and coercions.

By 1830, the Mill-Hegel construction had taken over English perceptions of India. Macaulay's minute of 1835 established English as India's language of higher education and the English achievement in civilization as the standard of excellence India must seek to approach. Utilitarians and Evangelists came together in a common zeal for reform by making use of the space of difference between "superior" and "inferior" cultures to argue that reform in the English direction was essential if India was not to be trapped in itself. The reform experiment, moreover, would be less contaminated than it might be, even in England, since custom and error, those twin sisters, could be disallowed any voice in the proceedings. A subjected country is not without its advantages as a laboratory for the social scientist.[1]

The "obligation of benevolence" for Hastings[2] consisted of those responsibilities (unilaterally determined) which made power seem respectable to itself. More self-righteously, it was presented by Evangelicals as an atonement for past injustices, including those for which Hastings was responsible.[3] "We cannot now renounce them without guilt," Grant said of the Indians in 1792, halfway through the Hastings impeachment. He went on to add prophetically that "we may contract great guilt in the government of them."[4] His agenda for atonement consisted of the "moral improvement" of those subject to British rule in India and the rooting out of the "internal principles of depravity" in their cultures.[5]

It cannot be said that India was particularly eager to accept Grant's atonement; it was inflicted moreover on hundreds of thousands of square miles of territory which had been spared the original sins of Clive and Hastings. The point to be made is about effectiveness, not justice; two converging movements of reform produced a momentum difficult to resist, particularly in the exclusive boardrooms of a private company which could still take decisions affecting the future of a subcontinent. Yet the reforming impetus, though vigorous, was short-lived, impeded from the beginning by institutional resistances both Indian and English. Two decades later, the events of 1857 shifted the emphasis from social engineering to the preservation of law and order.

Mill's own agenda, before reformist zeal enlarged it, had sought no more than peace preserved and justice impartially dispensed. The Olympian aloofness offered by this formula fitted the British mood after 1857. The introduction of English as India's higher language and the beckoning possibilities of conversion to Christianity had been presented as the means for collapsing the otherness of India into a space of difference that could be progressively reduced. The original otherness that had been conceived so as to justify these measures was now reinstated in all its intractability. Bengali Babus could never be honorary Englishmen. Imitation had been amusing once, notably in Emily Eden's journals. But imitation could be parodic as well as flattering. More threateningly, it could be a form of usurpation.[6]

On the whole it was better for East and West not to meet. It was preferable for India to be a place of exile where the Great Game was played on a frontier resembling the American West, with the English identity realized on a periphery and not at a center lost to the cosmopolitan. To manage India, the site of passion, deceit, and irrationality, with firmness and with wisdom, was to enact in the theater of empire the conquest of the self.

There could be alternatives, even for the same author. In Kipling's world India is not the madwoman in the attic but a prized possession to be cared for and guarded, externally from rapacious Russians and internally from the wildness in herself. Dryden's Nourmahal, it will be remembered, anticipates that wildness side by side with Indamora's embodying of India's desirability. We can see the wildness as amiable rather than hysterical. We can see the desirability as dangerous rather than rewarding. Perceptions can shift widely between these elasticities, leaving their containment discursively in place. India can also be a jungle where we discover reassuringly that the fundamental law, as in civilized societies and empires, is the obedience of the lower to the higher. On the other hand, Kim can live in an enclosed garden where the events of 1857 have left no scar upon the smiling earth. As with the view of Chandrapore from the cantonment in Forster's novel, more than one construction can be shaped and sustained by the gaze of the beholder. But India, endearing or dangerous, reticent or treacherously secretive, India as not a promise but an appeal, or as a promise that becomes an appeal, remains consistently feminine India.[7]

Perceiving India as feminine is a familiar practice of the literary imagination. Scholarship should be a different matter. It is factual and not fictive, neutral and not partisan, entrenched protectively in that disinterestedness which Matthew Arnold once called the Indian virtue. Claims to this effect have not ceased to be heard but they are considerably less persuasive than they once were. It is not easy after Said to believe fervently in the disinterestedness of scholarship though a mild persuasion along these lines may be desirable in order to continue with these pages. Inden's important study, *Imagining India*, provides little ground for reaffirming scholarly impartiality.[8] The various scholarly disciplines as they apply themselves to India consistently devalue it; and they all eventually do so by subscribing to the fictive dispositions they might be expected to resist. They provide different scholarly names for India's femininity.

India is the *anima* and the *id*. It is a proliferating jungle where the garden of civilization must be maintained with great difficulty against the invading undergrowth. It is prolixity instead of order, wayward passion and wild extravagance instead of purposive reason, and serpentine Oriental deceitfulness instead of straightforward Western candor. It is tribal and inherently fragmented. It is the primitive feminine, masculinized too late. It is the Aryan ship foundering in the Dravidian ocean. It is tropical rather than temperate; the very word-play in this contrast underlines the nature of Indian irresponsibility.[9]

A common rhetoric sustained by metaphors both explicit and buried, percolates through the discourse formation of religious, philosophical, socio-economic, anthropological and psychoanalytical scholarship. There is an impressive homogeneity in the findings which may mean that the truth identifies itself by remaining the same irrespective of the approach to it, or may simply mean that one usually finds what one is looking for and that the Western gaze looks only in one direction. But of course, in a hegemonic era it is the cumulative concurrence that counts and not the cautionary scepticism which is becoming audible only after the passing of territorial empires.

The solidarity of the discourse formation facilitates migration from one discipline to another and increases the coercive force of each discipline. Investigations can lead to vigorously disputed conclusions which seem to bear witness to the integrity of scholarship; but there is no real disagreement on how the investigations are to be channeled. India is a stage on which the feminine can be enacted and given its full range of representations with a luxuriance of rendering that is itself feminine in its elaborations. The elaborations feed back into the originating principle so that the relationship between gender, culture, and race becomes symbiotic rather than overlapping. When Inden tells us that Mill and Hegel are hegemonic within Indology[10] we have to recognize that Indology is not just the study of the history and culture of a specific geographical area. If India is thought of as the theater of the Other, Indology can appropriately become the didactic productions mounted in that theater.

The completeness of envisaging which characterizes feminine India, the comprehensiveness and the interlocking nature of its rhetoric, makes escape from its constraints remarkably difficult. The directing strength of discourse, its writing of the self that writes the novel and the heavy investment of identity in the assumptions of empire, are particularly to be borne in mind when we consider women writers on India. A subjected femininity might be expected to reach out to a subjected India, defined as meriting subjection because she is feminine. But Benita Parry finds very little of this empathizing in her chapter on women novelists of the Kipling era.[11] Brantlinger's fine chapter on 1857 suggests that the rhetoric enveloping those tragic events remained much the same irrespective of the sex of the author.[12] In the most recent and probably the most thoughtful consideration of this problem Jenny Sharpe recognizes that "a rejection of the gender hierarchy the domestic ideal enforces does not similarly negate the racial superiority it implies. It may in fact, reinforce it."[13]

These are not findings that should surprise us. The sacrifice of family life and the self-effacing exile in an ungrateful land that were needed to maintain British supervision of a wayward and potentially vicious India enshrined Victorian domesticity by immolating it on the altar of empire. The Englishwoman in India was thus captured and sometimes captivated by a discourse which offered her both heroic dignity and limited empowerment. A double seduction was held out in return for that compliance with the script which the discourse expected from participants in its theater. The reward was more than sufficient to contain and render insubstantial, any potential generosities of gender.[14]

To study the feminine view of India's femininity under conditions less warped by the pressures of discourse we must return to an earlier phase of Britain's relationship with the subcontinent. The sudden elevation of India's past in the first wave of Oriental scholarship opened a moment of opportunity for understanding between peoples. The moment passed almost before it had articulated itself. 1785 and 1810 might be said to mark its limits, and even during that brief period the view from the window was clouded. The literary attractiveness of William Jones's perception of India merely meant that for the time being literature would be one step behind in the imperial march. It was the swiftly changing power relationship between England and India that mattered and that relationship was obliged to place out of bounds the mutual respect which is a condition of dialogue. Subject peoples are to be educated, not listened to. Indeed the very decisiveness with which the moment was sealed off makes apparent the priorities which it threatened.

The first novels in English about India began to be written during this moment. The earliest may have been *Hartley House, Calcutta* (1789). It was published anonymously but because of the epistolary form and because the letters are from Sophia Gildborne to a close friend in England, we can conjecture that the author was a woman.

A. L. Basham, who draws attention to the novel, finds it of "small literary merit."[15] Nevertheless, it was of sufficient interest for a pirated edition to appear in Dublin during the year of its publication and for a German translation to appear two years later. The novel seems to have attracted a reading public which expanded notably for Elizabeth Hamilton's *Translation of the Letters of a Hindu Rajah*, five editions of which were published between 1796 and 1811. Lady Morgan's *The Missionary*, published in 1811 (the year after Southey's *The Curse of Kehama*), was reprinted no less than four times in the same year, in three elegant volumes with a portrait of the author, as the publisher, Stockwell, enticingly chooses to put it. The title-page also assures us that a portrait of the author will be among the reader's rewards for putting down his guinea. The novel's literary, as distinct from its commercial, success was not restricted to the Shelley Circle. Schwab notes that in France the "stir regarding Sanskrit" began with Bernadin de Saintpierre's *Chaumiere Indienne* in 1794 and also included *The Missionary*.[16] Indeed, the currency of the novel was such that Owenson, at the time of her death nearly half a century later, was working on a revised version of it (*Luxima the Prophetess*) responding to the events of 1857.

The novel about India was originated by women. It found a significant reading public before the genre (including unfortunately, the work of those women writers who practiced it) was made to collaborate in the masculine domination of a feminine Orient, now stereotyped so as to make that domination desirable. Part of the attraction which these early novels held for their public was the displacement of gender-relationships on to an intercultural plane where issues not otherwise easily negotiable could be discussed through surrogate representations. Sophia Gildborne's admiration (Letter XII) for the mildness, gentleness, and inoffensiveness of the Hindus (Mill, thirty years later, is an instructive contrast)[17] recognizes not only a feminine nature that has yet to be given its due but also the capacity of that nature to engender a civilization worthy of respect. Sati can be taken as implying that a woman exists only as the wife of her husband and that her life ends when that meaning is extinguished. Sophia treats it as evidence that heroism of the highest order is not excluded by gentleness. Her platonic attachment to a teacher at the University of Benares foregrounds the *idea* of India rather than its bizarre customs or exotic fascinations. In her conversion to Hinduism (Letter XXVI) she rejects not only the West but the masculine principle which the West embodies, in favor of a feminine alternative. When her friend and teacher dies and she marries an official of the East India Company, the highly artificial and almost peremptory closure recognizes a fiction which one can entertain but which it is not as yet possible to inhabit. In an intercultural relationship the contestation of boundaries characteristic of the feminine affirmation within a masculine culture is reconfigured as the choice of a different site.

Elizabeth Hamilton's *Translation of the Letters of a Hindu Rajah*[18] is a more sophisticated novel than *Hartley House, Calcutta*. Its ironic manners are in striking contrast to the lush prose of *The Missionary*, written fifteen years later. The novel is dedicated to Warren Hastings and is in memory of Hamilton's brother, whom Hastings had assisted toward a position in the East India Company. He is not to be confused with that more distinguished Alexander Hamilton who, marooned in France during the Napoleonic wars, whiled away the tedium by cataloguing the Indian contents of the *Bibliothèque Nationale* and by giving Friedrich Schlegel lessons in Sanskrit.

The word "Translation" in the title is significant. Since the translator is also the author (and the editor) the multiple roles can suggest that there is a part of the self sufficiently alienated from the socially constructed and acceptable self to be regarded as "foreign" and to require translation, supplemented by editorial mediation, if its now "strange" voice is to be understood. The co-presence of the familiar and the unrecognized is obviously appropriate to a feminine affirmation within a masculine environment. India provides the theater for a narrative of that self-affirmation which can be offered as history and read for what history can teach us.

A "Preliminary Dissertation" by the "Editor" emphasizes by its length and care in exposition the distance that necessitates translation. As a setting for the Rajah's letters it acts in conjunction with them by specifying, in a manner which is highly individual, a historical and religiophilosophical context for their reading. Hamilton begins by drawing attention, not simply to the antiquity of Indian civilization, but to its remarkable continuity (vii–viii). She then proceeds to argue (quite unlike others who take up this subject) that this continuity must be due to the inherent stability of Indian institutions. The caste system, for instance, is perceived as socially cohesive rather than paralyzing (xv–xvi). A loose federation of rajahs governed by a maharajah represents a monarchic structure that is responsive to autonomy, rather than one which is inflexibly totalitarian (viii–ix). This is a perception interestingly close to the "revised" view now offered by the New Cambridge History.[19] Monarchs in Hamilton's presentation are governed not by unregulated caprice (the Hindu State in Hegel exists only for the freedom of the single person at the head of it) but by inherited principles, laid down in primary texts, which have gained authority by being practiced through the centuries.

A further stabilizing characteristic of Hindu civilization is the firmly marked identity that results from its being tenacious of its own doctrines, "in a degree that is unexampled in the history of any other religion." This cultural cohesiveness is accompanied by an "unbounded toleration" that enables it to live in peace with others (xvi–xvii).

There can be objections to the view of Hindu India which Hamilton offers, but it deserves consideration as much as the view which overwhelmed it and which dominated discussions of India for over a century. In any case, our concern is not with the accuracy of the representation but with the forces that result in its being what it is. Hamilton's unstated intention is to argue that a civilization built on feminine prin-

ciples can succeed in being just and enduring and that to say so is not
to voice a pious hope; a demonstration of the proposition is to be found
in India's history. When a society embodying these principles is subjugated, it is by forces superior only in strength and determined to use
strength for the ends of subjugation.

Hindu India was conquered by Muslim invaders of whom Hamilton
has nothing good to say. She is less than fair to Islam but her voice is
in refreshing contrast to the chorus of voices denigrating Hindu civilization as weak, vicious, self-wounding, and largely responsible for its
own fate. This is an all too familiar characterization of the feminine
and one can even argue that its export to India enables it to be displayed with a clarity and invested with an opprobrium not altogether
possible in more familiar settings. Hamilton offers a different view of
India as the site of an authentic femininity that calls out to be heard
from rather than sequestrated. Subjected to a power of oppression that
is both unjustified and unrelieved, India is also presented within a theater of gender with Islam installed as the male force. Disinterestedness
may be deflected by the requirements of this theater but the moral
made available for domestication would not have been lost on an English audience.

The British, in Hamilton's scenario, cannot be successors of the
Mughals. Their contribution is to produce a hero capable of playing
St. George to the Muslim dragon. He must liberate an imprisoned femininity and restore it to the status it once occupied, and deserves to
occupy in other countries as well as India. Hastings's role in India was,
to put it charitably, more complex, but Hamilton takes a straightforward view of how the obligation of benevolence is to be exercised. Her
political naïveté may be in the end a reproof to those who did things
differently in India and in the theater of gender in nineteenth-century
England.

Hastings as liberator and dragon-slayer is too much a part of the
golden world to be credible in the bronze one where Sidney placed
the fictions which mediate our understanding of history. Like Rushdie,
blithely altering the date of Mahatma Gandhi's death,[20] Hamilton
places the logic of fiction and perhaps the form of romance on a higher
plane than the awkwardness of fact. The correct date would not have
affected Rushdie's fiction. He makes an issue of his right to be wrong
simply to remind us that chronological accuracy is not the most important of a writer's responsibilities. With Hamilton, the investment in re-
fusing to see what is embarrassing is heavier and the Hastings she invents is essential to the integrity of her fiction. Her book, published the
year after the impeachment ended, must proceed as if it never took
place.

Hastings's treatment of the Rohillas was a prominent feature in the impeachment. Macaulay's dramatic account of the injustices perpetrated in "Rohilkund" has been found too severe by some historians and it is true that Macaulay tends to write as if the darkest hour came before Macaulay. In Hamilton's novel, the Rajah passing through Rohilkund finds it a place of almost idyllic bliss. The author (as editor) concedes that the account differs strikingly "from that tale of horrors which has been generally received." Eyewitnesses of the scene can best determine, she adds confidently, "which account comes closest to the truth" (I, 202–203n).

The passage through Rohilkund with its living proof of the beneficence of British administration is a prelude to the Rajah's meeting with Hamilton's idealized Hastings. It is preceded significantly by a description of an exemplary Indian monarch taken from the *Hitopadesa*, which Wilkins had translated nine years earlier. Hastings, needless to say, conforms fully to the description. The "pure and blessed spirit of humanity . . . has distinguished every act of his administration" (I, 219–20). The Rajah is confirmed in his desire to visit an England that can provide India with such flawless exemplifications of her own ancient texts. He undertakes the perilous voyage which was not actually undertaken until Ram Mohun Roy crossed the "dark waters" to die at Bristol in 1833. The Rajah arrives a quarter of a century earlier in an England where the impeachment ought to be in progress. No trace of it is to be found in his letters.

Cultures, precisely because of their distinctiveness, cannot be transparent to other cultures but the vantage point of another culture can generate a critique not easily possible from within the culture being viewed. As in Montesquieu's *Lettres persanes*, Hamilton's letter-writer is nominally a "foreigner" but a foreigner listened to as a voice in a contested self, the exclusions of which are questioned by that foreignness, the partition of the self between two sites. Both difference and similarity are implied by the circumstances of the act of composition. Opportunities even exist for a two-way traffic, which Hamilton must ignore because her vantage point is presented as an unwavering idealization, positing not only praiseworthy principles but an implausible congruence between principles and practice. Distancing this vantage point by locating it in India allows the implausibility to be fictively entertained. Feminizing it provides an indication of the extent to which England has marginalized and psychically distanced forces that should remain important within herself.

The Rajah cannot conceive of any cleavage between social philosophy and its implementation. Fortified in his innocence by the unimpeachable integrity displayed by Hastings, he proceeds on the basis that if English social behaviour seems inconsistent to him it can only be because he has not read it with sufficient care. There must be hidden significances and patterns of cohesiveness with which he, as a foreigner, cannot be familiar. If people's lives do not follow the texts of their religion it can only be because those texts are modified by other texts which, at this moment, are not known to the Rajah.

There is a caste system in England, but instead of being functionally aligned, it consists of People of Family, People of No Family, and People of Style. The last category is the highest but the principles of election to it are unclear. Nevertheless it is more than self-proclaiming. The validity of the entire caste system, including its indeterminate upper tier, is attested to by the consensus which supports it and which must have a foundation in hidden understandings.

Poojahs exist in England, the most important among them being the Poojah of Cards. Its mystic dimensions are evident from the concentration and intensity of commitment displayed by participants in the poojah and by the manner in which all other concerns are put aside in deference to its imperative.

The Bible calls for equality between the sexes (the Rajah's reading seems politically correct rather than textually indisputable) but this is apparently not the case in England. The inference should not be that sacred texts are being disregarded but that a secondary revelation is in place which provisionally tolerates inequality and also makes poverty not a matter for compassion, but the most heinous of offences (II, 161).

The Rajah's hermeneutic procedures are throughout designed to deny the existence of fissures in the social fabric of a country as exemplary as England and to see that fabric as a seamless rendering of the doctrinal patterns that are woven into it. If the procedures are extreme to the point of being comic, that is a comment on the "strangeness" of England to the idealized integrity which Hindu India has been constructed to represent. India's return to itself under Hastings is an augury of what can happen in England—but only if those seeking liberation live according to standards instead of according to the casteism of style or the frivolity of the Poojah of Cards.

The important feature of the novel for our purposes is that Hinduism is treated as capable of yielding the paradigms of ideal behaviour; that it is regarded as an oppressed and silenced voice, liberated so as to be listened to once more in the counsels of understanding; and that its restoration argues for the restoration of other voices that are in harmony with it and are not being heard. On the other hand, the contrast between Muslim tyranny and British benevolence is insensitive to the realities of dominance; the stain of power is not materially altered by the moral pretensions of those who enjoy the use of it. Even as a fable of the maiden in distress rescued from the Muslim dragon's clutches, the book is not appropriate to a more realistic era, where rescue has to be earned by the inner strength and perseverance of the oppressed. One has to read the novel to recognize that these failings are not fatal. From a vantage point that is uncontaminated much can be seen that is quietly comic, suggesting how being uncontaminated is itself comic in an up-to-date world. There is a need for integrity, and Hindu India, as the site of its realization, is perceived with a sympathy and insight that is an important corrective to the hostile perceptions beginning to gather force.

Both *Hartley House, Calcutta* and *Letters of a Hindu Rajah* are cast in the epistolary form which Lady Morgan (Sydney Owenson) also uses in the best known of her novels, *The Wild Irish Girl.*[21] It is a form that is naturally conversational and indefinitely extensible. Though it can sustain a narrative and be brought to closure by it, it is not necessarily dominated by narrative requirements. Multiple correspondents can generate a criss-cross of interpretations, with each interpretation weighed and sifted by the necessity of committing it to writing. The relationships between the author, the editor, a possible translator, and the writer or writers of the letters can introduce layers of commentary that do not have to culminate in judgment by a fixed standard. If our aim is a thoughtful open-mindedness, the form has advantages not easily dismissed.

It cannot be said that the authors being discussed make anything like full use of these opportunities. Owenson's novel has only one letter-writer. Hamilton has two, but the second disappears as the novel proceeds. The editorial role is used by Hamilton largely to provide us with the Preliminary Dissertation. Owenson furnishes us with ample notes, sometimes speaking in the first person as the author and more frequently signing herself as the editor. Both figures provide documentation for what is said in the text; but the Editor can sometimes differ from the text on scholarly grounds or be critical of its extravagance of style (57, 61, 100, 175).

In her introduction to *The Wild Irish Girl*, Brigid Brophy comments that "the epistolary convention, which in the course of the eighteenth century, Samuel Richardson had used with extreme emotional power and Chaderlos de Laclos had made into an ironic gallery where correspondent flashes ironic light on correspondent, is here flattened into a ribbon of first person narrative, chopped into roughly letter lengths" (viii). The peripheral maneuvers of Editor and Author make this judgement a trifle harsh but it is true that Owenson is either unable to engage or is not interested in engaging the more serious possibilities of the form. In *The Missionary* she turned to an impetuous narrative.[22] She could have done this because the epistolary form no longer appealed to her. Alternatively, she could have made her decision because a form which may have suited the relationship between Ireland and England did not seem to her to suit the relationship between England and India. With its emphasis on closure and containment and on a dominant narrative order which its divergent constituents must not only accept but promote, the narrative form is closer than the epistolary to the form of empire and more receptive to collaboration with the latter's coercive forces.[23]

In *The Wild Irish Girl*, a hoped-for marriage which cannot materialize is taken to be "prophetically typical of a national unity of interests and affections between those who may be factitiously severed, but who are naturally allied." In this unity "the distinctions of English and Irish, of Protestant and Catholic" will be "for ever buried" (253). The union here is between equals, or at least functions as an equalizing force. Though Glorvina (cum Ireland) is seen through the eyes of a male correspondent, the male correspondent is constructed by a female author and Glorvina is the center of attention of the novel as well as of her suitor. The marriage is presented not as the acceptance of differences which enrich each other, but as the burying of distinctions. Its "unity" arises from the binding force of what is held in common.[24]

In *The Missionary*, Hilarion, who combines total dedication to his calling with an appropriately majestic Western presence, meets Luxima (a corruption of Lakshmi, significant in its elision of luxury and light) in that Kashmiri valley which ever since Bernier had been the fashionable site of Paradise. The occasion is momentous. It is the meeting of East and West and Owenson depicts it so that its symbolic significance cannot escape even the most casual of readers.

> Silently gazing, in wonder, upon each other, they stood, finely opposed, the noblest specimens of the human species as it appears in the most opposite regions of the earth; she like the East, lovely and luxuriant; he, like the West, lofty and commanding: the one radiant in all the lustre, attractive in all the softness which distinguishes her native regions: the other, towering in all the energy, imposing in all the vigour, which marks his ruder latitudes: she, looking like a creature formed to feel and to submit; he like a being created to resist and to command: while both appeared as the ministers and representatives of the two most powerful religions of the earth; the one no less enthusiastic in her brilliant errors, than the other confident in his immutable truth. (I, 149–50)

This is not simply the meeting of East and West. It is also the meeting of Adam and Eve and a meeting arranged under Miltonic auspices. In *The Wild Irish Girl* Owenson quotes Milton frequently (39, 40, 42, 52,

82, 195), though Tasso is the poet she most often cites. In *The Mission-ary*, she quotes Milton almost to the exclusion of everyone else. The tableau she devises for us here vividly recalls Satan's (and the reader's) first sight of Adam and Eve in Paradise (IV, 288–301). In particular, it circulates obsessively around two lines delineating the difference be-tween them

> For contemplation he and valour formed,
> For softness she and sweet attractive grace.

The Eastern Eve in Owenson's tableau is lovely, luxuriant, radiant in her lustre and attractive in her softness. The Western Adam is lofty, commanding, towering and imposing. All of these epithets are evoca-tive of a natural right to dominance; and all of the epithets surrounding Luxima evoke a natural propensity to subjection. Owenson does not shrink from the conclusion which follows:

> She, looking like a creature formed to feel and to submit; he like a be-ing created to resist and to command.

To describe Hilarion as a "being" and Luxima as a "creature" is to go beyond any hierarchic principle that Milton may have espoused. Milton moreover makes poetry of the principle only in a prelapsarian world. The relationship of Adam and Eve in the world we inherit from them is dialogic rather than hierarchical. In the Kashmiri paradise, the rela-tionship as Owenson here formulates it seems to proclaim itself as the engendered prologue to the imperial theme. Though Hilarion and Luxima are placed before us as "the noblest specimens of the human Species" (a reminiscence of *PL* IV, 321–24) the best that the East can offer seems created only to yield to the "towering" superiority of the West. It can come as no surprise that Christianity is presented as a re-ligion of "immutable truth" and Hinduism as a religion of "brilliant errors" to which commitment is enthusiastic rather than rational.

Enthusiasm is not limited to Luxima, and Owenson can be the will-ing victim of her own prose, as some of her editorial comments in *The Wild Irish Girl* suggest. More persuasively we can argue that Owenson writes for an audience (as her publisher's advertisements of her book make clear) which can be tentatively characterized as literate, affluent and given to the fashionable. She is writing in fact for those People of Style whom Hamilton's Hindu Rajah places in the top tier of the En-glish caste system. The set-piece invokes a discourse then making its claim to dominance, endowing it with the finish of style and the bless-ing of voguishness. Having met the expectations of the salon which she continues to regale with a love story, Owenson is then free to follow a route which fortunately for the real worth of the novel, complicates as well as confirms the original tableau.

Enthusiastic co-operation with a discourse humbly endorses its fictions of self-justification; but it also offers an irreproachable way of subverting those fictions, a possibility appealing in its potential for mockery to women writers and to subject peoples. It appears moreover that *The Missionary*, as it progressed, was read repeatedly after dinner to "distinguished guests" who insisted on making their own contribution.[25] Subversive surrender may have been the only way to cope with the unwanted views of experts. Owenson's novel can and perhaps should be read along these lines though, as will be suggested later, she is drawn into and does not merely adopt the discourse she both affirms and interrogates.

Compliance with the discourse is foregrounded in the emphasis on Hilarion's invincibility, which is strongly announced not only in the set-piece but throughout the early pages of the novel. He displays "the heroic fortitude of the martyr" (I, 28) and combines the "piety of the saint with the energy of the hero" (I, 52). Yet the doctrines he preaches are later described as "rigid" (II, 29). The "chill hand of religion" checks the rise of "human feelings" in him (II, 7–8). Reluctant even to touch a wreath which Luxima has made part of an "idolatrous ceremony," he finds within himself "a fastidiousness which almost resembled bigotry" (I, 154). He is prepared to perceive that "a pure system of natural religion" is innate in Luxima's "sublime and contemplative mind" (I, 227). But he refuses to build on the common ground which this perception uncovers. Instead, he concentrates obsessively on Luxima's idolatrous practices. It becomes apparent that his repudiation of the priestess is in proportion to his attraction to the woman:

> . . . when the Priestess disappeared, the woman stood too much confessed; and a feminine reserve, a lovely timidity, so characteristic of her sex overwhelmed the Missionary with confusion. (I, 151)

> He would not submit to the analysis of his feelings, and he was determined to conquer, without understanding their nature or tendency. *Entombed* and *chained* within the most remote depths of his heart, he was deaf to their murmurs and resisted their pleadings with all the *despotism* of a great and lofty mind, created equally to command others and itself. (II, 4, italics added)

Hilarion undertook to win over Luxima to Christianity because a Kashmiri Pandit, displaying the opportunism that is all too characteristic of the clerisy, had assured him that Luxima's conversion would bring about mass defections from the Hindu faith. Conversion now becomes the conversion of the Other within himself. Listening to Luxima is "dangerous." On the other hand, arguing with her is impossible because there is "an incoherence in her ideas" which is "not to be reconciled or replied to" (I, 220).

Significantly, this finding comes after a perfectly cogent passage in which Luxima has expatiated on the difficulty of seeing God face to face and on the desirability of knowing him in his works. This is standard Christian thinking, except in India, with *PL* V, 507–12 providing the most convenient locus. Hilarion's refusal of a dialogue based on the common ground which Luxima's statement uncovers is one more erosion of the dramatic contrasts proclaimed in their original encounter. Luxima's enthusiasm includes more than a hint of rational understanding and Hilarion is considerably less than dispassionate in protecting his immutable truths from an Other who seems well on her way to sharing them.

Unfortunately, conversion is not usually a matter of building on common ground. Its drama and justification can be more compelling if common ground is minimized, if Christianity is exhibited not as the final step in a ladder being ascended, but as the only means of deliverance from continuing incarceration in a prison house of error. When cultural differences are widened to this degree by the refusal to recognize shared understandings, the two cultures involved can only meet within a pattern of dominance and tutelage. That fact returns into and forces apart the gender differences with which cultural differences are intertwined.

Hilarion's invincibility is now under duress because of his "entombment" in himself in a manner ironically reminiscent of Mill-Hegel perceptions of India. It is time to turn to the lovely and luxuriant Luxima, a character truly designed to excite the wrath of Hegel. Hughes points to her as Shelley's archetypal heroine[26] but at least in her interrogation of Demogorgon, Asia seems made of sterner stuff.[27] Luxima professes a religion which, as with Hamilton's Hindu India, "unites the most boundless toleration to the most obstinate faith" (I, 213). She may abandon the name of Hinduism but she clings tenaciously to its essence. Nevertheless, abandoning the name in a world largely constituted by naming, is sufficient to ensure her ruin.

In a capacious generalization the Pandit tells Hilarion that "in all the religions of the East, woman has held a decided influence, either as priestess or as victim" (I, 95). This is a statement as erroneous as it is comprehensive but it defines the alternatives before Luxima, making it clear that to renounce one role is inexorably to choose the other. When she accepts Christianity and prefers a platonic life with Hilarion to a fuller one with Suleiman Shikoh (with whom she would not have done any better) she surrenders herself to victimization. Once made, the choice is irreversible. To have second thoughts is only to be placed in double jeopardy:

> . . . the unfortunate Indian was now alike condemned by the religion of truth and the superstition of error. Driven with shame and obloquy from the altar of Brahma, her life had become forfeit, by the laws of the Inquisition as a relapsed Christian. (III, 160)

When truth and error concur so felicitously in their consequences we can legitimately ask what the difference is between them.

Meanwhile, Hilarion has himself become a prisoner of the Inquisition as a result of charges brought against him by a Franciscan monk whom he had dismissed from office in an excess of "fastidiousness."[28] In an unexpected flurry of action Luxima escapes from prison with the assistance of the Pandit and audaciously rescues Hilarion from the stake. She is dangerously injured in the process but the two are able to flee in one of Shelley's boats to a friendly island where Luxima expires, mistakenly believing Hilarion to be dead.

After Luxima's death, Hilarion no longer finds himself "a being created to resist and command." He retires to an icy grotto in the fastnesses of Kashmir. His life as a *Sanyasi* duly comes to a self-effacing end, but not before Aurangzeb has "waded through carnage and destruction to the throne of India," seizing "a sceptre stained with a brother's blood" and wearing "the diadem torn from a priest's brow" (III, 217). The destructiveness of history contrasts with the seclusion of the missionary's cave. Hilarion's dead body is discovered there, holding an urn which contains some ashes, a significantly blood-stained crucifix, and the sacred thread of Luxima's ordination. Inscribed on the urn are the following words:

> . . . thou wilt say "that having gathered a *dark spotted flower in the garden of love*, she expiated her error by the loss of her life; that her disobedience to the forms of her religion and the laws of her country was punished by days of suffering and by an untimely death; yet that her *soul* was pure from sin, as when clothed in transcendent brightness, she outshone in faith, in *virtue*, all women of her nation! (III, 213)

Few writers remember Milton as vividly and thoughtfully as Owenson. Her opening set piece, already discussed, extends the hierarchic principle to a point where it can be brought under interrogation by the rest of the novel. Her description of the banyan tree (II, 8–10) washes away the Satanic propensities with which it had been invested and makes it resplendently emblematic of created order.[29] In using descriptions of Satan to characterize Hilarion (e.g., III, 157, 158) she questions as Milton does, not the nobility she affirms, but the underlying dedication which may support or subvert that nobility. Here, in her association of the unspotted soul with *virtue*, she is remembering the *Ludlow Masque* and adding the contrast with the "*dark spotted flower*" gathered in "*the garden of love.*" Hegel took up that last phrase with contempt.[30] Luxima puts it in tragic opposition to the forms of her religion, the laws of her country, and the womanhood of her nation.

Though the Ludlow Masque is remembered in Luxima's final statement, it is Satan's remembrance of Beelzebub in his unfallen glory that is called into life most strongly by her last words:

> If thou beest he; but O how fallen! how changed
> From him who in the happy realms of light
> Clothed with transcendent brightness didst outshine
> Myriads though bright. (*PL*, 85–88)

Luxima is a name written in light. Her disobedience consigned her to ruin, but it was disobedience only to forms and to laws. She turned away from her religion, not to self-love but to the love of another. If Hilarion composed the inscription (the urn is made from the materials of the grotto), it is an ironic end to the missionary's mission. He has in effect become what he beheld.

Owenson's dramatic unraveling of her novel's beginning raises troubling questions about the possibilities of relationship between cultures. Those possibilities could be considered more carefully if they were not deflected and indeed overwhelmed by a love story in which religious institutions are too readily foregrounded as the main obstacles to human relatedness. The main obstacle remains the symbiotic alliance between dominance and discourse, with gender added to the imperial family.

Owenson's tribute to this family is not without significant reservations. Like Shelley and Southey, whose work I discuss elsewhere, her novel is both fissured and enriched by its participation in two discourses—a literary discourse of world humanism for which William Jones provides an Indian scholarly foundation and an imperial discourse gendered so as to offer India the enlightenments of feminine submission to Western overlordship. Her conspicuously enthusiastic cooperation with the second discourse is partly so that she can seek out the openings in it and make use of those openings to let in the possibilities of the first discourse. But she also endorses what she resists and carries forward what she moves against. Her subversive surrender is a surrender despite its subversiveness and testifies, not for the only time, to the coercive strength of a way of viewing India which it is not possible to bypass and which must hereafter be propitiated.

The propitiation can be deemed more than sufficient in Owenson's remarkable rendering of the first meeting between Hilarion and Luxima— an encounter which the Edenic and Miltonic setting endows with an almost ancestral authority. Her styling of this encounter is extraordinarily and eloquently representative; but the very success of her composition of two essences, which can only be fitted to each other hierarchically, makes her the hostage of a characterization from which she must thereafter struggle to ransom herself. The sculptured antitheses so vividly prominent in her tableau rule out the possibility of any equitable relationship between their "finely opposed" polarities. An East which is totally feeling and a West which is totally intelligence can only meet on a basis which projects the regulative ordering of the psyche on to an intercultural stage.

Owenson does make evident in Hilarion the disabilities of an intelligence that shuts out feeling. Luxima is not subjected to the same critique and her languid passivity fits a regrettable stereotype that licenses domination of the East by the West. The stereotype is also precisely that image of the feminine against which feminine protest has been consistently directed. It is striking that Owenson should choose to lavish upon it so much of her undoubted skill in writing the wrong kind of prose. One might almost conclude that the stereotype is exported to India so that an identification with it can be both allowed and resisted, leaving Europe free for the emergence of a different model of womanhood. Unfortunately, several of Luxima's attributes are shipped back to England after appropriate enrichments to become incorporated into Victorian imaginings of the feminine.

A gendered relationship between cultures might be more easily negotiable if our perception of the genders were changed. The time can be judged as propitious for such changes. The recuperation of India's femininity has been attempted in nationalist counter-constructions of her history. Those in the West who have come to see its past as predatory rather than masterful may find it desirable to recognize a different tradition on a site that has been differently gendered. The question is whether the many injustices of appropriation can be successfully barred from entering the future by re-envisaging the very figures which functioned as the vehicles of those injustices. We can argue that the figures are too contaminated to serve as a basis for the difficult task of understanding between peoples. We can also argue not for a cleansing which may no longer be possible, but for a radical re-appropriation based on the distinctive ontological status which Indian philosophy gives to the feminine principle.[31]

India is not Ireland in Owenson's imagination and if the Celt knew the Indian as Shelley advises us,[32] that understanding is not easily to be found in her work. Glorvina has little in common with Luxima. Much is said in *The Wild Irish Girl* about British injustices in Ireland, but with *The Missionary* set in a period nearly a century prior to the battle of Plassey, not a word needs to be said about British injustices in India. England's prophetical marriage to Ireland was envisaged as a marriage between equals on the shared ground of what those equals held in common. India's marriage to England is projected as an adoring discipleship, a union of sensibility with the West's towering intelligence. India is not a real country but a contrivance, seen through the spectacles of Orientalist books which are actually projected back into an era more tolerant than the Evangelicals of Hindu religious practices.

One might argue that Owenson distances Evangelical constructions so that they can be disowned as Portuguese mistakes. We can allow this defense some weight. The historicizing of a current discourse is one way of suggesting that it may no longer be current. But the novel subscribes and perhaps subscribes heavily to the discourse it also interrogates. The inequality of the relationship it enshrines is never seen as the root of the intercultural failure.

Feminine constructions of India's femininity not only differ from male constructions, but differ in the difference they allow among themselves. Male constructions of India as feminine have one aim that persists through their range of variations—it is to appropriate gender characteristics to political objectives and thereby to find India ineligible for self-government. Owenson does not support this finding—the havoc the missionary wreaks implicitly condemns interference by one country in the culture of another. Nevertheless, her emphasis on Luxima's clinging passivity can be appropriated to an argument for dependence and her frequent references to Hinduism's idolatrous rites underwrite the evangelical view of India. It is Elizabeth Hamilton's novel which, despite its irritating unrealities, sees India as possessing a capacity for self-government which her own history has enduringly demonstrated. A century and a half was to pass after the publication of her novel before that capacity could be reluctantly recognized.

NOTES

1. India as a laboratory for canon formation and for the pedagogical practices surrounding the canon is studied by Gauri Viswanathan in *Masks of Conquest* (New York: Columbia University Press, 1989), throughout and esp. p. 65. As Viswanathan notes, the idea of India as a testing-ground was originally explored by Eric Stokes in *The English Utilitarians and India* (Oxford: Oxford University Press, 1959).

2. See P. J. Marshall, *The British Discovery of Hinduism in the Eighteenth Century* (Cambridge: Cambridge University Press, 1970), 185.

3. Francis G. Hutchins, *The Illusion of Permanence* (Princeton: Princeton University Press, 1967), 5.

4. Quoted in Javeed Majeed, *Ungoverned Imaginings: James Mill's The History of British India and Orientalism* (Oxford: Clarendon Press, 1992), 80.

5. Ibid.

6. The subversiveness of mimicry is addressed by Homi K. Bhabha in "Of Mimicry and Man: The Ambivalence of Colonial Discourse," in *The Location of Culture*, 85–92. Although imperial discourse is both subtended and subverted by the mimicry it calls for (I take this discrimination from Diana Fuss), the feminization of subjected peoples rests on a hierarchic relationship that discourages mimicry. Thus even in its primary figurations, imperial discourse can be found at odds with itself.

7. For the different modelings of Chandrapore, see *A Passage to India*, ed. Oliver Stallybrass (London: Penguin, 1985), 31–32. For the promise and the appeal see 148–49.

One could say that the paragraph on pp. 148–49 puts to work yet once more the much-used trope of India's femininity. The observation would be correct but worse than worthless. Forster's rendering of a figure too familiar to call for attentiveness is deeply eloquent in its immediacy but also in its evasiveness. "How can the mind take hold of such a country?" suggests at once exasperation with colonial nonsense, fortification of the mind against that nonsense and, at the same time, the mind's need for an incomprehensibility in which it seeks to find, yet fears to lose itself. India's hundred mouths are a multiplied invitation, a monstrous polyvalency, the embodiment of the voracious feminine and, at the same time, the multitude of forms which infinity requires to make itself manifest. The mouths speak through objects "ridiculous and august," inviting us to reflect on a separation which becomes no longer easy to maintain. Their "promise" was, historically, opulence and the seduction of the exotic. Their "appeal" can be India's vulnerability, a claim upon the exploitative conscience, proffered under the cloak of a contiguous naming that calls for the imperial burden to be shouldered. India is what is beheld in India, the terrain of the gaze, the discovery that changes as we grasp it, the unveiling of the knower in the knowing.

These recognitions, which do not merely traverse an imperial trope but open out its possibilities even as they encapsulate its history, give substance to Sara Suleri's caution against crude transpositions of gender into empire (*The Rhetoric of English India* [Chicago: University of Chicago Press, 1992] 15). At the same time we have to take account of Laura Brown's justified finding that the discursive intertwinings of the sexual, the commercial, and the imperial have yet to be adequately explored (*Ends of Empire* [Ithaca: Cornell University Press, 1993]). Essays such as this, cognizant of both warnings, must come to rest along a line which only tact and attentiveness is capable of drawing convincingly.

8. Ronald Inden, *Imagining India* (London: Basil Blackwell, 1991).

9. These characterizations are all offered by Inden. Inden stops short of calling them different names for India's femininity.

10. *Imagining India*, 4, 45–48.

11. Benita Parry, *Delusions and Discoveries: Studies on India in the British Imagination, 1880–1930.*

12. Patrick Brantlinger, *Rule of Darkness. British Literature and Imperialism 1830–1914* (Ithaca: Cornell University Press, 1988), 199–224.

13. Jenny Sharpe, *Allegories of Empire. The Figure of Woman in the Colonial Text* (Minneapolis: University of Minnesota Press, 1993), 96. See also 93–94.

14. Sara Suleri's consideration of this matter (*The Rhetoric of English India*, 75–110) is appropriately complex but does not deny that subjugation in the domestic order, limited dominance in the imperial one, and the valorizing of empire by the sacrifice of family life required to maintain it constitute a configuration too tightly interlocked to be easily pried open and one in which the opportunities for maneuvering are restricted.

Most forthright of all is Antoinette M. Burton in "The White Woman's Burden," *Western Women and Imperialism: Complicity and Resistance*, ed. Napur Chandur and Margaret Strobel (Bloomington: Indiana University Press, 1992), 151–52.

15. A. L. Basham, ed., *A Cultural History of India* (Oxford: Clarendon Press, 1975), 373–74. Basham describes the work as the first novel about India written in English. Mrs. Francis Sheridan's *The History of Nourjahad* (1767) can be regarded as belonging to another genre.

16. Raymond Schwab, *The Oriental Renaissance: Europe's Rediscovery of India and the East*, trans. Gene Patterson-Black and Victor Reinkins. Foreword by Edward W. Said (New York: Columbia University Press, 1988), 102.

17. Mill's derogatory comparison of Hinduism to Islam puts an end to the Jonesian interregnum, that brief period during which Hindu religion and culture could be sympathetically viewed. Before the interregnum, Islam was seen as India's official religion. After the interregnum, it became India's preferred religion and a Hinduism first merely colorful and then inconveniently invested with classical authority was increasingly perceived as chaotic and dangerous.

18. References in the text are to the fifth edition (London, 1811).

19. See in particular, C. A. Bayly's volume in the Cambridge History: *Indian Society and the Making of the British Empire* (Cambridge: Cambridge University Press, 1988).

Hamilton's novel was written in the middle of the Jonesian interregnum but one should not forget that only eleven years earlier, Beckford's *Vathek* had treated Hinduism as the infernal circumference of an Islam already circumferential to Christianity. The interregnum was a fragile affair, with Evangelical imaginings of India luridly at work during its span.

As has already been suggested, the quarter-century after 1785 provided a narrow time-frame of opportunity during which Hindu culture could be sympathetically examined. Hamilton may go further than anyone else in endorsing that culture and in urging its reinstatement. We can attribute the strength of her commitment not solely to a detached esteem for things Hindu, but also to a desire to idealize Hindu India as a site of the culturally feminine; but this explanation though plausible, is perplexed by her defense of caste hierarchies to which gender hierarchies can be deemed analogous.

The forces at work during the interregnum are examined in an important study by Rosanne Rocher: "British Orientalism in the Eighteenth Century: The Dialectics of Knowledge and Government," in *Orientalism and the Postcolonial Predicament: Perspectives on South Asia,* ed. Carol A. Breckenridge, and Peter van der Veer (Philadelphia: University of Pennsylvania Press, 1993), 215–49 and esp. 225–31 and 240–44.

20. Salman Rushdie, *Midnight's Children* (London: Jonathan Cape, 1981, Pan Books edn. 1982), 166.

21. References within the text to *The Wild Irish Girl* are to the 1986 Pandora Press (London) edition with an introduction by Brigid Brophy.

22. References to *The Missionary* are to the three-volume 1811 edition (London: Stockwell) reprinted in Scholar's Facsimiles (Delmar: 1981).

23. In *Revolution and the Form of the British Novel, 1790–1825: Intercepted Letters, Interrupted Seductions* (New York: Oxford University Press, 1994), Nicola J. Watson connects the decline of the epistolary novel and the rise of more authoritarian third-person narratives to the remodeling of British national identity during the Napoleonic period.

24. In one of the few articles of note on Owenson's ideology, Joseph W. Lew argues that *"The Wild Irish Girl, Ida of Athens* and *The Missionary,* different in technique as they may be, form an imaginative unit. In these three novels, Owenson explores the range of possible 'outcomes' to imperialism: from euphoric union to dysphoric mutual destruction." "Sydney Owenson and the Fate of Empire," *Keats-Shelley Journal* 39 (1990), 43–44.

The problem remains of why Ireland should be the site of the euphoric and India of the dysphoric construction. In so far as India is a surrogate for Ireland, *The Missionary* can be read as reassuringly distancing the uneasy possibility of a dysphoric text that might still be written about Ireland. Such a reading might contest a more immediate reading which puts it to us that a different site and a different cultural relationship are likely to lead to a different outcome. The pages that follow pursue the second reading, particularly because of its responsiveness both compliant and subversive, to a discourse being developed specifically in relation to India.

Yet as Katie Trumpener argues, the "central political tendency" of the national tale "shifts gradually from a celebratory nationalist politics, which both recognizes cultural distinctiveness and believes in the possibility of trans-cultural unions, towards another, more separatist politics, in which a history of cultural oppression makes rapprochement and reconciliation more and more inconceivable. The national tale's marriage plot and its national characters are deeply affected by these shifts." "National Character, Nationalist Plots: National Tale and Historical Novel in the Age of *Waverley,* 1806–1830" *ELH* 60 (1993), 703.

If we are witnessing an ideological shift rather than the composing of an "imaginative unit," the unfortunate outcome of *The Missionary* becomes a less distant intimation of what the future could hold in store for Ireland.

25. Campbell, Mary, *Lady Morgan: The Life and Times of Sydney Owenson* (London: Pandora Press, 1986), 108.

26. Hughes, A. M. D., *The Nascent Mind of Shelley* (Oxford: Clarendon Press, 1947), 90–2.

27. Echoes of *The Missionary* in Shelley's poetry were considered by
S. R. Swaminathan, "Possible Indian Influence on Shelley" *Keats-Shelley Memorial Bulletin* (1958), 30–45, in the context of the writings of William Jones
and of Moor's *Hindu Pantheon* (1801), a work which Shelley owned. John
Drew carries the study considerably further in his extensive examination of
the presence of *The Missionary* in *Prometheus Unbound: India and the Romantic
Imagination* (Delhi: Oxford University Press, 1987), 240–82.

There are iconographic similarities between Shelley's Asia,
Botticelli's Venus, and traditional depictions of Lakshmi which, taken together, might make Asia a statement of the Romantic movement toward a
world-humanism enlarged beyond Greco-Roman boundaries. If Asia is in
herself the marriage of East and West, and if she is that world conscience
which she seems ardently to be in her strongly-phrased encounter with
Demogorgon, she has to be distinguished from Luxima, who represents
only one side of that marriage and who represents it moreover in a hierarchical relationship for which Milton's pre-lapsarian Eve clearly provides the
model.

In *British Romantic Writers and the East. Anxieties of Empire* (Cambridge: Cambridge University Press, 1992), Nigel Leask finds "Shelley's radical scepticism regarding Hindu culture" to be "offset by his admiration for
Luxima, a character type to which he returned obsessively in his oriental poems" (102). It is possible that that scepticism is let into the revisionary version of Luxima which Asia might be taken to represent.

28. The Goan Inquisition, established in 1560, was not abolished until
1812, the year after the publication of Owenson's novel. Its special objects
of hatred were Portuguese who Indianised themselves excessively and those
converts who reverted to Hinduism or never really renounced it. For a
graphic account of the Inquisition's cruelties, see Paul William Roberts, *Empire of the Soul. Some Journeys in India* (Toronto: Stoddard, 1994), 85–89.

29. The tree had been the emblem of feminine prolixity and wantonness, a forest of excess (anticipating the jungle as a metaphor for India)
which, "strangled by its waste fertility" could also be regarded as a desert of
barrenness. Milton's ambivalent perception of the tree questioned the justice of these usages; but his highly specific location of it in "Malabar or Deccan" also linked India to the original shame and to a fallen femininity.
Owenson's recuperation of the tree as a temple of natural religion is not unusual; but her boldly enthusiastic presentation of the tree's self-sufficiency,
its power to create and sustain its own world of companionship, takes us
back powerfully to Adam's dialogue with his maker (*PL* VIII, 380–436) and
to the deficiency within him that led to the creation of Eve. The extent to
which the tree thus recuperated can be read as the emblem of a cultural
self-sufficiency that can only be marred by external efforts to reform it may
be a problem raised by the momentum of the text rather than by the intentions of its author. Nevertheless it is a possibility that once excited, need not
be dismissed.

30. *The Philosophy of History*, trans. J. A. Sibree, (New York: Dover, 1956),
140.

Hegel may well have been aware of *The Missionary* and could be alluding to it in this passage. Luxima might be India incarnate, a temptation
to be sternly rejected and the marriage of East and West even in its hierar-

chic modeling, a proposition to be resoundingly denounced. Hegel's overall objection however, extends to much more than the possible castigation of a literary heroine; it is to an Indic-Orientalist infatuation particularly noticeable in Germany which may place in danger the West's assumption of its proper place in world history.

31. The functional division between male and female in Hindu thought is between concept and implementation and not between *natura naturans* and *natura naturata*. The relationship between Prometheus and Asia seems to approximate this functional division as does the relationship between the Father and the Son in *Paradise Lost*.

32. *Prometheus Unbound*, 11, IV, 94. The allegedly Oriental origins of the Irish were used by Spenser as evidence of Ireland's otherness and by Byron (in the Dedicatory Epistle to *The Corsair*) as indicating that to write about India is also to write about Ireland.

Seven

JOSEPH LEW

The Necessary Orientalist? The Giaour *and Nineteenth-Century Imperialist Misogyny*

[Y]ou had formed a surmise of such horror as I have
hardly words to—Dear Miss Morland, consider the dreadful
nature of the suspicions you have entertained. What have you
been judging from? Remember the country and the age in which
we live. Remember that we are English: that we are Christians.

—Jane Austen

IN RECENT YEARS, *The Giaour* has resurfaced from relative critical oblivion. Its new critics find it uncanny. Scott Simpkins notes its "radical dislocation amid killings, dismemberment, vampirism, and chase scenes," and views its genre as "infidelic" and a "seductive outlet for lawless projects";[1] for Daniel Watkins, it is "disturbingly fragmented."[2] Stuart Curran writes that Byron "exploit[s]," and his "power lies in . . . arousing fantasies that prove distasteful even as they entrance."[3] Removed from their context, Curran's words take on a double-edgedness which is itself disturbingly perverse. Byron's "exploits" or adventures are also exploitative: one thinks not just of his reading public or the many women in his life, but also the fact that he got to see the Elgin Marbles as they were being shipped from Greece. These adventures cast a spell over us, but they also provide an "entrance" into another world, a sadistic or "distasteful" one of which Curran writes, "The role of women in this world is to be abused by masculine dominance."[4] One thinks of the undeterminable suffering of Leila, who (a narrator hints) may have still been alive when sewn into her sack and dropped into the sea: "methought / Some motion from the current caught / Bestirr'd it more."[5]

173

The 1980s saw the rebirth of scholarly interest in *The Giaour* and its companion Tales, focusing particularly on their form, orientalism, and heroines.[6] To date, however, no one has tried to bring these admittedly diverse and complex issues together. Why should not just Byron but his readers of 1813 have thought that it was so appropriate that this poem should be a fragment? What connects the form of this poem (which became longer in subsequent editions as additional fragments bubbled to the surface of Byron's mind) to its subject matter: not just the Orient in general but the body of a particular woman who has been sewn into a bag and made to disappear? This female orientalized body is, I will argue, crucial to the poem: so crucial that it will appear (or rather disappear) time and time again in Byron's Oriental poems.

I write 'orientalized' because I wish to include among these women Julia and Haidée, both "tainted and graced by an ancestral infusion of Moorish blood,"[7] as well as the Astarte of *Manfred*—whose name, as Alan Richardson first pointed out, derives from the tale of the brother-sister Guèbres embedded in Montesquieu's *Lettres persanes*.[8] And strictly speaking, many of the other women (including Leila and Myrrha) are not 'oriental' but Greek; however, they and Greece itself have been subjected to a process of 'orientalization' because of their political subjection to an Oriental master, whether it be the Turk or Sardanapalus. This 'orientalization' can even effect a Western (Italian) heroine such as Francesca, contaminating her and leading to her death by the mere fact of her residence at Corinth. What is striking about all of these women is the dreary monotony of their fates. Curran notes that "none of the early Oriental Tales ends in marriage";[9] Franklin points out that "all the heroines of the Oriental tales die except Gulnare and Kaled";[10] Mellor adds that both the Byronic hero of the Turkish Tales and Don Juan "leave in their wake a series of female corpses, from Medora and Kaled to Haidée."[11] One could add Myrrha, the Greek slave who commits suttee at the end of *Sardanapalus* to this list. The bodies of the few who don't die literally disappear (Gulbeyaz, Dudú, the child Leila), while *The Giaour*'s heroine both dies and disappears. At times, criticism kills those Byron allows to live; one scholar successively transforms Adah, the heroine of *Cain*, from a woman of "limited intelligence" into an animal (she becomes "bovine") and then into a "zombie," or reanimated corpse.[12]

This fate is the more striking when one compares it to the fates of Byron's more purely European heroines: in *Don Juan* alone, Donna Inez, Catherine the Great,[13] and the trio of women at Norman Abbey are very much alive when the poem halts. What I am suggesting is that, beginning with *The Giaour*, Byron helped to create an expectation

based not on genre but on geography: that Oriental women in literature would die—most often by violent means. Moreover, this generic
expectation was not merely unusual, it was new. Byron's immense European and American popularity encouraged (if it did not in some places
create) the obsession with beautiful, dead, and particularly Oriental
women which, from the 1820's, litter the stages, poems, fiction, and
movie screens of the West. I pose a different answer to Jerome Christensen's (and the *Christian Observer*'s) question, "by what devices is an
Oriental tale 'constituted for popularity'?"[14]

My strategy is derived from a hint of Jerome McGann, who asserts
that "a framework of interpretation was gradually formed from 1806
onwards in which Byron's readers were trained *not* to take his works as
textually autonomous structures. The works continually solicited the
reader to observe, and elaborate, various referential connections: political, biographical, historical."[15] In this essay, I attempt to examine a
few of the "various referential connections" which inform *The Giaour*,
including questions of gender, genre, and geography and the significance of the fragment form for Orientalist poetry.

GENDER, GENRE, GEOGRAPHY

The bodies of beautiful but dead Oriental women litter modern Orientalist writing. Travelogues, histories, and other types of writing contain at least one beautiful corpse *de rigeur*. Lady Mary Wortley Montagu related the finding of "the body of a young woman, naked, only
wrapp'd in a coarse sheet, with 2 wounds with a knife, one in her side
and another in her Breast. She was not yet quite cold, and so surpriz-
ingly Beautifull [sic] that there were very few men in Pera that did
not go to look upon her."[16] The last words of Montesquieu's *Lettres persanes* are literally the last words of that novel's most beautiful woman,
Roxane. In what would, if the chronology were not wrong, seem a
Sadian parody of Richardsonian "writing to the moment," Roxane describes the effect of the poison she has swallowed.

It may seem that the mutilating murder of women was part of a
genuine 'oriental' tradition as conveyed to England and France through
The Thousand and One Nights, first translated by Galland (between 1704
and 1708, translated into English by 1710).[17] The frame opens with a
Sasanian king, Shahzaman, who, upon finding his wife in the arms of
a cook, strikes them with his sword, then drags them by the feet to the
roof of the palace and throws them into a trench below. His brother,
Shahrayar, executes his wife for having had sex with a slave who has
been dressed as a woman (shades of *Don Juan*). Shahrayar determines
to allow no other woman to deceive him: he marries in the evening

and executes the woman the next day; this continues "until all the girls perished, their mothers mourned, and there arose a clamor among the fathers and mothers, who called the plague upon his head" (11).[18]

Although this is the way the frame begins, the narrative is about the manner in which Shahrazad, the frame's heroine, manages first to postpone her fate and then to convert the king, who spares her life and makes her his queen (426). At least some of the eighteenth-century Western writers inspired by Galland's translation got the point. Voltaire's *Le taureau blanc* opens with the threat of what seems inevitable death for its heroine; the *conte*'s interest hinges upon the undoing of that inevitability.[19] Beckford's *Vathek* is remarkable in the way it manages to avoid the spectacle of dead bodies: Vathek, Carathis, and Nouronihar live eternally albeit in torment in the subterranean halls of Eblis; the fifty boys supposedly sacrificed to the Giaour, we later learn, have been snatched from his jaws to live in eternal felicity in the clouds with Gulchenrouz; Carathis even cures the noblewomen she has had deliberately stung by scorpions, "for this good princess abhorred being indolent."[20] Only the unhappy citizens of Samarkand who attempt to rescue Vathek from the supposed inferno of his tower actually die, but their bodies are consumed before we have a chance to visualize them. Curran describes how the eponymous heroines of Hugh Mulligan's "The Virgins, An Asiatic Eclogue" (1788), "flee from the British despoiling their temple and comfort each other in their ruin."[21] Southey provides an important link between the increase of female corpses in poems of the 1790s and Byron's orientalized heroines.[22] In his oriental epics, Oneiza dies (*Thalaba the Destroyer*, 1801), as does "presumably"[23] Kailyal (*The Curse of Kehama*, 1810)—but so do many other of his heroines in a variety of geographic locales. Despite the popularity of Byron's tales, other poets would resist his example; Thomas Moore "manages to preempt" a Haidée/Lambro-like "clash of wills between father and daughter" in *Lalla Rookh*, "since the poet Feramorz turns out to be the bridegroom in disguise."[24]

Even more interesting is the fact that the genre we might most associate with the death of women—and particularly the death of Oriental women—opera, scrupulously avoided the very spectacle that, from the 1830s, drew the largest crowds. Eighteenth-century practitioners of opera often went out of their way to avoid the deaths of their female characters. Glück, for example, does not simply arrange to have Iphigeneia's life saved in both of the operas he wrote on this theme, he also has Eurydice returned to life *twice*. It was only in the late 1820s, with the productions of *Norma* and the various versions of *The Bride of Lammermoor* (including the still-popular Donizetti setting) that the craze for mad and dying heroines began.[25] And can it be coincidental that the dying heroines of what are sometimes called the 'ABC' of opera are all Oriental? (Aïda is Ethiopian—both 'eastern' and 'southern'; Butterfly is Japanese; Carmen is a gypsy, a term derived from popular beliefs that 'gypsies' had migrated from Egypt.)

Beginning with *The Giaour*, Byron transformed the Oriental tale in the West and became a precursor to the creators of the Aïdas, Butterflys, and Carmens. This is not to say that women—whether Oriental or not—had not died violently in early literary works. In the works of earlier writers it was a matter of genre. Heroines of tragedies died; heroines of comedies survived. "Mixed" genres might have mixed fates for female characters: in *The Monk*, Antonia is raped and then brutally stabbed to death by her own brother and the wicked Prioress is torn to pieces by the mob, but Agnes emerges from her living-death in the catacombs and the rather non-descript Virginia is rescued from the mob and marries the man Antonia had loved. But in Byron a female character's fate is determined by geography; Western heroines tend to survive, while orientalized women die or disappear.

This is also not to say that, before *The Giaour*, women were not portrayed as being generally mistreated. Every female character in *The Monk* is either physically or verbally abused: Leonella is baited mercilessly by Lorenzo and Raymond and the demoness Matilda is subjected to the Inquisition. In her novels, Burney invents ever more excruciating tortures for her heroines, even subtitling her last novel "Female Difficulties" (published in 1814, the year after *The Giaour* but completed by 1812).

From 1789 on, female characters seem to have begun to die more frequently (although I do not know of any statistical studies of this). In fact, as I will argue in a later section, there were important cultural forces favoring such an increase in fictional female suffering. Here I wish only to illustrate this increase. Mellor points out that "almost all Wordsworth's women are dead, either literally (as in the cases of Lucy, Margaret, and Martha Ray) or figuratively (they are mad, or allowed to live only vicariously through the words and experiences of male narrators)."[26] Coleridge published an untitled collection of sonnets which featured dead women by Charles Lamb and Southey.[27] Deserted or dying wives and mothers were staples of regency verse romances and "antagonistic male critics [of Byron] were wont to point out that such pathetic victimized heroines abounded in Regency periodicals catering specifically for female readers."[28]

FRAGMENTS POLITICAL AND POETICAL

A century before Byron's birth, although western Europeans confidently if wishfully predicted the collapse of the Ottoman Empire, the

Ottomans were capable of besieging and almost taking Vienna in 1683; about the same time, the first efforts of the East India Company under Josiah Child to create a land empire in India were ignominiously defeated by Aurungzebe. In the eighteenth century, however, the Ottoman Empire declined suddenly and the Mughal Empire actually collapsed. In the late seventeenth century, the Mughals exercised at least suzerainty over all of modern India except the very south and a small territory around Goa, as well as Pakistan, Bangladesh, parts of Afghanistan and Iran. By 1798, the map resembled a patchwork quilt, with more than half a dozen British territories widely separated by various Hindu and Muslim territories. Similarly, the Ottoman Empire, during Byron's sojourn there, presented a bewildering variety of emergent 'states.' Lord Eversley describes the condition of the empire at that time:

> In every part of [the Ottoman Empire in 1808–1812] turbulent and rebellious pashas were asserting independence. In Epirus the celebrated Ali Pasha of Janina had cast off allegiance, and was threatening to extend his rule over Greece, Thessaly, and the Ionian Islands. At Widdin on the Danube, at Bagdad on the Tigris, at Acre in Syria, the same process was being pursued by other pashas. In Egypt, Mehemet Ali had assumed the position of Governor and was creating an army and a navy independent of the Porte. In Arabia, the sect of Wahabees had attained a virtual independence, and had obtained possession of the holy cities. Other provinces, such as Serbia, Wallachia, Moldavia, and Greece, were seething with disaffection.[29]

Thus, by 1813, there was ample ground for Byron and his reader to make political and historical "referential connections" between a disintegrating empire and the fragment as verse form.

In its peculiar eighteenth-century development, the literary fragment, the idea of which "was apparently unknown" to the ancients, became defined as 'female': "The partial, the incomplete, the disruptive, the 'hysterical' is the feminine; the whole, the rounded-off, the ordered, the sane is the male."[30] The reader of the fragment adopts the 'male' perspective; 'he' must avoid the threat posed by that fragmentation. Levinson notes that the reader of romantic fragment poems must do a great deal of labor: 'he' must be "willing and able to generate contexts from internal textual signals as well as from accompanying authorial-editorial commentary. Second, the reader would have to work these contexts no less aggressively than he worked the primary or nuclear textual material." The fragment rewards the "reader who can revise the poem into a unity."[31] The fragment requires the masculine-coded reader to intervene in the poem which otherwise will "frustrate his claims to mastery."[32] Implicitly, the fragment poem 'wishes' to be violated by the reader.

Only after this development was well under way did the fragment begin to achieve a very specialized usage by Orientalists. After 1750, Europeans developed "the ability to decipher unknown alphabets"; with the arrival of Sir William Jones in Calcutta and the foundation of the Asiatick Society, western Europeans first became aware of the wealth of Hindu literature. Thus began what Raymond Schwab (after Quinet) calls "The Oriental Renaissance."[33] Some of this material was at first only available in fragments, but by the time of the huge success of Sacy's *Chrestomathie arabe* (three volumes, 1806), this process of collecting Oriental fragments became more than just customary or convenient.

Sacy's new or "special genre," the chrestomathy, is a collection of fragments, but also a "theory of fragments" significant for understanding *The Giaour*. The Orientalist, like Byron, is a mediator. He does "necessary" on-the-spot work (somehow even if he never leaves home); he "fishes some useful gems out of the distant Oriental deep." He is "*required* to *present* the Orient by a series of representative fragments, fragments republished, explicated, annotated, and surrounded with still more fragments."[34] The order and choice of fragments are "not chosen for their chronological development," but must "embody a certain Oriental naturalness, or typical inevitability."[35]

As I have argued elsewhere, *Orientalism* often seems to have one eye on 'scientific' Orientalists and the other on Western poets and novelists.[36] The resemblance between Said's description of Sacy's "theory of fragments" and Byron's practice in *The Giaour* is astounding. Leila, of course, is the "gem" which we would like to have "fished" from "the distant Oriental deep." When she is dropped into the sea, presumably still alive, she leaves behind "a speck of white / That *gemm'd* the tide" and promises to undergo a Tempest-like sea change among the "Genii of the deep" in "their *coral* caves" (II. 382–86, my emphases). The poem consists of fragments not presented chronologically, but the number of voices is meant to produce a "certain . . . naturalness," while our early knowledge of the drowning of Leila and the death of Hassan produces a sense of "inevitability." In his edition of the poems, McGann maps out the very complicated process by which Byron himself initiated the continuing process of 'representing' this Orient as a series of "fragments republished, explicated, annotated, and surrounded with still more fragments"[37]—a process to which, of course, I contribute. But I hope that the representation of fragments in this essay might be a way to "dis-orient" the power structures embedded in the fragmentary gesture.

Such, then, are some of the political and poetical ramifications of the fragment form for an orientalist poem. Important questions remain. What effect did this geopolitical situation have on the British men "on the spot"? Why, in the early nineteenth century, did the invasion of the East need to take the specific form of an 'abduction from the seraglio'? And what biographical and cultural imperatives caused Byron compulsively to rewrite this scenario in a dysphoric form, specifically producing the death or disappearance of the Orientalized heroine? I turn to these questions in the next segments.

INSTANT ARISTOCRATS

Instead of ingenious essays, elegant pieces of gallantry,
and witty satires . . . we have . . . the exploits of buccaneers,
freebooters, and savages . . . and the tragedies of a vulgar atrocity.
—*Edinburgh Review*

Byron's elevation to the peerage was through accident.[38] The intertwining of life, poetry, and 'myth' is only one early nineteenth-century example of 'self-fashioning,' if one of the most prominent ones, and needs to be read as a response to the role of 'accident.' But the accidents which made possible the myth of Lord Byron were not unheard of in his generation, and Napoleon was not alone in dreaming of glory in the East. Men—particularly northern English and Scottish men—could exercise talents unsuspected and achieve unprecedented power in the East. A man of the middling classes, if he had some connections, skill, and luck enough not to die of dysentery or other diseases, might become, like Byron's older contemporary Sir John Malcolm, ambassador to Persia or, even more ego-gratifying, the British Resident and *de facto* ruler of a nominally independent state in India. This section will chart the impact of this aspect of the expansion on British power on some typical British men—and on Byron himself.

Byron and his contemporaries grew up in a world in which it seemed, once again, as if a 'common' English *man* could make a difference. While the French Revolution could be seen as an irresistible, anonymous, feminine, and almost shapeless force finally brought under control by the man who was also its embodiment (Napoleon), it is remarkable how often single Englishmen could deflect and occasionally even halt that force. Nelson's victory over the French fleet at Aboukir Bay affected Napoleon's supply route, but did not in itself stop his Eastern plans. Rather, Sidney Smith's timely arrival at Acre and his directions of the fortification and defense of that stronghold prevented Napoleon from marching on undefended Constantinople. Toynbee imagined the encounters of British and French forces; his rhapsody is a double mirroring, that of a twentieth-century don imagining Egyptian fellahs and perhaps even the Mamelukes watching the battles between men who (Toynbee believes they must have believed) were literally from out of this world: "At the first onset, these Occidental 'Martians' carried all before them, and Oriental mankind was stunned. Egypt became a battleground on which superhuman Frenchmen and superhuman Englishmen fought one another."[39]

While Toynbee's account seems self-serving from our post-colonial perspective, it probably crystallized from events like one described by Colonel James Welsh. In *Military Reminiscences*, published in 1830, Welsh recalls an incident from February 1806, when several Indians wished Welsh and his company to cast a "niggah, or look" to cure a horse of a broken back:

> This was the only favour they had to ask, and a very simple one it was, certainly. It was, however, very difficult for us to persuade them that we by no means possesed that virtue. With such ideas of Europeans, and such they were in days of yore, pretty generally, what might we not have effected, with such simple people! and to what noble account might we not, as Christians, have turned such a confidence and estimation![40]

Welsh's account is interesting because, for his historically-minded readers it must have recalled "the king's touch": the belief that English monarchs could, by merely touching, cure scrofula—a practice only finally abandoned in the eighteenth century. For men of Byron's generation, and particularly those from the Border regions and Scotland proper, a career in 'the East' became *the* albeit physically hazardous way to short-circuit the hierarchical oligarchy that was Great Britain. Relatively impecunious, if financially well-connected men like Lord Clive, Sir William Jones, and Sir John Malcolm made fortunes and titles in India. The possibilities of 'the East' (despite frequent complaints of the climate) unleashed vast and unexpected amounts of energy: energy that was sometimes simultaneously military, commercial, sexual, linguistic, and poetic. In one unusual case, Pitt's niece, Hester Stanhope (whom Byron met in Athens), dressed as a man and for a time wielded political influence in Lebanon. For men, the effect could be even more drastic: in India they could have all the trappings of a lord, innumerable servants and a zenana; the most intelligent and most dedicated of them received a training in alternative 'classical' languages that put the public schools and even Oxford and Cambridge to shame. In the words of Francis G. Hutchins, "India's function was to turn Englishmen into 'instant aristocrats.' This passion for gentility was prevalent even among the middle and lower classes of Europeans in India, every one of whom considered himself a 'Sahib' or gentleman."[41] They could even write poetry—which they did in increasing quantity, if not necessarily with increasing talent. In one poem Leyden (d. 1811) describes the Battle of Asseye in terms reminiscent both of Toynbee's fantasy and the battle between the Giaour and the Pasha.[42]

Although Byron was never particularly interested in India, during his Eastern Tour he benefited greatly from increased British prestige, which at no time had been higher in the Ottoman Empire and its provinces. Ottoman attitudes towards Napoleon waffled after the Egyptian expedition, but matters were scarcely helped by attacks on the Ottoman Empire by France's ally, Russia. Byron wrote from Constantinople on July 4, 1810, "The Russians and Turks are at it, and the Sultan in person is soon to head the army. The Captain Pasha cuts off heads every day, and a Frenchman's ears; the last is a serious affair."[43] The quasi-independent provincial strongmen, particularly Ali Pasha of Albania and his son in the Morea had no desire to come under Napoleon's sway, and turned to the British. In fact, Ali Pasha "was particularly anxious to conciliate the English, for he wanted their co-operation against the French in the Ionian Islands." Albanians and Turks cooperated with Lord Elgin; Byron saw some of the Elgin Marbles being loaded.[44]

Byron "was immensely flattered by the attention."[45] By 1810, the half-century string of broadly "oriental" victories of small numbers of European and European-trained forces against numerically vastly superior "native" forces meant that the arrogance of an Elgin or the "flattered" state of Byron were beginning to be seen, by the British themselves, as typical of Europeans in the East. The "courting" (in both the political and the sexual senses of the term) of young Byron by Ali Pasha and his son, Veli, was strong wine indeed for the twenty-two-year-old peer who had taken his seat in the House of Lords but was "deeply mortified that he was forced . . . to go through the formalities of proving his legitimacy to the Chancellor before he could take his seat, something that rarely happened to a young lord,"[46] and who had no idea of the lionization that awaited him upon returning to England and publishing *Childe Harold*.

Men of Byron's generation performed the 'experiments' which enabled the worldwide expansion of the British Empire in the nineteenth century. These included experiments in education inspired by Macaulay's famous 'Minute'[47] and in the military training of 'natives' (Sepoys), and the beginnings of modern anthropology. They also had more immediate benefits: the military experience acquired by Richard Wellesley, the later Duke of Wellington in India (1798–1805), was useful developing strategies to defeat Napoleon in the Iberian Peninsula and then at Waterloo, as John Malcolm (d. 1833) asserted in a poem celebrating the Battle of Asseye.[48]

Accounts, often self-authored, of these men's lives began appearing with increasing frequency from the later eighteenth century. In them, the roles of "scientist," "capitalist" and "poet" which Marlon Ross links metaphorically[49] were physically embodied, as if Mary Shelley's characters of Walton, Clerval, and Victor Frankenstein were rolled up in one. Moreover, the lives of most of Byron's readers were 'invested,' in one way or another, in Britain's 'eastern adventures.' Two London-based E.I.C. Servants (Charles Lamb and Thomas Love Peacock) alone knew most of the canonical Romantics; one might also cite Medwin, Trelawney, James Mill, and Charles Dilke.

MISOGYNY, PUBLIC AND PRIVATE

The death . . . of a beautiful woman is, unquestionably, the most poetical topic in the world—and equally is it beyond doubt that the lips best suited for such topic are those of a bereaved lover.

—Edgar Allan Poe

Marlon Ross reminds us that feminist criticism has taught us "to question the *absence* of women as active subjects in any phenomenon, for that reputed absence may be an effect of the fear of their actual presence."[50] In this section I would like to apply this insight to Byron's life and to his culture. It is now generally accepted that wife-beaters can and too often do become wife-murderers. Here I would like to twist that argument, claiming that a writer who could verbally abuse real women as soundly as Byron did (and I will rely primarily on comments made in the correspondence after the separation) suffered from deeply-ingrained misogynistic feelings. Such a man could not only kill off fictional women, as Byron did so often before and after the separation. His veritable obsession with the deaths or disappearance of young orientalized women combined with the 'historical' status of the poems in which these women appear suggest a nostalgia for a place not Christian, not English, and not the present, when unwanted women could be disposed of with relative impunity.

That a man as promiscuous as Byron should harbor a deep dislike of and fear of women should no longer surprise us. Pop psychiatrists explain this syndrome regularly on daytime talk shows. What comparatively little we know of Byron's early years illustrates that he had reason for such fear. There was the torture of the various machines and shoes which were meant to straighten Byron's foot (and it is likely that, although such devices were prescribed by men, their day-to-day use was supervised by a woman, whether Byron's mother or a servant). Byron's mother alternately praised him extravagantly and subjected him to extreme verbal abuse. David Erdman sums up the alternating, unpredictable extremes of reactions by Mrs. Byron: "If he disobeyed the authority of 'Mrs. Byron *furiosa*,' she might slap him or she might fondle his pretty hair. If he did just what she told him to do, he might receive a smile or he might receive a bit of crockery in the side of his head."[51] When Byron was eleven, a servant named May Gray was dismissed for sexually abusing the boy; we can have no idea over how long a period of time this abuse occurred.

Abused children can grow up to become abusers themselves; even Augusta, who he claimed "handled him best," had to put up with his tantrums. Before and for some time after the separation, Byron seems to have had only one close female friend: Lady Melbourne, the mother-in-law of Lady Caroline Lamb and aunt of Lady Byron. Lady Melbourne was past sixty when she and Byron met. With this one exception, Byron seems to have had little time for older women.

After the separation proceedings began, Byron's wrath was not directed against Lady Byron's father, Sir Ralph Noel, but against the two elderly women involved: Lady Noel and Mrs. Clermont. Had it not been for Sir Ralph's acquiescence in and active support of the separation, it is likely that Lady Byron would have been persuaded or forced to return to her husband unless she had found other male protectors. Lady Byron had been and still was the legal property of a man; the current question was simply whether her husband or her father currently had the strongest rights. Byron directly addressed this issue, writing to his father-in-law that he "doubt[ed] the propriety of [Sir Ralph's] interference" (*BLJ* 5:21). The decision to prevent even a meeting after Lady Byron left on January 15, 1816 unpleasantly echoes the legal proverb "possession is nine-tenths of the law." The generality of Byron's references to Sir Ralph are respectful. Byron later wrote to Thomas Moore that he even felt "sorriest" for Sir Ralph (*BLJ* 5:36).

In striking contrast is Byron's attitude toward Lady Noel and Mrs. Clermont, two elderly women who on their own could legally have done little to keep Lord and Lady Byron separate. Byron's wrath fell immediately upon the least protected of the two: Mrs. Clermont, who was Lady Noel's maid. He immediately vilified her in "A Sketch." In correspondence, he refers to her as a "spy," an "Honest—Iago," and even hints at sexual perversion: "once Lady Noel's maid then her—God knows what" (*BLJ* 5:36; 5:56; 5:31). As long as there was some hope for a reconciliation, Byron treated Lady Noel with kid gloves. When hope was gone, however, his comments about her evince a settled rage. His favorite term for her was "bitch" (*BLJ* 5:231; 6:138; 7:179; 7:214) and he often expressed a wish for her death and damnation, but feared that "Malice will keep her alive, the bitch is but a bare Seventy and a mere Minor in longevity" (*BLJ* 6:138). Only when Byron took on her name after her death do such references cease. Strikingly, Lady Noel seems not to appear in any of Byron's satires: a point which suggests that his hatred was too intense to allow even the moderate distancing given to Mrs. Clermont and even Lady Byron.

Byron's skewering of his wife was more famous and sustained both in purely chronological occurrence and in its continuing impact. Besides the famous caricature as Donna Inez, there are at least twenty insulting references to Lady Byron in the index to the *Letters & Journals*. These include "fool," Byron's "worst enemy," "mathematical Medea," "a cold blooded animal," "fiend," the "White Devil," "that mathematical Blue Devil,"[52] and Byron's favorite, "moral Clytemnestra." Byron repeatedly blamed Annabella for the failure of their marriage because he believed himself "easily managed" (nine references). Of his future wife, he wrote to Lady Melbourne "it is her fault if she don't govern me properly— for never was anybody more easily managed" (*BLJ* 4:199 and 4:258), and he repeated that sentiment to Lady Melbourne (*BLJ* 4:218) and to Annabella Milbanke herself (*BLJ* 4:219). If he terrorized his wife late in her pregnancy and after Ada was born, it was Lady Byron's own fault. Marchand writes that Byron "confessed later to only one *really brutal* outburst against his wife, though there may have been more."[53]

Byron's favorite epithet for Annabella, "moral Clytemnestra," has more complex resonances than simply to the legendary Greek woman and her murdered husband. The earliest reference to the "moral Clytemnestra" occurs in the excerpts from Moore's manuscript journal printed by Marchand and is dated September 19, 1818. The first Canto of *Don Juan* was completed the very same day. Byron's somewhat odd denial, Donna Inez "is not meant for Clytemnestra—and if She were— would you protect the fiend?" ironically suggests that the identification should be made (*BLJ* 6:131). Juan's mother, Inez, is a caricature of Lady Byron; but as Peter Graham points out, Don Jóse [sic] resembles Captain Byron more than it does his poet son.[54] Juan, of course, resembles Byron both in his penchant for travel and his relative passivity in his early sexual experiences. Franklin suggests "The underlying suggestion is, of course, that hero and narrator are age-related aspects of the same man (the poet)."[55]

If this identity of Byron/Juan and Lady Byron/Inez is possible (and Byron himself makes the suggestion, not I), then in what Graham calls the "associative ingenuity"[56] of *Don Juan*'s world, Lady Byron becomes the mother of the poet. If, as a "moral Clytemnestra," she is responsible for Don Jóse's death in stanza 32, then Byron is no longer Agamemnon but Agamemnon's son. By painting himself as Clytemnestra/Inez's son, Byron may have engaged a fantasy that, like Orestes, he could return from his exile, kill Clytemnestra—and get away with it. (In Aeschylus,

Orestes was finally exonerated after an apparently 'hung jury' when Athene cast the deciding vote in his favor.) The Juan/Orestes parallel is even stronger, considering that both youths are sent away from home to allow their mothers' infidelity to continue. The Orestes/Byron relationship is inverse: Orestes is exiled because his mother has an 'incestuous' relationship with her husband's brother; Byron, because of his relationship with his half-sister.

The case of Byron, as I have sketched it out, may seem extreme, but it was neither individual nor isolated. Almost the whole of Byron's life was spent in a period of intense reaction—a reaction that was not just political but also gendered in the way that Susan Faludi labeled "backlash." Although Faludi concentrates on what she calls the "All-American Repeating Backlash," she asserts that "this pattern of women's hopes raised only to be dashed is peculiar neither to American history nor to modern times." She suggests the existence of "different kinds of backlashes against women's mostly tiny gains—or against simply the perception that women were in the ascendancy."[57] The entire generation—on both sides of the English Channel—that lived through the Revolutionary and Napoleonic era was shaped by such a backlash. The most prominent victim of this fear of women in the ascendancy was, of course, Marie Antoinette. Although I have seen no comparisons of the queen to Clytemnestra, she was called the "new Agrippina"—whom Suetonius accused both of incest (with her son, Nero, but also with her uncle, Claudius) and of murdering her husband, Claudius—and compared to Messalina, Brunhilde, Fredegond, and Catherine de Medici.[58] Women played important roles not only in the course of the Revolution (the March on Versailles, the assassination of Marat), but in its iconography as well. Franklin notes that "the Napoleonic Civil Code of 1804 actually rescinded the rights of woman gained in the Revolution, reinstituting unequal standards of divorce, and forbidding women to act as witnesses, to plead in court in their own name, or to own property in their own right."[59] In England, the well-known case of the posthumous vilification of Mary Wollstonecraft (whom Horace Walpole once called a "hyena in petticoats") illustrates my point. Even a prominent conservative like Hannah More could be attacked from the right as a "tyrant" and as fomenting revolution.[60]

Despite the efforts of William Wilberforce, Hannah More, and Elizabeth Hamilton to reform the morals of aristocrats, throughout the period of the Regency the upper crust, perhaps following the scandalous lead of the Prince of Wales, remained largely untouched by proselytization efforts. The misdeeds of female aristocrats were public and even self-publicized (Caroline Lamb in *Glenarvon*). In circles like these,

Mansfield Park's Mary Crawford would not have been alone in viewing "the detection, not the offence" of Maria Rushworth's adultery the true matter of "reprobation."[61]

Questions of morality aside, as mistresses, wives, and hostesses, titled women exercised a certain amount of power in visible and obviously *ancien régime* ways. *The Giaour* was "composed during the months of Byron's liaison with Lady Oxford, whose political influence was substantial, and immediately after that liaison."[62] This coterie of powerful women Byron would label "the Gynocrasy": women "who obtain a modicum of political influence through their participation" in the exchange of women between men.[63]

Paradoxically, at this same time, Britain prided itself on its treatment of women, deciding even that the status of women directly indicated the quality of a civilization; foreigners agreed that "in no country do women possess more rational liberty . . . than in England."[64] It is hard to imagine a politician becoming as rhapsodic about the plight of an Imelda Marcos as Burke did about Marie Antoinette or Sheridan about the Begums. But Byron's contemporaries often used the (alleged) mistreatment of women as an excuse to meddle in the internal affairs of other nations. Marie Antoinette was the sister of both Joseph and Leopold, the Austrian monarchs, and the Austrian declaration of war against Revolutionary France was justified in part as vengeance for outrages perpetrated against the French queen.

Later, Britain's decision to abandon the principles of the Holy Alliance and to intervene in the Greek War of Independence was justified by personifying Greece as a woman caught between two physically abusive "suitors," as in the 1828 R. Seymour print Franklin reproduces, "Mrs. Greece and Her Rough Lovers." The Ottoman Empire is openly abusive; he has a noose around Mrs. Greece's neck and brandishes a scimitar. Russia (Tsar Nicholas) only seems more civilized, for he holds the "imperial knout" behind his back.[65] In the background we see a thinner woman fleeing from another bescimitared male. To the right, three British men (including what seems to be a 'tar' and John Bull himself) observe the scene and seem to be contemplating action. This print appeared at least one year after Delacroix painted his famous "La Grèce expirant sur les ruines de Missolonghi"; the differences are informative. Delacroix's Grèce is young, beautiful. Her breasts are almost exposed, and her arms are open. She faces away from the black man in the background, toward the (presumably) white male viewer. It would be difficult to realize that she is "expiring" were it not for the title. The white man (presumably Byron) who has come to help her is crushed beneath a tombstone-like slab; only his hand protrudes—an odd reminiscence of Hassan's severed hand. R. Seymour's Mrs. Greece, in contrast, is much older, short, and quite fat—not at all like Leila, whom Watkins describes as "the woman every man dreams of,"[66] and who appears with her breasts revealed for the white male eye in the print published by Murray and reproduced in the McGann edition.

There is one other area where the brutality against Oriental women aroused widespread concern in Britain and even justified colonial intervention: the supposedly voluntary immolation of Brahmins' wives on their husbands' funeral pyres. Drawing on Gayatri Spivak, Eric Meyer points out the intellectual relevance of drawing parallels between *The Giaour* and suttee.[67] In what remains of this section, I would like to argue that making such a connection is not just intellectually valuable, but historically justified as well. For from Byron's return from his tour in 1811, the question of suttee received increasing amounts of attention from the British and Anglo-Indian press as well as from the British Parliament, especially by those who wished revisions in the charter of the East India Company, which was to expire in 1813. Important emendations concerned the support of Christian missionaries and the exertion of unspecified kinds of "influence" to prevent this practice and/or convert the Hindus. And while I will draw on slightly later documents as well, the particular campaign relevant to *The Giaour* culminated in a speech by William Wilberforce to the House of Commons in June 1813.

Although suttee had long fascinated men from outside the subcontinent, British obsession with the practice stems from the 1760s. Zephaniah Holwell, for example, described the "pitiable dread, tremor, and reluctance, that strongly spoke repentance for their declared resolution," but also wrote of his own "commisseration [sic], awe and reverence" of some *"women in the bloom of youth, and beauty"* who underwent this death with "astonishing fortitude."[68] Witnesses drew attention to the noise which accompanied the immolation: "It was impossible to have heard the woman had she groaned, or even cried aloud, on account of the mad noise of the people."[69] After the 1790s (and this coincides with not just the rise of Evangelicalism in England but with the appointment of men such as Sir John Shore to responsible positions in the East India Company and the increasing but not strictly legal presence of missionaries in India), such accounts reached an increasingly numerous audience in England. In 1810, William Ward described many incidents of suttee in *History, Literature, and Mythology of the Hindoos,* often with epithets such as "most shocking and atrocious murder."[70] Missionaries began keeping statistics, which were published in 1811 by Claudius Buchanan in *Christian Researches in India*. In a speech delivered to the House of Commons on June 22, 1813 (only three weeks after Byron's last speech in the House of Lords), William Wilberforce quoted statistics of 275 widow-burnings within 30 miles of Calcutta for 1803, and summarized one eyewitness account: "To have seen savage wolves thus tearing a human body limb from limb, would have been shocking; but to see relations and neighbours do this to one with whom they had familiarly conversed not an hour before, and to do it with an air of levity, was almost too much for me to bear."[71] It is to be suspected that Wilberforce's informant allowed his rhetoric to carry him away, for I have seen no other accounts where suttee was preceded by (accompanied by?) dismemberment.

Such accounts were bound to cause a clamor for intervention. In 1789, M. H. Brooks requested approval from Governor-general Cornwallis to prevent a widow-burning; Cornwallis refused permission for Brooks to act officially, but suggested Brooks use his "influence."[72] In the early 1800s, interventions increased. In 1830, J. Peggs published or reprinted statistics, descriptions of suttee, a "pathetic" poem called "The Infant Hindoo Mourner." His *Cries of Agony* not only called for further British intervention, but was greeted by reviewers with similar calls: "we hope that, in behalf of the widows in India, he will not plead in vain"; "We beseech our readers . . . to let no opportunity be neglected of advancing his benevolent aim."[73]

This interest in the sufferings of these young women could have sadistic overtones, as the image of white males dashing around the environs of Calcutta in search of burning widows suggests. In a poem by "Ellen" called "A Voice from India; or The Horrors of a Suttee,"[74] "Ellen" draws attention to the body of the woman, (seeming to forget that often-reported noise of the crowd): "See how she writhes! hark to her screams, / As now the lurid flames enfold her!" She is surrounded by unfeeling relatives, whose very unfeelingness allows or perhaps produces her suffering: "Her kindred stand with hearts of stone, / Cased by the demon Superstition." Oddly enough, it is the very capacity of "Ye British matrons, husbands, sires," to feel for the widow which promises to put a stop to such events—and only because the apostrophized British (and the women listed are outnumbered by men) can empathize with the widow because they, too, can feel (in a dim way) her pain: they have "souls with soft compassion glowing." (Presumably, maids would need to be protected, or it might be dangerous for them to "glow" in any way.) And of course, one would have to *want* to read a poem called "The Horrors of a Suttee" (and perhaps pay for it as well) before one could, unlike the relatives, first "heave a sigh at her condition," and then "haste to quench the horrid fires," presumably by military-backed intervention.

A COMPULSION TO KIDNAP

I have entrusted to you the most valuable thing that I have in the world.
—Usbek to the First Black Eunuch[75]

As my reference to Mozart at the end of section two made clear, 'abduction from the seraglio' plots were not new, but it is more likely that Byron knew Elizabeth Inchbald's 1784 farce on this theme, *A Mogul's Tale*, than Mozart's opera. In Inchbald as in Mozart, however, the woman who must be gotten out of the seraglio is a Western European. Inchbald's *Gilligan's Island* atmosphere has the heroine take a hot-air balloon pleasure trip in England, then blow off-course to land inside the seraglio in Delhi. These eighteenth-century farces develop from the genre G. A. Starr calls "Escape from Barbary."[76] Early "escape" narratives (which are not gender-specific) focus on the power of the Orient and the necessity of providential intervention to make escape possible. In short, Western Europe is besieged, and can scarcely protect its own. It is hard to imagine (and I am not aware of) any seventeenth-century farces on this theme; farcical treatments begin to appear when the threat is clearly receding into the past.

Byron's version of this plot, as typified in *The Giaour*, functions as a kind of fantasy-revenge for centuries of Ottoman (and other Islamic) dominance. To understand the dynamics of this situation, we must first get an overview of Ottoman conceptions of space (particularly of "harem") and Western European "misunderstandings" of that space.

Although Western societies have characteristically shared a predominantly hierarchical or vertical structure, perceptive Western writers have long been aware that Eastern, and particularly Islamic or Islamic-dominated societies, have been marked less by a vertical structure than by one which can best be mapped out by concentric circles. Traditional Muslim states have attempted to prevent the development of powerful 'families' with regional powerbases (typical of feudal Western Europe) by denying the principle of private and inheritable property, especially in land. In the Ottoman Empire (the Muslim state pertinent to this study), *all* subjects of the Empire were theoretically the Sultan's slaves; any property they amassed during their lifetimes theoretically, at least, reverted to the Sultan at their deaths (a theory which led to judicial abuses by unscrupulous Sultans or their subordinates who wished to 're'- acquire the property of a wealthy subject). In Ottoman society, since all subjects (male and female) were 'slaves' of the Sultan, all were roughly equal. A rich and powerful vizier, for example, might be bowstrung, his property confiscated, and his relatives left in poverty. The difference between a grand vizier or provincial military governor or 'pasha' and his slaves and slave-concubines was hence (in theory if not always in practice) purely nominal. 'Birth' in the Western sense scarcely mattered. A man— or a woman—could rise from abjectness to incredible heights in this society where 'upward mobility' had connotations and legal-political realities entirely different from the West. What mattered in the Ottoman Empire was not the ability to get to the top of the ladder or 'wheel' of Fortune, but the ability to safeguard the "inner sanctum," which is the etymological meaning of the term "harem." Although the west has conventionally naturalized just one narrow meaning of the Arabic root "h-r-m" as a group of women (or occasionally men) kept for the sexual pleasures of a dominant male, the term "harem" is, in Leslie P. Pierce's definition:

> a sanctuary or a sacred precinct. By implication, it is a space to which general access is forbidden or controlled and in which the presence of certain individuals or certain modes of behavior are forbidden. That the private quarters in a domestic residence and by extension its female residents are also referred to as a 'harem' comes from the Islamic practice of restricting access to these quarters, specifically access by males beyond a particular degree of consanguinity with the resident females. The word *harem* is a term of respect, redolent of religious purity and honour, and evocative of the requisite obeisance. It is gender-specific only in its reference to the women of a family. . . . The most sacred or exalted places in the sixteenth-century Ottoman world were harems. The holy cities of Mecca and Medina and their environs were, and remain, the two most revered harems in Islam.[77]

Pierce notes a fifteenth-century Anatolian text which links the Akkoyunlu dynasty's "claim to 'distinguished origin' " to "the fact that 'the hand of a conqueror never touched their spouses,' "[78] and Westerners soon became aware that Turks linked sovereignty with the ability to protect the sacred center, as personified by women. From Gibbon, Byron would have known of the taunt allegedly made by Bayezid I to Tamerlane: "If I fly from thy arms. . . . may *my* wives be thrice divorced from my bed: but if thou hast not courage to meet me in the field, mayest thou again receive *thy* wives after they have thrice endured the embraces of a stranger."[79] When the Ottomans stopped marrying (with remarkably rare exceptions), Europeans mistakenly believed it to be a response to the 'poetic justice' meted upon Bayezid I by Tamerlane: "the sultans did not wish to repeat the agonizing and ignominious experience of Bayezid I," who "suffered the insult of having to watch one of his wives, the Serbian Maria, forced to perform menial tasks. This unendurable shame is supposed to have contributed to the sultan's suicide in captivity."[80] The tale of the humiliated Sultan was immensely popular in the West, being recounted in histories of the Ottoman Empire (several of which Byron owned) as well as on the British and French stage.

In short, to penetrate the seraglio is to hurt the enemy where he is most vulnerable; to steal one of his women is to take from him what is "most valuable in the world." It is also, as I have hinted, to detach one of those lush and inviting provinces from the grasp of what was becoming known as the "old" or the "sick" man of Europe. Hence, the West could turn even its misunderstandings to ideological advantage. The nominally Christian but increasingly secular Western empires, in reducing or fetishizing "harem" as merely a collection of female bodies, facilitated the symbolic representation of the geographically scattered process of empire building. What endangered polities such as the Ottoman Empire (or later, Siam and China) might experience as dismemberment could be seen, through Western eyes, as "liberation," a freeing from "captivity."

LEILA'S DILEMMA

Yet did he but what I had done
Had she been false to more than one.

—*The Giaour*, 1062–63

Leila, the slave-concubine and not the wife of Hassan, has often, and wrongfully, been accused of adultery. Repeatedly, she has been the victim of rape—sexual, but also in the older sense of *raptus*, which includes the likelihood that she was carried away as a result of war—just as is her namesake in *Don Juan*.

Eric Meyer points out that, in Delacroix's treatment of *The Giaour*, the "battle between Hassan and the Giaour as world-historical agents of East and West . . . is generally seen . . . as the central narrative image."[81] While I agree generally, I would like to change the focus to discuss the absence of Leila. She cannot be present in the painting for she is already dead, and her death provides the pretext for the 'world-historical' battle.

The Giaour, it seems to me, fights Hassan not just because Hassan has killed Leila (which Hassan has the legal right to do), but because Hassan has killed Leila *before the Giaour has had the chance to do so himself.* It has never been entirely clear to me why the Giaour manages to have his sexual tryst with Leila and escapes, leaving her behind. In leaving Leila behind, the Giaour leaves her in a position where her death is exceedingly probable, if not quite inevitable. For, as Franklin points out, even though the Giaour claims to possess Leila's affections, Hassan possesses her "physical being."[82] If Hassan had not murdered her, he may decide to enjoy her despite his suspicions—as Seyd in *The Corsair* threatens Gulnare. In other words, if Hassan had decided to rape Leila (thus causing her to be "false to more than one"), the Giaour by his own admission would have been 'forced' to kill her himself. By this account, his strange delay in coming to Leila's rescue becomes psychologically motivated, as does the excessiveness of the numerous wounds he inflicts upon Hassan: not merely cutting off Hassan's hand and probably inflicting a severe head injury when he "cleft" Hassan's turban "in twain," but also stabbing him in the breast "unnumber'd" times (665–67). Projecting his own murderous desire upon his oriental double,[83] he can then not simply kill, but wantonly mutilate that externalized desire.

Attempting to increase the aura of authenticity and historicity of *The Giaour*, Byron gave two accounts of his having "witnessed" the events which inspired the tale. The differences between these accounts and *The Giaour* are instructive for tracing the development of the fantasy. In both accounts the girl is rescued on the condition of leaving Athens, although in the (later) Medwin account she dies of a fever in a few days. Meyer underlines the concealed reference to suttee: "How eminently gratifying to the imperial ego to save the submissive colonial 'girl' from the barbarians only to have her *voluntarily immolate herself* for sheer love of her dashing white savior!"[84] I distrust this account published in the year of Byron's death, and not simply because Byron could not have refuted it if he wanted to. For, in 1821, he had published an account of a Greek "girl" who rejects freedom in order voluntarily to commit suttee on the pyre of her extremely Byronic imperial master, Sardanapalus.

HAIDÉE'S CHILDREN

The bleeding flower and blasted fruit of love.

—*Don Juan*, V.70

Ruth Perry has argued that historians and historically-minded literary scholars alike must be careful about the evidentiary uses they make of literary documents.[85] It would be absurd to assert that many readers of Defoe were interested in finding out how others dealt with the familiar experience of shipwreck or with inadvertent marriage to a sibling. Clearly, Defoe's readers were not looking for 'reflections' of their daily lives, but in the reactions of ordinary people to extraordinary circumstances. Perry argues that later eighteenth-century narratives featuring the mysterious 'call of the blood' reflected not an increased sense of kinship ties, but rather anxiety about the weakening of such ties.

Perry's insights are useful in considering British reactions to Muslim 'atrocities' against women and the institutionalization of such atrocities in Western literature. Byron's traveling companion, Hobhouse, recounts a 'typical' example of such brutality in *A Journey through Albania* (1813),[86] which Hobhouse says is "very well-known, and . . . secretly talked of at Ioannina." According to Hobhouse's account, the wife of Monctar Pasha complains to Ali Pasha that her husband "paid . . . attention to . . . other women." She wrote down "quite at random, it is said . . . the names of fifteen of the most beautiful women . . . of Ioannina. The same night they were all seized . . . , carried in boats on the lake, and after being tied up in sacks, were thrown into the water" (111). Hobhouse asserts that this "is a trait of Turkish ferocity, rather than of a savage disposition peculiar to Ali." As proof, he provides an account (which I have not seen elsewhere) that the Grand Vizier "disposed of many of Sultan Mustapha's harem by the same death, in order to decrease the expenses of the seraglio, or, as some say, to punish them for supposed court intrigues" (112).

Clearly, the Albanians are fascinated and "secretly" discuss such accounts because they are atypical. But as the century progressed, readers and interlocutors of Western travelers came not simply to expect but to demand tales of atrocity and of amorous intrigue with secluded women. Norman Daniel describes how writers were 'forced' to fabricate such adventures or sheepishly admit they had had no such experiences themselves.[87]

The Byronic/Imperial obsession I have briefly attempted to sketch here is, of course, part of a larger cultural phenomenon which includes the numerous suffering and dying white women of nineteenth-century literature and the continuing fascination with Jack the Ripper and his numerous progeny, fictional or otherwise.

In Byron's oeuvre (and for many of that oeuvre's readers), I believe, the death and/or disappearance of orientalized females performs particular psychic services. I have already discussed the geo-political connotations of 'penetration of the seraglio' plots. Here, I would like to speculate upon the 'individual' functions of the fantasy. Although accurate knowledge to the contrary was readily available, it was still widely believed in Western Europe that Muhammed enjoined that women had no souls.[88] To abuse a woman (under this moral system) was little different from popular British sports such as foxhunting, bear-baiting, or cockfighting, let alone such amusements as torturing cats. Contingent upon this belief, it seemed, were such Muslim practices as polygamy (a Muslim male might have up to four wives and as many concubines as he could afford) and the ease with which divorce might be attained. We might expect easy divorce to appeal to British men (and women) for whom divorce could only be obtained by Act of Parliament; interestingly, however, divorce rarely occurs in Orientalist narratives. British and Frenchmen alike prefer having their Muslim counterparts give 'the sack' to unwanted sexual partners in the literal, not figurative manner.

As Edward Said has taught us, traveling to the Orient involves not just spatial but also temporal displacement. To travel to the East was to enter a past realm, one in which a Rackrent or a Rochester could still totally seclude a disobedient wife or a General Tilney might dispose of one by poison. Many of Byron's contemporaries did, in fact, take advantage of such 'time-travel.' Servants and soldiers of the East India Company did establish zenanas (the term used in Bengal) of local women. And although I have not seen evidence of brutality toward these women (they were, after all, secluded), the mistreatment of 'native' servants by their British employers is well-documented.[89]

How much simpler Byron's life would have been if, as he once wrote, he "might and should have become a Pasha" by the age of 26? (*BLJ* 3.246). *Glenarvon* would not have been written, for Lady Caroline Lamb would have been disposed of by her husband. Byron's separation from his wife would have been easily preventable. And yet, anxieties would still remain. Even the 'good' orientalized woman must somehow be encased in immaturity, lest she become a Roxana, who deceives Usbek and then commits suicide; a Gulnare or a Clytemnestra, who murders her sexual master; or a Sowdanesse or Medea who murders her own children in the pursuit of power or of revenge.

Ironically, some at least of Haidée's children were doing quite well during Byron's life. In the eighteenth century, East India Company servants commonly "liked . . . *Nautch* [Indian dancing] girls, and otherwise borrowed whatever Hindu and Muslim customs they fancied."[90] 'Half-caste' need not be hidden away: Zoffany painted the Palmer family, an Englishman with his native wife and children, and a relative of Jane Austen's was the guardian for what may have been Warren Hasting's illegitimate, Anglo-Indian child.[91] Lord Liverpool, nominal prime minister from the assassination of Spencer Perceval until after Byron's death, was himself the grandson of an Indian woman, although historians rarely mention this fact.

In this context, Byron's famous portrait in Albanian dress is itself simultaneously deliberately anachronistic or 'nostalgic' and an affront to what would become the racial morality of the Victorian Empire. Nostalgic in its self-conscious references to other notorious portraits of English aristocrats and empire-builders 'going native' to greater or lesser extent: Lady Mary Wortley Montagu of course, but also Lady Impey supervising her Indian household and numerous other Levantine and Indian merchants and soldiers. This tradition would continue with 'Chinese' Gordon,[92] Lady Hester Stanhope cross-dressing in Lebanon, Sir Richard Burton (who shocked the Victorians with his sexually explicit translations) and Lawrence of Arabia. An affront, because it played upon the growing sense of the specifically sexual dangers of even Oriental dress: in *Cosi fan tutte*, which had its London debut in 1811, Dorabella and Fiordiligi fall in love with each other's fiancés when they appear in Albanian drag.

For proto- and actual Victorians, eager to convince themselves of some innate superiority, of the 'white man's burden' which they invented for themselves, "distance" of all kinds must be maintained, even "cultivated" and "magnified":

> Hence the abhorrence of Europeans who 'went native', hence in the British empire the psychological importance of private rituals such as the afternoon tea, and customs of dress, manner, and language, and of public rituals displaying the splendor of British might. Social distance between the rulers and the ruled was cultivated precisely for fear that if it were allowed to break down, to the point of admixture, the superiority of the rulers would crumble and vanish; for in essence it was not built on any true and lasting difference such as could withstand the effects of proximity.[93]

Disraeli, who began publishing only a few years after Byron's death and who would become one of Victoria's favorite prime ministers, could, despite his own obvious lack of racial purity, claim that the British Empire had been created by "an unmixed race of first-rate organization."[94] Oddly enough, Celts predominated in the Crown forces in 1815.[95] Far from being a "hiatus between the irresistible waves of liberal reform," Bayly argues, the Scots and Irish were interested in establishing "colonial despotisms . . . characterised by . . . aristocratic military government . . . which emphasised hierarchy and racial subordination."[96]

Miscegenation became a problem precisely when the British abandoned the rather clear-headed thinking of Warren Hastings and many of his contemporaries, who realized that the British had conquered and ruled parts of India because of temporary technological and organizational advantages, who were able to see themselves as just one more in a long line of foreign adventurers which included Persians and Afghans, and indeed the Mughal dynasty itself. Only a self-righteous religiosity as twisted as that of Byron's mother could claim "God made the Whites, God made the Blacks [i.e., Indians], but the Devil made the Half-Caste,"[97] when it was perfectly obvious that white men such as Byron shared some of "the Devil's" responsibility.

The impossibility of Haidée's child being born prophetically 'solves' certain problems of the nineteenth-century British Empire. People of "mixed breeds," according to the new racial philosophy, were odd and anomalous conglomerations: "they belong to no *single* race, but are a kind of monster."[98]

The stillbirth of Juan and Haidée's child, the half-caste, the monster, is the 'unwriting' of *Frankenstein*. Read 'against' *Frankenstein*, the end of Juan's Greek Idyll becomes strangely overdetermined: Juan is a Victor who remains blissfully unaware of the consequences of his creative activities; he is not responsible for those consequences because he is removed from the scene against his will; and in his absence, those consequences are aborted anyway. Mary Shelley's creature (as I point out elsewhere, himself iconographically similar to the millions of new British subjects in India),[99] of course returns to wreak vengeance upon his irresponsible progenitor, but the Byronic imperialists are wiser. The monsters they and the Devil (pro)create are fatally flawed, are a kind of monster whose "every cell is the theater of a civil war"[100]—a metaphor which is echoed even in post-independence description of fictional Anglo-Indians.[101] This, then, is the Byronic rationale for Stuart Curran's observation that, even in Byron's Oriental Bowers of Bliss, "no children are ever born," let alone reared.[102] Their bodies are quite literally the battlefields into which those Devils their fathers have turned the lush and feminine Orient. Children of unbridled economic and sexual lust, they would perhaps too literally and truly mirror the image of their creators. It is better—for their fathers—that they never be born. As Byron teaches us, in literature, at least, that can be arranged.

NOTES

1. Scott Simpkins, " 'The Giaour': The Infidelity of the Romantic Fragment," *Approaches to Teaching Byron's Poetry*, Frederick W. Shiltone (New York: Modern Language Association of America, 1991), 89–93.

2. Daniel P. Watkins, *Social Relations in Byron's Eastern Tales* (Rutherford: Fairleigh Dickinson University Press, 1987), 35.

3. Stuart Curran, *Poetic Form and British Romanticism* (New York: Oxford University Press, 1986), 143–44.

4. Curran, *Poetic Form*, 143.

5. All quotes from *The Giaour* are from George Gordon Lord Byron, *The Complete Poetical Works*, ed. Jerome McGann (Oxford: Clarendon Press, 1981), vol. 3.

6. Besides works cited elsewhere in this paper, the reader may wish to consult the following: For fragments, David Seed, " 'Disjointed Fragments': Concealment and Revelation in 'The Giaour,' " *The Byron Journal* 18 (1990), 13–27. Ian Haywood, *The Making of History: A Study of the Literary Forgeries of James Macpherson and Thomas Chatterton in Relation to Eighteenth-Century Ideas of History and Fiction* (Rutherford: Fairleigh Dickinson University Press, 1986), investigates relationships between 'authenticity' and the famous literary hoaxes of the 1760s, many of which were fragmented. For Orientalism, see two important related articles by Marilyn Butler, "The Orientalism of

Byron's 'Giaour,' " in *Byron and the Limits of Fiction*, Bernard Beatty and Vincent Newey (Liverpool: Liverpool University Press, 1988), 78–96, and "Byron and the Empire in the East," in *Byron: Augustan and Romantic*, Andrew Rutherford (New York: St. Martin's Press, 1990), 63–81. On heroines, see Malcolm Kelsall, "Byron and the Romantic Heroine," in *Byron: Augustan and Romantic*, 52–63.

7. Peter W. Graham, *'Don Juan' and Regency England* (Charlottesville: University Press of Virginia, 1990), 7.

8. Alan Richardson, "Astarte: Byron's *Manfred* and Montesquieu's *Lettres persanes*," *Keats-Shelley Journal*, 10 (1991), 18–22.

9. Stuart Curran, *Poetic Form*, 143.

10. Caroline Franklin, *Byron's Heroines* (Oxford: Clarendon Press, 1992), 35.

11. Anne K. Mellor, *Romanticism and Gender* (New York: Routledge, 1992), 26.

12. Bernard Blackstone, *Byron: A Survey* (Bristol: Longman, 1975), 249. Franklin also draws attention to this in *Byron's Heroines*, 233.

13. Catherine II, it must be remembered, was a German princess who gained power when her Russian husband, Peter III, was deposed. She died in 1796, but is left very much alive in the poem.

14. Jerome Christensen, *Lord Byron's Strength* (Baltimore: Johns Hopkins University Press, 1993), 96.

15. Jerome J. McGann, "Lord Byron and 'The Truth in Masquerade,' " in *Rereading Byron: Essays Selected from Hofstra University's Byron Bicentennial Conference*, Alice Levine and Robert N. Keane (New York: Garland, 1988), 1–19.

16. Lady Mary Wortley Montagu, *The Complete Letters of Lady Mary Wortley Montagu* (Oxford: Clarendon Press, 1965), vol. i, 407. Byron owned a copy of Montagu's letters: A. R. Kidwai, "A Bibliography of Byron's Oriental Reading," *Notes and Queries*, 39 (237) (1992), 167–68.

17. Curran refers to the 1812 publication of a Weber's three-volume *Tales of the East* "brought the Arabian Nights, greatly expanded back into the national consciousness." *Poetic Form*, 131. Kidwai, "A Bibliography," shows that Byron owned a copy of Jonathan Scott's six-volume *Arabian Nights*, published in London in 1811.

18. *The Arabian Nights* (New York: W. W. Norton, 1990), 4, 11.

19. Thomas M. Carr, Jr., "Voltaire's Fables of Discretion: The Conte philosophique in 'Le Taureau blanc,' " *SECC*, 15 (1986), 47–65.

20. William Beckford, *Vathek. Three Gothic Novels*, E. F. Bleiler (New York: Dover, 1966), 136.

21. Stuart Curran, *Poetic Form*, 97.

22. Both Nigel Leask, *British Romantic Writers*, and Peter W. Graham, *'Don Juan'*, demonstrate Southey's pervasive and continuing influence on Byron's work.

23. Franklin, *Byron's Heroines*, 18.

24. Franklin, *Byron's Heroines*, 24.

25. See Catherine Clément's *Opera: The Undoing of Women* (Minneapolis: University of Minnesota Press, 1988), for an excellent discussion of this aspect of nineteenth-century operas.

26. Mellor, *Romanticism and Gender*, 19. Mellor's point is well taken, but I wish to emphasize the difference between "literal" and "figurative" deaths. A character "allowed to live only vicariously through the words and experiences of male narrators" is still allowed to live.

27. Stuart Curran, *Poetic Form*, 36.

28. Franklin, *Byron's Heroines*, 19, 35.

29. Lord Eversley, *The Turkish Empire: Its Growth and Decay* (Lahore: Premier Book House, 1959), 272.

30. Elizabeth Wanning Harries, *The Unfinished Manner: Essays on the Fragment in the Later Eighteenth Century* (Charlottesville: University Press of Virginia, 1994), 12, 137–38.

31. Marjorie Levinson, *The Romantic Fragment Poem: A Critique of a Form* (Chapel Hill: University of North Carolina Press, 1986), 49.

32. Harries, *Unfinished Manner*, 138.

33. Raymond Schwab, *The Oriental Renaissance* (New York: Columbia University Press, 1984), xxiii, 11.

34. Edward Said, *Orientalism* (New York: Pantheon, 1978) 128; first emphasis mine, second Said's.

35. Said, *Orientalism*, 129.

36. Joseph W. Lew, "The Deceptive Other: Mary Shelley's Critique of Orientalism in 'Frankenstein,' " *Studies in Romanticism*, 30 (1991), 255–83.

37. Needless to say, this was also a savvy commercial move. The poem continued to grow through seven editions. William St. Clair estimates a production of 13,500 copies of *The Giaour* through fourteen editions. It is likely that some of the sales were to repeat buyers. Murray used this strategy to get customers to buy an extra copy of *Childe Harold* I and II simply to obtain the 52-line "To a Lady Weeping." "The Impact of Byron's Writings: An Evaluative Approach," *Byron: Augustan and Romantic*, 1–25.

38. In *Lord Byron's Strength*, Jerome Christensen charts how Byron's life and poetry is shaped by the fact that he was neither born nor bred to be Lord Byron.

39. Shafik Ghurbal, *The Beginnings of the Egyptian Question and the Rise of Mehemet Ali* (London: Routledge & Sons, 1928), xi.

40. Colonel James Welsh, *Military Reminiscences: Extracted from a Journal of Nearly Forty Years' Active Service in the East Indies* (London: Smith, Elder, 1830), vol. i, 266.

41. Francis G. Hutchins, *The Illusion of Permanence: British Imperialism in India*, (Princeton: Princeton University Press, 1967), 108, quoting John Beames, *Memoirs of a Bengal Civilian* (London: Chatto and Windus, 1961), 132.

42. Rukmini Bhaya-Nair, "Fictional Selves, Empire's Fictions: The Poets of John Company," *Tropic Crucible: Self and Theory in Language and Literature*, Ranjit Chatterjee and Colin Nicholson (Singapore: Singapore University Press, 1984), 193–217.

43. George Gordon Lord Byron, *Letters and Journals*, ed. Leslie Marchand (London: John Murray, 1978), 1: 234. All further references will be cited in the text as *BLJ*.

44. Leslie A. Marchand, *Byron: A Biography* (New York: Alfred A. Knopf, 1957), 204, 222.

45. Marchand, *Byron: A Biography*, 222.

46. Marchand, *Byron: A Biography*, 168.

47. Gauri Viswanathan, *Masks of Conquest: Literary Study and British Rule in India* (New York: Columbia University Press, 1989).

48. Rukmini Bhaya-Nair, "Fictional Selves."

49. Marlon B. Ross, *The Contours of Masculine Desire: Romanticism and the Rise of Women's Poetry* (New York: Oxford University Press, 1989), esp. 26–27.

50. Ross, *Contours*, 3, original emphasis.

51. David V. Erdman, "Byron's Flirtation with His Muses," *Rereading Byron*, 119–31.

52. This is not in the Index, but can be found among the "Excerpts from Moore's Manuscript Journal" (LBJ 11, 197).

53. Marchand, *Byron*, 556, my emphasis.

54. Graham, *'Don Juan'*, 28.

55. Franklin, *Byron's Heroines*, 144.

56. Graham, *'Don Juan'*, 27.

57. Susan Faludi, *Backlash: The Undeclared War against American Women* (New York: Crown, 1991), 47.

58. Lynn Hunt, "The Many Bodies of Marie Antoinette: Political Pornography and the Problem of the Feminine in the French Revolution," *Eroticism and the Body Politic*, Lynn Hunt (Baltimore: Johns Hopkins University Press, 1991), 108–30.

59. Franklin, *Byron's Heroines*, 111.

60. Ross, *Contours*, 209.

61. Jane Austen, *Mansfield Park* (Oxford: Oxford University Press, 1970), 415.

62. Watkins, *Social Context*, 49.

63. Franklin, *Byron's Heroines*, 155.

64. Franklin, *Byron's Heroines*, 108 and 115.

65. Franklin, *Byron's Heroines*, points out this much in her discussion, 73.

66. Watkins, *Social Context*, 40.

67. Eric Meyer, " 'I Know Thee Not, I Loathe Thy Race': Romantic Orientalism in the Eye of the Other," *ELH*, 58 (1991), 657–99. Both Meyer and Christensen (*Lord Byron's Strength*) provide good exegeses of the nature of desire in the Oriental Tales, but they do not emphasize the significance of the dysphoric nature of such plots.

68. Ray, *Widows*, 15, my emphasis.

69. William Carey to Andrew Fuller, 1 April 1799, quoted in Ray, *Widows*, 85.

70. Ray, *Widows*, p. 30.

71. House of Commons. Debates. V. 26, Col. 862.

72. Sakuntala Narasimhan, *Sati: A Study of Widow Burning in India* (New Delhi: Viking, 1990), 61.

73. J. Peggs, *Cries of Agony: An Historical Account of Suttee, Infanticide, Ghat Murders & Slavery in India* (Delhi: Discovery Publishing House, 1984), xi, xii.

74. Peggs, *Cries,* 112

75. Montesquieu, *Persian Letters,* (London: Penguin, 1973), 41.

76. G. A. Starr, "Escape From Barbary: A Seventeenth-Century Genre," *Huntington Library Quarterly,* 29 (1965), 35–52.

77. Leslie P. Peirce, *The Imperial Harem: Women and Sovereignty in the Ottoman Empire* (New York: Oxford University Press, 1993), 4–5. Throughout this section I have silently standardized transliterations.

78. Peirce, *The Imperial Harem,* 37.

79. Edward Gibbon, *The Decline and Fall of the Roman Empire,* (New York: Modern Library, n.d.), 3.663.

80. Peirce, *The Imperial Harem,* 38.

81. Meyer, "I Know Thee Not."

82. Franklin, *Byron's Heroines,* 40–41.

83. This is a major point of Meyer, "I Know Thee Not."

84. Meyer, "I Know Thee Not," 676, my emphasis.

85. Defamiliarizing the Family" (paper delivered at the Twenty-fifth Anniversary Meeting of ASECS, Charleston, South Carolina, March 10, 1994).

86. J. C. Hobhouse Broughton, *A Journey through Albania* (New York: Arno Press and the *New York Times,* 1971). All references are to this edition.

87. Norman Daniel, *Islam, Europe and Empire* (Edinburgh: University Press, 1966), esp. 36–61.

88. For a history of such misapprehensions, see Norman Daniel, *Islam and the West: The Making of an Image,* (Edinburgh: University Press, 1962).

89. See especially Dennis Kincaid, *British Social Life in India, 1608–1937,* (London: G. Routledge and Kegan Paul, 1938).

90. Angus Calder, *Revolutionary Empire: The Rise of the English-Speaking Empires from the Fifteenth Century to the 1780s* (New York: E. P. Dutton, 1981), 407.

91. Here I use the term in its legal, racial sense as defined in the Constitution of India.

92. For Lady Impey and Gordon, consult the plates in John Bowle, *The Imperial Achievement: The Rise and Transformation of the British Empire* (Boston: Little, Brown, 1974), after pp. 180 and 244.

93. Pieterse, 256.

94. Quoted in Hannah Arendt, *The Origins of Totalitarianism* (New York: Harcourt, Brace, Jovanovich, 1966), 73.

95. C. A. Bayly suggests that Scots formed close to 20 percent and the Irish well over 50 percent, particularly if the East India Service is included. *Imperial Meridian: The British Empire and the World, 1780–1830* (London: Longman, 1989).

96. Bayly, *Imperial Meridian,* 8.

97. Jan P. Nederveen Pieterse, *Empire & Emancipation: Power and Liberation on a World Scale* (New York: Praeger, 1989), 250.

98. Pieterse, *Empire & Emancipation*, 250.

99. Lew, "The Deceptive Other."

100. Pieterse, *Empire & Emancipation*, 250.

101. The only discussion of this point I have seen is in Kathleen Cassity, "Voices from the Shadows: Locating the Anglo-Indian in Post-Colonial Texts," unpublished Honors Thesis, University of Hawaii, 1994.

102. Curran, *Poetic Forms*, 143.

Eight

SAREE MAKDISI

Versions of the East:
Byron, Shelley, and the Orient

> The settler makes history and is conscious of making it.
> And because he constantly refers to the history of his mother
> country, he clearly indicates that he himself is the extension of
> that mother country. Thus the history which he writes is not the
> history of the country which he plunders but the history of his own
> nation in regard to all she skims off, all that she violates and starves.
>
> —Frantz Fanon, *The Wretched of the Earth*

JAMES MILL WRITES in his *History of British India* that "whatever is worth seeing or hearing in India, can be expressed in writing. As soon as every thing of importance is expressed in writing, a man who is duly qualified may obtain more knowledge of India in one year, in his closet in England, than he could obtain during the course of the longest life, by the use of his eyes and his ears, in India."[1] Mill argues that the entire reality of what was for him an "object" called "India" can be defined by being captured in writing, just as its territory had been defined by being captured by the armies of the East India Company. He is "correct" to the extent that imperial rule from London relied upon the minute documentation of the endless activities of the Company in India, so that what was being judged and decided upon by the Directors in London were not the material activities themselves, but rather the documents produced alongside them—not, in other words, the "realities," but the "representations." During the course of the late eighteenth and early nineteenth centuries, not only the British Empire itself but the territories over which it had or sought dominion—as well as

their peoples—were re-invented. A series of Oriental realities was produced, partly through the discursive networks on which Mill places
such heavy emphasis. Frantz Fanon once wrote that it is "the settler
who has brought the native into existence and who perpetuates his existence."[2] And yet neither the native nor the settler is or can be a static
being: caught in the violent "dialogue" of imperialism, settlers and natives, Europeans and others, have been—and still are—ever-changing
and turbulent, non-identities rather than identities.

As Edward Said has argued, the Orient "as such" only exists—and
has only ever existed—as a spatial construction endowed with a series of facts, essences, histories, etc., a space that could be known, controlled, exploited and developed by Europeans.[3] Byron's Orientalism
has often been compared to Shelley's, but while the two poets undoubtedly have much in common, I believe that it is of crucial importance to
distinguish between Byron's East—as produced in the first two cantos
of *Childe Harold* (1812)—and the vision of the East first produced by
Shelley in *Alastor; or, the Spirit of Solitude* (1816). Underlying each of
these versions of the Orient there are radically opposed concepts of
empire, of Orientalism, and of history—concepts that would become
more defined in Shelley's (and, though to a lesser extent, Byron's) later
works.[4] What I want to propose in the present essay is that the Oriental
space developed in *Alastor* represents a reclamation of an Oriental terrain from previous visions and versions of the East and its incorporation into the emergent space-time of modernity. Thus it not only anticipates the paradigms of Orientalist discourse associated both with
James Mill and with late nineteenth-century English Orientalists (many
of whom were inspired by Mill's *History*) but it contributes to the historical production of the Orient as a space for European knowledge,
discipline, and control. The version of the Orient that is produced in
Childe Harold II—the Orient as refuge from and potential alternative to
modernity—was contested and redefined in later spatial productions;
its critical and imaginary terrain had to be siezed, cleansed, and totally
reorganized and reinvented. The Oriental space produced in *Alastor*
symbolizes the beginning of that reclamation, the production of a new
Orient that the poem "discovers," which would later be embellished,
developed, augmented, and improved in succeeding visions and versions of the East.

Even if Byron never ventured farther into Asia than the eastern outskirts of Istanbul, he had certainly ventured to the "Orient." For in
the first two decades of the nineteenth century, Albania and Greece
were merely outlying provinces in a farflung Asian empire. Europe did
not simply grow gradually "less European" toward the East, as Victor

Kiernan has argued, for the very identity of a geographical or spatial entity called Europe was still in the process of development.[5] Nevertheless, at a certain point "European" travelers crossed an indefinite symbolic "frontier." For Byron, that frontier was the Albanian coastline, which he first viewed from the decks of the Royal Navy frigate that carried him eastward from the British colony of Malta. As his alter ego, Childe Harold, wanders on that shore, he finds "himself at length alone, / And bade to Christian tongues a long adieu; / Now he adventured on a shore unknown, / Which all admire, but many dread to view."[6]

Harold's arrival in the East represents a passage across a multidimensional "border" into the space and time of the Orient, a space-time that has its own distinct pattern of temporal ruptures and losses, but, on its own terms, is a discrete spatial-temporal sphere, different from that of the West which Harold leaves behind. Thus the space-time of Byron's Orient exists alongside that of the Occident, in apposition to it, rather than as a rupture contained by—or within—an otherwise homogeneous Western *jetztzeit*. This East is then not simply a repository of some mythical Western "past"; it exists as its own space, on the fringes, perhaps, of a power that threatens it with annihilation, but nevertheless still clinging to its own life, its own structures, its own meanings, distinct from the homogenizing modernity of the West— and hence profoundly attractive to exiles attempting to flee that modernity. Byron conceives the historical relationship between East and West in synchronic, rather than diachronic, terms. Indeed, he could conceive of the Orient as a spatial alternative to Europe precisely because he sees European and Oriental histories as distinct—as synchronic *histories*, rather than one diachronic *History* narrated and controlled by Europe.

"Byron's is a poetry of trajectories," Bernard Blackstone argues; "we travel far afield, but always on a return ticket. *The Ancient Mariner*, not *Alastor*, is the paradigm of *Childe Harold, Lara, Mazeppa, Don Juan*."[7] As a self-constituted pilgrimage (even if in the end it proves to be aimless), *Childe Harold* has its basis in what Johannes Fabian argues is the concept of "sacred" as opposed to "secular" time, depicting a movement *toward* some central spatial objective from elsewhere. According to Fabian, the creation and development of secularized time was inextricably caught up with a gradual shift in European concepts of travel, away from an outmoded version in which travel involved a movement *to* the centers of religion (e.g., Rome, Jerusalem, Canterbury) *from* everywhere else; and instead towards a notion of travel *from* the new centers of learning and power (London, Berlin, Paris—acclaimed in later Eurocentric views as the "capital" of the nineteenth century itself) *to* "places where man was to find nothing but himself."[8] In this new topos of travel, the old model of Judeo-Christian time was simultaneously secularized and gradually universalized, so that time became a more or less uniform natural essence, pointing to and "culminating" in a (nevertheless developing) modern Europe. This new formation of time was fundamental to the formation of a properly evolutionary temporality, through which difference was understood as, or expressed in terms of, temporal distance from a standard point of reference (modern Europe).[9] In a "quest," like that of *Alastor* (to which I will turn shortly), which has no delimited spatial objective, the movement represents a turn outwards, away from the center, and in search of some outside fulfillment. But *Childe Harold's Pilgrimage*, by contrast, implicitly affirms a belief in, or a claim to, sacred (or at any rate pre-modern) time. Childe Harold, in leaving Europe, leaves behind the slowly-universalizing temporality of modernity and enters a synchronous structure of time, space, and history; not a *premodern*, but an *antimodern* Orient.

Byron's meditations on Greece in canto II are interwoven with his "discovery" of the space of the East. The text of his musings on Hellenic antiquity is shaped by the context of the Oriental world within which he finds the ruins of ancient Greece; at the same time, this context itself is altered by Byron's nascent philhellenism. The Greek ruins of *Childe Harold* II are inseparable yet distinct from their Oriental surroundings—so that Byron's discovery of what Robert Gleckner terms "the ruins of paradise"[10] and Harold's contact with the Asiatic other are in symbiosis: the one is written in terms of the other. And yet the contemporary Orientals in Byron's vision seem not to see the ruins, or at least not to pay them any heed. From their standpoint, the days of Hellenic antiquity are as remote as they are from Byron's—even if they do not participate in the modernity whose homogenizing sameness drove the Englishman into his exilic search for alternatives to it, a search which eventually brings him to their world.

For the space-time of the contemporary Orient that canto II produces is neither modern nor ancient; it is as distinct from the ruins that mark its terrain as it is from Europe, as though these ruins had been left there by a society whose lost heirs have not yet come to claim their heritage. The history of this space, in other words, is alien to the people currently inhabiting it; or, rather: the space-time of Hellenic antiquity is somehow buried beneath the space-time of Byron's contemporary Orient, figuratively existing in a planar dimension whose ruins protrude through the latter, marking and scarring it in places—marks and scars that Byron can emplot on his imaginary map of this contemporary Oriental space, whether or not they are seen, felt, and recognized by the natives. His is a pilgrimage, however, not an excavating archaeological expedition; and though he points out and traces the "ruins of paradise," he does so not in order to retrieve them, but in order, once again, to "remember" the imaginary past in which they were produced and for which, hence, they are memorials: "Come—but molest not yon defenceless urn: / Look on this spot—a nation's sepulchre! / Abode of gods, whose shrines no longer burn."[11] Byron's anxiety pertains not to the spatial zone that he has discovered (the Orient), but to the scattered relics of a space that once was, or in other words, a previous spatial production of the (Hellenic) East. His admonition is, moreover, directed not at the "ignorant" Greeks and Turks—ignorant insofar as they apparently ignore the ruins—but at Lord Elgin and his antiquary relic-collectors.

The dark sepulchral tone of canto II is thus restricted to the dream-like "memories" and memorials of Greece, rather than to the living Oriental pageant of the present (although his admonition "not to molest" may also be applied to the Oriental space, rather than solely to the ruins). The ghosts and specters haunting the tombs and temples do not torment the Orientals, by whom they are not seen. They are, rather, the private projections and possessions of the European tourist, even if they are his as an individual, and not simply as a European, for not all Europeans acknowledge or feel the sepulchral gloom that pervades Byron's Greece.

Although there is a sense in canto II that the ruins of paradise ought to be exclusively appreciated by those who hold a cultural claim to a right of inheritance (i.e., modern Europeans, not the "fallen" Greeks, and certainly not the Turks), this sense is tempered by Byron's insistence on the sepulchral nature of the ruins. The canto's claim is that the relics of Greece ought to be preserved just as graveyards and tombs are preserved, as relics and reminders of a previous age forever irretrievable from modernity, and not as treasured kindling for some Promethean fire of European cultural renewal (which I will argue is what they would become for Shelley and others after 1815: see below). Greece is finally, utterly and irrevocably dead, though its traces are immortal; it can be remembered, perhaps, and its passing can be mourned, but it can never be revived or excavated from the crushing historical weight of the other civilizations that have come to claim its terrain.

The death of Greece is redeemed, though, by the Oriental presence on its terrain. Byron's and Harold's thrilling contact with this other civilization easily rivals Byron's "memories" of Hellenic antiquity; so that the space of Hellenic "memories" and that of Oriental contact both afford zones of escape from modernity. Canto II thus structurally distinguishes—and even segregates—Harold's expedition from what we may term Byron's philosophical and political musings on Greece.

The version of Oriental space that the canto produces is both structurally and spatially separated from the monuments of antiquity against which it is juxtaposed. Harold's arrival in the Orient takes place after crossing the symbolic frontier (the Albanian coast) dividing East from West, Europe from Asia. But the ruins of paradise are neither "here" nor "there"; separated from modern Europe by a gulf, they are also opposed to the contemporary Greeks and Turks, whose spatial structures and assemblages are superimposed upon them.

Harold's pilgrimage is thus twofold: on the one hand, it is a trip to the space-time of Hellenic antiquity; and, on the other, it is a journey to the East. The canto begins with the first journey, "rewinds," then begins again with Harold's arrival in the East; the two dimensions of Byron's East (Hellenic and contemporary) occupy the same space, the one displacing the other. Access to either dimension requires a leap across the frontier and away from the space-time of modernity and modernization. The contradictory and even mutually exclusive relationships connecting the space-time and history of modernity with the space of (on the one hand) the Hellenic past and (on the other) the Oriental present are not at all coincidental to Byron's anxious production of these spaces. In his mourning for the Hellenic past and in his indignant attack on Lord Elgin, Byron is affirming or positing a historical and cultural continuity between modern Europe and not only ancient Greece but the rest of the (premodern) Levant; yet in constucting (and turning to) the contemporary Oriental Levant as a space distinct from modern Europe, he is affirming a rupture and dislocation between East and West, Orient and Occident, Asia and Europe— as spaces with synchronic histories, rather than one diachronic history.

When I say that Childe Harold's pilgrimage is twofold, what I mean is that Byron narrates a voyage to two different and mutually exclusive spatial-temporal constructs (that he himself produces): first, the Levant as the cultural and historical ancestor of Europe; and second, the Levant as the space and territory of the Oriental other. The first is an affirmation of a diachronic historical continuity between modern Europe and ancient Greece, while the second is an affirmation of a synchronic historical separation between modern Europe and an antimodern Orient. In other words, the first implies the repossession and the appropriation of the space of the Levant for a Eurocentric vision of history, in which Europeans claim to assimilate other peoples, cultures, and histories into the history of modernity—a history to be narrated and understood from the standpoint of Europe; while the second implies the coexistence of distinct though related cultures and histories, spaces, and times.

Byron's anxiety here stems from his simultaneous participation in both projects—viewing the East as the site or birthplace of Europe's great cultural heritage, while at the same time viewing the East as a site into which one could escape from modernity, a site from whose vantage point one could critique both modernity and Europe itself. For while Byron views the East as such an alternative synchronic space, he sees its possibilities and its very existence (as such a space) threatened by its appropriation and re-constitution in European colonial projects— colonial projects he both participated in and at the same time opposed and contested.

For Byron arrived in the Levant along with the first wave of intense European colonial activity in the heart of the Muslim world, and his first trip to the East took him not only to the very fringes of Europe, but close to the freshly-captured—and at the time still hotly-contested— easternmost European possessions on and off the Mediterranean coasts of Africa and Asia. These territories, including Sicily, Malta, and the Ionian islands, as well as Egypt and Syria (from 1798 to 1801), were neither the first nor the most valuable European colonial prizes, though they represented the beginning of the intense European imperial investment in the region. On the other hand, they were unlike all other colonial territories inasmuch as they were virtually extensions of Europe, lying within quick and easy reach across the various straits and channels of the Mediterranean.

During his sojourn in the East, hence, Byron was never very far from the scene of colonial rivalries. In spite of the rapidly-unfolding European involvement in the region, however, Byron's 1809–11 Levantine tour was a voyage into territory still largely "unknown" and "unexplored" by Europeans, and Gibbon's famous remark about Albania ("a country within sight of Italy is less known than the interior of America") still held true in Byron's time, at least from a Eurocentric standpoint. The Levant was—for the most part—still neither occupied nor firmly controlled by any of the various competing European powers. In 1809, still mired in the war with France, Britain was unable and unwilling to fully commit itself to large-scale interventions in the area, except where the French directly and immediately threatened the overland routes to India (most notably in Egypt).[12] The Ottoman Empire was, despite its weakness, still intact, and certain semi-independent Ottoman provincial governors would become or were already major forces to be reckoned with even on their own. Britain's main imperial policy in the region, at least until the end of the war with France, was to back up the steadily-weakening Ottomans in order to safeguard the approaches to India from both the Russians and the French. The Ottoman territories, from North Africa to Palestine and from Palestine to the Balkans, were held in a kind of political vacuum: a space still decidedly "Oriental," but one which no longer posed a significant threat to Britain. Hence it was an ideal space to tour the exotic East without, on the one hand, having to see the obvious deployment of British imperial power needed to keep it under control (as in India); or, on the other hand, feeling threatened by what even some contemporary critics *still* refer to as "the austere ferocity of Islam."[13] While the integration of the local economies of Southwest Asia and North Africa into the capitalist world-economy would radically and permanently transform the region, beginning after 1815 and accelerating in the 1830s, they were not yet fully locked into the Eurocentric structures of capital. In other words, while this region *would become* crucially important to, and dependent on, European industry from the 1830s onwards—when, e.g., the intensification of cotton production in Egypt and silk production in what is today Lebanon would gradually force Egypt and Lebanon into dependence on the textile industry of Lancashire and the silk industry of Lyon—the Ottoman Levant was in Byron's time still largely a "neutral zone" lying outside the circuits of industrial capitalism's unequal exchange.[14]

At length, Harold bids to Christian tongues "a long adieu" and *"finds himself"* alone. Canto II has been called "Byron's 'self-discovery' canto," or the poetical narrative space in which Byron "invented the myth of himself."[15] It is, as both McGann and Blackstone observe, not coincidental that Byron's self-discovery or self-invention—for they are one and the same—takes place in the fantastic Orient produced in *Childe Harold* II. In the very process of producing an Oriental other, Byron has to produce an image of himself: a narrative persona of himself as a man, an Englishman, a European. Even if one of the aims of Childe Harold and of Byron's flight and exile from England in 1809 was to escape the realities of his self-identity and his status as an Englishman and a modern European, his voyage to the Orient only forced him into greater awareness (or, rather, the "discovery") of those identities and realities. His despair stems in part from the realization that any attempt to escape self-recognition only strengthens it, especially in the narrative field of the other. For it is when he is most overwhelmed by the surrounding presence of others—in and among whom he tries to lose himself—that Byron can declare, "This is to be alone; this, this, is solitude!"[16] Byron's alter ego, Childe Harold, is even more lonely than Byron was on his Levantine trip, since the entourage of servants, followers, and friends that had journeyed with Byron from England is nowhere to be found in the pages of the *Pilgrimage*. Indeed, Harold's existential loneliness is an important structural and thematic component of the Albanian narrative—a narrative of a single European's visual discovery of the Orient and its mysteries. Childe Harold's pilgrimage is necessarily a private, if not quite secretive, tour; his tourist's "consumption" of the landscape and people of the East (in an imaginary space of his own equally private production) is a deeply personal, private, and even selfish affair, to which no other tourists or wanderers can be admitted. Indeed, the narrative of Harold's pilgrimage to the East takes place almost entirely in a visual register, and hence his consumption of the Orient is doubly private in that it takes place through and in his own eyes (". . . let me bend mine eyes / On thee . . . ").

The very privateness of this visualized touristic consumption is of more importance, in and of itself, than the space that it consumes. Moreover, the uniqueness of the consumed space does not matter as much as its radical difference from the modernizing culture and historicity of the tourist: a difference that, on its own terms, makes the distinction between, for example, Scottish Highlanders and Albanians (compared in Byron's poetic vision) fade into obscurity. The attraction of these other cultures, in other words, lies first and foremost in their sheer difference from the standard of emerging European modernity, and only in a secondary sense in each culture's unique features. In another sense, however, the radical alterity of a particular anti-modern culture could be rendered more comprehensible by comparison to one more familiar—but still different; or, inversely, a culture that might otherwise seem to be dangerously "familiar" could be distanced (from "us") by a comparison to a more unfamiliar group. Thus, although in *Waverley* Walter Scott repeatedly uses Oriental allusions and references to accentuate or exaggerate his Highlanders' radical difference from some standardized Lowland-English culture of modernity, Byron makes his Albanians seem more knowable by assimilating them to the familiar alterity of Highlanders: a group that, for all that remained of its exoticism in Byron's time, had already been purged of whatever hostile threat it might contain in the aftermath of Culloden. Hence, just as Oriental allusions are repeatedly invoked in Edward Waverley's tour of the Scottish Highlands, the Highlands and Highlanders are repeatedly invoked in Byron's stanzas on Albania. Such reassurances notwithstanding, the central parts of canto II are about contact—beyond the safety delineated by the frontiers of modernity—with an otherness whose appeal would possess Byron for the rest of his life, and whose influence would shape his poetry more profoundly than by merely offering him exotic thematic material.

Byron never ventured farther east than the western territories of the Ottoman Empire, Greece, Albania and Turkey; yet, as I have already suggested, he did not need to in order to "discover" the wonders of the East. In canto II of *Childe Harold*, Albania—the westernmost and northernmost of those territories—is the most significantly Oriental, or, to use Said's term, Orientalized space. Indeed, Byron's spatialized vision of the East and his production of an Oriental space is largely confined to Albania, although that confinement does not by any means prevent Albania from standing for and representing the "Oriental" nature of spaces farther east. On the contrary; in *Childe Harold*'s imaginary map of the East, Albania is a synechdochical space for the representation of the greater Orient; the former's exoticized character-types (the despot, the eunuch, the harem-girl, the janissary) and spaces (the harem, the emir's palace, the mosque) are not only "found" in the rest of the Orient: they are specific cases or illustrations of the Oriental "truths" and essences that would be generalized through the later nineteenth century by the institutions and discourses of modern European Orientalism.[17]

This imaginary Oriental terrain can never be defined, let alone invested and captured, insofar as it defies encapsulation in a single field of vision; rather, its spatial-visual field is defined by the infinite series of barriers that not only invite, but necessitate discovery. The rich and colorful Oriental collage describing Ali Pasha's enclave is a visual encapsulation of the sights, colors, odors, and sounds of the Orient. It is a complex space, marked and defined by a honeycomb of walls, courtyards, doors, gates, passageways, layers within layers. The most impenetrable space—that of the harem—is not seen by Childe Harold, who merely pauses outside its "silent tower," though the ultimate voyeuristic vision of the harem's "sacred" space would later be famously provided by Byron in *Don Juan*. Nor is Ali Pasha himself encountered in these stanzas; he remains an unseen presence, whose invisible power nevertheless invests all the activity and bustle that Harold does indeed encounter. Apart from the flow of "typical" Oriental types in a "many-hued array"—slaves, eunuchs, santons, etc.—Ali Pasha's domain brings together exotic and exoticized people from all over the Orient: Tartars, Moors, Nubians, Indians, Turks, and, more locally though no less exotically, Greeks and Albanians as well. Over this "motley scene" of preparations for feasts and battles—this crowd of "strange groups" adorning Ali Pasha's corridors of power, this collage of smokers and players and prayers arguing and talking and babbling in a mix of Eastern tongues, this moving panoply of Oriental shapes and colors—floats the *muezzin's* distant call to prayer, rendered here in *very* Anglicized terms, "There is no god but God!—to prayer!—lo! God is great!" Byron's visual and spatial portrait of the Orient is an alluring series of images of the exotic Orient drawn by a charmed and attracted European "caught in its spell." Once again, Byron here anticipates later developments and uses of colonial imagery and visuality in the nineteenth century, as for instance in the Great Exhibitions of the second half of the century, which,

in part, render the experience of colonialism in iconographic and visualized—and, later on, cinematic—terms.[18]

The space of Ali Pasha's enclave in Albania is an exemplary and
representative space; "defining" the Orient, it is "purely" Oriental in
the sense that the purest essences of the Orient are spatially and visu-
ally represented in it. Yet, precisely because of its Edenic quality, and
despite the protection and insulation afforded by the layered boundaries separating it from the impinging outside (Western/modern) world,
this perfect and exemplary space is threatened with penetration, "discovery," and destruction by the forces against which it is momentarily
and even fleetingly defined. Robert Gleckner argues that the reader's
final impression of Ali Pasha's enclave "is of an Edenic, sublime land
surrounded by the awe-inspiring, terrible, and destructive power of the
Pasha, a panoramic image of one of Byron's major themes, the ruins
of paradise."[19] The isolation of this Oriental space, however, is as yet
an *unruined* paradise, not one that has been destroyed, pillaged, and
only then touristed. Ali Pasha's paradise, in other words, is encircled
and threatened by outside penetration, but the enabling condition for
Harold's (and through him Byron's) entry into that space is that its
essential property as an exemplary Oriental space not be physically
touched, materially altered, or tangibly affected. This is strictly a visual
tour of an imaginary space, leaving no trace of its own passage on the
terrain that it voyeuristically describes. Thus the lone European who
ventures silently into the realm of the Oriental other virtually lifts himself out of his own voyage, and the process of self-discovery once again
slips into one of "selfish" self-negation. The Orientalism of Byron's production of the Orient is therefore not simply visual or even thematic—
its distinction between East and West is simultaneously a spatial and an
epistemological structure.[20]

While the threat of destruction is the price to be paid for visiting
this forbidden Oriental space, the reward, on the other hand, is the
viewer's access to a pristine, and Edenically inviolate otherness. The
space of this otherness, whose silent Western viewer/voyeur can observe almost without being observed, once again becomes a "theater"
for individual Western discovery of self (a discovery whose significance
for Byron in particular has been pointed out by Jerome McGann and
others), or for the freedom and refreshing independence of a lonely
Western tourist.[21] At the same time, Byron's Orientalism—quite apart
from its litany of authenticating devices and references—claims to represent to Western readers the multitudinous realities of the East in its
scenes and images that are not only taken from the land of the other,
but even reproduce (at a distance) the experience of that otherness
on its own terms. Marilyn Butler argues that Byron tended to respect

"the autonomy of other cultures, but was inclined to admire them precisely for their otherness, their unreformed 'romantic' features."[22] Indeed, Byron's Orient claims to be the Orient's Orient—the real Orient "out there," and not only some vaguely-realistic figurative landscape produced by a Western imagination.

For, ultimately, Byron's attraction to and obsession with the East is driven not only by a deep-felt interest in non-Western structures and spaces, but also with the desire (however chimerical) to experience the East "as such," on its own terms and in its own sphere of existence— a sphere preferably, for Byron, protected from European incursion and imperial investment. Butler points to the central importance of Southey in the early nineteenth-century literary production, and especially to what she argues are "the reappearances of Southey's structures and images in the nineteenth-century literature of colonialism, high and low, beginning with Shelley and Byron."[23] She insists, however, that much of Byron's poetry, including *The Giaour*, can be read as an explicit contestation of Southey's interventionist and evangelical attitude towards empire, as exemplified in *Madoc* (1805) and *The Curse of Kehama* (1810).[24] Drawing upon a contrast between Byron and later English writers on the Orient (e.g., Burton, Thackeray, and Disraeli), other critics, including Patrick Brantlinger, have discussed what they see as Byron's "anti-imperialist message," a "message" predicated upon the contrast that they establish with the paradigms of imperialism supported by the later figures.[25] That Byron did not share the kind of imperial attitudes expressed by Disraeli and Burton does not, however, necessarily mean that he opposed imperialism altogether.[26] Indeed, it seems to me that the question at hand is not *whether* a politics of imperialism underlies Byron's vision of the East in *Childe Harold* II, but rather what kind of politics it is.

"Fair Greece!" Byron writes in canto II, "sad relic of departed worth! / Immortal, though no more; though fallen, great! / Who now shall lead thy scatter'd children forth, / And long accustom'd bondage uncreate?" The next stanzas propose two answers to this question. On the one hand, and in striking contrast to what a Burton, a Disraeli, or a Lawrence might answer, Byron insists that only the Greeks can free themselves ("Hereditary bondsmen! know ye not / Who would be free themselves must strike the blow? / By their right arms the conquest must be wrought?"). On the other hand, he is certain that "ne'er will freedom seek this fated soil: / But slave succeed to slave through years of endless toil." Thus, the sepulchral tone of the opening stanzas of canto II—in which Byron mourns for the ruins of paradise—is, at the end of the canto, tied not only to Byron's analysis at the time (for it would later change) of the prospects for Greek rebellion against the

Ottomans, but to his views of the Greek nation and the Greeks themselves. These views, in turn, are inextricably caught up with Byron's
uneasy and ambivalent early attitudes toward empire and toward empire-building in the "boundless East," as he was writing in the years
before the triumphant victory of 1815: a victory that would forever alter
British attitudes toward the rest of the world. Among the notes to canto
II, Byron has a lengthy reflection on Greece and the Greeks:

> The Greeks will never be independent: they will never be sovereigns
> as heretofore, and God forbid that they ever should! but they may be
> subjects without being slaves. Our colonies are not independent, but
> they are free and industrious, and such may Greece be hereafter.

Byron continues:

> The English have at last compassionated their negroes [NB: only the
> slave trade was abolished in 1807, not slavery itself], and under a less
> bigoted government, may probably one day release their Catholic breth-
> ren; but the interposition of foreigners alone can emancipate the
> Greeks, who, otherwise, appear to have as small a chance of redemp-
> tion from the Turks, as the Jews have from mankind in general. . . .
> To talk, as the Greek themselves do, of their rising again to their pris-
> tine superiority, would be ridiculous: as the rest of the world must re-
> sume its barbarism, after re-asserting the sovereignty of Greece; but
> there seems to be no very great obstacle, except in the apathy of the
> Franks, to their becoming a useful dependency, or even a free state,
> with a proper guarantee;—under correction, however, be it spoken, for
> many and well-informed men doubt the practicability even of this.

It is well known that Byron would not only later change his views of the
Greeks and their rebellion against the Turks, but that he would give
his own life in their cause. Nevertheless, at this earlier moment (at least
up to his return to England in 1812), he was clearly doubtful both about
the Greeks' "national character" and about their chances for freedom.
Byron here neither advocates Greek independence, nor does he call
for immediate British intervention in the cause of a struggle whose
prospects he believes are hopeless, or, at best, doubtful.

Byron's assertion, earlier in the canto, that there is no hope for a recuperation or regeneration of the Hellenic monuments is by the canto's
end tied to his assertion that the Greeks of his time have lost virtually
all claims to their fabled Hellenic ancestry. Like Africans and Irishmen,
he argues, contemporary Greeks are "afflicted" with certain "ailments"
(principally moral ones) as a result of their treatment and their historical condition. Yet his position in the notes is not that England ought to
intervene and "enlighten" these "degenerate" colonial or semi-colonial
peoples, let alone that England has some moral duty to do so, but—at

the most—that England might take it upon itself to remove the conditions that led to their "degeneration," through the abolition of slavery, through Catholic relief, and by ending the foreign domination of Greece. Although "only" foreign intervention could force the Ottomans out of Greece, such intervention could never truly liberate the Greeks; on the other hand, Byron is clear that ending the foreign domination of Greece might benefit England (because it would alleviate the prospects for French and Russian intervention which would destabilize Turkey). At most, Byron argues, Greece might be turned into a colony or protectorate under the benevolent guidance and care of a power like Great Britain. Thus Byron resigns himself to an ambivalent argument—the Greeks can only be free by freeing themselves, the Greeks cannot under their present conditions free themselves, therefore the Greeks will never be free—whose main thrust is not simply to defer intervention, but to assert that, if one day the Ottomans might be pushed out of Greece, on the whole it would be better for England if France and Russia were not behind the Ottoman defeat and the new Greek "state."

Byron does not, however, call in any way for British intervention elsewhere in the Ottoman Empire or in the rest of Asia. His fascination with the otherness of the Orient is predicated, as I have already mentioned, on its inviolate non-Westernness as much as on its own pure and essential Easternness—indeed these are, for him, one and the same. His belief (such as it is) in the Greek cause is not based upon assumptions of a wider British imperial destiny or mission in Asia and the world; rather, his equivocal support for English intervention in Greece is based as much upon his desire to keep the rest of the Ottoman Empire intact and free of Russian and French interference as it is upon his belief in Greek liberty. Byron's weakly-stated and deeply ambivalent philhellenism of 1812, in other words, has little to do with notions of innate European superiority over Turks and Muslims, and even less to do with a broader European *mission civilisatrice* in Asia. Indeed, Byron is very careful not to make sweeping pronouncements about Turkish or Oriental degeneracy, or to declare their "need" for moral "improvement," development, and evolution. "It is hazardous," Byron writes in his notes, "to say much on the subject of Turks and Turkey; since it is possible to live amongst them twenty years without acquiring information, at least from themselves. As far as my own slight experience carried me, I have no complaint to make; but am indebted for many civilities (I might also say for friendship), and much hospitality. . . . " He goes on to say that

> the Ottomans are not a people to be despised. Equal, at least, to the
> Spaniards, they are superior to the Portuguese. If it be difficult to pro-

nounce what they are, we can at least say what they are *not*: they are *not* treacherous, they are *not* cowardly, they do *not* burn heretics, they are *not* assassins, nor has an enemy advanced to *their* capital. They are faithful to their sultan till he becomes unfit to govern, and devout to their God without an inquisition. Were they driven from St. Sophia tomorrow, and the French or Russians enthroned in their stead, it would become a question whether Europe would gain by the exchange. England would certainly be the loser.

Byron's knowledge of the Turks is here defined in negative terms, rather than as the sort of positive knowledge that was already being advocated by James Mill; with the lack of such positive knowledge, there is a lack of explicit proscriptive or prescriptive emphases, and hence no effort to correct the deviation or the abnormality of another civilization. On the contrary; as spatial production, the East is for Byron not only a refuge from modernity—that is, a space from which to flee modernity—but also a space from which to critique modernity and the West itself. Byron's Oriental space, in other words, offers liberatory possibilities for the critique of Western, European, English concepts, taboos, norms, and standards—political, social, sexual, poetical, economic, and cultural. The concept of imperialism underlying Byron's early Orientalism is hence torn with anxiety. Sometimes in favor of intervention, and sometimes not, it is as though he were aware that Ottoman independence—and hence the kind of "pristine" or even Edenic Oriental realm that the Ottoman domains provided for Western tourism—could, paradoxically, be maintained only by a British intervention that would eventually undermine and erode it. Not seeing any need for a productive transformation of a cultural system that he in many ways finds admirable, Byron wants to preserve it intact, though it becomes increasingly clear that such "preservation" would be as fictive as declaring a regularly-maintained country park in England to be "natural." His desire to keep this space of non-Western and anti-modern otherness intact is thus contradicted by his increasing awareness that to do so would only accelerate its penetration by the West and by the forces and structures of modernity; such otherness would henceforth only be toured in the imaginary spatial productions of a poetry which might preserve it as an alternative space forever. Or else it would be abandoned altogether with a return to Eurocentrism—the sort of Eurocentrism advocated and typified by Shelley, but also by the later Byron, the Byron of *Childe Harold* III and IV, whose destination is no longer the East, but Italy—the "heart" of modern Europe.

Following hard on the tracks of its Visionary, *Alastor* takes us on a journey deep into the vast expanses of what Byron called the "boundless East."[27] Like *Childe Harold* II, *Alastor* faces the dilemma of having to create its own object, that which it wants simultaneously to describe and to "represent." It does so at a crucial historical juncture, in which the multiple conditions of that rapidly developing "object," the East— its location, its figurative and material possibilities, its value, its history, its peoples, its usefulness, its rule and above all its relation to "the West" and to Europe—were undergoing momentous changes. *Alastor*'s map of the East has no real referent: it does not and cannot simply "represent the Orient," a region and a space that did not and does not exist as such, but that had to be endlessly reinvented by its symbiotically-related opposite term, "the West," during the long and bloody history of imperialism. Inhabiting the form of a travel narrative, Shelley's poem is in large measure informed by the shock of (imaginary) encounter on the imperial frontier, a region in which, as Mary Pratt has observed, "Europeans confront not only unfamiliar others, but unfamiliar selves."[28] Torn by the anxieties of colonialism and of oppression, *Alastor* is a profoundly disturbed meditation on empire.

"The philosophical traveller, sailing to the ends of the earth, is in fact travelling in time; he is exploring the past; every step he makes is the passage of an age."[29] Joseph-Marie Degérando's observation, made in 1800 following his excursion from Europe into lands inhabited by "savages," provides a strangely appropriate description for *Alastor*'s Visionary. In the prime of his youth, the Visionary—just such a philosophical traveler—leaves "his cold fireside and alienated home / To seek strange truths in undiscovered lands." His thirst for knowledge is at first satiated by what he can grasp through intercourse with Nature and the magnificence of "the external world." But the charms and intellectual treasures of a sweet and domestic Nature are quickly exhausted, and the Visionary takes his search into lands "undiscovered" not by people, but specifically by Europeans. He pushes away from the tranquil scenes of domestic Wordsworthian Nature, and toward the (Byronic and Southeyan) realm of the foreign and distinctly non-European: "Many a wild waste and tangled wilderness / Has lured his fearless steps; and he has bought / With his sweet voice and eyes, from savage men, / His rest and food." Having pursued like her shadow "Nature's most secret steps," the Visionary leaves behind the familiar world of squirrels and deer and begins his fantastic adventure back in time, not only to Eden, but to what came long before. At the end of the poem, once he has reached the very heart of the East, the so-called "cradle" of (Western) civilization, and still in pursuit of the phantasmatic and elusive "veilèd maid" of his dreams, the pitch and velocity of his journey accelerate "beyond all human speed." A tiny boat carries him on to his destiny at the very origins of time: "Nature's cradle, and his sepulchre." This cyclical inversion of time, in which a cradle is also a sepulchre, in which the beginning is also the end (oddly reminiscent of Words-worth's "the child is the father of the man"), is accomplished precisely through the translation of a forward movement in space into a back-ward movement in time. For, propelled by a supernatural whirlpool, the quasi-magical boat is indeed a time-machine of sorts, taking the Vision-ary *up* the cavern of a river which pours *down* into the Caspian sea:

> Seized by the sway of the *ascending stream*,
> With dizzy swiftness, round, and round, and round,
> Ridge after ridge *the straining boat arose*,
> Till on the verge of the extremest curve,
> Where, through an opening of the rocky bank,
> The waters overflow, and a smooth spot
> Of glassy quiet mid those battling tides
> Is left, the boat paused shuddering.[30]

Having reversed and rewound time, having defied the laws of gravity and of physics, the Visionary's boat arrives at the source of space and time (to which I shall return a little later). This dizzying upward and backward journey bears a synecdochical relationship to the entire poem's spatial-temporal flow, especially that of the section preceding this mystical last stage of his journey. For even before this apotheosis, each of the Visionary's steps toward the East is signaled as a troubled step "back in time." The passage recounting his travel to and arrival in *Alastor*'s Orient is worth quoting at length:

> His wandering step
> Obedient to high thoughts, has visited
> The awful ruins of the days of old:
> Athens, and Tyre, and Balbec, and the waste
> Where stood Jerusalem, the fallen towers
> Of Babylon, the eternal pyramids,
> Memphis and Thebes, and whatsoe'er of strange
> Sculptured on alabaster obelisk,
> Or jasper tomb, or mutilated sphynx,
> Dark Æthiopia in her desert hills
> Conceals. Among the ruined temples there,
> Stupendous columns, and wild images
> Of more than man, where marble daemons watch
> The Zodiac's brazen mystery, and dead men
> Hang their mute thoughts on the mute walls around,
> He lingered, poring on memorials
> Of the world's youth, through the long burning day
> Gazed on those speechless shapes, nor, when the moon

Filled the mysterious halls with floating shades
Suspended he that task, but ever gazed
And gazed, till meaning on his vacant mind
Flashed like strong inspiration, and he saw
The thrilling secrets of the birth of time.[31]

These passages, "set" in the Levant and northeastern Africa, are of course only the beginnings, the westernmost leading edges, of *Alastor*'s map of the East, for the Visionary will penetrate deeper still, beyond Arabie and Persia, beyond Kashmir, beyond the Caucasus, beyond the Caspian and Aral Seas. This eastward movement (the opposite of Keats's "westering") involves a complex and subtle temporal play. On the one hand, the Visionary has arrived in the space of Oriental and Hellenic antiquity, intact and laden with its tombs and palaces, its memorials and sphinxes, its columns and its halls. On the other hand, he has not quite gone back to the *time* of antiquity; or, rather—paradoxically—he has *and* he has not. Time has stopped: nothing has changed in this mythic Orient, nothing has altered the Roman temples of Baalbeck, the Phoenician palaces of Tyre, the temples of Athens, the towers of Babylon. The "eternal" pyramids are as they were when Cheops was entombed; Tyre has neither grown nor changed since Alexander's siege; Jerusalem's temples remain as they were left by the city's last pillagers or pilgrims; the Parthenon stands silently awaiting its sacrificial trains; Memphis, once the united capital of Upper and Lower Egypt, is frozen, its palace of Apis remaining as it was—though all of these places are desolate and depopulated, at once preserved and emptied out. And yet, of course, time has moved on: these are ruined temples, open wastes, fallen towers, mutilated monuments.[32] In other words, these "awful ruins of the days of old," these "memorials to the world's youth," have somehow been frozen in time—as though nothing has changed and no one has lived here since some vanished moment of antiquity— and yet they have also been inscribed by the movement of time and the passage of the ages: they are ruins, they are memorials. *Alastor*'s map undermines and contradicts itself. If this *is* a move back in time, why are these temples and palaces not alive, rather than being dead? And if this is *not* a move back in time, then where are the living people of the present? How can great and living cities—Athens, Tyre, Jerusalem—be reduced to ruination and to waste, to the eternal silence of death? The difference between this vision of the Levant and that of *Childe Harold* II is striking, for this is ostensibly the same landscape in which Harold finds both the same ruins *and* the civilization that has developed in the Levant since the temples and palaces were destroyed. Where Harold sees the ruins of paradise mingled with the signs and peoples of the contemporary East, however, the Visionary sees only ruins—not only because the narrator has effectively obliterated the people of the present from the Visionary's field of vision, but *because this is indeed not the Orient toured by Childe Harold.* Having been reinvented, it is an altogether different space, one that cannot be reconciled with the latter, but that can only take its place—for these visions and versions of the East are mutually exclusive and all-demanding.

Thus, while Byron and Childe Harold retrospectively mourn the passage of time from their inescapable standpoint in the present, viewing the Levantine ruins as the traces of premodern and bygone times, Shelley's East is always already in ruins, the flow of history—impossibly and paradoxically—having inexorably moved on to the future, in order to leave behind ruins, and at the same moment having ground to a halt in some fixed and immutable space of the past. "The waste where stood Jerusalem" presents the exalted city itself as at once preserved as a trace, and simultaneously cancelled and blasted out of existence, its inhabitants written over and hidden away, vanished refugees banished from their land. "The eternal pyramids" are eternal, living forever before and after, and yet at the same time they are consigned to the oblivion of the past. Such ruins are in one sense the "concretization" of history, bearing in their very materiality the inscriptions of the passage of time; that is, the movements and flows of historical events. Temples, castles, memorials, columns, statues, tombs stand as placemarkers on imaginary maps, the signposts of spots of time which open up from present and future moments to past ones—each is a space that has been temporalized. The spots of time in *Alastor*'s map of the East are, however, fleeting and illusory, sometimes reactivating and reanimating the glories of the past—so that the Visionary can literally "see" the birth of time—and sometimes falling short and yielding nothing but mute and non-signifying memorials, piles of barren and silent rocks. While each of the signposts on the map ("Tyre," "Memphis," "Babylon," "Jerusalem") might open to a different temporal level, none allows for the reactivation of events, so that they finally succeed one another as a series of flashes which flatten out into a more or less uniform time and space of a "past" seemingly without history. There is a certain order of succession, however, for they form a series that describes a gradual curve, an inverted "fertile crescent," first toward the southeast (Athens–Tyre–Baalbeck–Jerusalem–Babylon) and then toward the south (Babylon–Giza–Memphis–Thebes[33]–Ethiopia). At a more abstract level this series also describes a temporal trend, with every shift south or east marking a corresponding move "back" in history; that is, roughly from Ancient Greece to Phoenicia to Sumer to Ancient Egypt. Yet this temporal hierarchy breaks down and dissolves, not least because each of these civilizations had (spatially) moved out of its area of origin and (temporally and historically) mingled with the others. Again, *Alastor*'s map is undecided and unclear, and what we are left with is a more or less haphazard spatial identification of the Orient with the past. It is a will to render it past, despite the awareness that Athens and Tyre and Jerusalem live on into the poem's own historical present, the one in which Childe Harold encounters them. Shelley's vision of the East is ruthlessly violent, for he symbolically depopulates a space in order to establish the possibility (or even inevitability) of its reclamation as part of some suddenly invented "Western" heritage. For *if* this journey to the Orient is a journey back in time, its condition of possibility is the annihilation of the present Orient, which is necessarily reduced to desolation and ruin, not to life and "living history" but to spatialized and ossified, "dead" history—or rather to a place altogether without history (i.e., outside the diachronic and universal history of modernity and Europe).

Emptied of their peoples, the living cities of the Orient are rendered as tombs of the dead, frozen museum-piece images, icons of antiquity—as if Tyre and Athens and Jerusalem exist not for the sake of their own peoples and cultures, but for the sake of the European explorer who "discovers" them, indeed as if they would not exist at all without this explorer and discoverer who, even if he does not actually bring them into being, at least confirms their existence (as "dead civilizations," as more than one contemporary critic has put it). These cities, in other words, exist as signs to be read and suddenly understood, like statues or columns or paintings, by the European explorer, the "philosophical traveller": marks upon a suddenly aestheticized landscape.

Alastor, however, again undermines itself, for the Visionary does indeed encounter one inhabitant of the present Orient on his eastward journey:

> Meanwhile an Arab maiden brought his food,
> Her daily portion, from her father's tent,
> And spread her matting for his couch, and stole
> From duties and repose to tend his steps:—
> Enamoured, yet not daring for deep awe
> To speak her love:—and watched his nightly sleep,
> Sleepless herself, to gaze upon his lips
> Parted in slumber, whence the regular breath
> Of innocent dreams arose: then, when red morn
> Made paler the pale moon, to her cold home
> Wildered, and wan, and panting, she returned.[34]

But the Arab maiden is (paradoxically) out of place in this Orient, a disruptive eruption, interfering with the Visionary (who resolutely ignores her as if she were not there at all), just as the phantasmic Arab horseman intrudes on Wordsworth's dream of the East in *The Prelude*. The maiden is not part of the (dead) past, she shares the present with the Visionary. Or does she? She can see him; but does he see her, does he recognize her presence? For their encounter is non-synchronous, not as if they were in separate spatial compartments, but on the contrary as if they "share" or overlap in the same space but at different times, and hence as if they do not share it at all. She is like a ghost from the past who remains unseen and whose presence goes unrecognized in the present; she is there and yet not there; she is in the Visionary's time and yet not in it, she is simultaneously absence *and* presence, a kink, a distortion in an impossibly convulsed and twisted imaginary map. The maiden is like one of Byron's voluptuous Eastern women, but where Byron's Eastern poems are tales of encounter with the other, *Alastor* is a narrative of non-encounter. While the maiden, hence, cannot be accommodated or reconciled with the map, and remains an intrusion on its surface, *Alastor* is nevertheless uneasy in its treatment of the peoples of the East, principally their representative, this maiden who falls in love with the Visionary and who tends him, feeds him, clothes him only to be mutely and carelessly unacknowledged as he moves on in search of his ideal and phantasmatic love—a gesture of which the Narrator is highly critical.

The ruins of the East are silent and deserted, places where dead men hang their *mute* thoughts on the *mute* walls around. Byron's Childe Harold, in Greece, mourns for the fact that "these proud pillars," which to him are laden with all the meaning of Hellenic antiquity, "claim no passing sigh; / Unmoved the Moslem sits, the light Greek carols by."[35] In *Alastor*, though, Orientals are not just unmoved—they are altogether absent from the stupendous ruins of the days of old, where the "speechless shapes" of the East are finally unveiled, unlocked, understood by the silent gaze of the European, upon whom alone inspiration can flash and to whom alone visual and graphic meanings can be transmitted from these memorials of the past. *This* Orient, in other words, is a vacancy and an absence to be filled in (a "land without a people," to cite the planners of a later episode in the region's colonial history) to be brought to life by the European, who alone can fulfill its hidden potential and make this symbolic desert "bloom." Unlocking this Orient's potential wealth, both material and figurative, in other words, fundamentally requires the intervention of Europe, without which this wealth would go unappreciated and hence unexploited.

In his 1820 essay "A Philosophical View of Reform," which is often taken to be the poet's greatest political statement (though indeed its explicitly imperialist orientation usually passes unnoticed), Shelley argues that "the Turkish Empire is in its last stage of ruin, and it cannot be doubted but that the time is approaching when the deserts of Asia Minor and of Greece will be colonized by the overflowing populations of countries less enslaved and debased, and that the climate and the scenery which was the birthplace of all that is wise and beautiful will not remain forever the spoil of wild beasts and unlettered Tartars."[36] This view of Britain's and indeed Europe's colonial project (one which prefigures later developments in colonialism, not least in its evocation of Zionism), contributes also to the shaping of *Alastor*'s map of the East, though in the poem it is to a certain extent qualified and undermined. In either case, the appreciation of the Orient's monuments comes to stand for the awareness and productive exploitation of its *other* resources, so that what European intervention accomplishes is not the *creation* of wealth, but its actualization and realization, its redemption. In his "Philosophical View of Reform," Shelley goes on to argue that the introduction of "enlightened" European institutions, literatures and arts into Egypt "is *beginning* that change which Time, the great innovator, will *accomplish* in that degraded country; and by the same means its sublime and enduring monuments may excite lofty emotions in the hearts of the posterity of those who now contemplate them without admiration."[37] Without this European impetus, time would not be able to accomplish anything; or, rather, it is the arrival of Europe in the Orient that activates "History" and allows time to begin moving and accomplishing "historical" and modernizing change there—*the very change from which Byron, for his part, had turned to the Orient as a refuge in* Childe Harold *II.*

Alastor's map of the East emplots the creation of an altogether new Orient through the arrival there of European influence and empire. This is at once a spatial creation, insofar as a new Oriental space has been "discovered," and a temporal one, insofar as this new Orient is determined by the beginning of a new temporal structure: not the time— or timelessness—of the old Orient toured by Childe Harold, but the time of the "new" Europe (which would not include places like the Scottish Highlands, Ireland, Sicily, etc.), or in other words the time of modernity from which Harold and Byron had fled. Shelley's poem charts out a polymorphous and multidimensional Orient, only one "layer" of which is occupied by its Visionary. It constructs a spatialized map of time that effectively opens a fourth dimension, which for want of some more appropriate language I find myself forced to describe three-dimensionally as the "layers" and "levels" of an imaginary map.

The Visionary's push into the East involves the penetration into and literally the discovery of a previously hidden—*because not yet invented*—layer of the Orient, a layer that *Alastor* "peels" away from other versions and visions of "the" Orient. What the poem maps out is thus a new space-time of the Orient, "outside" or "underneath" of which other Orients (that is, the Orients inhabited, lived, and experienced by others and by European tourists in search of an Orient of difference) still manage to "exist," though they are inaccessible to the Visionary, just as *his* Orient is spatially and temporally forbidden to these others. The Arab maiden is a troubling and even transgressive figure who undermines and threatens the coherence of this structure: she is a refugee, a vagrant in space-time who floats in between the different dimensions of *Alastor*'s East, coming to "haunt" the poem in his own private Oriental space, only to finally give up and return to her father's tent, or in other words, to her "proper" space, that Orient where she "belongs."

Alastor concerns itself with and limits itself to the Orient that its Visionary has discovered, explored, appreciated, and above all understood. The "living" Orient of the poem's own present, as opposed to the "dead" Orient of ruined temples and palaces, is not seen (just as the Visionary does not really see the Arab maiden). Thus when the Visionary explores the "waste where stood Jerusalem," or the deserted and dust-blown ruins of Tyre or Athens or Memphis or Thebes, it is *his* own Jerusalem, his own Tyre, Athens, Memphis, and Thebes, that he sees—Oriental spaces upon which he meditates and ruminates. There are other visions and versions of these places, inhabited (though apparently not appreciated) by others. *Alastor*, a travel narrative of sorts, commemorates a certain type of tourism in which the tourist is "free" to consume the objects of his contemplation in his own private way, though unlike Childe Harold's tourism, which involves a private voyeuristic consumption of the otherness of the (contemporary) Orient. On its own terms, *Alastor*'s vision or re-vision of the East is *the* East, which is being "faithfully" re-presented to its Western readers. In other words, *Alastor* makes a claim about the universality and the truth of its vision and re-presentation of the Orient. Its Orient is the Orient; there is no other. Or: the Orient which *Alastor* discovers—i.e., invents—is not just cut off, isolated and placed in radical opposition to other versions of the Orient: it is linked to, and placed in continuity with, a larger vision of the world which lies to the west. *Alastor*'s East does *not* exist in isolation from some putative West; if it dives underneath other layers of the Orient, it does so partly in order to establish connections and continuities between *its* Orient and what lies to the west of this Orient, as though this (equally invented) West had seeped or pushed eastwards along with *Alastor* to claim this other Oriental space as its own, as part and parcel of the space that it had left "behind"—as an extension, or better yet, a colonial possession, of the West and of Europe.

In this sense, *Alastor* maps out a temporal colonization coinciding, complementing and constituting European spatial and material colonizations of the Orient in the late eighteenth and early nineteenth centuries. On the one hand, this involved the process that Johannes Fabian has identified as the simultaneous secularization and universalization of time (see section II, above).[38] On the other hand it involved a colonial reclamation and appropriation through the invention and spatial production of a certain version of the Orient as Europe's source of origin ("the birthplace of all that is wise and beautiful"). Not merely the "cradle of civilization," but the site, the scene, of Europe's heritage, this space suddenly needed to be understood and explained in terms of a (fabricated) historical and cultural "continuity" with modern Europe. It was gradually appropriated by the universalizing European claims that time and history are uniform natural "essences" that point to modernity and to Europe.

What *Alastor* does, then, is to re-orient the East in terms of this newly-developed universal essence of time. I say re-orient, because the other Orients (or older visions and versions of the Orient), including that of *Childe Harold,* cannot be accommodated in this newly-produced configuration of the East. Indeed, this Orient—*Alastor*'s East—has to be fundamentally reinvented in a recuperative gesture that removes it from the claims of the other Orient. One can posit a temporal divide separating these Orients from each other, as I've already suggested, the dimension of the East which the Visionary discovers and explores being neatly cut off from and made inaccessible to Orientals themselves, so that the Visionary is free to appreciate and understand it on his own. What I am arguing involves the production of an analogue to Frantz Fanon's great dictum that "the colonial world is a world cut in two."[39] For Fanon, the profound dividing line is spatial, as expressed in the violent division of the colonial city (of which French-occupied Algiers is his prime example):

> . . . The zone where the natives live is not complementary to the zone inhabited by the settlers. The two zones are opposed, but not in the service of a higher unity. Obedient to the rules of pure Aristotelian logic, they both follow the principles of reciprocal exclusivity. No conciliation is possible, for of the two terms, one is superfluous. The settlers' town is a strongly built town, all made of stone and steel. It is a brightly lit town; the streets are covered with asphalt, and the garbage cans swallow all the leavings, unseen, unknown and hardly thought about. . . . The settlers' town is a well-fed town, an easygoing town; its

belly is always full of good things. The settlers' town is a town of white people, of foreigners.

The town belonging to the colonized people, or at least the native town, the Negro village, the medina, the reservation, is a place of ill fame, peopled by men of ill repute. They are born there, it matters little where or how; they die there, it matters not where, nor how. It is a world without spaciousness; men live on top of each other, and their huts are built one on top of the other. The native town is a hungry town, starved of bread, of meat, of shoes, of coal, of light, a town on its knees, a town wallowing in the mire. It is a town of niggers and dirty Arabs.[40]

Alastor's map of the East is not only an intervention in the Orient and hence (which is to say the same thing) in the imaginary terrain produced by Orientalism; it produces a new version of Oriental space-time that must be placed in radical opposition to previous European conceptions, versions, productions, of this space, not least that of *Childe Harold*. Its logic of separation and division is not solely spatial, but simultaneously spatial and temporal. The natives, the Orientals themselves, are consigned to their own version, their own space, their own time—none of which concern *Alastor* or its Visionary, as they are displaced beyond the poem's rigorously self-imposed limits and remain ghosts hovering on the edges of the poem, haunting it. They exist on the multiple other sides of this interdimensional frontier: in the Orients of Beckford's *Vathek*, of Southey's *Thalaba* and *Kehama*, of Byron's *Corsair*, of de Quincey's opium-induced Asiatic nightmares, in the worlds of European penetrations and visits to the Orient of the other, as opposed to this newly-invented "European" Orient. And yet, of course, both these Orients are produced, and policed, by Europeans— by the Orientalists, the colonial administrators, the armies of occupation. This amounts to something more than what Fabian terms the "denial of coevalness," through which Europeans distinguished themselves from their colonial interlocutors according to their supposed relative positions on the stream of evolutionary time, so that European ventures into the colonial realm were seen as voyages "back" to the time of the other.[41] Thus the clash of cultures on the imperial frontier is also a clash of temporalities: this newly-invented Orient, and hence this whole new set of relations between Orientals and Europeans (which is what the Orient and Orientalism always imply and delineate, as Said argues), could thus be opposed to older versions, older and now-subsumed "layers" of this imaginary map of the imperial domain.

In the meantime, this new Orient could be excavated and explored, could be recuperated, redeemed, put to good use, saved from itself and

from degradation and waste. And indeed its inhabitants could and
even had to be re-invented as well. They had to be re-Orientalized.[42]
Europe's colonial project could change to a benevolent mission of salvation, by which the Orientals could be given aid and allowed, through
"catching" what Shelley called a "contagion of good," to break out of
the prison of their old space and hence into "our" world, "our" world
history, and the stream of evolutionary time which is warily patrolled
by "our" gunboats. While this vision of the colonial mission anticipates
the Victorian conception of empire, in Shelley it is still premature, as
if the terrain on which its great drama will eventually unfold has only
just been captured, and hence is still composed of ruins and deserts in
urgent need of repopulation and reconstruction. In a long and careless,
though impassioned, paragraph of his 1820 essay, Shelley writes:

> Revolutions in the political and religious state of the Indian peninsula
> seem to be accomplishing, and it cannot be doubted but the zeal of the
> missionaries of what is called the Christian faith [allowed into India for
> the first time as late as 1813] will produce beneficial innovation there,
> even by the application of dogmas and forms of what is here an out-
> worn incumbrance. The Indians have been enslaved and cramped in
> the most severe and paralysing forms which were ever devised by man;
> some of this new enthusiasm ought to be kindled among them to con-
> sume it and leave them free, and even if the doctrines of Jesus do not
> penetrate through the darkness of that which those who profess to be
> his followers call Christianity, there will yet be a number of social forms
> modelled upon those European feelings from which it has taken its col-
> our substituted to those according to which they are at present
> cramped, and from which, when the time for complete emancipation
> shall arrive, their disengagement may be less difficult, and under which
> their progress to it may be the less imperceptibly slow. Many native Indi-
> ans have acquired, it is said, a competent knowledge in the arts and phi-
> losophy of Europe, and Locke and Hume and Rousseau are familiarly
> talked of in Brahminical society. But the thing to be sought is that they
> should, as they would do if they were free, attain to a system of arts and
> literature of their own.

The arrival of Europe in the Orient thus suddenly and even violently
wrenches the latter into "the" stream of history. Not only does it begin
the process of freeing the Orientals literally from themselves (from
their culture, their social institutions and organizations), but it begins
their gradual and total re-development, through which they have to
begin from nought, leaving behind the cultural products of their past
only to hope for the vague possibility of some day developing "their
own" arts and literature. What has been used up and rendered outmoded in Europe, including for instance Christianity, thus has some

usefulness and applicability to this region which can now aspire to cultural, philosophical, economic and political handouts, aid, and encouragement from Europe. Whereas Byron turned to the East, in *Childe Harold* and his Tales, as a space toward which to escape—and from which to critique and contest—modernity and its claim on the space of Europe, this newly produced Eastern terrain is effectively an extension of Europe, no longer an opposite, but a space which Europe could colonize and thus use to re-produce itself. In other words, the supposedly specific, cyclical and even centripetal time and history of the East can now be opened up and channeled into the uniformationist, unilinear, and universal time and history of modernization and development.[43] I have already said, however, that *Alastor* is not quite so straightforward as this later summary of the dubious benefits of colonization. If the latter is reminiscent of a retrospective history of contact on the imperial frontier, *Alastor* represents a first glimpse at a new space that would be elaborated in later visions of the East, including Shelley's 1820 essay.

These possibilities of the new East exist not merely for the Orientals themselves (if at all), but for the Europeans who have captured this terrain by the act of having defined it. Greece, in particular, becomes a site which had to be cut off from its Oriental affiliations and completely redeemed as a part of Europe, thus pushing the imaginary frontier between East and West further east, toward Turkey. In a now often-quoted claim, Shelley argues in the preface to *Hellas* (1821): "The apathy of the rulers of the civilised world to the astonishing circumstance of the descendants of that nation to which they owe their civilisation, rising as it were from the ashes of their ruin, is something perfectly inexplicable to a mere spectator of the shows of this mortal scene. We are all Greeks. Our laws, our literature, our religion, our arts have their roots in Greece. But for Greece—Rome, the instructor, the conqueror, or the metropolis of our ancestors, would have spread no illumination with her arms, and we might still have been savages and idolaters; or, what is worse, might have arrived at such a stagnant and miserable state of social institution as China and Japan possess." And yet, when he was writing those words, in 1821, Greece was still a part of the Ottoman Empire, and hence merely one of the many parts of the Orient which Europeans were gradually beginning to claim for themselves. As he announces in *Hellas*, the modern Greeks ("descendants of those glorious beings whom the imagination almost refuses to figure to itself as belonging to our kind"), through their revolution against the Turks, are somehow reinventing themselves, rising as reincarnated Europeans from the ashes of Oriental despotism: "Greece, which was dead, is arisen!"[44] And yet in this reinvention lay opportunity not only for the Greeks, but for the other Europeans, who could now establish their claims to an "authentically" Greek (as opposed to Egyptian, Persian, or Arab) heritage. Indeed, this reclamation and recuperation of "our" heritage establishes, on this Romantic Hellenophilic (or, rather, Helleno-maniac) view, not only a claim to some past, but the basis for security for the future, almost a renewal, or rather re-beginning of time and of history; "The world's great age begins anew, / The golden years return, / The earth doth like a snake renew / Her winter weeds outworn."[45] This is precisely the standpoint on Greek renewal and rebirth—a reawakening of Hellenism—denied and rejected by Byron in *Childe Harold* II and its notes (see above), which instead insist on the final death of Greece, albeit as one that ought to be commemorated.[46]

Elsewhere in the East, Europeans were laying their claims to have derived their heritage from certain "pure" strains of Indic civilization, leading ultimately to the construction of an "Indo-European" language family, civilization, and race, supposedly distinct from the taints and impurities of Africa or the rest of Asia. This newly-discovered Orient, however had first to be separated from the old Orient (that is, other "layers" of the imaginary map), and purged of its influence, whether through the fires of revolution (as in Greece) or through the discipline of archaeological or philological research (as in India). Thus, as Martin Bernal has suggested, in the late eighteenth and especially the early nineteenth centuries, Europeans began to fundamentally re-cast their relations with and to the Orient, selectively claiming heritage from this or that corner of the East, while separating these putative heritages from less convenient or desirable cultural, historical, and political attachments and associations (e.g., the enormous influence of Egypt on classical Greek culture, or the interpenetration of Indian cultures with Arabic, Persian, and Chinese civilizations).[47] Indeed, the Orient itself, as a space of material, discursive, and figurative opportunity, had to be entirely re-invented and re-discovered. It had to be altogether reproduced, and Orientals, born "anew," had to begin their "progress" from scratch, the cultural productions and achievements of their previous incarnation being not merely devalued but, in the course of their new development, inappropriate, as the outworn remnants of a bygone age. As Shelley puts it in his essay, they could now only "aspire" to arts and literature "of their own," like good pupils who have plenty of potential and yet have not actually produced anything to show for themselves. For (as I've already said) in Shelley's terms, the arrival of European influence "begins" the change that time "will accomplish." Until then, time was unable to accomplish anything: not only had the Orient "stopped developing," but time itself had stopped there, and had thickened and congealed into endless and everlasting ruin and decay without or outside of history. Yet even if it opens up into the "new" Orient, *Alastor* marks a transition between Orientalist structures and paradigms, and the supposedly displaced other returns in the form of the Arab maiden, a haunting presence who is recognized by the Narrator and not by the Visionary—as though the Narrator could see the "old" Orient inhabited by this other, whereas the Visionary can only see the ruins and temples of the "new" Orient which are there for him to understand, to know, and to map on his journey and his quest into the Orient.

Perhaps for obvious reasons, I have not been concerned in this reading of *Alastor* with an examination of this quest itself, or in other words with an examination of the poem's narrative. Instead my analysis has been restricted to the terrain on which the narrative takes place, a terrain that has more or less been taken for granted by recent critics, whose readings uncritically reproduce Shelley's vision of the East as a tantalizing imaginary space, which serves—for them as well as for the poet—merely as a necessarily silent surface for (Western) inscriptions and interventions. For insufficient critical attention has been given to the imaginary terrain on which the Visionary's (I use Earl Wasserman's terminology to avoid confusion)[48] quest unfolds. Instead, critics have focused on the nature of the quest. Thus, while Earl Wasserman's reading of the poem has become one of the central landmarks on the terrain of these critical debates, and if more recent critics try either to support, to attack, to refine, or to develop Wasserman's careful and nuanced reading of the quest, the poem's historical ground—and, again, the terrain on which the quest is written—recedes further and further from view. That is to say, this "critical" terrain supplants the imaginary Oriental terrain produced in the poem as a basis for readings and re-readings of *Alastor*. The main issue at stake in the critical discussion of the poem has recently shifted toward a debate over whether *Alastor*'s narrator and the Visionary are two different characters (which is what Wasserman proposes), one character struggling with himself, two different versions of the same persona (as Christopher Heppner argues), or indeterminate identities (the position taken by Martyn Crucefix and Frederick Kirchhoff).[49] For all the critics' disagreements about the similarities or differences between the Narrator and the Visionary, they seem to be virtually unanimous in their view of *Alastor*'s representation of the Orient, almost entirely taking for granted the poem's assumptions about Asia and the peoples and civilizations that happen to be there—whose existence and history make it difficult, in my view, to take Shelley so easily and uncritically at his word. Harold Bloom, for instance, writes simply that the Visionary "moves on to the foothills of the Caucasus, retracing in reverse the march of civilization,"[50] a march that in this view "obviously" took a westward course, reaching its height in Europe and America, so that the Visionary, going back in time, goes back to the cradle of (ultimately a Western) civilization. Heppner writes that the Visionary tours the ruins of "Nature and past culture"; Strickland says that the voyage is to "dead civilizations . . . away from civilization altogether"; while John Reider, offering his reading as "a politicizing supplement to other interpretations," has little difference with other critics on this point. In the poem's own terms, of course, these critics' claims have truth-content; but it seems to me that one must question and interrogate not merely the poem's narrative, but its very terms and conditions of possibility. My own reading of *Alastor* proposes that the quest and the terrain on which it unfolds are not coincidental to each other and must be read together; a detailed reading of the quest, which lies outside the scope of this essay, must be informed by a reading of the terrain, by placing both in an historical and historicized perspective.

The Narrator's reappearance and intervention in the text of the poem highlights the Visionary's death and the total failure of his quest. Up to that moment, however, the Narrator's involvement complements the Visionary's voyage. It is the Narrator who translates the spatial production of the East undertaken in the poem into visual terms, and hence it is structurally and formally through the device of the Narrator that the Visionary is placed on *Alastor*'s map of the East. Until that final moment, therefore, the Narrator and the poem both enable and participate in the Visionary's quest through and across the space of the Orient. The Narrator's "reversal" of position—even if it had been anticipated and prepared for in the preface and the opening lines of the poem itself—retroactively and retrospectively unravels and condemns the Visionary's quest. *Alastor* produces an imaginary map of the space of the East and then consumes it. It puts it forward and then withdraws it and cancels it out. Put in slightly different terms, the quest that takes place—a quest for a self-projected and self-confirming other (in other words, a version of the self *itself*)—is enabled and sustained by the terrain on which it takes place, i.e., the particular version of the space of the East that the poem itself produces. In simultaneously producing this terrain and narrating the quest that it finally condemns, the poem rewrites and destroys itself.

Alastor produces a version of the Orient in which otherness has been all but obliterated (save for its traces and vestigial hauntings, e.g., the Arab maiden), and in which a search can take place for images and reflections of Europe; this new Orient is thus no longer a refuge offering and containing the other, it is a cleaned-out slate ready for European colonization and inscription—even if these processes are condemned by *Alastor*'s Narrator. In *Childe Harold* II, Byron produces a spatial version of the Orient as a refuge from modernity; he and his alter ego venture into that space in search of otherness, and precisely in search of the sort of exchange and reciprocity with otherness that the Narrator of *Alastor* affirms. Against *Childe Harold*'s dreams of an immortal, everlasting and immutably different East, Shelley's poem puts forward a vision of the East as a space for European redemption in evolution and in progress, in the development and improvement of others who turn out to be merely inferior versions of "ourselves."

NOTES

Copyright © Saree Makdisi 1995. This essay has been adapted from a book-length study, which is being prepared for publication, of the emergence of modern imperial culture and of British representations of Nature and the colonial world in the Romantic period. A version of the second half of the essay was presented at a conference, "Changing the Subject," held at the University of Glasgow, Scotland, in July 1992; a version of the first half was presented at the British Association for Romantic Studies conference at the University of Strathclyde, Glasgow, in July 1993. I am deeply indebted to Fredric Jameson, Robert Gleckner, Marjorie Levinson, Barbara Herrnstein Smith, Kenneth Surin, Cesare Casarino, Rebecca Karl, and James Chandler for invaluable comments on and criticisms of earlier drafts.

1. James Mill, *The History of British India* (1837; Chicago: University of Chicago Press, 1975). Preface, p. 13.

2. Frantz Fanon, *The Wretched of the Earth*, translated by Constance Farrington (New York: Grove Press, 1991), p. 36.

3. See Edward W. Said's *Orientalism* (New York: Pantheon, 1977).

4. See, for example, Shelley's *The Revolt of Islam* (1818) and *Hellas* (1822).

5. See Victor Kiernan, *The Lords of Human Kind* (New York: Columbia University Press, 1986), p. 13.

6. Byron, *Childe Harold's Pilgrimage*, canto II, XLIII.

7. Bernard Blackstone, " 'The Loops of Time': Spatio-Temporal Patterns in 'Childe Harold'." *Ariel*, 2 (1971), 5.

8. Johannes Fabian, *Time and the Other: How Anthropology Makes Its Object* (New York: Columbia University Press, 1986), p. 6.

9. See Stephen Jay Gould, *Ever Since Darwin: Reflections in Natural History* (Now York: Norton, 1977), pp. 147–52; also see Fabian, pp. 6–12.

10. See Robert Gleckner, *Byron and the Ruins of Paradise* (Baltimore: Johns Hopkins University Press, 1967), esp. pp. 69–90.

11. *Childe Harold* II, III.

12. Indeed, Britain did not invade Egypt again until 1882; elsewhere in the Arab world, it made various "arrangements," e.g., with the emirs of the Gulf—mostly concerning the overland and maritime approaches to India. Thus it is not a coincidence that the first two major conquests of Arab countries were by the French, in Egypt (1798) and Algeria (1830), while Britain

intervened in the Mediterranean region mostly in response to French or Russian advances. See Hourani, *A History of the Arab Peoples* (New York: Warner Books, 1992), pp. 265–314.

13. As Bernard Blackstone puts it. See Bernard Blackstone, *Byron: A Survey* (London: Longman, 1975), pp. 88–89. The significance of such latter-day "Orientalizing" among Romanticists (Blackstone is by no means alone in this regard) cannot be overestimated.

14. According to Hourani, there was, for instance, little or no direct merchant traffic between the Levant and Britain before 1815; following the wars, and especially in the 1830s, shipping lines connected the ports of the southern and eastern Mediterranean with London, Liverpool, and Marseille—and, while exports of Egyptian cotton to Lancashire increased dramatically following the wars (tenfold from 1800 to 1850), British exports to the Levant increased by some 800 percent in value between 1815 and 1850. At the same time, the Ottoman sultans (notably Selim III and Murad II) and their governors—once again, especially Muhammad Ali of Egypt—began undertaking "Westernizing" reforms, and European cultural production had a direct and enduring impact on the region. See Hourani's *A History of the Arab Peoples*, and also his important book *Arabic Thought in the Liberal Age: 1798–1939* (Cambridge: Cambridge University Press, 1988).

15. See Blackstone, *Byron: A Survey*, p. 93; and Jerome McGann, *The Beauty of Inflections* (Oxford: Oxford University Press, 1989), pp. 255–62.

16. "To withdraw myself from myself (oh that cursed selfishness!) has ever been my sole, my entire, my sincere motive in scribbling at all." Journal entry, 27 November 1813. See Marchand, ed., *Selected Letters and Journals* (Cambridge: Harvard University Press, 1982), p. 360. Also see *Childe Harold* II, XXV–XXVII: "But midst the crowd, the hum, the shock of men, / To hear, to see, to feel, and to possess, / And roam along, the world's tired denizen, / With none who bless us, none whom we can bless; / Minions of splendour shrinking from distress! / None that, with kindred consciousness endued, / If we were not, would seem to smile the less, / Of all that flatter'd, follow'd, sought, and sued; / This is to be alone; this, this is solitude!"

17. See Said's *Orientalism*.

18. See Timothy Mitchell, *Colonising Egypt* (Berkeley: University of California Press, 1991).

19. Gleckner, p. 81.

20. Here I would qualify Marilyn Butler's observation that "Orientalism is a major theme of English Romanticism," a statement that limits Orientalism to the status of a narrowly-considered "theme." See Marilyn Butler, "The Orientalism of Byron's *Giaour*," in *Byron and the Limits of Fiction*, edited by Bernard Beatty and Vincent Newey (New York: Barnes & Noble, 1989), p. 78.

21. Patrick Brantlinger argues, for instance, that *Childe Harold* and the Turkish Tales "seem to celebrate a barbarism identified not only with Oriental despotism but with the desire for personal liberty and national independence from empire." See Patrick Brantlinger, *Rule of Darkness: British Literature and Imperialism, 1830–1914* (Ithaca: Cornell University Press, 1988),

pp. 140–41. McGann makes a similar point; see *The Beauty of Inflections*, p. 200.

22. Butler, p. 85. Note, however, that Butler elsewhere contrasts Byron's Orientalism with that of Shelley, whose works, she says, "display a kind of Orientalism with more complex potential than Byron's." See Marilyn Butler, *Romantics, Rebels & Reactionaries* (New York: Oxford University Press, 1980), p. 121.

23. Marilyn Butler, "Plotting the Revolution: The Political Narratives of Romantic Poetry and Criticism," in *Romantic Revolutions: Criticism and Theory*, ed. Kenneth Johnston, et al., 1990, p. 142.

24. See, e.g., Butler's essay on *The Giaour*, where she observes that Southey was one of the first writers of the time who believed that evangelical missions ought to be sent to India: a position that she contrasts with Byron's.

25. See Brantlinger, pp. 141–45.

26. Indeed, in his *Hebrew Melodies* (1815), Byron is evocative of a premature Zionism, one which predates the colonialist project of the mature Zionism developed by Theodor Herzl and others from the 1890s onwards (a project formally launched in 1897 and formally given the support of the British Empire in the Balfour Declaration of 1917).

27. Byron, *The Giaour*.

28. Mary Louise Pratt, "Scratches on the Face of the Country; or, What Mr. Barrow Saw in the Land of the Bushmen," in *"Race," Writing, and Difference*, ed. Henry Gates Jr. (Chicago: University of Chicago Press, 1986), p. 140.

29. Joseph-Marie Degérando, *The Observation of Savage Peoples* (1800). Quoted in Fabian, *Time and the Other*, p. 7.

30. *Alastor*, lines 387–93. My italics.

31. *Alastor*, lines 107–28.

32. The sphinx was damaged by Napoleon's artillery in 1798.

33. Not the Thebes in Greece, but the Thebes in Upper (i.e., southern) Egypt, which was the Greek name for the capital of Upper Egypt, Luxor.

34. *Alastor*, lines 129–39.

35. Byron, *Childe Harold*, canto II, X.

36. Shelley, "A Philosophical View of Reform," p. 225.

37. Shelley, p. 226. My emphasis.

38. See Fabian, pp. 1–35.

39. Frantz Fanon, *The Wretched of the Earth*, p. 38.

40. Fanon, pp. 38–39.

41. Fabian, p. 30.

42. To use one of Said's terms. See Said, pp. 49–72.

43. Sentiments which are echoed in a more elaborate form by Marx in *Capital*, vol. 1, where he says that capitalism will finally provide the key to the "riddle of the unchangeability of Asiatic societies." See Karl Marx, *Capital*, vol. 1, translated by Ben Fowkes (1867; New York: Vintage Books, 1977).

44. Shelley, *Hellas*, line 1059.

45. *Hellas,* lines 1060–65.

46. As my distinction between Byron and Shelley suggests, the relationship between different versions of Philhellenism and imperialism needs to be examined much more closely. On the one hand, I am uneasy with Jerome McGann's proposition that Shelley's ideals, as expressed in his proclamation that "we" are all Greeks, are "typical philhellenist illusions, and, as such, were open to political exploitation by Europe's imperialist powers, as well as by poetical exploitation by writers like Shelley and Byron." On the other hand, I have grave disagreements, some already outlined above, with Mark Kipperman's reductive assertion that, in the context of the eastern Mediterranean in the 1820s, "philhellenism could be seen as nothing less than a challenge to the global order of empires negotiated in 1815." Kipperman goes on to say that, "Within its own forms and the real historical context it evokes, Shelley's idealism in *Hellas* does reflect the constitutionalist, nationalist, and essentially anti-imperialist progressivism of his time." I believe that Shelley represents a much more aggressive form of colonialism than Byron, precisely because his imperial world view is fired by progressivism, whereas Byron's is sustained by some sort of respect in the inalterable otherness of other cultures, a respect that, at least in his 1812 *Childe Harold,* tempered his philhellenism. But the point is not that Shelley was imperialist and Byron was anti-imperialist; as I have tried to suggest, their different approaches to and versions of philhellenism and Orientalism correspond to different moments or phases of imperial development. See Jerome McGann, *The Romantic Ideology* (Chicago: University of Chicago Press, 1983), p. 125; and Mark Kipperman, "Macropolitics of Utopia: Shelley's *Hellas* in Context," in *The Macropolitics of Nineteenth Century Literature,* ed. Jonathan Arac (Philadelphia: University of Pennsylvania Press, 1991), p. 92.

47. See Martin Bernal, *Black Athena: The Afroasiatic Roots of Classical Civilization* (New Brunswick: Rutgers University Press, 1985), pp. 189–245.

48. See Earl Wasserman, *Shelley: A Critical Reading* (Baltimore: Johns Hopkins University Press, 1971), pp. 3–46.

49. See Martyn Crucefix, "Wordsworth, Superstition, and Shelley's *Alastor,*" *Essays in Criticism,* 33 (1983): 126–45; Christopher Heppner, "*Alastor:* The Poet and the Narrator Reconsidered," *Keats-Shelley Journal,* 37 (1988): 91–109; Frederick Kirchhoff, "Shelley's *Alastor:* The Poet Who Refuses to Write Language," *Keats-Shelley Journal,* 32 (1983): 108–22; John Rieder, "Description of a Struggle: Shelley's Radicalism on Wordsworth's Terrain," *Boundary* 2, 8 (1985): 267–87; Edward Strickland, "Transfigured Night: The Visionary Inversions of *Alastor,*" *Keats-Shelley Journal,* 33 (1984): 148–60.

50. Harold Bloom, *The Visionary Company: A Reading of English Romantic Poetry* (Ithaca: Cornell University Press, 1971), p. 289.

Nine

NANCY MOORE GOSLEE

Hemans's "Red Indians": Reading Stereotypes

IN 1824 Felicia Hemans published a poem in the *New Monthly Magazine* which begins, "Is not thy heart far off amidst the woods / Where the Red Indian lays his father's dust . . . by the rushing of the torrent floods . . . ?"[1] Doubling her characteristic gestures of melancholy, she asks her addressee whether he yearns for a "far off" place; and that place, in turn, is characterized by a figure in the landscape, a "Red Indian" who mourns his dead father. Because of a gesture toward sublime expansion in the "rushing of the torrent floods," these layers of mourning can find a release from a fixed despair that would cling to the image of the lost beloved. If we can appreciate Hemans's lyric skill at evoking and placing emotion, however, her phrasing disturbs a twentieth-century reader. The first troubling aspect is one of style: Hemans characteristically uses broad categories of description that evoke stock visual images, almost icons, for generating emotional responses. This style is neither the simplified yet occasionally abstract and philosophical diction of the "high Romantic" lyric, nor the quotidian depiction of domestic responsibilities which Stuart Curran and Marlon Ross praise in women romantic writers.[2] Though economic in its gestures and accessible in its vocabulary, Hemans's poetry risks stereotype both in its melodic rightness and in what now seems to us a conceptual and emotional expectedness. If we accept this aspect of style as an effective means of communicating to her audience—and, to judge by her popularity, it was very effective—then we face the more troubling political or ideological question of how her generalization of a marked racial otherness should be read. "Red" makes the figures "far off" and other to most of Hemans's early readers—and many of them now—who are white Europeans and Americans; "Indians" brackets together very diverse groups and does so, of course, under a European expectation of discovering the Orient by westering.[3]

Though the aesthetic problem of a stereotypical phrasing exists all through her poetry, only fourteen of her many poems represent or refer to the groups Europeans then called "red" or American Indians. These poems, then, might seem unrepresentative of her work's wider political and ideological implications. Yet much of her work explores the consequences of patriotism and imperialism for women, and the European colonizing of America extends these consequences by confronting racial differences along with gender differences. Further, attitudes of melancholy or mourning are pervasive in Hemans's poetry; and these "Indian" poems re-appropriate a barely post-colonial treatment of American Indians as lost and yet redemptive figures for the culture of the early United States. Representing the often conflicting values of exile from a homeland, liberty in a new land, terror of the vast wilderness, and a nurturing, maternal nature, these figures embody a complex ideological representation of melancholy. Many of these representations, moreover, involve women either as literal and symbolic victims or as mythic redemptive forces such as liberty or nature.[4] Through Hemans's "red Indian" poems, then, we can explore how this already multiply-determined and to some extent already Anglo-American interpretation of "Indians" as simultaneously alien, uncivilizable objects and universally-feeling subjects relates to interpretations of Hemans's own melancholy, a melancholy usually linked more exclusively to gender.

In "Race and Sensibility in the Early Republic," Julie Ellison argues that Indians and women shared a melancholy prompted by their marginalization, and thus that race and gender can figure each other's anxieties. Ellison's readings show how complex such an equation can become, and in Hemans's poems such an alignment becomes complicated even further by her own position on another shore. Two recent interpretations of Hemans's "British" melancholy can help us explore her almost contrapuntal portrayal of race and gender in these poems. Anne Mellor proposes that Hemans's own broken marriage created a yearning for familial unity and domesticity, yet that this yearning found all too much reinforcement in the anti-Jacobin backlash that supported separate spheres for men and women.[5] Tricia Lootens's more recent essay argues that Hemans's melancholy is generated both from the patriotic, public mourning for soldiers in the Napoleonic wars and other military ventures, and from a powerful undercurrent criticizing the costs of this military and political empire-building for individuals and families.[6] Both of these critics suggest that we read Hemans for ironic subtexts of meaning beneath the blandly affirmative surfaces of her patriotic and domestic affect, yet both seem uncertain about whether or to what extent Hemans controls her ironic subtexts. I would suggest that she does indeed control a complex ideological effect, but that this effect might better be described as synthetic than as ironic. By carefully circumventing or omitting contested territory, by universalizing common affective ground, and by generalizing descriptive details, she extends sympathy in ways that begin to transform the very generalizations she works with. We might interpret this extension of sympathy as an emotional or spiritual colonizing, and indeed it appears that way in some poems. She mourns for a lost American empire, a symbolic or allegorical place "far off amidst the woods" in which the actual colonists' violent expropriation of Indian territory and now the expropriation of British territory by actual republican settlers does not exist. Familial, even domestic affections exist there, but almost without domiciles, and with few "quotidian" details; and though the European characters yearn for home, that yearning is ambivalent, for it sometimes fuses with the Indians' journeys either to westward exile or to a "spirit land." Though using the language of sensibility and not that of irony, these poems create a version of what Homi Bhabha calls "the hybridity of imagined communities," through the "emergence of the interstices—the overlap and displacement of difference" where cultures and selves are worked out.[7]

The 1824 lyric I began with illustrates very effectively the way Hemans creates a gap where more explicitly contested territory is redefined as a more symbolic, sympathetic affective terrain. Titled "Child of the Forests," the poem is later subtitled "Written after reading the Memoirs of John Hunter." In 1824 her original readers would have supplied this gloss, for Hunter's *Memoirs of a Captivity among the Indians of North America, from Childhood to the Age of Nineteen,* published in Philadelphia and London in 1823, were widely read and reviewed in both countries.[8] In early 1824, Hunter was in London, an object of fascination as a white captive who both valued Indian culture and yet could wield "civilized" culture. Yet when her poem describes him as "mingling with the city's throng" and asks, "Doth not thy soul o'ersweep the foaming main, / To pour itself upon the wilds again?" Hemans leaps over the intervening territory that almost immediately made Hunter and his *Memoirs* controversial: the territory of an expanding United States, with its land-exacerbated tensions of "red, white, and black."[9]

The metaphor of Hemans's title has a complex history I will only touch on. In 1818 John C. Calhoun, then U.S. Secretary of War and thus in charge of Indian affairs, wrote, "to use a figure drawn from their own sublime eloquence, the poor children of the forest have been driven by a great wave which has flowed in from the Atlantic ocean to almost the base of the Rocky Mountains and [is] overwhelming them in its terrible progress" (Dippie, 8). When Calhoun adapts that eloquence and ironically makes them infants who cannot speak for themselves, he avoids his and his government's own agency, naturalizing the Indians' loss of territory and cultural continuity into inevitability. Intense British interest in Hunter's book was prompted in part, as it was for the *Quarterly*'s reviewer, by admiration for the Indians and in part by a desire to criticize U.S. policies that were fast making them only "a living ruin." A former British army officer who had served in Canada in 1812–13, the reviewer champions a British paternalism that rewarded the "children of the forest," led by Tecumseh, for "tak[ing] up the hatchet with their British Father, against the Long Knives, as they termed the Americans."[10] In the name of the "British Father," the reviewer attacks a "republican government," unable to control "the recklessness of all human restraint and compunction which distinguish [the] . . . lawless and ferocious body" of "the mass of outsettlers." It is "American policy" to advocate "extermination of all the Indian nations east of the Rocky Mountains." He has, of course, ample evidence of abuses and atrocities, especially "the recent and authorised horrors of General Jackson's Seminole War."

Like many American writers in the northeastern and middle Atlantic states where the immediate threat of Indian hostility had eased by the 1820s, British conservatives were freer to sympathize with, instead of demonizing, "red Indians." Furthermore, such sympathy could ease the anxieties posed in several other "Indian" territories, over which they retained a troubling control: the British West Indies, and, in the Far East, the "real" India. In the West Indies, the 1807 bill abolishing the slave trade had ended the importing of Africans to replace the virtually destroyed "red Indians" as labor on the sugar plantations, but agitation for total emancipation continued in England through the 1820s. In the southern and "old southwestern" states of the U.S., from Jackson's campaign against the Seminoles in Florida through his ousting of the Cherokees from Georgia, the Carolinas and Tennessee in 1830, Indian policy became increasingly entwined with an agricultural economy that justified black chattel slavery on grounds of an increasingly fixed racial difference. Black Africans might be civilized, though civilized as slaves, befitting their "nature"; while Red Indians, befitting their nature, should be "saved" in their supposedly primitive, non-agricultural state by westward removal across the Mississippi.[11]

Discussing this growth of British agitation for the emancipation of slaves in the 1820s, Moira Ferguson mentions in passing that "Popular contemporary poets, Letitia Landon . . . and Felicia Hemans underscored bondage in their verses."[12] Yet the silence of the latter on the more specific issue of black chattel slavery in the Americas is striking in contrast to the work of the other women writers Ferguson discusses. Though her *Records of Woman* and her other poems range as far afield as Bengal, Hemans never takes up the cause of African enslavement nor even the representation of Africans other than Moors. Her family background and her father's business connections in Liverpool must have made her acutely aware of that city's involvement in the slave trade, though this very closeness may have encouraged a discretionary silence.[13] We might also argue that Hemans uses "red Indians" as a more acceptable way of developing toleration for racial difference than a direct discussion of black chattel slavery would have been. Yet no simple equation that substitutes one "alien" race for another will work here, even if similar fears and projections work in each confrontation of Europeans with others[14] and even if American whites were constantly struggling with such comparisons and contrasts. Instead, we might hypothesize that a strong awareness of how powerfully charged racial issues and images can be emerged from Hemans's Liverpool background and influenced her careful manipulation of stereotypes of Indians. Further, we might speculate that the very lack of a neat equation between "red" and "black" situations and responses encouraged her to draw upon highly—but not explosively—charged images of race to destabilize stereotypes of gender—and that, in turn, she negotiates the apparently contradictory pulls in her portrayals of race between a universalizing "otherness" and a universalizing sentiment that suggests a common subjectivity through the apparently more familiar terrain of gender.

In Hemans's "red Indian" poems, these charged images show a range of functions from poem to poem. In some poems they seem only scenic markers to signal the alien if sometimes soothing vastness and emptiness of the landscape for European refugees from persecution and imprisonment. In other poems, the "red Indian" figures reveal universal human sentiments, especially spiritual and domestic sentiments, even within cultures represented as alien and untouched by European influence. As if developing out of a confrontation between these two roles is a third one, in which the figures are more explicitly caught in the clash between their own native culture and that of the expanding European settlements. In this third category are two captivity narratives that warrant close comparison to other examples of that genre.

Though she first published many of her poems individually in periodicals, Hemans organized them for republication in thematic collections or wrote them specifically for such collections. These collections, or a longer poem or play, often made up half of a volume; "miscellaneous" or "other" poems filled the backs of those volumes. For each of these collections, Hemans works out carefully modulated emphases that influence our interpretation of race and gender in individual poems. A further formal context to consider is Hemans's editorial framing, a citing of authorities that evokes historical and geographical specificity and yet sometimes evades it by elision of multiple places and cultures as if there is no difference between them—as if Hemans "orientalizes" the blank spaces of the West. While this essay will use Hemans's formal contexts to interpret her poems, its own organization will follow these descriptive categories based on complexity of representation.

In my first group, four poems present white Europeans who see only glimpses of "red" figures or recognize only their traces—graves by lakes that the settlers, a "fearless race," will rename, or arrows that fly past the grave of an unhappy emigrant. In each of these four poems the vanishing Indian is interpreted by the land's new occupants more as an image or icon that marks their own state of exile than as an actual person. The two I have just quoted from—"Song of Emigration" and "The Exiles' Dirge"—are included in *Songs of the Affections* (1830), but were written earlier.[15] A third is Hemans's long Spenserian poem *The Forest Sanctuary*, published in 1825;[16] and a fourth appears as a "miscellaneous" poem in the back of Hemans's thematic collection *Records of Women*.

Although it covers a vast American territory, *The Forest Sanctuary* avoids all but the most elusive representation of Indians. The terrible record of Pizarro's conquests in the Andes is recalled only as the narrator reduces the Inca civilization to "Indian bow and spear" or "a javelin shower" that turned the Spanish troops to innocent "mountain deer / Hemmed in our camp" (30). This focus contrasts to that in R. B. Sheridan's long-running *Pizarro*, a 1799 play that championed the Incas by identifying them with the invasion-fearing British and identifying the Spanish with Napoleon and his armies.[17] Hemans implicitly, I think, alludes to the question of Catholic emancipation by saving her representations of horror for the Inquisition. Her Protestant protagonist eventually returns to the New World as an exile, to wander with his young son through its vast and empty forests, which become a "sanctuary" for his individual religious spirituality. In *The Forest Sanctuary*, the "wild Indian" has no direct voice, only a momentary gesture; and he has virtually no social existence.

Other than the unnamed Incas, the most highly-organized society of native Americans at the time of the conquest was the Aztecs. From her

reading of Robertson and Bernard de Picart, and her probable reading
of Southey's 1809 *Madoc*, Hemans must have been well aware of that
society and the difficulties its highly organized and extremely violent
culture would present for her treatment of Indians in this poem as
meditative icons such as Wordsworth's shepherds or leech-gatherers.[18]
The narrator and his child have apparently left the tropics for a more
temperate and northern climate, for " . . . those deep southern shades
oppressed / My soul with stillness. . . . I sighed to hear / Once more
earth's breezy sounds, her foliage fanned / And turned to seek the
wilds of the red hunter's land" (II, 72). Yet Hemans posits no more
specific geography that might force her travelers to confront Mexico
and its populations.

Not only does Hemans detour around the violence of the Aztecs, she
also detours around any suggestion of Indian society that includes
women and thus any suggestions of intermarriage. Southey has his villain hint at the possibility, and the myth he works from of course assumes it, because traces of the Welsh emigrants are supposedly found
hundreds of years later among "light" Indian tribes in North America.
A positive model of interracial marriage is central to Sheridan's play,
to show European support of Inca culture and rights. As a number
of critics have pointed out, the subject of interracial sexuality and
marriage is both fascinating and threatening for white American writers, who confront it with attitudes ranging from horror to positive if
wary acceptance in fiction and in the borderline fictions of the captivity
narratives.[19] Sollors reads this pattern as a "national allegory" of "the
search for republican legitimacy in the world. The oceanic daughters
of England . . . break out of the arranged marriage with old-world aristocracy and rank in order to wed the 'natural' republican system of
America that they so dearly loved," represented as "the ancient Indian
traditions," and passed on often by a solitary, mournful older Indian
(123). Thus a new system is reconceived as an ancient and natural one,
framed in a mourning which marks both the cost of their own separation from European roots and the Indians' recognition that their land
and culture are being appropriated along with their values of freedom.

Hemans might well be acknowledging and repudiating such a political liberty as too republican, or too distracting from her theme of religious liberty. Surely, though, she is also revising the allegory even
more common among early conquerors, that of the virgin land figured
as an Indian woman.[20] Hemans avoids the exploitative aspects of this
mythology by removing the actual woman from the landscape and allowing the landscape to offer an equal, if melancholy, companionship.
The cabin in the cathedral-like wilderness has a maternal-enough father and a child, but no social or sexual affiliations with other settlers

or with Indians. Instead, the narrative closes, "I am here, / Living again through all my life's farewells, / In these vast woods" (II, 74). Turning to his sleeping child, he says he is learning "the might / Of solitude . . . While thou art breathing soft / And low, my lov'd one! on the breast of night" (II, 76). Maternal, sexual, and natural merge as "night" fulfills all possibilities with its dark vacancy. Marlon Ross's point that Hemans has educated her hero to take on female values (294) is appealing, but in the context we might better read that feminizing as split between affective domesticity, preserved in an androgynous, nurturing father, and a female sexuality that is displaced and depersonalized in the natural setting.

A fourth poem, published in the back of the *Records of Woman* volume in 1828, celebrates a "band of exiles" of less divided mind: the "Pilgrim Fathers." Praising their spirituality and their search for freedom, the poem's speaker asserts that they have reached "holy ground." When Hemans first published the poem in 1825 in the *NMM*, she prefaced it with a quatrain from "an American poet" that intensifies this praise (*NMM* 14, Part II [1825]: 402). Yet in the 1828 volume, she changes the prefatory lines, now quoting William Cullen Bryant. These lines see the landing from the Indians' point of view: "Look now abroad— another race has fill'd / Those populous borders—wide the wood recedes. . . . "[21] By placing these lines before her celebratory poem, Hemans not only reinforces the barely-suppressed theme of exile, identifying Puritans with Indians, but subtly raises questions about how "holy ground" might conflict with prior claims to the land.

Two other groups of poems follow *The Forest Sanctuary* in Hemans's 1825 volume. Most had already been published in *The New Monthly Review*, she explains in a prefatory note, but she groups them here as *Lays of Many Lands* because "each is intended," following Herder, "to be commemorative of some national recollection, popular custom, or tradition."[22] In *Lays*, she places her three "Indian" poems in sequence, from pages 131–41. In all three, the Indians themselves speak, as a communal "we" or folk. Thus they gain a voice, or an imputed voice, denied them in my first group of poems. In the second and third of these poems in the *Lays*, the community addresses a "stranger" and raises complex issues of shared or alien beliefs; yet the "stranger's" difference is not marked as racial. In all three, as well, a paradisal "spirit land" is evoked, and defines a different kind of strangeness. For each, Hemans cites one or two sources that we might term ethnographic, to authorize her representation of their voices and cultures. Both her choice of beliefs to represent and her synthesizing or extrapolating of the sources, however, deliberately universalize these particulars, first in the attitude toward "otherness" that assumes a unity of all Indian cultures, and second—and simultaneously—in the universality of loss, mourning, and longing for a reconciling afterlife. The first two—"The Messenger Bird," based on a Brazilian Indian belief described by Picart, and "The Stranger in Louisiana," also based on Picart and seemingly confirmed by Chateaubriand—emphasize the community's longing to speak to and join those already dead. The third, based on an account from William Bartram's travels in Florida, describes a paradisal but entrapping island. I will consider only the third of these in detail.

Her "ethnographic" preface to "The Isle of Founts" is a long paragraph from William Bartram's *Travels* reporting a Creek Indian belief about a specific "terrestrial paradise" which can be glimpsed somewhere in the wetlands of a Florida river but which "like an enchanted land, . . . seemed to fly before" the Creeks who search for it.[23] The speakers in Hemans's poem are the Creeks as if speaking to Bartram. By calling him "Son of the stranger!" they set up two frontiers: one outside their territories, though not necessarily outside their race, and one mysteriously islanded inside both their race and their tribe's geographic territory. That geographic territory is extended, however, by Hemans's inclusion of beliefs from other tribes, represented in the poem's text as the speakers' own but carefully footnoted to show their diverse origins. If she generalizes these beliefs into a synthetic "Indian" mythology within the poem, a mythology of "strangers" to her European readers, she nevertheless preserves a framework of specific tribal and geographic difference.

In an even more striking difference from Bartram, Hemans's island contains no "incomparably beautiful women" encountered by the Creek hunters, but instead only strangely compelling natural forces that are gradually revealed as both supernatural and demonic in their transformative power. In Hemans's poem, the Creek speakers describe an abstract and mythic form of desire. "Woe for him who sees" the "flashing ray / Of joyous waters," for "Earth has no spring to quench the thirst / That semblance in his soul shall work, / For ever pouring through his dreams, / The gush of those untasted streams!" Once returned from "their long and weary quest," warn the speakers, "Our hunters . . . dwelt among us as the dead," wasting away "With visions in their darkened eyes." The final comment in Hemans's headnote, "The additional circumstances in 'The Isle of Founts' are merely imaginary," states her highly Romantic theme as much as her use of sources.

As in the two preceding poems, these hunters, too, suffer a loss—but their visionary loss is not shared by the narrators, and the narrators mourn the loss of the haunted, enthralled hunters to their community. Partially displacing the sexual and imaginative transgression of social bonds, so that she can represent the ambivalence of condemnation and attraction more fully than her audience might otherwise tolerate, Hemans seems to deny gender difference, while simultaneously evoking myths that would essentialize it. We can see this maneuver as a making chaste, if not quite a chastening, of a woman writer's ability to represent traditionally-formulated sexuality; or we can see it as an eliding or overcoming of difference in order to open the imaginative quest and the sexual transgression to women writers and readers alike.

Her treatment of tribal and cultural difference here works as a model for gender difference: that is, a fluctuating set of boundaries for "strangers" forces us constantly to redefine what is the "other" and what is a part of ourselves. In these poems spoken from within "Indian" culture no strong racial difference, no "red" against "white" is marked, even toward the various strangers; and this sense of cultural variety with an underlying similarity extends to the collection as a whole.

Two other "Indian" poems that might well fit into this group of lyrics voiced by Indians also point ahead to the third of my descriptive groups, in which opposition between "red" and "white" races is strongly marked. Spoken by an unidentified narrator and "sung" by an Indian, the "Indian Woman's Death Song" is one of Hemans's *Records of Women*, a thematic collection which also includes two narratives of whites captured by Indians. "The Aged Indian," another death-song spoken or sung by the Indian from within his own culture alludes rather ambiguously to "races." Both death song and captivity narrative entered Anglo-American literature through reports of actual occurrences, of whites hearing the Indians' death-songs and experiencing and reporting their own capture by Indians. By the time Hemans writes, however, literary versions had established themselves as flourishing sub-genres with author and audiences aware of their conventions.

The pressures and codifications of an established genre, then, as well as their firm thematic link to American "red" Indians, link the two death-songs to the captivity narratives, even as the specific shapings of the two genres divide them into opposing dramatic voicings—the death-song from within Indian culture, the captivity narratives from those forcibly drawn into it. A further set of formal and thematic influences, however, ties the "Indian Woman's Death Song" to the two captivity narratives: their status as "Records of Woman." This thematic collection was evidently conceived as a group because even the first one, published in *NMM* as early as 1825, is marked "Records of Woman No. I, Imelda." One of the captivity narratives I will discuss is "Records of Woman No. XI, Edith" (*NMM* 20 [1827]: 33–37). In *Records of Woman*, as in *Lays of Many Lands*, Hemans explores similarities that cross racial and cultural differences, and these similarities include, indeed are dominated by, mourning for lost affective relationships. Yet that underlying similarity is based upon what Hemans apparently sees as the universality of gender difference. We might call this difference a "separate sphere," but it more often appears to be a separate vulnerability to, and victimization by, men's violent social practices. Like cultural differences, racial difference becomes one more way of showing the negative, dehumanizing universality of these social practices. Yet in two of the three "Indian" poems in *Records*, racial difference appears heightened, at least initially, as if to use its potentiality for alienating and demonizing to represent all the more strongly the gender differences caused by social practices. To begin the reading of these poems without a context of the other poems in the collection might lead to seeing them as racist and as distancing male violence from its practitioners closer to home. Yet the universality both in Hemans's framing apparatus, in the other "records," and in the narrative turns she gives to these two poems suggest that she evokes such a sharply-defined racism to represent a sharply-felt gender difference—and then to ask if the conditions leading to gender difference might be changed by universalizing the behavior shown by the women in these poems who have challenged racial stereotypes. These poems do not support, though they do not explicitly deny, a biologically-based essential difference between women and men. The two already mentioned imply that the virtues of a nurturing, pacifist womanhood as English culture had increasingly come to define it are not limited to that culture alone. Yet the third, set wholly within the "red Indian" culture as Hemans's sources defined it, presents a less nurturing, what we might call a more aggressively passive response to women's victimization.

As Julie Ellison and other literary and cultural critics have noted, the supposedly Native American genre of the death song becomes popular as a literary genre among white American and white British writers alike.[24] Speaking in the voice of the dying Indian, though sometimes with other voices framing the song, these lyrics tend to sum up cultural values for individual behavior at crisis-point, expressing different degrees of defiance, melancholy, and prophetic vision. In "The Aged Indian," the first of Hemans's two death-songs I will consider, Hemans's speaker pleads with some unidentified "Warriors" who withhold the final stroke that would kill him, telling them he is ready to join his ancestors. The solitary survivor of his tribe, he then tells the dead "heroes of his youth" that "His [own] eyes . . . Have seen, since darkness veiled your fame, / Another, and another race, / Rise to the battle and the chase" (*Works*, 333–34). Here "race" may mean successive Indian tribes, or those tribes succeeded by successive waves of Europeans. Hemans gives no more details than this haunting phrase, and no identifying colors. In either case, the apparently inevitable succession has doomed his own tribe, and has doomed, as well, his own sublime strength and liberty: "in his flower of days," he was "strong to stem the torrent's force . . . his way was an eagle's course! . . . and the wild hurricane's delight!"

Gender is even less an issue in this poem than is the evoked but ambiguous category of race. True, a woman writer preserves the imagined voice of the speaker, and thus of his tribe, speaking out of a silence created by a confused, endlessly repeated "race" for arms and glory. She speaks as if on behalf of other silenced groups, of women and others who lament such "races." Yet she does not exploit the tradition of far more specific, situated polemical prophecy that already exists in the American versions of this sub-genre.

Hemans's second death-song in *Records of Woman* is the first of this sub-genre I have found in which a woman sings in her own voice about her own death. In it, the Indian woman does not "stem the torrent's force" but rides it to her death "Down a broad river of the western wilds" toward the "cataract's thunder"—because, as Hemans's epigraph from Cooper's *The Prairie* says, "sad is the life of a woman." Revising the topos of the melancholy Indian prophesying his own death and that of his race, Hemans domesticates it, to focus upon a melancholy based upon the social and emotional circumstances of gender. Because the young woman carries with her "a babe, born like me, for woman's weary lot," her sorrow extends to affect future generations. Yet she is not described as "red" or as "dark" or "dusky." Her "weary lot" seems influenced by race only to increase the sublime freedom of her gesture and to make her protest more permissible because partially but not irrevocably distanced: "upon her Indian brow / Sat a strange gladness, and her dark hair wav'd / As if triumphantly."

The source Hemans cites in her footnote in the back of the volume, though not in her epigraph, is a report of Stephen Long's expedition to the northern Mississippi. Arrived at the Falls of St. Anthony on the Mississippi, Keating recounts an episode told by their Dakota host. In this story, an Indian woman, despairing when her husband marries a second wife, "launched her light canoe, entered into it with her children, and paddled down the stream singing her death song. . . . finally her voice was drowned in the sound of the cataract."[25] In Cooper's *The Prairie*, the Dakota Sioux woman who speaks that despairing line fears that her infant son is to be raised by the Hispanic woman her husband has captured from some white settlers. Though Cooper sets the woman's betrayal within the customs of a "suffering, female, savage life" often criticized by white writers for its fluidity of marital arrangements and the otherwise low status of women, he makes her relinquishing of her son symbolic of the Dakotas'—and other tribes'—loss of their future to the white invaders.[26]

Though Hemans's epigraph from Cooper would raise the issue of intercultural conflict and interracial marriage for those readers familiar with *The Prairie* (published in 1827, when Cooper was living in Europe), and possibly also for readers who had seen a remarkably similar story by Lydia Child (also published in 1828),[27] she narrows the focus of her poem to a record of woman's plight. Thus the Indian woman does not stand for the virginal new-found land exploited and wasted by Europeans nor for a race driven in its proud isolation into exile or self-destruction. Instead, recasting these motifs along with *Childe Harold's* images of a melancholy sublimity, Hemans transforms allegories of culture into allegories of gender, in which the woman's plight is primary and the other interpretations subordinate to, as well as contributing causes of, her exploitation. Her immolation in the "great river's" cataracts is a defiant claim for a freedom elsewhere denied.

If Hemans's treatment downplays or rebalances the well-established mythic equation of Indian woman with dark wilderness, to be sexually and economically conquered, her heroine's ecstatic merging with the river's cataracts suggests her own and perhaps Hemans's own substitution of natural for human merging—a defiant claiming of her own sexuality as, and in, death. If the stranger in "The Isle of Founts" is warned away from a vision of water that only creates restless desire, here the desire is celebrated and climactic—though both displaced to natural images and made suicidal, and thus socially acceptable. A less subversive reading, one Hemans might have felt less uneasiness in having her readers elaborate upon, would be one in which the Indian woman retreats from husband to father. Committing herself to "the Father of ancient waters," "Father of waves," she tells her child that they go to "where the soul shall find its youth, as wakening from a dream— / One moment, and that realm is ours."

Cooper's epigraph links this poem to an episode in his novel which forms a captivity narrative. Hemans's other two "red Indian" poems in *Records of Woman* are versions of this other major genre that emerged from the European encounter with American natives. Both "The American Forest Girl" and "Edith, a Tale of the Woods" represent this encounter in highly-colored contrasts of red and white, or dark and "fair." Yet each seems written to establish, then dissolve or blend those contrasts.

"The American Forest Girl" opens with a terrifying abruptness characteristic of the captivity narratives[28] and with the powerfully simplified iconography and compressed emotions characteristic of Hemans's poetry:

> Wildly and mournfully the Indian drum
>   On the deep hush of moonlight forests broke; —
> 'Sing us a death-song, for thy hour is come!' —
>   So the red warriors to their captive spoke.

In the next four lines her depiction of the captive sharpens her opening contrasts between "wild . . . drum" and "deep hush," "red warriors" and "moonlight forests": "Still, and amid those dusky forms alone, / A youth, a fair-hair'd youth of England stood / Like a king's son. . . . " While we admire her images, the coloration that seems to convert race into abstract and traditional Eurocentric codes, even hierarchical, heraldic flags, surely makes us question the neatness with which color assigns value. The opposition of captors and captives has sharpened this difference, for the "mantling crimson" that marked the youth as "island-born" has left his cheek, suggesting a delicate sensibility not expressed in the Indians' constant "red"; and his tension turns him into a classical statue, as "his press'd lips look'd marble" (131).

Yet dating from Captain John Smith's own narrative of his release by Pochahontas, the story Hemans tells is a familiar one, repeated in fact as well as in literature (see Picart III, 106, for example). She gives us no local habitations, names, or chronology. Either because her own patriotism dominates her vision or because she deliberately uses the captive's yearning for "that happy hall in England" to avoid the tangled complexities of the actual settlement process—a view I prefer to argue—Hemans also avoids, as in *Forest Sanctuary*, the motif of the cultural marriage. Here the Indian woman mediates between cultural differences instead of representing one of the opposed groups. For the "youth's" rescuer is "a young slight girl—a fawn-like child / Of green Savannahs and the leafy wild, / Springing unmark'd till then, as some lone flower / Happy because the sunshine is its dower"—a Wordsworthian nature-spirit. Both the epithets of the poem's title and her physical description mediate between races and cultures. Though "American" refers to "Native Americans" as late as Bernard de Picart, by the early nineteenth century the term as well as the territory had begun to shift to the white colonizers.[29] Further, as she pleads for the soldier's life, thinking of her "playmate brother dead," "her cheek flush'd thro' its olive hue, / As her black tresses to the night wind flew." If the second line confirms an ecstatic wildness, the first suggests both a sensibility like that of the soldier's "mantling crimson" and white and an ethnicity without sharp racial difference.

The poem ends with the girl's success: " 'Away!' they cried, 'young stranger, thou art free!' " Though this follows the Smith narrative, it was in fact, as Hemans knew from her reading of Hunter's *Memoirs* and other works, a less usual outcome than adoption into the tribe or marriage into it. She defines a spiritual adoption, an assertion of emotional siblinghood with no restraining bonds, and no complicated future of further sexual or territorial disputes, or of their mythical resolution in the motif of the cultural marriage.

Hemans's second captivity narrative develops this motif of a spiritual adoption to reverse many of the conventions of that genre. Beginning her narrative after one scene of violence and allowing her heroine's unconsciousness to account for the poet's lack of narrative specificity at the beginning of the next scene, she avoids the typical pattern of a sudden, terrifying onslaught and a violent wrenching of the captives away from the bodies and the homes of their families. Instead, a mutual acceptance by captive and captors allows the development of a common emotional bond. In fact the "death song" for Edith sung at the end of the poem by the aged Indian who has become her adoptive father enacts in its strategic omissions precisely what Hemans brings about in the poem as a whole.

When this narrative opens, the battlefield is already silent and nearly empty of living figures. This tableau of emptiness paradoxically suggests both the loss of self in a sublime nature and the loss of others to a mourning central sensibility: " . . . solemn are the boundless woods / Of the great Western world / . . . Awful it is for human heart to bear / The might and burden of this solitude! / Yet . . . midst those green wastes, there sate / One young and fair." The next lines go on to fill in the foreground with "pale and silent" forms and a suffusion of red colors—"crimson light" and "high cedars"—that bleed metonymically into suggestions of red skin as cause. The "many" who "lay around" the central figure "on the bloody ground . . . Were severed from her need and from her woe, / Far as Death severs life." An abstract Death becomes the agent, and the repeated verb "severs" is displaced from limbs or scalps to emotions. All we know is that "Combat," another subdued personification, "had rag'd, and brought the valiant low, / And left them, with the history of their lot, / Unto the forest oaks."

This abstraction, this shadowy displacement of actual human agency, allows Hemans to schematize and naturalize the "dark and bloody" middle "ground" of colonial settlement and of the mutual, often painful interchanges of native and newer Americans and to turn to their emotional and spiritual consequences. For she goes on to complete the center of her tableau, a blood-stained pieta or liebestod: "Of him alone she thought, whose languid head / Faintly upon her wedded bosom fell

... heavily she felt his life-blood well / Fast o'er her garments." Yet Hemans does include a few cultural or political markers. Again, as in "Forest Girl," the male figure is a "warrior," and the woman's "home of other days had been / Midst the fair halls of England." A footnote explains that her source is *Scenes of Connecticut*, "published in America," but nothing in the poem locates the setting that specifically.[30] If Hemans were more precisely describing a characteristic Indian attack, the attackers would have quickly carried off the woman as a captive. Instead, the most pressing antagonist to the "fair" young woman seems to be the alien silence of the "Western world."

Yet even with this permeation of the landscape with colors that carry racial coding, the poem does not essentialize race so much as it establishes a psychological mood of alienation in order to dispel it. For her version of the captivity topos deracinates Indians as well as white captive. A more typical captivity narrative would begin its "removes," to use Mary Rowlandson's term, with a forced march further into the wilderness. In this poem Edith faints at her husband's death, then wakes to find her "glance" falling "on faces dark and strange, / And dusky forms" (73). Yet this awakening to marked difference of color and culture, still building on the expected terror of the genre, immediately changes to a recognition of shared humanity through shared grief: "An aged chief, / Whose home look'd sad—for therein play'd no child—" has carried her home to his wife, "touch'd with thoughts from some past sorrow sprung."

A part of Edith's consolation is the parental role of her rescuers: she escapes back into the childhood they long to replace and yet she is free to preserve the image of "Love and Death" from the preceding tableau. Not only does the old couple live in a "lone cabin in the woods," absent from a tribal society that might pressure her into marriage with one of the younger warriors, but their cabin is surprisingly near "her soldier's lonely grave." Thus she has not undergone any physical removes farther into the wilderness, and it is not even clear that she is a captive. She seems to have links to no American settlement—we scarcely ask whether she wants to return to Mystic or Meriden or Wethersfield.

Instead, her earlier home in England is conflated with her ultimate home. She brings renewed life to the old Indian couple, a "power of love . . . which . . . Gives the glad soul its flowering time again." Through this renewal, but even more through her "sweet mournfulness" and her "child-like piety," Edith leads her "Indian fosterers" to "heaven-born truth" and "to the cross." Once she does so, she dies: "The broken flower of England might not stay / Amidst those alien shades" (77). Hemans's rhetoric of spiritual enlightenment is surely Eurocentric in its imagery of dark and light, but the colors of racial difference are only a starting-point for humans universally capable of the same spiritual journey. Yet when she gives the Indian father the last word, or better, the last song, we can read that song not only as a universalizing lament but also as a subtle voicing of Native American spirituality that claims its own dignity and merely shares some attitudes with Christianity: "Thou'rt journeying to thy spirit's home, / Where the skies are ever clear. . . . " Bound by their common mourning and their common search for a place "where farewell sounds are o'er" and "Thou shalt see / No fear of parting more," they too will follow to "the happy dead," to "that shining band. . . . " So he ends, "Go to the better land!" Though we can argue, as Hemans may intend us to, that Edith is a kind of Christ, redeeming others through her suffering, the old chief's song is not precisely Christian.

"The Cross in the Wilderness," written in 1823 and published in 1824 in *The Amulet* (Boyle, 121, and Chorley, I, 116), contains a religious imperialism similar to that in "A Tale of the Woods," but it is less synthetic: no song of mourning reconciles Christian and Indian versions of the "spirit land." Or rather, it needs no synthesis: surprisingly, both speakers in the poem, an old Indian chief and a traveler of unspecified race but of urban and Christian origins, find the solution to "the cloud settled o'er thy [the Indian] nation's lot" in Christianity. As the traveler consoles the chief mourning the long-ago death of a priest, he asserts, "Yet shall the gloom which wraps thy hills be broken, / And the full dayspring rise upon thy race. . . . "

The poem's first stanza, with the dignified old chief sitting "By a grassy tomb" with his "bow unstrung," sounds like the beginning of a typical mourning-song or a death-song; but the "mound" he sits beside "sanctified the gorgeous waste around," not quite like Stevens's jar in Tennessee, "For a pale cross above its greensward rose." Surprisingly, the "grey chieftain" mourns the death of a priest: "I mourn the clear light taken / Back from my people, o'er whose place it shone." Now only he remembers those "true words . . . faintly sounding from the past, / Mingled with death-songs in each fitful blast." The already-receding loss of Christianity fuses with his earlier cultural loss, signaled by the "death-songs." The traveler reassures him that his race will have a new birth, "And the desert blossom as the rose," but he returns to his city with no practical answer as to how that promise might be realized on earth. As if to suggest subtly that the only solution is spiritual and otherworldly, "the forest's child," the old man, is left with "memories" beside the stream's "lonely way," and the traveler carries into the city "Deep thoughts and sad, yet full of holiness." Hemans may intend the pious hopes of the chief, the millennial promise of the traveler, and their mutual respect as a scene of instruction not only for each of them but for the readers—especially American readers—who should act as Christians and treat Indians as humans worthy both of spiritual and of material salvation. Yet as she draws attention to the duplicitous confusion of spirit land and actual land that haunts many of these poems—hers and those of other writers, both British and American—her instruction becomes a recognition of irony.

A fourth poem in this final group that directly if schematically represents cultural and racial conflicts in the colonizing and settlement of America is, like the captivity narratives, included in a larger thematic group, the 1830 *Songs of the Affections*.[31] Answering, in effect, the emigrants' refusal in "Song of Emigration" and "The Exiles' Dirge" to see more than fleeting glimpses or the abandoned graves of their land's earlier owners, "The Indian with his Dead Child" also answers, as its affective bonds parallel, the father-son link in *The Forest Sanctuary*. The father speaks as he carries his child, whom he has "raised . . . from the grave-sod," back "to th'ancestral wilderness," where his burial will not be "defiled" "By the white man's path": "I have left the spoilers' dwellings, / For evermore, behind; / Unmingled with their household sounds, / For me shall sweep the wind." Though he thought himself "established . . . in a township in Maine," as Hemans writes in her headnote, his cultural alienation was also personal, for as his child died, none of his neighbors of the "pale race" came to help. Again, the return to his homeland and its "chainless host" of waters is a turn from a version of "civilization"—though a cold version—to a paradisal wilderness that seems like a world of the dead: "In the silence of the midnight / I journey with the dead; / . . . . My father's path I tread" (51).

As if echoing the phrase describing the gray chief in "Cross in the Wilderness" as a primitive or renewed child, "The Child of the Forests," written several months later, identifies a closeness to nature with a positive primitivism. In this case, though, Hemans also refers to John Hunter's upbringing by a succession of Indian tribes. Beginning as a mourning-song in which those tribes lament his absence, the poem concludes with alternate calls. In the fifth stanza, the English, urban speaker asks, "Comes not the sound of forests to thine ear . . . ? / They call—wild voices call thee o'er the main, / Back to thy free and boundless woods again." In the sixth, this imaginative sympathy turns out to be a taunting, or rather a temptation:

> Hear them not! hear them not! —thou canst not find
>   In the far wilderness what once was thine!
> Thou hast quaffed knowledge from the founts of mind,
>   And gathered loftier aims and hopes divine.
> Thou knowest soaring thought, th'immortal strain —
> Seek not the desert and the woods again!

Yet this is the imagery of "The Isle of Founts," and "th'immortal strain" seems an insidious, life-threatening poison leading to a fall from innocence or an enthrallment to prevent a return to his own world. His own world is more obviously the unburdened paradise that the speaker seems also to long for. Though the first stanza evokes that world in terms deliberately alienating to the poem's readers by evoking race—the "Red Indian" with whom I began—no racial difference appears in the rest of the poem; Hunter's own success in Indian culture also creates an imaginative way for us as readers to share the same simplicity, sublimity, and freedom. In this poem the nostalgia for the "fair halls of England" is, if not fully reversed, surely made ambiguous, and Hemans's fascination with a forested freedom "beneath the giant pine" speaks more clearly than usual.

With their competing claims for a European-centered "civilization" and sublime American liberty, the trans-Atlantic voices of Hemans's poem to Hunter return us to the problems of interpreting her apparently contradictory—or paradoxical—re-colonizing of America, her establishing of a synthetic, universal, and conveniently non-particular common ground. The pressures of two kinds of post-colonial viewpoints urge me, and probably many of Hemans's modern readers, to question this synthesis. First, however critical we may be of our own particular national histories, we'd like to see those particularities addressed as a way of beginning to understand past blindnesses or paralyses. Second, from a more explicitly post-structuralist view, we may well question the bases both of the universal human values, especially the universal spiritual impulses, she finds underlying racial and cultural differences, and the universal similarity of gender *difference* she also finds underlying cultural differences. To what extent is the perception of woman's universal victimization by the effects of male-dominated cultural practices a confirmation, even if unintentional, of some innate psychological or biological difference?

Granted these twentieth-century questions, however, we should go on to recognize Hemans's early nineteenth-century intentions, as they are manifested in her shapings of genre and theme, to make her re-colonizing a critique of exploitation based on race and gender differences. Through her appropriation of an American cultural myth of Indian melancholy, she defines several levels of a hybrid territory, to use Bhabha's term. First, she maps out a physical territory of conflict between races and between genders that in its schematic focus largely ignores political, economic, and class differentiation. Second, she interprets that generalized physical territory and its conflicts as a psychological conflict between two desires, two longings that also threaten to redefine gender—a "westering" longing for a sublime wilderness, with its energies and its freedoms; and an "eastering" longing for the familiar gardens, flowers, "halls," and affectionate familial links of European homes. The loss of either of these loci for desire, these apparently irreconcilable alternatives, might well lead the author, as it leads the characters and speakers of her poems, to mourning. The recognition of their irreconcilability leads, I think, to a more fixed melancholy that subsumes and is intensified by the American melancholy that the American writers project onto and draw from the Indians.

I have borrowed Geoffrey Hartman's term "westering" from his analyses of European "progress" odes both because of its geographic handiness and because of its resonance for the "child of the forest" motif. With that pattern, northwestern Europeans allayed their anxieties about the priority and preeminence of Greece and Rome in poetry and in liberty by imagining a westward "progress" of a deified Poesy or Liberty. Through it they claimed for later, more western generations a progressive development and improvement. The primitive or childlike barbarian grows up, with the westering light of a fostering deity, into an ever-better adulthood surpassing their progenitors to the east. Yet this enlightenment myth of progress that draws value from the east while looking westward is most useful in the ways that it fails to fit the American situation, or for that matter, any colonizing situation, more closely examined. For it repeatedly breaks apart in Hemans's poems, as it does in Bryant's "The Ages," which Hemans used as epigraph to the "Pilgrim Fathers," and just as its Christian version, with Christ as "dayspring," breaks apart and is only memorialized in "Cross in the Wilderness." For it both values and justifies the western "children" only as they are able to grow into or revitalize the "eastern" patterns of colonization that they claim as descendants. While longing still for the eastern, European values of Christianity, for a civic liberty based on male claims to public spaces, and for an affective domesticity, Hemans turns toward two different versions of the west as a positive goal. Yet both of these versions are affected by her backward longings. Like many white American colonists, she has her characters claim or be claimed by "grey chieftains" as foster-parents and thus claim or at least recognize a moral and spiritual value in the living cultures of "red Indians." Yet such a specific liberation from eastern longings is continually erased by a longing for a more complete, more sublime liberty that does not recognize the specific otherness of Indian cultures but only an undifferentiated freedom from European restraints. This sublime longing might be interpreted as a feminist longing for an apparently less constrained or mediated mode of subjectivity and sexuality, a moving from Burkean domestic beauty to a more traditionally masculine wilderness sublime—a complex topic I can only touch on here. Ironically, however, it is also the very liberty claimed by the early American colonists who described the

North American lands as empty or "virgin" wilderness. Further, it is the liberty attributed to "red Indians" by the U.S. policies which pushed them westward from their own farmland to vast, "free" spaces, in order to preserve their "way of life."

As if recognizing both the psychological and the political dangers of this longing for a more spacious, untrammelled and yet almost phantasmal sublimity, Hemans then in her third stage of "common ground" seeks to reshape or colonize it from both western and eastern perspectives into a still infinite but more normative vision of an afterlife—a release in which the "dayspring" of eastern origin and a "spiritland" of western journey, merge into a "better land."

This dialectic or rather this near-impasse of melancholy longing for "eastern" and "western" in Hemans's "red Indian" poems might seem to obscure the tensions within her eastern, domestic poems that also generate melancholy, tensions arising from women's emotional focus upon affective bonds that are both strengthened and broken through the separation of public and private spheres. Yet by watching her stretching and testing of those affective bonds in the formally and generically varied, if still relatively undetailed voices and territories of "red Indians" and white colonists, by seeing her appropriation of American cultural melancholy to explore the not quite overlapping problems of racial and sexual differences, we can return to those home-poems with a clearer sense that her melancholy is not only individual and expressive but consciously explored as a more collective cultural phenomenon—or rather as several overlapping phenomena or patterns that in their differences shown from poem to poem, genre to genre, collection to collection, may create spaces for an artist's deliberate imagining and negotiating of solutions. Moreover, the various structures of melancholy in her "Indian" poems seem to function not only as recognitions of impasses, of conflicts in allegiance, but also as ways to preserve these schematic borderlands as places for negotiation. Though Hemans does not acknowledge Britain's political loss of the American colonies in these poems, but only the more personal losses that take place there, her imaginative re-creation of colonialism occurs under the protection of a patriotic melancholy that sees her poems only as fictions of loss and thus as less threatening—even as disarming—to the actual structures of empire. Her domestic melancholy may protect similar mild-voiced revolutions disguised as losses.

NOTES

1. The text for this poem comes from *The Poetical Works of Mrs. Hemans*, preface by Michael Rossetti (New York: Hurst, n.d.), pp. 381–82. Original publication in *NMM* 10 (1824):282; I was directed to the journal by

Richard Drinnon, *White Savage: The Case of John Dunn Hunter* (New York: Schocken, 1972), pp. xiv and 153.

2. See Stuart Curran, "The 'I' Altered," in Anne Mellor, ed., *Romanticism and Feminism* (Bloomington: Indiana University Press, 1988), pp. 185–207, and Marlon Ross, *The Contours of Masculine Desire* (Oxford: Oxford University Press, 1989), esp. p. 291.

3. See Robert F. Berkhofer, Jr., *The White Man's Indian* (New York: Knopf, 1978), pp. 3–13.

4. See Brian W. Dippie, *The Vanishing American: White Attitudes and U.S. Indian Policy* (Middletown, CT: Wesleyan University Press, 1982), pp. 17–24; Werner Sollers, *Beyond Ethnicity* (New York: Oxford University Press, 1986), pp. 115–18; Mitchell Robert Breitwieser, *American Puritanism and the Defense of Mourning* (Madison, WI: University of Wisconsin Press, 1990); and Julie Ellison, "Race and Sensibility in the Early Republic: Ann Elizabeth Bleecker and Sarah Wentworth Morton," *American Literature* 65, no. 3 (Sept. 1993):445–48.

5. Anne K. Mellor, *Romanticism and Gender* (New York: Routledge, 1993), pp. 24, 143.

6. Tricia Lootens, "Hemans and Home: Victorianism, Feminine 'Internal Enemies,' and the Domestication of National Identity," *PMLA* 109, no. 2 (March 1994):238–53.

7. Homi Bhabha, *The Location of Culture* (London: Routledge, 1994), pp. 5, 2.

8. John Dunn Hunter, *Memoirs of a Captivity . . .* , a new edition, with portrait (London, Longman, 1823; facsim. rpt. New York: Johnson Reprint, 1970); for the reviews and the intercontinental controversy, see Drinnon, p. 262.

9. See Gary B. Nash, *Red, White, and Black: The Peoples of Early America*, 2nd ed. (Englewood Cliffs, NJ: Prentice-Hall, 1982).

10. "The North American Indians" in *Quarterly Review* 31 [actually 33], no. 61 (April 1824):76–111. The author, who gives his credentials in the review, is George Procter; see Drinnon, pp. 102–103.

11. See Dippie, chaps. 5–6; Nash, 291–98; Drinnon, p. 272; and Francis Jennings, *The Invasion of America: Indians, Colonization, and the Cant of Conquest* (1975; rpt. New York: Norton, 1976), pp. vi, 8. See also Timothy Flint, *Recollections of the . . . Valley of the Mississippi* (Boston: Cummings, Hilliard, 1826), p. 137; Hemans cites Flint as source for "The Exile's Dirge."

12. Moira Ferguson, *Subject to Others: British Women Writers and Colonial Slavery, 1670–1834* (New York: Routledge, 1992).

13. For lingering sensitivity on this issue in Liverpool, see Gomer Williams, *History of the Liverpool Privateers . . . with an Account of the Liverpool Slave Trade* (London: Heinemann and Liverpool: Howell, 1897, rpt. London: Frank Cass, 1966), p. x. See Mellor, *Romanticism and Gender*, p. 124; see also Henry Chorley, *Memoirs of Mrs. Hemans*, 2nd ed., 2 vols. (London: Sounders and Otley, 1837), I, 1–15; she visited the abolitionist Roscoe in 1830, and they admired each other's work (II, 79).

14. See Edward Said, *Orientalism* (1978; rpt. New York: Vintage, 1979), chap. I and esp. p. 120.

15. These songs were contributed as a series to *Blackwood's Magazine* before being published as a separate volume; "Song of Emigration" appears in 22, no. 128 (July 1827):32. See Chorley I, 292. "The Exile's Dirge" appeared in *Winter's Wreath*, a Liverpool annual, in 30:322; see Andrew Boyle, *An Index to the Annuals 1820–1850* (Worcester: Andrew Boyle, 1967), 122. The volume is *Songs of the Affections, with Other Poems*, facsim. rpt. intro. Donald H. Reiman (Edinburgh: Blackwood, and London: T. Cadell, 1830; rpt. New York: Garland, 1978).

16. *The Forest Sanctuary and Other Poems*, by Mrs. Hemans, facsim. rpt. intro. Donald H. Reiman (London: John Murray, 1825; rpt. New York: Garland, 1978).

17. Richard Brinsley Sheridan, *Pizarro*, in *The Dramatic Works*, ed. Cecil Price (Oxford: Clarendon Press, 1973), II. 629–30.

18. *Madoc*, in *The Poetical Works of Robert Southey*, 10 vols. in 5 (Boston: Houghton, Mifflin, n.d.), III. 11–439; see also Bernard de Picart, *Ceremonies and Religious Customs of the Various Nations*, tr. into English by a gentleman, 6 vols.; III (London: W. Jackson for Claude Du Bosc, 1734); and William Robertson, *The History of America*, 3rd ed., 3 vols. (London: W. Strahan, T. Cadell, 1780).

19. See Richard Slotkin, *Regeneration through Violence* (Middletown, CT: Wesleyan University Press, 1973), pp. 125, 376–77; Annette Kolodny, *The Land before Her: Fantasy and Experience of the American Frontiers, 1630–1860* (Chapel Hill: University of North Carolina Press, 1984); Kathryn Zabelle Derounian-Stodola and James Arthur Leverer, *The Indian Captivity Narrative 1550–1900* (New York: Twayne, 1993), p. 56; June Namilias, *White Captives: Gender and Ethnicity on the American Frontier* (Chapel Hill: University of North Carolina Press, 1993), pp. 120–36; Lydia Child, *"Hobomok" and Other Writings on Indians*, ed. Carolyn Karcher (New Brunswick, NJ: Rutgers University Press, 1986), introduction; and Catherine Maria Sedgwick, *Hope Leslie*, ed., intro. Mary Kelley (New Brunswick, NJ: Rutgers University Press, 1987). Hemans had read *Hope Leslie*; see Chorley I, 290.

20. See Louis Montrose, "The Work of Gender in the Discourse of Discovery," in Stephen Greenblatt, ed., *New World Encounters* (Berkeley: University of California Press, 1993), 177–217 for a discussion of Raleigh's manipulation of these metaphors. See also Laura E. Donaldson, *Decolonizing Feminisms: Race, Gender, and Empire-Building* (Chapel Hill: University of North Carolina Press, 1992), esp. pp. 4–6, chap. 1, and 133–35.

21. *Records of Woman, with Other Poems*, facsim. rpt. intro. Reiman (Edinburgh: Blackwood, and London: T. Cadell, 1828; rpt. New York: Garland, 1978). The Bryant poem is "The Ages" (1821), stanza 32, in *The Poetical Works of William Cullen Bryant*, ed. Parke Godwin, 2 vols. (New York: Russell and Russell, 1883, rpt. Atheneum, 1967), I, 66. For similar Bryant poems, see "The Disinterred Warrior" (1827) and "An Indian at the Burial Place of His Fathers" (1824), I, 191–92 and I, 92–96.

22. "Isle of Founts" in *NMM* 8 (1823):298; "The Messenger Bird," 10 (1824):538; "The Stranger in Louisiana," 13 (1825):496.

23. William Bartram, *Travels through North and South Carolina, Georgia, East and West Florida* (London: J. Johnson, 1792; facsim. rpt. Savannah, Ga.: Beehive Press), pp. 24–25.

24. See Ellison, pp. 461–62, Sollers, pp. 104–108, Dippie, pp. 12–14; Picart, III.105. Because Ellison, Sollers, Dippie, and others have described a range of American and British examples, I will mention here only two additional ones they do not discuss, both by British male writers. Robert Southey's *Songs of the American Indians* (1799; in *Works* I[II]: 203–14) include several songs mourning the dead, including one in which a "Chik-kasah" widow incites her tribe to revenge: "The stake is made ready, the captives shall die; / Tomorrow the song of their death thou shalt hear; / Tomorrow thy widow shall wield / The knife and the fire: be at rest!" As in *Madoc*, Southey gives us exact details of the material and emotional economy in this revenge-culture. In some sense mourning poems, these songs incite an active rage in their supposed Indian listeners and an alienating but fascinated horror in their European readers, instead of a more easily acceptable cross-cultural sympathy and melancholy or a suicidal despair. Thomas Campbell's 1809 *Gertrude of Wyoming*, set in Pennsylvania during the 1760s and 1770s, concludes with an aging Oneida's death song that combines anticipatory defiance for the next day's battle that may bring his own death and an elegy for the dying white settler, Gertrude, like him a supporter of the American Revolution, who has been wounded by Mohawks allied with the British. As Gertrude dies, the sympathetic Oneida mourns the widower's now-desolate homestead, and as in Philip Freneau's earlier poems contemplates crossing "yon mountains blue" to a western exile that would be "desolation" and "despair," a kind of hellish afterlife. Cultural and personal displacement merge as adoptive Indian father and widowed white foster-son face a sterile land. In *The Complete Poetical Works of Thomas Campbell* (Chicago: Belford, Clarke, n.d.), pp. 75–106. Campbell became editor of the *NMM* in 1823; intro. to *PW*, p. 21. See *NMM* 4 (1822):97 for Campbell's response to the children of Joseph Brant, the Mohawk he had made the villain in his poem; they had read it, and they complained.

25. William Hypolitus Keating, *Narrative of an Expedition to the Source of the St. Peter's River . . .* , 2 vols. (Philadelphia: H. C. Varey and T. Lea, 1824), I, 299–301; for other discussions of Indian women's suicides, see I, 284 and I, 394; for another version of the Lake Pepin "lover's leap," on p. 284, see also Lewis Deffebach, *Oolaita* (Philadelphia: printed for the author, 1821); Sollers directed me to this play (p. 107).

26. James Fenimore Cooper, *The Prairie* (1827), intro., notes by Donald A. Ringe (Oxford: Oxford University Press, 1992), pp. 292–94.

27. Child, "A Legend of the Falls of St. Anthony," in *Hobomok*, ed. Karcher, pp. 202–12. Child's story, like Cooper's, involves interracial and cultural conflict.

28. See Child, *Hobomok*, p. 176; Slotkin, 256; Hunter, pp. 32–33 and 330; and n. 19. See also Nancy Armstrong and Leonard Tennenhouse, "The American Origins of the English Novel," *American Literary History* 4 (Fall 1992):386–410, for an argument that seems to undervalue Puritanism as a common factor in Rowlandson's narrative and eighteenth-century English novels but that rightly emphasizes the trans-Atlantic cultural influences that we too often consider separately.

29. See Berkhofer, p. 15; Jennings, vi–vii, and Bernard de Picart, passim in vol. III.

30. I have been unable to locate Hemans's source for this poem, *Sketches of Connecticut,* "printed in America," according to her note.

31. First published in *Blackwood's* 25, no. 151 (April 1829):498–99, with an epigraph from Bryant omitted in the volume: "Then the hunter turn'd away from that scene, / Where the homes of his fathers once had been, / And burning thoughts flashed o'er his mind, / Of the white man's faith and love unkind."

PART THREE

Resituating Romanticism

Ten

ALAN RICHARDSON

Epic Ambivalence: Imperial Politics and Romantic Deflection in Williams's Peru *and Landor's* Gebir

"EMPIRE IS NO MORE!" Blake ominously thunders in the "Song of Liberty," the radical prophecy that concludes *The Marriage of Heaven and Hell* (1793). Blake was only one among a number of British poets to assail empire in the years between the American Revolution and Waterloo, a period of colonial wars and rebellions, slave uprisings and maroon revolts, agitation in England over the slave trade and the East India Company's management of Bengal, and a transglobal struggle with France which placed the entire British colonial system in crisis— though it would end with Britain unrivalled as an imperial power. Helen Maria Williams in *Peru* (1784), Walter Savage Landor in *Gebir* (1798), Thomas Campbell in *The Pleasures of Hope* (1799), James Montgomery in *The West Indies* (1809), and Samuel Rogers in *The Voyage of Columbus* (1810) all condemned European imperialism in its various forms, with explicit or implicit reference to Britain. Their complaints made part of a larger anti-colonialist discourse which was first making itself felt in modern Europe, whether posed on radical Enlightenment grounds, as with Raynal in France or Godwin in England, or on economic grounds, as with the challenges to mercantilist ideology and colonialist policy developed by Turgot and Adam Smith.[1]

And yet the question remains open whether it was indeed possible to write anti-imperialist poetry in Britain during the Romantic era. Nigel Leask, in his groundbreaking study *British Romantic Writers and the East*, has claimed that to "speak of manifestly anti-imperialist discourse in the Romantic era" would be a "misnomer," since criticism of

the more crudely oppressive aspects of the British imperial system—
mercantilism, wars of colonial expansion, the slave trade—was inevitably accompanied by an endorsement of European cultural and economic hegemony, what Campbell, in *The Pleasures of Hope*, terms simply
"Improvement."[2] Although Leask nowhere mentions Blake, one can
readily construct a case demonstrating that even the "prophet against
empire" comes up against this discursive bind. The "Song of Liberty"
expresses Blake's own quirky version of Enlightenment universalism
("The Eternal Female groand! it was heard all over the Earth"), and
draws unabashedly on racial stereotypes in the process: "O African!
black African! (go. winged thought widen his forehead.)" The "Song
of Los" assumes that Oriental despotism (the "darkness of Asia") can
be pierced only by a Volneyan cry from the West, Orc's Revolutionary
"howl . . . from Europe."[3]

If the treatment of empire in Romantic-era poetry is characteristically ambivalent, however, each poem manifests this ambivalence
in its own manner, beginning with the obvious distinction between
works with anti-imperialist agendas that nevertheless take up a colonialist rhetoric or harbor colonialist paradigms, and those which, like
Southey's international epics, are more overtly committed to the imperial enterprise.[4] Southey's adaptation of the epic genre in poems like
Madoc (1805) and *The Curse of Kehama* (1810) is significant in itself,
given the close association between epic and empire in the European tradition running back to Virgil's *Aeneid*, which establishes a master narrative of heroic colonization that later poets—Ariosto, Tasso,
Camões, Milton—would draw upon. As David Quint has shown in compelling detail, *The Aeneid* inaugurated the celebration and ideological
justification of empire as the "defining tradition of Western epic," yet
this tradition has been shadowed almost from the beginning by a
counter-tradition which attempts to throw the ruling terms of the imperial epic into question. The subversion of imperial epic is undertaken
by means of a generic swerve that Quint has traced from Lucan's *Pharsalia* through Macpherson's *Ossian*: a turn from the universality and
remorselessly teleological structure of epic proper to the contingency
and open-endedness of romance.[5] A similarly romantic deflection of
epic design characterizes, though in signally different ways, the generic
ambivalence of the two works considered here: Landor's *Gebir*, often
considered the earliest significant example of Romantic literary Orientalism, and Williams's *Peru*, a moving and long-neglected poem that
brings terms from "sentimental" discourse to bear on the anti-imperialist project.[6] Both poems posit an oblique relation to the epic tradition
that manifests itself, most obviously, in their ambivalent generic status

as "brief" epics with pronounced elements of romance; both also feature explicit denunciations of European colonialism with evident relevance to British policy. Williams's turn to romance, however, makes part of the self-consciously feminine, domestic rhetoric with which she frames her condemnation of imperialist violence, whereas Landor distances himself from the feminine connotations of romance through a prefatory disavowal of his "incoherent" "female" source, Clara Reeve's *Progress of Romance*. Issues of gender, no less than questions of ideological and political allegiance, further complicate the generic hybridity and discursive tensions informing (and deforming) these works. Finally, the two works are distinguished by the complex interplay in each case between historical setting—sixteenth-century Peru for Williams and Pharaonic Egypt for Landor—and their respective production histories in the early 1780s and late 1790s, divided by a period which included the French Revolution and the British reaction, as well as such colonial developments as the impeachment and trial of Warren Hastings and the massive British losses in the West Indies.

Williams's choice of the conquest of Peru as her epic subject might be seen as minimizing the relevance to Britain of her critique of imperialist violence. The "Black Legend" of the Spanish conquest of the Americas had, after all, long served the purposes of English nationalist and anti-Catholic propaganda, and had historically been used to justify British expansion at the expense of the "Bloudy and Popish" Spaniards.[7] Given that *Peru* was published the year after Britain signed the Peace of Paris, however, acknowledging the independence of the thirteen colonies and throwing its own transatlantic empire into crisis, an anti-imperialist poem set in the Americas could hardly fail to suggest a home application. The major Peruvian Indian uprising of 1780–81, which Williams celebrates in the conclusion to her poem, poses a more overt connection between South and North American revolutions and anti-colonial movements. Moreover, in referring to the leader of the Peruvian revolt (Tupuc Amaru II) as a "chief of India's royal race" (VI.323) in a poem that appeared the same year the East India Act was passed, Williams suggests an association between Spanish conquest in the Americas and the consolidation of British control over Bengal, where Haidar Ali had been decisively defeated only in 1781.[8] This topical link between the Americas and India should be seen as embedded within a longstanding discursive association between the Americas and the Orient, the East and West Indies, in the European mind. That 1492 witnessed not only Columbus's first encounter with the New World but also the final battle against the Moors and the expulsion of the Jews in

Spain, which has become something of a cliche in recent cultural studies, was already a commonplace for Romantic-era writers: Rogers makes the connection in the notes to *The Voyage of Columbus*, for example, and Montgomery refers to the military experience of the conquistadors in battles against the Moor in Part I of *The West Indies*. Raynal opens the *Histoire des deux Indes* (as it was known) by describing the "discovery of the New World, and the passage to India by the Cape of Good Hope" five years later as a single world-altering "event" which inaugurated a truly global "intercourse" for the first time.[9]

Memorializing the conquest of Peru at a time when British colonial enthusiasm, in the aftermath of the successful American rebellion, was at a singularly low ebb, Williams could give voice to a rising tide of British anti-imperialist sentiment, which was becoming a legitimate if decidedly minority position. She does this at the generic level through a studied evasion of epic, organizing the poem into six rather than twelve cantos and making her poem's lack of epic sweep an explicit issue in the "Advertisement," promising not a "full, historical narration" of Peru's "fall" but a selection of "some few incidents that make a part of that romantic story." Williams chooses the episodic over the totalizing form of historical narrative, "sufferings" over heroism, "pathos" over telos, the "romantic" over the epic: in short, the losers over the winners.[10] The heroic values of Virgilian epic are caricatured in the "martial band" under Pizarro (II.1), whose "savage pomp of armour" (II.13) and "dire weapons" (VI.8) not only render the disproportion of numbers irrelevant, but sap the "unequal" contest of any chivalric glory (IV.60). The Indians, on the contrary, embody feminine-coded virtues—nurturing and sympathy, "melting charity" and "ardor warm" (I.43); their virtue is in being unheroic.

Williams hints at the feminine character of Peruvian culture at the outset in her description of the exotic hummingbird, which might initially seem included, along with the "guava" and the "soft ananas," the "Pacos, and Vicunnas" (I.13, 23), as an instance of the "new and ample materials for poetic description" furnished by the Incas' "climate"— Williams is by no means above the exercise of *literary* colonization. As the passage unfolds, however, it becomes clear that Williams values the hummingbird more for its androgynous character than for its local color:

> He sees the flower which morning tears bedew,
> Sinks on its breast, and drinks th' ambrosial dew:
> Then seeks with fond delight the social nest
> Parental care has rear'd, and love has blest:
> The drops that on the blossom's light leaf hung,

He bears exulting to his tender young;
The grateful joy his happy accents prove,
Is nature, smiling on her works of love.   (I.33–40)

The male hummingbird nurses his young with a quasi-maternal ambrosia gathered from a flower's breast, with a feminine nature alternately weeping and smiling over the scene. In an extended simile later in the poem, the Peruvian army will be compared to an amorous hummingbird intercepted by a "savage" condor (IV.169–78), implying—as do images and descriptions throughout the poem—that Peruvian culture is no less feminized than Peruvian nature.

The very fact that the Spanish travel without women, in contrast to the salient presence of women in Peruvian society (at least as Williams represents it), sets up a gendered dichotomy throughout the text between "Iberia's ruthless sons" (V.53) and the "gentle tribe" (I.115). In her portrayal of Ataliba (Atahualpa), the Peruvian leader, Williams strategically elides the background material supplied in her principal historical sources, Raynal and William Robertson, relating to his dispossession of his elder brother and the civil war which left the Inca Empire weakened and divided. Instead she expands on Raynal's idealized picture of the Incas as "one single family" guided by mutual love, and presents Ataliba ruling less through authority and open force than parental guidance—his "mild behest the willing heart obey'd" (I.56).[11] Ataliba's political virtues are inextricable from his love for (and psychic interpenetration with) his wife Alzira—"His gentle spirit, love's soft power possest, / And stamp'd Alzira's image on his breast" (I.65–66)—a dynamic repeated throughout the poem. Ataliba's successor, Manco-Capac, is guided by "tender Cora, partner of his breast" (IV.66); the love of Aciloe humanizes (and feminizes) the Peruvian "Bard" Zamor, whose "early passion's pure controul . . . Bids her soft sympathies the bosom move / And wakes the mild emotions dear to love" (V.32–34). Williams's Peru—pacific, communitarian, harmonious—exhibits what Britain might become if feminine "influence" should hold sway.[12] The Spaniards, on the other hand, exemplify the perversity of a culture bereft of feminine values, as with the "fanatic" priest Valverde, whose "bosom never felt another's woes" (III.15, 29).

Williams's domestic revision of epic heroism—with an important precedent in *Paradise Lost*—follows Milton as well in problematizing the distinction between heroic and familial, public and private, representing the Peruvian revolt under Manco-Capac as an expression of the incomparably "gentle" and affectionate national character which, for Robertson, made the Incas both unusually virtuous and easily conquered.[13] The Indians persist in "dire, unequal war" because they are motivated by "every tender, human interest" (IV.60–61); when they have succeeded in taking half of Cusco, their capital, they welcome Capac with a "gen'rous tear" and hail his restoration as a "tender child" torn from home would view

> His mother's form, when in her arms she folds
> The long lost child, who bathes with tears her face,
> And finds his safety in her dear embrace.   (IV.112–14)

In defeat, however, the Indians follow the precedent of the archetypal epic loser, Dido, who exemplifies, for Virgil and for the poets who follow his lead, the epic counter-values of femininity, exoticism, peaceful negotiation, and romantic love, terms the Virgilian epic takes up in order to demonize and expel.[14] The presence of Dido is particularly strong in the poem's first such suicide, that of the Indian queen Alzira, who has helplessly seen Ataliba captured, ransomed, betrayed, and murdered:

> Distraction throbb'd in every beating vein:
> Its sudden tumults seize her yielding soul,
> And in her eye distemper'd glances roll.   (II.84–86)[15]

When an Indian youth is slain attempting to save his lover's father, an Inca priest, from Valverde's "fanatic fury," a second youth stabs himself (like Alzira and like Dido) with his enemy's sword, out of a passionate friendship at once quasi-erotic and quasi-familial: "The first pure passion of my infant breast; / That passion, which o'er life delight has shed" (III.58–59). These romantic suicides align the Incas with the losers of Virgilian epic—Dido, Cleopatra, Antony—in an attempt, analogous to the stoic suicides in such anti-Virgilian epics as Lucan's *Pharsalia* and Ercilla's *Araucana* (set in Chile and commemorating Indian resistance to Spanish dominion), to invert a colonialist trope and evince sympathy for the anti-heroic values that the imperial tradition entertains only to disarm and abnegate.[16] In recounting the Inca rebellion's ultimate defeat, Williams self-consciously deflects epic description—"But from the scene where raging slaughter burns, / The timid muse with pallid horror turns" (VI.13–14)—to recount instead the sufferings of the defeated, particularly of the women; the poem proceeds to one of its most remarkable (and lushly sentimental) passages, Cora's dying speech to her infant, which reads in part:

> When my chill'd bosom can no longer warm,
> My stiff'ning arms no more enfold thy form,
> Soft on this bed of leaves my child shall sleep,
> Close to his mother's corse he will not weep:

Oh weep not then, my tender babe, tho' near,
I shall not hear thy moan, nor see thy tear;
Hope not to move me by thy piercing cry,
Nor seek with searching look my answering eye. (VI.73–80)

Capac arrives in time to fuse once more with Cora as she dies ("their melting souls unite") and take up the "lov'd babe," again assuming a maternal role (VI.99, 123).

If the trajectory of epic is as linear and end-directed as that of romance is circular and non-sequential, epic clearly aligns itself with history, at least with the totalizing style of history endemic to writing in the West.[17] In taking on a historical subject, Williams can be seen as deflating the grandeur of epic by underscoring the painfully contingent nature of the brutal acts of imperial violence which epic mythicizes and ennobles, yet at the same time aligning herself with the victors' teleology, for all her sympathy with their victims. The conquistadors import history into the Edenic, cyclical world of Peru, and European norms tacitly define the relative cultural status of the Indians, who are drawn inevitably into a progressive historical schema aligned with the "improvement" ethos of the West. Williams's discursive subordination of the Incas to a Eurocentric progressive history is hardly crude: she goes out of her way to expatiate on the "cultur'd" fields, the religious practices, the erotic and tragic poetry mentioned by Raynal; it is the bloodthirsty and venal Spaniards who merit the epithet "savage" (I.3, II.13). But in representing Peru as a luxuriant garden of "simplicity" and "innocence," and the Peruvians as "artless" and "unsullied" (I.42–49, 74), Williams adapts the well-known Eurocentric trope by which geographical distances become temporal ones, and newly encountered peoples are represented as somehow living in a chronologically junior, "primitive" era in relation to their European contemporaries.[18] The tragedy of Peru is that, "Consum'd, and fading in its early prime" (I.175), it will suffer European corruption before it can mimic European progress.

This sense that the Incas' exemplary social virtues depend on their cultural backwardness—the irony that vitiates all forms of European primitivism, however apparently generous or self-critical—is intensified in the scenes set in a pristine Andean valley, a garden of romance that helps bring out the literary character of Williams's Peru, based as much on European epic and romance traditions as on the historical sources.[19] The valley appears as a literally "new" world—"like nature rising from the breast / Of chaos, in her infant graces drest" (IV.149–50)—and its denizens, "gentle natives of the mead" (IV.161), are helpless before the European invaders who happen across them naively culling gold from the crystal streams. The valley boasts a bard, Zamor, but he is explicitly presented as what Southey would call an "uneducated poet," his "wild warblings" unalloyed by "art" (V.5, 21). The weakness of the Peruvians' infantile culture becomes an issue not simply because a handful of desperate Spaniards, cut off from the main army, can instantaneously conquer the valley, but because the Peruvians' only recourse is to another European, the saintly Las Casas, who appears seemingly out of nowhere (certainly not out of the historical accounts) to rescue Zamor's beloved from a forced marriage to one of the conquistadors. A "pitying angel" (III.97), more specifically a Gabriel to Valverde's Satan (III.121–26), Las Casas's role as deus ex machina underscores Williams's difficulty in breaking out of a colonialist mentality, however benevolent. When Las Casas dies (his eulogy spoken by "Sensibility" herself), his place is taken by "mild Gasca" (VI.271), who comes to soften Spanish dominion with progressive policies.

Williams's elisions from her sources can be as revealing as her embellishments to them. In her version of the historical encounter between Atahualpa and the Spaniards, which begins with Pizarro's chaplain, Valverdo, demanding in the style of the *Requerimiento* that the Indians embrace Christianity and submit to the king of Spain, to whom the Pope has granted Peru, Pizarro is represented as an adept in "eloquence" and the display of superior European knowledge and "Ataliba" as his naive, dumbfounded victim:[20]

> Unfolding to the monarch's wond'ring thought,
> All that inventive arts the rude have taught:
> And now he bids the purer spirit rise
> Above the circle of surrounding skies;
> Presents the page that shed religion's light
> O'er the dark mist of intellectual night;
> While thrill'd with awe the monarch trembling stands,
> He dropp'd the hallow'd volume from his hands. (II.17–24)

In both Raynal's and Robertson's accounts, however, Atahualpa is presented as anything but credulous. Rather, he explodes the fiction of the *Requerimiento* and puts the Spaniards' religious claims into perspective: "I am very willing to be the friend of the king of Spain, but not his vassal; the pope must surely be a very extraordinary man, to give so liberally what does not belong to him. I shall not change my religion for another; and if the christians adore a God who died upon a cross, I worship the sun, who never dies."[21] Atahualpa does not drop the breviary out of awestruck fumbling, but throws it to the ground in scorn when he is told that Valverdo's religious knowledge is contained in the book, and on examining it laughingly declares: "This book tells me nothing of all this." Rather than being intimidated by the "advanced" technology of European writing, that is, Atahualpa subjects it to a test on his own cultural ground and finds it wanting.[22] Williams has so thoroughly adopted the Enlightenment ideology, exemplified by Robertson, of "stages" of development through which various civilizations pass, providing a basis upon which they can be compared (to the advantage of Europe and above all of Britain), that she can find no room for the moment of "native" resistance and mocking deflation which Robertson himself records, despite its ironizing relation to his own historical project.[23]

Put another way, Williams's romantic deflection of the epic masterplot is disarmed by her tacit adherence to an epic vision of history, teleological, Eurocentric, constructing its others as "rude" "natives" if not as barbarians proper. Although free of any overt or crudely biological racism, the poem's underlying ideology groups various peoples into racial categories, distinguished as much by "climate" as by economic arrangements and social institutions.[24] Moreover, the conventionally feminine "relational" virtues which set the Incas above the conquistadors in moral terms—charity, nurturing, "melting" love, self-abnegation—stand in an uncomfortably close relation to the "primitive" virtues—simplicity, purity, innocence, artlessness—that set them below the Spaniards in the hierarchy of races and civilizations.[25] The romantic values enabling Williams's critique of imperialism become entangled in the colonialist tropes that ultimately bleed the critique of its force. Yet, as we will see, Williams's primitivism is not the only instance in the poem of temporal derangement, which does not always have to work to the colonizer's advantage. Moreover, the very distinction between epic and romance upon which Williams's poem may be seen to founder is one which Williams herself takes pains to erode.

Clara Reeve, in the *Progress of Romance* (1785), risks shocking the classically educated men among her readers by calling this very distinction into question, disarming their spokesman in her dialogue of a prime argument against romance—its association with undisciplined female reading and its lack of a classical pedigree—at the outset.[26] If the romance has its "extravagant" elements so does the epic, its "parent"; as both share heroic elements as well, the romance might best be termed an "epic in prose" (13, 20, 25). Reeve also challenges the distinction between European and Oriental literary modes, claiming a kinship between Odysseus and Sinbad and noting that, if the European romance has a classical father in epic, it has a foster-mother in the "Moorish" models which the "Saracens" brought from Africa to Spain in the eighth century (ix, 35). "The History of Charoba, Queen of Aegypt," which Reeve appends to her dialogue, is offered as an example of the ancient Egyptian narratives preserved in the "traditions of the Arabians" (2: 105); rich in biblical allusions and classical parallels along with its "Oriental" motifs, it is meant to exemplify cultural as well as generic hybridity.[27]

Landor, dismissing "Charoba" as a "wild and incoherent" fiction and finding *The Progress of Romance* remarkable only for the "pertness and petulance of female criticism," might be seen as reasserting the claims of the Western epic tradition in developing Reeve's "Arabian Romance" into his heroic poem, *Gebir*.[28] His revisions include the addition of an epic descent into the underworld, a self-conscious deployment of the Dido and Aeneas motif, a vision of future history granted to the founder of a conquering race, and passages describing the building of a North African city and the celebration of athletic-military games. And the "Miltonic and Virgilian flavor" of the style is, as one scholar of the Romantic-era epic points out, "absolutely unmistakable."[29] Williams and Landor both commingle heroic and romantic modes, but Landor seems less bent on feminizing epic than on masculinizing romance.

One of Landor's more salient changes, however, would indicate that his relation to the Virgilian tradition is anything but filial. In transforming Gebir from a Chaldean (or "Metaphequian") into an Iberian, changing his lineage from Asiatic "Gadite" nomads into colonists based in "Gades" (Cadiz), Landor underscores the association of the European epic with European imperialism, to which his poem bears an ambivalent relation in its 1798 version, further vexed in the revision of 1803. Stuart Curran rightly remarks that "no reader of 1798 could miss the implications of a colonial power in Egypt, where Napoleon had just landed his armies and usurped the Mameluke government."[30] Yet Landor could scarcely have known about Napoleon's designs on Egypt in 1796, when *Gebir* was mostly drafted; the Egyptian destination of Napoleon's invasion force (which had been initially assembled with England in mind) remained secret until well after its departure in May 1798, and *Gebir* was apparently published the same month (July) that Napoleon landed near Alexandria.[31] Landor was more likely drawn to North Africa as a traditional site for crossings (in both directions) between the Iberian peninsula and the Maghreb, a region at once African and "Oriental," a point where Europe, Africa, and the East converged. Gebir's Iberian invasion anticipates, in reverse, the "Saracen" occupation of the peninsula that would bring (according to Reeve and Thomas Warton before her) the romance to Spain, initiating a long period when European territories were incorporated into Muslim empires, rather than the other way around. More obviously, *Gebir* evokes the various Iberian counter-incursions into North Africa beginning

with the epochal Portuguese seizure of Ceuta in 1415 and extending
to strategic European outposts from Tunis—the modern site of Dido's
city—to Tangier, which had passed to England (along with Bombay)
as part of Catherine of Braganza's dowry at the time of the Restoration.
Although Tangier was soon abandoned, Britain's interest in this strategic border area was manifested in its continuing occupation from
1704, against intense Spanish opposition, of Gibraltar, across the Strait
from Ceuta. And Gibraltar, according to Landor's fanciful etymology
(I.15), had been named for Gebir.

Transforming Reeve's Gadite giant into an "Iberian king" (II.173)—
the Egyptians hail him as "King of the western world" (IV.223)—sets
up a critique of European colonialism which, as Leask suggests, bears
an undeniable if "elliptical" relevance to British empire-building.[32] Landor's extensive use of epic motifs and devices can thus be seen as bearing an ironic or inverted relation to the Virgilian imperial tradition,
perhaps most obviously in portraying Gebir as a more crudely manipu-
lative Aeneas to Charoba's warier Dido, who views Gebir less as her
suitor than as her "conqueror" (IV.139).[33] In fact, Landor's early poetry
shares a number of ideological valences with that of Williams, despite
the quite different tonal qualities of their brief epics: both attack the
slave trade, celebrate the independence of the North American colonies, and strongly sympathize with the ideals of the French Revolution,
their misgivings about empire arising from republican, egalitarian, and
pacifist inclinations. Gebir's epic descent should (but fails to) teach
him to distrust Virgilian epic values: his ancestors have discovered the
emptiness of "trophies, tributes, colonies" (III.72), and are exposed
as tyrants in vignettes meant to evoke George III and prior British sov-
ereigns, leading the young De Quincey to admire the "audacity" of a
"*Tom-Painish*" poet "whom the Attorney-General might have occasion
to speak with."[34] Epic heroism is deflated ("Go mighty men, and ruin
cities" [II.33]) and "compassion" is valorized in its stead (III.275). Local patriotism (of the sort encouraged under monarchies) is dispar-
aged, in one of the poem's many striking passages, for devaluing the
"Sympathies / Divine":

> those Sympathies whose delicate hand
> Touching the very eyeball of the heart,
> Awakens it, not wounds it nor inflames.   (IV.72–75)

At such points in the text, Landor's rhetoric seems no less "feminine"
than that of Williams.

Gebir also manifests, however, a residual colonialist rhetoric that undercuts its anti-imperialist agenda. Whereas the primitivist associations
of *Peru* rendered Williams's feminization of her idealized Indians sus-

pect, Landor's reliance on related Orientalist tropes in *Gebir* still more dubiously aligns the feminine with the monstrous, dangerous, irrational Other, an association all too familiar from the Virgilian epic. If Charoba evokes Dido, she also recalls a third North African queen, Cleopatra—"tho' indeed she never drank / The liquid pearl" (IV.44–45)—the exotic seducer of Antony, the dabbler in charms and poison, the embodiment of luxury and "Oriental" slothfulness. Landor's Egyptians are superstitious, "extravagant," "wild," "luxuriant," and "wanton," and Egypt is a land of "incantation; demons rule these waves" (II.205–6, Book IV, passim). The Iberians are, in contrast, "brave" and "frugal" (IV.201, VI.16), and Gebir himself shares the characteristic "flatness" of the Virgilian hero and his predilection for duty over desire: "My people, not my passion, fills my heart" (II.90).[35] According to the Enlightenment schema of racial hierarchies upon which both Williams and Landor tacitly draw, an "ancient race" like the Egyptians (V.13) fares still worse than a "primal" one like the Incas. If the Incas have not had sufficient time to match European progress, the Egyptians have had more than enough time to regress under "despotic" institutions.[36] Europe's others are found either infantile or degenerate, and to Europe alone belongs the present.

Landor can therefore imagine, following Volney, a democratic, universalist impulse arising out of the French Revolution and imposing the most progressive aspects of European ideals and institutions—renewing "Time himself"—first throughout the West, and then around the globe, in an enlightened version of imperialism:[37]

> Captivity led captive, War o'erthrown,
> They shall o'er Europe, shall o'er Earth extend
> Empire that seas alone and skies confine,
> And glory that shall strike the crystal stars.   (VI.305–308)

For Landor in 1798, these ideals and their radical contemporaneity seem to be embodied in Napoleon Bonaparte, "a mortal man above all mortal praise" (VI.193), whose military prowess will hasten the "Hour" when "Justice shall unite the Iberian hinds, / And equal Egypt bid her shepherds reign" (VI.226–27). Although Landor here is presaging rather than reacting to Napoleon's invasion of Egypt, in the fragmentary "Extract from the French Preface" written for his *Poems from the Arabic and Persian* (1800), Landor praises Bonaparte's "deliverance" of the Egyptians from their own "prejudices" and "weakness"; "conquerors like him, posterity will declare it, have never been the enemies of the human race" (2: 549–50). Three years later, however, in the 1803 revision of *Gebir*, Landor has come to see Napoleon himself as a tyrant, and his endorsement of "enlightened" imperialism becomes qualified in a manner which entails rethinking the poem's heroic allegiances as well as unsettling its East/West polarities.

Much of the revisionary material appears in the preface, the new "arguments" to each book, and the notes, bringing the margins of *Gebir* into an antithetical relation with the body of the poem. A note to the line praising Bonaparte—whose elevation to First Consul for Life had been witnessed by a disgusted Landor in 1802—reads it as stating only "what might have been," and reinterprets Bonaparte as exemplifying not progressive change but a program of restless innovation, "to overthrow by violence all the institutions, and to tear from the heart all the social habits of men" (1: 479). The radical "Empire" arising from the energies of the French Revolution is now qualified as the "empire of justice and equality," only to be dismissed as a delusory hope, the reality being "internal and external subjugation" which Britain would do better not to emulate, "God forbid" (1: 47). The revised "Preface" designates a newly specific meaning for Gebir's death (by a poisoned garment) at the end, now less a lamentable result of tragic misprision (and Egyptian sorcery) than an event pointing the work's "moral," the "folly, injustice, and the punishment of Invasion, with the calamities which must ever attend the superfluous colonization of a peopled country" (1: 474). The epic venture of building empire through the military defeat of colonized peoples, whether in the name of "progressive" values or not, is now definitively rejected, though the option of developing allegedly "vacant" lands—in emulation of the virtuous North American republicans—remains open as a vehicle for Landor's "rational" colonialism.[38]

If the epic pretensions of the 1798 *Gebir* sit uneasily with its critique of manifest imperialism, the 1803 additions effectively ironize the Virgilian references and topoi and shift the poem's generic balance decisively in favor of its romance elements. Virgil, in Curran's brief but suggestive reading, is the "model who is dethroned, and with him the value of an imperialist mission and the warfare that sustains it," and the "pastoral romance" associated with Gebir's brother, Tamar, takes precedence over the epic values exemplified by the poem's nominal hero. Although Curran is evidently thinking here of the revised *Gebir*, the valorizing of pastoral romance over epic is already latent in Landor's seemingly odd decision, in the first published version, to transform Reeve's anonymous "young shepherd" into a major character and the brother to a king (though no less a shepherd for that). Tamar's amorous adventure with a sea-nymph, which mainly serves to advance the plot in "Charoba," is greatly expanded by Landor in 1798, and it is Tamar's bloodline, rather than Gebir's, which will eventually come to flower in Bonaparte and realize the Iberians' colonial ambitions in a finer tone. The disavowal of Bonaparte (and the demotion of Gebir) in the 1803 revision underscores the benign, pastoral quality of the promised victories of Tamar's progeny—enfranchising "hinds" and "shepherds" under a world republican alliance. In lines added in 1803, the heritage of the "nymph divine" further softens the benign character of Tamar's side of the Iberian royal family, for nymphs represent the leveling properties of water: "By every lake's and every river's side / The Nymphs and Naiads teach Equality" (VII.14–15). The "watery element" which, in the Virgilian tradition, is associated with the Orient, with chaos, flux, purposelessness, and femininity, is reclaimed by Landor as an image of democracy and of the principle that peopling a desert remedies a void whereas "colonization in peopled countries" is "hostile to equality" and inevitably tyrannical ("Argument" to Book VII).[39]

In addition to the awkward fact that so-called "desert colonies" such as North America and Australia *were* more often than not "peopled," if not so densely as Egypt or Peru, a problem arises for Landor's revised position in its very reliance on a pastoral-romance mode. Landor seems unable to imagine an egalitarian future without drawing (like Williams) on a primitivist lexicon—nymphs and hinds, shepherds and antique virtue—which, particularly in a work concerned with colonialism, carries troubling discursive resonances. ("Pastoralism" was the next lowest "stage" in the hierarchy of civilizations which played so crucial a role in late eighteenth-century attempts to place exotic cultures in relation to a British norm.)[40] On the other hand, the temporal dislocations proliferate in *Gebir* (particularly in the 1803 revision) to the extent that a simple binary opposition between the contemporary West and the untimely rest becomes difficult to maintain. Napoleon's imagined descent from the Iberian Tamar participates in a patently Eurocentric vision. Yet it also aligns the benign empire of the future with the utopian atemporality of pastoral romance ("Time himself throws off his motley garb" [VI.301]), rather than with the linear, teleological movement of the epic mode, disturbing any simple equation of history with progress. Gebir's "fathers" (III.35), in contrast, are identified with the (future) kings of the British past, from the headless Charles I to a doomed George III (III.187), equating Gebir's heroic genealogy with a line of English tyrants whose time has run out. Epic lines lead not to a universal empire but to a dead end, and "futurity" (VI.289) emerges from the timelessness of pastoral romance.

In *Peru*, prophecy similarly disrupts epic closure, unsettling that work's starker opposition between more and less advanced civilizations.[41] The Andean rebellion heralded at its close allows Williams to move from "dear remembrance of the past" to envision Peru's "future triumphs" (VI.304, 356) as the progressive force of liberty jumps the Atlantic to reside among the Incas: "O Freedom, may thy genius still ascend, / Beneath thy crest may proud Iberia bend" (VI.339–40). Williams's Iberians, like Landor's, represent in the end a passing order, and freedom proves—however transiently—an uncontainable and promiscuous force, its European pedigree in no way obviating its migration from Spain to Peru (or from England to North America). Landor and Williams remain wedded, of course, to distinctly European liberal ideologies, and neither proves willing to maintain a coherent radical critique of British imperialism, displaced though it is onto "Iberia," the dominant European colonial power of the past. Both poets short-circuit their attempts to frame an anti-colonialist rhetoric through continuing to rely, perhaps inevitably but nonetheless incongruously, on colonialist figures of savagery, primitivism, and the primacy of the West. We may hesitate, nevertheless, to categorize their condemnations of empire as simple matters of disavowal or liberal bad faith, if we wish to keep sight of the ambivalences and hesitations that mark the inchoate anti-imperialist discourse of a quite different historical moment. Though the British Empire was on the eve of its period of unrivalled world dominance, there was no way of knowing this at the close of the eighteenth century, a time when, on the contrary, the empire may well have seemed more fragile and transient than it had since its inception and would for over a century to come. The fracturing of epic form, with all that it traditionally represents, in *Peru* and *Gebir*, attests to the "sense of crisis" which characterizes British imperialism toward the end of the eighteenth century; the Romantic poet's notoriously vexed relation to epic may proceed no less from geo-political anxieties than from literary-historical ones, registering the psychic costs of empire-building as much as the "burden of the past."[42] Fully assimilable neither to imperial nor anti-imperial ideologies, *Peru* and *Gebir* prove most compelling in their discursive incoherence, and their formal interest resides in their generic hybridity, their disruptive temporality, and their studied failure as imperial epics.

NOTES

1. See Glyndwr Williams, *The Expansion of Europe in the Eighteenth Century: Overseas Rivalry, Discovery, and Exploitation* (New York: Walker, 1966), 232–38; R. L. Schuyler, "The Rise of Anti-Imperialism in England," *Political Science Quarterly* 37 (1922): 440–47; and P. J. Marshall, "Empire and Authority in the Later Eighteenth Century, *Journal of Imperial and Commonwealth History* 19 (1991): 1–23.

2. Nigel Leask, *British Romantic Writers and the East: Anxieties of Empire* (Cambridge: Cambridge University Press, 1992), 92–94; see also 25–33.

3. Blake is quoted from *The Complete Poetry and Prose of William Blake*, ed. David V. Erdman, rev. ed. (Garden City: Anchor, 1982). On Blake's anti-imperialism, see David V. Erdman, *Blake: Prophet against Empire* 3rd ed. (Princeton: Princeton University Press, 1977). For the parallels with Volney on Oriental despotism ("All Asia lies buried in profound darkness") and the "cry of liberty" from the West, see Constantin Francois Volney, *A New Translation of Volney's Ruins*, 2 vols. (1802; rpt. New York: Garland, 1979) 1: 134, 1: 138.

4. For Southey, see Javed Majeed, *Ungoverned Imaginings: James Mill's The History of British India and Orientalism* (Oxford: Clarendon Press, 1992), 47–86.

5. David Quint, *Epic and Empire: Politics and Generic Form from Virgil to Milton* (Princeton: Princeton University Press, 1993), 8. Stuart Curran notes that the "signal difference between epic and romance" within Romantic-era poetic practice is that epic is meant to embellish upon "historical truth" whereas romance is associated with the "improbable," the latter form tending "in the abstract" toward pure, undisciplined fictionality, *Poetic Form and British Romanticism* (New York: Oxford University Press, 1986), 131–32, 147.

6. Marlon Ross has read the romance form, as developed by Scott and Wordsworth in the early nineteenth century, in terms of the "ideology of nationalist evolutionary growth" and as exerting a "call to British imperialism" in "Romancing the Nation-State: The Poetics of Romantic Nationalism," *Macropolitics of Nineteenth-Century Literature: Nationalism, Exoticism, Imperialism*, ed. Jonathan Arac and Harriet Ritvo (Philadelphia: University of Pennsylvania Press, 1991), 75, 84. That romance can, at least in critical juxtaposition with epic, militate against a call to imperialism in Romantic-era works (no less than in Quint's epic "counter-tradition") is manifest in *Peru* and *Gebir*; it is perhaps significant that the works Ross principally analyzes, *Rokeby* (1813) and *The White Doe of Rylstone* (1815), were published at a time when British imperial confidence was rapidly becoming restored.

7. The quotation is from the dedication to Oliver Cromwell, on the eve of the Jamaica expedition, in the 1656 English translation of Las Casas's *Brevissima Historia*: Bartolomeo de las Casas, *The Tears of the Indians*, trans. John Phillips (Stanford: Academic Reprint, n.d.); see also William S. Maltby, *The Black Legend in England: The Development of Anti-Spanish Sentiment, 1558–1660* (Durham: Duke University Press, 1971).

8. *Peru* is cited (by canto and line) from Helen Maria Williams, *Poems*, 2 vols. in 1 (London: Rivington and Marshall, 1786).

9. Abbe Raynal, *A Philosophical and Political History of the Settlements and Trade of the Europeans in the East and West Indies*, trans. J. Justamond, 3rd ed., 5 vols. (London: Cadell, 1777) 1: 1–2.

10. Quint, *Epic and Empire*, 9.

11. Raynal, *Philosophical and Political History* 2: 481–82; cf. William Robertson, *The History of America*, 2 vols. (London: Cadell, 1777) 2: 165–66, where Inca rule is described as "beneficent" though as "absolute" as the "despotism of Asia."

12. On the development of a "feminine" reformist discourse in late eighteenth-century and early nineteenth-century Britain, with particular reference to the early career of Williams, see Gary Kelly *Women, Writing, and Revolution 1790–1827* (Oxford: Clarendon Press, 1993), 3–79; the "feminine" rhetoric of *Peru* is briefly discussed on pp. 22 and 32.

13. Robertson, *History* 2: 310–13, 326. Quint writes that "just as Milton reverses epic tradition by giving the private world of Eden priority over a public arena of military and political exploits—a reversal so remarkable that it almost seems to create a new genre—he also disputes the conventional epic wisdom that separates them," *Epic,* 283.

14. Quint, *Epic,* 182–5.

15. Cf. *Aeneid* IV.642–47.

16. Quint, *Epic,* 29, 101–103.

17. Quint, *Epic,* 30; see also Robert Young, *White Mythologies: Writing History and the West* (London: Routledge, 1990).

18. See Eric R. Wolf, *Europe and the People without History* (Berkeley: University of California Press, 1982) and Johannes Fabian, *Time and the Other: How Anthropology Makes Its Object* (New York: Columbia University Press, 1983).

19. See Henri Baudet, *Paradise on Earth: Some Thoughts on European Images of Non-European Man,* trans. Elizabeth Wentholt (New Haven: Yale University Press, 1965) and A. Bartlett Giamatti, *The Earthly Paradise and the Renaissance Epic* (Princeton: Princeton University Press, 1966).

20. On the significance of the *Requerimiento* see Tzvetan Todorov, *The Conquest of America: The Question of the Other,* trans. Richard Howard (New York: Harper, 1984), 146–49, and Stephen J. Greenblatt, "Learning to Curse: Aspects of Linguistic Colonialism in the Sixteenth Century," *Learning to Curse: Essays in Early Modern Culture* (New York: Routledge, 1990), 28–30.

21. Raynal, *Philosophical and Political History* 2: 477; cf. the similar account in Robertson, *History* 2: 175.

22. The claim for writing as an "advanced" technology of communication is made by Todorov, *Conquest,* 160. It is important to note that Pizarro's own illiteracy is stressed in the accounts both of Raynal (*Philosophical and Political History* 2: 471) and Robertson (*History* 2: 183).

23. On the "stages of development" ideology, see C. A. Bayly, *Imperial Meridian: The British Empire and the World 1780–1830* (London: Longman, 1989), 152–53, 213. Robertson gauges the "progress" of the Peruvians and finds that they have hardly "advanced beyond the infancy of civil life," *History* 2: 269.

24. Note Williams's rather anxious remark at the outset that Peru's "favour'd clime" might be expected to diminish the virtue of its natives (I.41).

25. Together the two lists of virtues are familiar attributes of the ideal lady of the eighteenth-century conduct book, who was herself explicitly infantilized throughout the conduct-book tradition, as early feminists such as Wollstonecraft and Hays pointed out in Williams's era and as feminist critics have reiterated in our own. See, e.g., Leonore Davidoff and Catherine Hall,

Family Fortunes: Men and Women of the English Middle Class, 1780–1850 (Chicago: Chicago University Press, 1987), 28, 346.

26. Clara Reeve, *The Progress of Romance and the History of Charoba, Queen of Aegypt* (1785; rpt. New York: Facsimile Text Society, 1930), 2. Hereafter cited in the text.

27. See the introduction to "Charoba" in Robert L. Mack, ed., *Oriental Tales* (Oxford: Oxford University Press, 1992), xxxviii.

28. Walter Savage Landor, *The Poetical Works of Walter Savage Landor*, ed. Stephen Wheeler, 3 vols. (Oxford: Clarendon Press, 1937) 1: 473. Hereafter cited in the text; *Gebir* is cited by book and line.

29. Brian Wilkie, *Romantic Poets and Epic Tradition* (Madison: University of Wisconsin Press, 1965), 52.

30. Curran, *Poetic Form*, 168.

31. R. H. Super, in *Walter Savage Landor: A Biography* (New York: New York University Press, 1954), writes that *Gebir* was printed "in the late spring of 1798" and "seems to have been published" in July 1798 (40); as far as the London *Times* was concerned, the goal of Napoleon's "Toulon expedition" was still a mystery at the end of June, and Egypt is mentioned as a destination "asserted by several of the Paris papers" only on 5 July (The *Times* 26 June 1798 and 5 July 1798). Yet Marilyn Butler, in "Plotting the Revolution: The Political Narratives of Romantic Poetry and Criticism," *Romantic Revolutions: Criticism and Theory*, ed. Kenneth R. Johnston et al. (Bloomington: Indiana University Press, 1990), declares that "*Gebir* (1798) turns Napoleon's adventure of that year into a primitive epic" (144), and Leask writes that Landor, in his "bizarre poem of 1798," is "lauding Napoleon's . . . Egyptian expedition of the same year" (*British Romantic Writers*, 93).

32. Leask, *British Romantic Writers*, 26, 93.

33. Wilkie writes that Landor "reverses" the "traditional values" of the Dido and Aeneas motif: "Pacifism, renunciation of ambition, withdrawal from the world of action—these are the virtues endorsed in the poem" (*Romantic Poets*, 53).

34. Thomas De Quincey, *The Collected Works of Thomas De Quincey*, ed. David Masson, 14 vols. (London: Black, 1897) 11: 403–404.

35. Quint, *Epic*, 29 (on Cleopatra) and 95 (on the epic hero).

36. In lines cut from the 1798 *Gebir* which Landor appends to the 1803 revision, "Monarchy" is explicitly described as an "Asian" institution (1: 479).

37. Butler discusses Volney's importance for both Landor and Blake (as well as for Godwin, Southey, and Shelley) in "Plotting the Revolution" (148).

38. Leask, *British Romantic Writers*, 27.

39. Quint, *Epic*, 33.

40. Ronald L. Meek, *Social Science and the Ignoble Savage* (Cambridge: Cambridge University Press, 1976), 177.

41. Quint, *Epic*, 136.

42. Mary Louise Pratt, *Imperial Eyes: Travel Writing and Transculturation* (London: Routledge, 1992), 72–74; W. J. Bate, *The Burden of the Past and the English Poet* (New York: Norton, 1972), 61–62.

Eleven

A L I S O N   H I C K E Y

Dark Characters, Native Grounds: Wordsworth's Imagination of Imperialism

NEW ATTENTION TO the discourse of "imperialism" in the Romantic period has been challenging and reshaping critical understanding of that venerable institution, the Romantic imagination. The complex interpenetration of imagination and imperialism has been elaborated, for example, in John Barrell's brilliant and disturbing reading of the "psychopathology of imperialism" in De Quincey, whose imperialist fantasies Barrell shows to be part of an all-pervasive national imagination of imperialism;[1] in Nigel Leask's examination of the anxieties and instabilities of Romantic representations of the East;[2] and in Sara Suleri's analysis of Burke and the "Indian sublime."[3] Participating in a wider field of political and historicist approaches to Romantic texts, these treatments also build upon, react against, and complicate the framework offered by Edward W. Said's *Orientalism*, which posits an "essentially hermeneutical" relation between Orientalist and Orient, a relation in which the Orientalist endeavors to "translate" a "hard-to-reach object" that is in fact largely constructed by the Western imagination.[4] Treatments such as Barrell's and Leask's address ways in which writers depict their Eastern "subjects" as resistant to representation—as in Suleri's description of Burke's representative and influential model, "dissolving the stability of facts and figures into hieroglyphs that signify only the colonizer's pained confrontation with an object to which his cultural and interpretative tools must be inadequate."[5]

Wordsworth, unlike just about all of his contemporaries, eschews Eastern subjects, and so would seem to offer little material for an analysis of "imperial imagination" as played out in hermeneutic transactions with the East.[6] But although Wordsworth's withdrawal from encounters with the East—and with other "others"[7]—shifts the focus of an inquiry into Wordsworthian imperial imagination, it hardly renders the question immaterial. Wordsworth negotiates the hermeneutical relation between colonizer and colonized not on distant shores, but closer to home: in London, in familiar rural spots, in the territory of the mind. We would be mistaken to view such shifts of ground as simply constituting the poet's withdrawal to the margins of imperial history; the shifts are part of a displacement inward, a move by which Wordsworth acknowledges the hermeneutic encounter with the "others" of British imperialism to be central to himself.

A parenthesis on the term "imperial" is already overdue. It is, of course, a word that can have, and has had, numerous different meanings, many of them contradictory.[8] "Empire" has been invoked for centuries to serve a great variety of political ends, and has been variously assumed to be either "of the people" or of the emperor, favorable to the propagation of "liberty" or adverse to it, compatible with democratic ideals or contradictory to them. Reflecting these contradictions, an embracing definition of imperialism might include the endeavor to appropriate, incorporate, assimilate, or permeate communities or territories beyond one's proper borders; to extend one rule, one set of laws or ideals, one system of control, one character, one "influence" or "spirit"; to infuse difference with unity. Such a definition demonstrates the way in which the rhetoric of "imperialism" is itself imperial, infusing different meanings with the unity of a single term whose own laws are thus extended beyond its "proper borders." In turn, that very statement, extending imperialism from an economic to a linguistic arrangement (or, alternatively, extending linguistic modes of thought to an economic sphere not properly their own), suggests the inevitability with which an analysis of the rhetoric of imperialism extends itself beyond its own proper borders. But where, precisely, can such borders be drawn? Who can determine what is "imperial" and what is an imperialist extension of the term beyond its proper borders? At issue is the question of proper borders themselves. To contend that there is a definitive border separating, for example, a political or economic sense of "imperialism" from a linguistic one would be false. It is not that political or economic imperialism is "literal," while linguistic imperialism is "figurative"; rather, the categories overlap, and each can operate as a figure for the other. A standard romantic logic manifested in topoi of the excursive or permeable self, the projective or introjective mind, the creative or perceptive eye, and other disruptions of proper borders plays itself out in the actions and reactions of imperial practice.

Readers schooled in the tradition of the Wordsworthian imagination, as interpreted by M. H. Abrams and others, should find the notion of an imperial imagination readily comprehensible. Even if the Wordsworthian imagination has until recently rarely been viewed from an explicitly political perspective,[9] some sort of imperialism is implicitly ascribed to it by those diverse critical arguments that emphasize the appropriation or progressive "fitting" of the external world to the core world of the poet's maturing self. This theme threads its way through Abrams, de Man, Hartman, Bloom, and recent historicist and feminist readings. Imagination, according to the common assumptions of such diverse figures and approaches, is the incorporation of otherness, the forging of unity from difference. The imaginative triumph (whether the critic celebrates it or condemns it) consists in the appropriation of the "nether sphere" as a foundation and the suppression of its potentially threatening aspect; imagination is a powerful structure erected in triumph over the abyss, a product of and monument to the "drama of consciousness and maturation,"[10] which has been commonly accepted as the central Wordsworthian drama.

This essay sets out to rethink, though not to repudiate, the assumption of the centrality of that drama, looking closely at the strategies by which "the poet's mind" situates itself in relation to imperial practice. Superficially, the two passages on which I shall focus—from Book 7 of *The Prelude* (227–43) and Book 9 of *The Excursion* (437–51)—appear to have little in common. Yet the passages reflect upon a common set of issues and on each other. Both were probably composed during the period between early October and late autumn, 1804, an interval that probably included the composition of most of Books 7 and 8 of *The Prelude*; the *Excursion* lines were originally drafted for Book 8.[11] Both present striking figurative representations of the imperial encounter, in which the English subject that sets out to make the other a reflection of itself runs up against a powerful resistance to such mirroring, a resistance that lodges not just in the other, but "In the last place of refuge—my own soul" (1850 *Prelude*, 10.415). Taken together, these (mutually) reflecting passages from *The Prelude* and *The Excursion* represent an important moment in Wordsworth's movement toward a stabilized mirroring relation between self and other—a relation that would appear to "fit" his imagination to the project of British imperialism. But the movement is asymptotic: though he seems to approach ever closer to the goal of balanced reflection and fittedness, he can never arrive there, for every displacement of difference is countered by an irruption of difference in a new form. The otherness of the other repeatedly subverts the notion of perfect reflection, displaying in infinite regress the internal contradiction of the imperial project: its desire to view the other as at once "Another and the same" (*Excursion*, 9.442).

I have used the term "English subject" to register Wordsworth's blurring of the boundaries between self and nation. In the course of the essay I use the less cumbersome "self" broadly as a term in a dialectic that works both on an individual and on a collective level. Attempts to isolate self from nation would be misguided, not only because the individual imagination mirrors and reinforces the imperial aspirations of the nation, but also because, as we shall see, the troubling consequences of imperial practice, in returning to penetrate the borders of the imperial nation, necessarily penetrate the boundaries of the self that inhabits that nation. If "inhabiting" involves identifying oneself with the integrity and hopes of a nation, then imperialism's violations of proper borders result in a radical unsettling of "inhabiting," as self and nation reflect each other's penetrability.

Book 7 of *The Prelude*, though its London setting is well within England's proper borders, clearly concerns the nation's grappling with questions raised by its imperialist ventures and its participation in an expanding international market. "Residence in London" brings the encounter with racial and cultural otherness onto English ground, deconstructing notions of "residence" and proper borders. The city, with its endless stream of international inhabitants and visitors, strikes the poet as alien to his native ground and beyond the grasp of his interpretive tools—a sort of sublime Orient in the midst of England. It is first introduced as an exotic place of romance and "obscure delight," whose appeal to the poet's boyhood fancy surpassed

> whatso'er is feigned
> Of airy palaces and gardens built
> By genii of romance, or hath in grave
> Authentic history been set forth of Rome,
> Alcairo, Babylon, or Persepolis,
> Or given upon report by pilgrim friars
> Of golden cities ten months' journey deep
> Among Tartarean wilds. . . . (82–91)[12]

The "real scene" of London, when the poet finally views it for himself, substitutes actual "specimens" for the figures of romance:

> See—among less distinguishable shapes—
> The Italian, with his frame of images
> Upon his head; with basket at his waist,
> The Jew; the stately and slow-moving Turk,

With freight of slippers piled beneath his arm.
Briefly, we find (if tired of random sights,
And haply to that search our thoughts should turn)
Among the crowd, conspicuous less or more
As we proceed, all specimens of man
Through all the colours which the sun bestows,
And every character of form and face:
The Swede, the Russian; from the genial south,
The Frenchman and the Spaniard; from remote
America, the hunter Indian; Moors,
Malays, Lascars, the Tartar and Chinese,
And Negro ladies in white muslin gowns. (228–43)

Although the poet initially evokes London by clothing it in associations of romance, he swiftly finds that the habits of imagination gleaned from his childhood reading cannot adequately encompass the confusing immediacy of the city.[13] Romance relies on the distance of the object ("golden cities ten months' journey deep / Among Tartarean wilds") and on the assumption that, while the reader is free to travel in imagination beyond the boundaries of his everyday world, the object remains confined within its proper borders. In Book 5 of *The Prelude*, the poet blesses the writers of imaginative literature, whose "lawless tales," he says, make us feel

With what, and how great might [they] are in league,
Who make our wish our power, our thought a deed,
An empire, a possession. (548–53)

In London, that imperial power eludes him; the shadowy inhabitants of the distant world that he had considered as his imaginative empire have "lawless[ly]" violated the borders of fiction and nation to occupy his native ground as physical specimens. In the midst of the emporium, the poet tries to proceed as if confident that the colorful array of "specimens" has been provided for his imaginative consumption, but the somewhat forced insistence on delight and power of choice fails to mask his anxiety about these images: the "Babel din" (157) and the motley array of colors and forms confront him with a disturbing loss of distinction. Romance, the archetypal mode for appropriating, domesticating, or mediating otherness,[14] is here emptied of its power.

If romance collapses almost immediately as a mode of potential mastery, so do more detached ways of surveying mankind from China to Peru. The Johnsonian emphasis on the availability of the "specimens" to observation and classification has the effect of highlighting by contrast the unmanageability of the "random sights."[15] The "snarling muse" of Juvenalian satire lurks here, partly mediated by Johnson's Juvenalian surveys of "the busy scenes of human life" in "The Vanity of Human Wishes" and in "London,"[16] with a trace of Pope's *Dunciad* as well. Instead of serving as a means for Wordsworth to encompass the city, the satiric voice itself seems to render his subjection more complete, becoming part of the flood of "mockery" (263) that inundates him. The poet at first pauses to attach epithets to some of the "specimens," but the list quickly gathers speed, and references to distinguishing characteristics fall away,[17] creating a sense that it would be impossible to single out each of the diverse races, origins, and narratives represented by the faces in the crowd: Europeans and non-Europeans, permanent residents and visitors, people whose presence could likely be attributed to slavery or the slave trade, immigrants from British colonies, sailors, possibly servants, "exotic" visitors, people of different religions, people of "all . . . colours."[18] London mixes the native and the foreign; of these is neither, and is both at once. A threat to the idea, however delusory, of racial or national purity is here inseparable from hermeneutical crisis: London, a "thickening hubbub" (227) of indecipherable faces and mysterious tongues, is a semiotic Chaos and a breeding ground for anxieties about hybridity.

In *A Guide through the District of the Lakes*, Wordsworth admires the District's secluded vales for their history of isolation from the social and genetic impurity now resulting from their increased "connection" to the nation and thus to the "mighty empire": until recently, "many of these humble sons of the hills had a consciousness that the land, which they walked over and tilled, had for more than five hundred years been possessed by men of their name and blood."[19] London poses a threat to such supposed purity, providing an important context—one of many—for Wordsworth's (in)famous dismay at the "increasing accumulation of men in cities," which threatens to infect the English imagination with "loss of distinction" and "savage torpor" (*Prose Works*, 1: 128–29). In Book 7, the threat of uncontrolled mixing expresses itself as an embarrassment of unmanageable syntagmatic modes of perception—the capricious combinations of fancy run amok. It is telling that what most "baffle[s]" the poet's "understanding" is that in London "Even next-door neighbors, as we say" (he can hardly even see how the homely local phrase might apply), are strangers who do not know each other's names (119–20). The city's "endless stream of men and moving things" (158) is a continuous stream of difference: "The comers and the goers face to face— / Face after face—the string of dazzling wares, / Shop after shop, with symbols, blazoned names . . . " (172–74). Like walking personifications, like the "allegoric shapes" (179) of London's facades and signposts, the city's "living figures" (445) become part of a "second-sight procession" (602), a "moving pageant" (610) of signifiers, whose power and momentum threaten to engulf the user in a sublime agency that is alien to him, or at least to the conscious portion of his nature.[20] The more the mind scrambles to overmaster its uncontainable object, the more it risks adding itself to the endless stream, becoming part of the syntagmatic phantasmagoria. The ideal of an imaginative "fitting" of the scene to the poet's mind is ironized by the kind of mirroring that occurs here: the poet's mind as it struggles to control the "unmanageable sight" of forms "reduced / To one identity by differences" (709, 704) mirrors the chaos it set out to "survey" and is itself reduced to identity with its supposed object. We may view this as a reflection on the dangers of the imperial venture: the collective imposition of a mirroring role on the other is highly susceptible to figurative inversion, whereby the imperialist becomes the mirror of an object that makes him recoil.

The real anxiety about difference, then, arises from the fear that it will reduce the self to the other. This is the deeper terror underlying the poet's more apparent trepidation about the general blurring of difference *among* others. Blurring works as a defense, a way of keeping the concreteness of difference at bay. Indeed, the list of others whose "random[ness]" Wordsworth is at pains to emphasize is not so random after all: from its initially "stately" progression through predominantly European, relatively light-skinned "specimens," it moves into a more desperate rush through "Moors, / Malays, Lascars, the Tartar and Chinese, / And Negro ladies in white muslin gowns." The more different the "specimens" from the poet, the greater his anxiety, and the more he renounces the "stately" categorization to blur the boundaries between them. But the "Negro ladies," the ultimate incarnation of otherness—of gender as well as of race—shock the poet into specificity, putting an abrupt halt to the stream of figures. The formal discontinuity is striking: a stream of national and ethnic types, mostly from various recognizable places is suddenly interrupted by a racial type from no specified place. The poet's failure to acknowledge the difference brings him face-to-face with an other whose unmediated presence refuses mitigation through distancing national or ethnic stereotypes.

These women are no doubt perplexing to Wordsworth in many ways. The contrast between their blackness and the whiteness of their dresses seems to crystallize for him the oxymoronic, ironic, and potentially horrifying juxtapositions that are part of the imperialist project. But the image is still more complex in its social implications, as we may gather from a glance at the world of fashion at the turn of the century. Delicate material such as light muslin was the essential fabric of the new mode of dress for European ladies; the preferred color was white, and the dresses were sewn in simple styles "based on the classical in-spiration of Rome and Greece."[21] In Wordsworth's image, muslin—a product of the emporium, and perhaps of the labor of black slaves—is, ironically, worn by black women who have apparently joined, or who seek to join, European upper-class circles. In accentuating difference while pretending to cover it, the dresses epitomize imperial ideology. Wordsworth's complicity here seems to overflow its proper boundaries to engulf the Negro ladies themselves in complicity. One of the most significant features of the muslin gowns was that the flimsiness of the fabrics revealed the lady's body contours. Wordsworth's focus at once on black women (already a standard figure for body) and on muslin presents an overdetermined image of the threatening immediacy of the body of the other. In mirroring the dress of European women, the "Negro ladies" thus doubly embody to Wordsworth not only their own bodily otherness, but also that of European women, who are now shown to mirror the nakedness of the other. In certain other contexts, this disclosure could be the stuff of social satire, betraying the uncomfort-able proximity of European fashion, with its imperial pretensions and avowed classical inspiration, to its supposed dark opposite and suggest-ing that the paradoxical endpoint of imperialist high culture may be "going native" (naked): muslin gowns as the empire's new clothes.[22] But, as we have seen, Wordsworth, though he may grasp at such a satiric mode in a futile attempt to hide his exposure to the other, is doomed to call attention to his nakedness in doing so; in the context of Book 7, the "Negro ladies in white muslin gowns" epitomize the threat of the other whose violation of proper borders makes the self vulnerable. In this book, largely devoted to the condemnation of false representa-tions, the poet is arrested by the spectacle of otherness masquerading as sameness. His shock is a reaction not to the falseness of masquerade, but to its potential truth: the crossing by the other of the boundary that divides masquerade from identity. The imperial venture relies on the persistence of otherness: complete fulfillment of the goal of making the other a mirror would mean loss of self. Facing the prospect of an erasure of otherness, the imperial subject continues to posit or con-struct it.

Book 7, then, does not merely present an instance of Wordsworth's being, to use Coleridge's paradigmatic phrase, "out of his element";[23] much more is at stake than either the aversion to city life or the tem-peramental adversity to satire both commonly associated with him. In London, Wordsworth is overwhelmed by a perceived "loss of distinc-tion" between self and other. Moreover, the city-country dichotomy that marks Book 7, holding forth the delusory promise of a rhetorical con-tainment of corruption within the boundaries of "London," turns out to offer little protection against such loss, for city and country are themselves undergoing loss of distinction.[24] The dramatic transformations (most notably population growth and the attendant conditions) in eighteenth-century London and the surrounding countryside made it more and more difficult, as Raymond Williams documents, to think of the city as an isolable repository of disease and corruption. Commentators were increasingly forced to acknowledge the "wen" as an organic part of the body politic: the expansion of London was an indication of "the true condition and development of the country as a whole. If it was seen as monstrous, or as a diseased growth, this had logically to be traced back to the whole social order." London was "not just a city but the capital city, embodying and directing the whole country";[25] the poet of Book 7 (which Williams calls "one of the major early records of new ways of seeing the city," 149) recognizes this organic relation between head and body politic. Moreover, as Williams proposes in a subsequent chapter, "the system we now know as imperialism" becomes "one of the last models of 'city and country' "; the industrialized (in this case, rapidly industrializing) nations fill the role of metropolitan center, determining and being determined by what is made to happen in the figurative "country"—other people's lands (278).

In a passage originally written for Book 7,[26] Wordsworth offers a grand view of London as a metropolis[27] whose influence reaches beyond the "country" (in both senses) to encompass "the earth's" destiny:

> that vast metropolis
> The fountain of my country's destiny
> And of the destiny of earth itself,
> That great emporium, chronicle at once
> And burial-place of passions, and their home
> Imperial, their chief living residence. (8.746–51)

But this ennobling description does not correspond to the "real scene" of London as he experiences it in Book 7; there, difference threatens the purity of the fountain (which is perhaps why the poet transfers the passage to Book 8, whose distanced perspective enables him to deploy it). What Williams calls the "loss of connection" (150) in the metropolis threatens the poet's imagination, his native ground, his "country's destiny" and the earth's.

Wordsworth's response to this recognition is a further withdrawal within the boundaries of the self. Having failed to incorporate London's difference, the poet tries to totalize and marginalize it, as a way of reasserting the centrality of the mind: "yet all this / Passed not beyond the suburbs of the mind" (506–507). Neither can we: Wordsworth closes off further inversions by enclosing himself within boundaries be-

yond which we cannot pass to challenge his authority. This move gains
some of its apparent force by purporting to reconfigure the paradigm
of metropolis and outskirts:[28] "the mind," isolated from "all this" by
buffering "suburbs," displaces the city to become the metropolis at the
heart of Wordsworth's imperial realm, a new source of the imperial
capacity to unify difference:

> But though the picture weary out the eye,
> By nature an unmanageable sight,
> It is not wholly so to him who looks
> In steadiness, who hath among least things
> An under-sense of greatest, sees the parts
> As parts, but with a feeling of the whole. (708–13)

Even the syntax of these lines, contrasting with the endless lists that
dominate Book 7, works to infuse difference with similitude, in the
repetitions that insist on encircling London's "parts" within "whole-
[ness]." But the supposed conversion of fragmentation to wholeness
remains strangely unconvincing—a solution based on assertions whose
validity London has already challenged. Though the repetitions in
these lines attempt to enact wholeness, they also belie the assertion of
wholeness: if London is "not wholly" fragmented, neither is it wholly
whole. Indeed, what the poet learns from Book 7 is that "wholeness" is
a delusion or, to be Wordsworthian, a "feeling" that can only be imagined to exist in realms of "second sight" or "under-sense." Moreover,
though the number of figurative displacements by which the threat of
difference may be evaded is potentially infinite, no territory can remain
lastingly invulnerable. The poet's imperfectly grounded imperial assertion that London is manageable to those who have a "feeling of the
whole" is best explained not as a positive recognition, but as a reaction
of denial, a deliberate rejection of a potential infinity of inversions.

  This assertion, though it occurs at a point at which Wordsworth's
"empire" has been more or less reduced to the dimensions of the sole
self, is nevertheless foundational to a more expansive notion of imperial
imagination. Such willful suspensions between wholeness and fragmentation—familiar as strategies of the "reconciling and mediatory power"
of imagination described by Coleridge[29]—are a necessary condition for
the existence of an internally contradictory imagination of imperialism, whether widely or narrowly conceived. The imperial "center" and
"system" are founded on the tension between difference and similitude;
moving outward from a unified center, the imperial imagination continues to insist upon the difference that it sets out to incorporate.

  Book 9 of *The Excursion* presents another complex figurative mediation of the imperial project and its internal contradictions; this book

charts Wordsworth's continued attempt to work through difficulties that remain unresolved in *The Prelude*. Like Book 7 of *The Prelude*, the final book of *The Excursion* is concerned with realizing a mode of imagination that will counter "darkness" and "confusion." But, whereas *The Prelude* focuses on the struggle to fortify the single mind against a counter-invasion of confusion and difference, *The Excursion* focuses on the formation of a collective mind. In many ways, Book 9 of this poem, with its harangues on England's "glorious destiny" (408), is more explicitly imperialist than Book 7 of *The Prelude*. But if Book 7 of *The Prelude* displaces the encounter with otherness by bringing it onto native ground, Book 9 of *The Excursion* finds ways to mirror the confrontation still more obliquely, through picturesque representations and allusions to classical literature that present a seemingly triumphant vision of England's collective imperial future. For a moment in this final book of the poem, such strategies seem to culminate in a vision of the kind of perfectly balanced mirroring of self and other that eludes the poet in Book 7. Once again, however, such mirrorings are shown to be unstable projections of the imagination upon an object that proves resistant to incorporation.

It hardly needs mentioning that the emergence of a British concept of empire during this period of history takes place in the context of British relations to another self-proclaimed empire, that of France.[30] France as dark "other" excites more of Wordsworth's hermeneutical preoccupation than the non-European (and, for that matter, the European) lands that are the objects of France's and England's competing imperial claims. The image of France functions complexly in the representation of imperial imagination—as England's imperial rival, as an analogue to the colonized "other" that threatens to invade (or counter-invade) the colonizer, as a dark mirror of England's own imperial imagination, and sometimes, like London, as a troubling externalization of Wordsworth's mind engaged in a confused endeavor to assimilate confusion. Like the London of Book 7, France is often associated for Wordsworth with corrupt modes of representation. To oppose it is to oppose a "sickly" mode of fancy that, as Coleridge describes it, "consists in the confusion and subversion of the natural order of things in their causes and effects."[31] The association of the "infection of imperialism" with dangerous modes of fancy (an association common among Wordsworth's contemporaries, including Coleridge, De Quincey, and Southey, to name a few) converges with fancy's already well-established French affiliations to create a manifold spectacle of spreading corruption.

In Book 9, the Wanderer advocates the cultivation of "knowledge," both within England's borders and beyond, as the means for halting the spread of such "confusion." "From culture, unexclusively bestowed,"

the Wanderer expects "mighty issues" (392–94): education, which he
views as the "best protection" for the "imperial Realm," will also ensure
Britain's wider destiny. Looking forward to the elimination of Napoleonic "oppression" that spreads "like the Egyptian plague / Of darkness, stretched o'er guilty Europe" (409–10), the Wanderer envisions
the overthrow of this allegorical darkness by the "brightness" that he
says "invests" the "happy Island" of England:

> O for the coming of that glorious time
> When, prizing knowledge as her noblest wealth
> And best protection, this imperial Realm,
> While she exacts allegiance, shall admit
> An obligation, on her part, to *teach*
> Them who are born to serve her and obey;
> Binding herself by statute to secure
> For all the children whom her soil maintains
> The rudiments of letters, and inform
> The mind with moral and religious truth,
> Both understood and practised,—so that none,
> However destitute, be left to droop
> By timely culture unsustained; or run
> Into a wild disorder; or be forced
> To drudge through a weary life without the help
> Of intellectual implements and tools;
> A savage horde among the civilised,
> A servile band among the lordly free! (293–310)

The notion of the "imperial Realm" in these lines assumes an analogy
between Britain's subjects at home and its subjects abroad: just as those
"born to serve her and obey" may be found on foreign soil, so "savagery" may be found on native soil, where it is perceived as capable of
undermining an imperial destiny. Alan Richardson aptly summarizes
the fears that underlie Wordsworth's desire for the spread of knowledge and culture: "that those who are 'born to serve' will 'run / Into
a wild disorder'; that the colonial ambitions of 'this imperial Realm'
will be undermined by a 'savage horde' *within* England, its uncivilized
and restive lower orders."[32] Once again, the drama of the imperial encounter with "savage" disorder is enacted within England's boundaries.
The solution, then, must also begin at home: the savage horde on England's native ground must be given the rudiments of culture as a condition for the spread of the "civilization" of the "lordly free" to other
shores. Education now becomes the new paradigm for the growth of
"the mind," silently transformed from the individual "poet's mind" to
the collective mind of the British subject. Education "inform[s] / The

mind": imposes a form on it, or forms it from within, fitting it to the imperial purposes of the collective culture.

The program that the Wanderer advocates is based on the Reverend Andrew Bell's Madras system of education, first developed at Egmore, near Madras, to educate the "half-cast" male children of the European military.[33] Wordsworth, along with Coleridge and Southey, promoted the system in Britain, seeing it as (in Richardson's words) "a radical cure for England's social ills and political unrest, a means for facilitating and justifying colonial expansion, and . . . a prop for that great edifice of stability, the Established Church."[34] The Bell program aims to make the "yoke of learning" (*Madras School,* 3) easy by mutual instruction—arranging children in pairs made up of a tutor and a tutee (both pupils) under the regulation of an overseer. This monitorial system is based on a hierarchy of supervision: "The assistant sees, at every moment, how every boy in his class is employed, and hears every word uttered" (23); the monitors preside over the assistants; the schoolmaster "overlooks the whole school, and gives life and motion to every member of it" (27). (The parallel to Bentham's "Panopticon," explored by Foucault, is noteworthy.) The very economy of the Madras system implies its ripeness for "general circulation," first throughout England, and then more widely (5). " 'You will mark me for an enthusiast,' " Bell quotes himself as saying to a skeptical friend; " 'but if you and I live a thousand years, we shall see this System of Tuition spread over the world' " (ix). "Earth's universal frame shall feel the effect," the Wanderer echoes (*Excursion,* 9.386).

Perhaps the most problematic feature of Bell's model is its assumption that distinct subjectivities can be blended into each other in "happy union" (*Madras School,* 7): the bodies of individual "members" become limbs in the one great body of the school, whose "spirit" emanates from the eyes of the superintendent (28). At another point Bell describes the master as "transfusing a portion of his own spirit into the breasts of his disciples" (13). The emphasis on "happy union" distracts from the apparent contradiction between education as a "yoke" and education as an infusion of "spirit"—a reconciliation that Christianity helps to make easy. Bell moves with great facility between yoke and spirit, community and individual, presenting these poles as "indissolubly united" in the school's functions:

> to imbue the minds of my pupils with the principles of morality and of our own holy religion, and infuse a spirit and habit of diligence and industry; so as at once to supply the necessities of the community, and promote the welfare of the individual—two objects indissolubly united in every well-regulated state. (7–8)

Bell wishes to have the hierarchical system and a pervasive distribution
of "spirit" at once (again, a goal compatible with the Anglican mission
of which his system forms a part). Such ambiguities in the structure of
education mirror and reinforce the contradictions in the aspirations
of a nation that envisions the spread of its own "spirit" through education.

For Bell, these contradictions remain invisible; they are swallowed
up in the harmonious spectacle of the "whole machine" in motion (28).
Nor do they emerge as explicit concerns in the Wanderer's speech,
which at any rate focuses more on the projected results of the system than on the details of its operation. For the Wanderer, the imagined results constitute the spectacle. But though he "kindl[es] as he
[speaks]," his speech fails to transcend the bounds of imperalist harangue to issue in a dazzling imperial vision. The speech is tinged with
the fear of obstruction and (counter)invasion, perceptible in the Wanderer's very insistence on England's "safe[ty] / From interference of
external force" (331–32). The inevitable collapse of the Wanderer's
rhetoric coincides, significantly, with his launching into the imagery
of "oppression, like the Egyptian plague / Of darkness, stretched o'er
guilty Europe": even as he speaks of subsuming "darkness" in a generalized program of enlightenment, darkness seems to take on a life of
its own; radiant optimism about England's imperial destiny threatens
to flip over once again into its mirror image of fear. The speech is cut
off at its highest pitch of urgency: "Abruptly here, but with a graceful
air, / The Sage broke off" (416–17). The "graceful air"—hardly con-
vincing—is oddly reminiscent of the hedging move at the end of Book
7 that magically transforms an "unmanageable sight" into one that is
not "wholly so." The phrase, perversely signaling a discontinuity on the
extra-diegetic level (between the harangue and the ensuing landscape
description), tells us that at this juncture in the text the appearance of
continuity is being substituted for a rupture. The issues raised by the
Wanderer's aborted harangue, still unresolved, are displaced onto the
landscape. This introduces into Book 9 a sequence that is by now familiar: a vision of "happy union" gives way to intrusions of threatening
otherness; the disrupted vision, in turn, is followed by a figurative displacement that appears—only fleetingly—to resolve the problem of difference by presenting a new vision of unity at a further remove from
the original threat.

After the Wanderer's heavily allegorical speech, which concludes
with the exhortation, "Show to the wretched nations for what end /
The powers of civil polity were given" (415), the landscape around him
seems more than ever to be invested with political meaning. It tempts
us to read it as successfully "show[ing]" the ends of civil polity that the

harangue failed to show, in an image of reflection and blending that signifies the glowing future of a "happy Island" (412):

> Thus having reached a bridge, that overarched
> The hasty rivulet where it lay becalmed
> In a deep pool, by happy chance we saw
> A twofold image; on a grassy bank
> A snow-white ram, and in the crystal flood
> Another and the same! Most beautiful,
> On the green turf, with his imperial front
> Shaggy and bold, and wreathèd horns superb,
> The breathing creature stood; as beautiful,
> Beneath him, showed his shadowy counterpart.
> Each had his glowing mountains, each his sky,
> And each seemed centre of his own fair world:
> Antipodes unconscious of each other,
> Yet, in partition, with their several spheres,
> Blended in perfect stillness, to our sight! (437–51)

The ram, following upon the Wanderer's harangue, seems to present a visible sign for what he has earlier called "the sovereignty of these fair Isles / . . . entire and indivisible" (344–45), and for the capacity of these isles to forge the world into unity through universal education. The spectacle of the ram presents a compelling miniature of Albion's noble race, reproducing its own image on shores that, the lines suggest, will come to resemble the green shores of England. The ram's reflection is characterized as both "Another" and "the same"; the shadowy counterpart beneath the "Most beautiful" ram is said to be "as beautiful" as he; the creatures' "several spheres" are represented as separate but equal—paradoxes whose implications are problematic in the context of imperialism ("brightness" overcoming "darkness"). The structure of the ram image in many ways replicates the structure of the educational system that the Wanderer promotes. Both Wordsworth's image and Andrew Bell's Madras system present spectacles of happy union achieved by the infusion of "life" or "spirit" into separate "bodies" to blend them into a single whole. This is a blending that denies hierarchical and individual difference and uses metaphors of shared substance to mask an appropriation of otherness, or an imposition of sameness.

Indeed, the ram image is an overdetermined matrix of imperial signs, whose cultural heritage is especially significant in this book whose central topic is cultural heritage. The passage originally drafted for Book 8 of *The Prelude* was deleted from MS. Y and later slightly revised for *The Excursion*. In the earlier version, the poet snatches up a stone

and is about to act upon a temptation to "dissolve / The vision." But
then, for ambiguous reasons, he finds that he cannot throw the stone,
and it drops from his hand.[35] In that context, the image serves as an
emblem of autobiography, recalling the reflective image of the "Two
consciousness" in Book 2 (32); the unfathered impulse breaks in upon
the emblem and disrupts the framework of autobiographical temporality intended to incorporate such events. In *The Excursion*, the image still
stands out from its discursive environment, but the emphasis is on the
smoothing away of difference—both on the incorporation of the moment into its context and on the unity of the image itself. Two added
lines highlight the blending of the ram and its reflection: "Yet, in partition, with their several spheres, / Blended in perfect stillness, to our
sight." Moreover, the imperial language is newly insistent: "imperial
front / Shaggy and bold, and wreathèd horns superb," "Antipodes unconscious of each other." The image succeeds a stream of prophetic imperial language systematically invoking Virgil, and culminating in the
appropriation of an extended simile of industrious bees sent forth to
"establish new communities / On every shore" (369–82)—the builders
of civilization widely looked to as a type for England.[36] Rather than
being a complete nonsequitur, the image continues to allude to Virgil,
turning now to the prophetic image of the snow-white sow in Book 8
of *The Aeneid*:[37]

> But something suddenly caught his eye—a sign
> To marvel at: snow-white in the green wood,
> Snow-white as her own litter, lay the sow
> Upon the grassy bank, where all could see
> And grave Aeneas dedicated her
> To thee, Juno the great, to thee indeed,
> Lifting both sow and brood before the altar
> In sacrifice. Then all that night's long hours
> The Tiber quieted his swollen stream
> And countering his current with still water
> Slackened so, that like a tranquil pool
> Or placid marsh he smoothed his whole expanse
> And left no toil for oars. (*Aeneid*, 8.110–22)

Virgil's prophetic image effects an immediate slackening of the Tiber's
current, which both allows the prophesied future to unfold and alle-
gorizes the negation of temporality that constitutes prophecy. The
Aeneid, whose purpose is to show how Aeneas and his men long ago
built their destined future, depicts them moving against the prevailing
current—a move that, although it might seem to figure retrogression,
will in fact lead to that future, the building of Rome. The sign of the

snow-white sow occurs in a context of reflection ("cleft green forests in the mirroring water," 8.131) that becomes for subsequent texts a *locus classicus* of picturesque description, recurring in various forms in a wide range of topographical poetry[38] and (with its green shore) proving particularly fertile to the English imagination.

The moment in which landscape is first "cleft" by the human perception of reflection is the moment in which it is appropriated for history; the mirroring sets up a perspective system that extends to encompass later texts. If the image were all there were, deprived of the perspectival settings and constructed histories, the similarity of Wordsworth's and Virgil's passages would be of minimal interest, but the trope of reflection puts the text's surfaces into perspective, creating the possibility of looking before and after. Thus the mediating text of the *Aeneid* facilitates the appropriation of the ram image into signification and into the service of England's imperial history. *The Excursion* and the *Aeneid* communicate not through a glassy mirroring of two blank images that happen to resemble each other, but rather through a history of cultural representation that invests these images with transferrable significance: England takes Latin tradition as a type of its own imperial history. Wordsworth's image looks through time to reflect another imperial image and to annex the consequences of that image's revision of temporality: by looking backward into the mirror, he looks forward to a time when English imperialists, "reflecting" Roman ones, will bear their culture from England's own "delightful" grassy banks and establish it on distant shores through the machine of universal education, the engine that provides the foundation for all other structures of dominance over plurality.

The ram image unfolds the imperial implications of the "feeling of the whole" tentatively achieved at the end of *The Prelude*, Book 7. Both sets of lines rest upon acts of imagination that assert wholeness in the face of fragmentation. The Virgilian paradigm seems to provide Wordsworth with a model for sustaining the kind of mirroring that the Juvenalian paradigm withheld in Book 7. While Book 7's lines on the "feeling of the whole" seem to represent a retreat from the kind of adventuring imagination that tried and failed to master London's dark characters, the ram passage suggests that this retreat may be the counterpart or prelude to an excursive imagination whose unifying strategies are subtler and more pervasive. The chief difference between *The Excursion*'s imagination and *The Prelude*'s is epitomized by the textual changes that accompany the appropriation of the ram passage for *The Excursion*. In *The Prelude*, the vision is a solitary one; in *The Excursion*, the meanderers who start out as "a broken company, / Mute or conversing, single or in pairs" (435–36), are composed into a focused group by the arresting spectacle. The blending of the breathing creature and its reflection emblematizes not only the suppression of difference between the "imperial" ram and its shadowy counterpart, but also the blending of the spectators' perspectives "in perfect stillness, to our sight!" (a new addition of communal piety since MS. Y). Unlike *The Prelude*— whose "I," according to Alan Liu, "looks into the background of collective history, deflects upon nature's polish of objectivity, and at last sees itself reflected as the awesome, historically free personality of '*The mind*' "[39]—*The Excursion* does not imagine the creation of such an imperial "I." In this poem, the "I" does not see itself at all, least of all as an "awesome, historically free personality"; the poem dismantles that foreground and constructs a collective foreground in its stead. The spectators look together into the background of collective history, but, rather than deflecting upon nature's polish and seeing themselves reflected, they become mirrors, the latest repositories of a doubled-and-redoubled image whose accumulated signification is relayed from age to age along a set of prefigured sightlines. The perpetuation of this inheritance depends upon the continual reaffirmation of the initial act of imagination that perceived the twofold image as a breathing unity. The imagination, a "repetition in the finite mind of the eternal act of creation in the infinite I AM" (Coleridge, *BL*, 2:304), is redoubled in the idealizing and unifying imagination of the "WE ARE."[40]

Read as a complex locus of mirroring that reproduces the blending of difference, the image of the ram seems to belong to a spectatorial paradigm that models "power" as precariously secured upon the threat of subversion—a paradigm that, as Liu elsewhere points out, is common to many New Historicist approaches. Whether it takes the form of theatricality, surveillance, or perspectival regulation of landscape, Liu proposes, this spectatorial model of power stresses not simply dominance, but "the slender control of dominance *over* plurality."[41] Power thrives on threats to the cultural facade or backdrop; it finds its expression in the transformation of "another" to "the same." In Wordsworth's paradigmatic image, as in similar instances, these threats, if viewed from the prescribed perspective, are contained: every inversion turns out to be "merely the reversal or repetition of a previous facade" (724). The mirrorings and sightlines, the stations and perspectives, have already been set up, and only an infinite regress of inversions is possible. These inversions, contained within the initial configuration, preclude more truly radical departures from the static (or merely inwardly dynamic) structure. The ostensibly inclusive structure, rather than allowing itself to risk subversion by external forces, merely reproduces or mirrors similar structures from other spheres (like education or colonial expansion)—structures that are already founded on "the slender control of dominance *over* plurality." The blending of two things—the "breathing" and the "shadowy," the empowered sphere and the subordinated sphere—here implies the suppression of one of them, to be accomplished by the "blending" of the difference between them. Viewed from this angle, the possibility of real subversion is swallowed up in prophecy: the potential threat in Wordsworth's image is sacrificed to the one-sided progressive gloss of the Wanderer, as the sow in Virgil is sacrificed to the progress of empire.

Here, if anywhere, Wordsworth seems for a moment to have achieved a perfectly stable mirroring of opposed spheres that suspends the threat of otherness by incorporating it as "Another and the same." Whether this may be considered a moment of imaginative triumph depends in part on one's notion of how many displacements imaginative triumph may be allowed to involve. Wordsworth appears to have displaced the threat of difference so far into the figurative background of his landscape as to ensure its virtual invisibility. But once again the Lady (she functions in this text as a principle of interruption masquerading as social facilitation) disrupts the spectacle of unity.[42] "Ah!" she whispers, "what a pity were it to disperse, / Or to disturb, so fair a spectacle, / And yet a breath can do it!" This whisper, if it does not actually break the image, breathes doubt. The Lady appropriates the reflective image to serve as an emblem of the Wanderer's reading of nature: "How pure his spirit! in what vivid hues / His mind gives back the various forms of things, / Caught in their fairest, happiest, attitude!" The Wanderer's utterances are as beautiful—and as fleeting—as a reflection: while he is speaking, the Lady has "power" to see as he sees, but when he ceases, she remembers that "combinations so serene and bright" are easily broken asunder (452–69). "Combinations" refers both to the harmonies that we perceive between distinct "forms of things" (the ram and its reflection, a metaphor for the empire and its others) and to the linking of "the forms of things" to human interpretations ("human life" and the Wanderer's "descant" on it, for which the ram and its reflection are also a metaphor). The unstable relation between ram and reflection thus mirrors on two levels the unstable relation between the Wanderer's imperial aspirations and otherness.

The merest whisper of iconoclastic energy (a displacement from the rock-throwing impulse in the original draft) is enough to remind us of the unresolvable tensions at the core of "combinations so serene and bright." The image of imperial blending already harbors a resistance at its core, a gap that resists incorporation. The lines refer to the "Antipodes" (ram and reflection) as "unconscious of each other": just at the point of encounter between "Another and the same," the notion of shared spirit upon which the "happy union" of opposites depends (in

Wordsworth and in Bell) is blocked by this mutual "unconscious[ness]."
We may read the gap as an intimation of the inevitable frustration of
attempts to blend away otherness, but in doing so we must bear in mind
that for Wordsworth, and perhaps for the imperial subject in general,
this may be a saving frustration, guarding against a loss of self in other.
A fragile and flawed mirroring ensures that the self will remain "Most
beautiful," the reflection merely "as beautiful"—a barely perceptible
difference that upholds the "imperial" position of the self by preclud-
ing the kind of inverted mirroring whose prospect made Wordsworth
recoil at the "Negro ladies in white muslin gowns."

The dynamic of "another and the same," integral to Wordsworth's
imagination, recurs with great frequency in his writings, whenever the
inaccessibility of a child's thought, the troubling unreadability of an
"Old Man's shape, and speech" ("Resolution and Independence," line
128),[43] or the recalcitrant otherness of the "maternal passion" (*Prose
Works* 1:126) is dwelt upon as a way of shoring up the poet's integrity
of self. As these examples suggest, the resistance to incorporation is
complexly motivated, stemming both from the poet's awe for the singularity of others and from his stake in his own singularity, necessarily
a factor in his positions on the otherness of others. Indeed, the tension
between the impulse toward "system" and the resistance to it is a hall-
mark of Wordsworth's life project of incorporating diversity in unity:
"My guiding wish," he writes in the Preface to the 1815 *Poems*, "was, that
the small pieces of which these volumes consist, thus discriminated
[into classes], might be regarded under a two-fold view; as composing
an entire work within themselves, and as adjuncts to the philosophical
Poem, 'The Recluse.' " In the same breath he expresses his doubt as to
whether this twofold aspect is really possible:

> I should have preferred to scatter the contents of these volumes at ran-
> dom, if I had been persuaded that, by the plan adopted, anything mate-
> rial would be taken from the natural effect of the pieces, individually,
> on the mind of the unreflecting Reader. (*Prose Works* 3:28)

Wordsworth wishes to reconcile the "natural" and the systematic under a twofold aspect, but, granted only one alternative, he would far
rather preserve the poems' "natural" independent status. In valuing
the uniqueness of "the pieces, individually"—even to the point of ac-
cepting a "random" scattering—he expresses reservations about his
own systematizing impulse. Of course, from one perspective in his twofold view, what he is thus preserving against loss of distinction is himself, embodied in his own poems; his statement about the ways in which
the systematizing self threatens the "other" self with effacement lays
bare the dynamic that we have seen operating in Wordsworth's impe-

rial encounters: his reservations about incorporating otherness into wholeness coincide with his fear of being incorporated himself. That the dynamic can be reduced to a conflict between opposed aspects of the self only suggests its irreducibility: for every impulse toward "a feeling of the whole," there is a countering impulse toward "random" scattering of the parts.

Wordsworth's texts may harbor uneasiness or resist "imperial" appropriations at every level of representation, but uneasiness does not, of course, unfit a canonical author for imperialist uses. Gauri Viswanathan's account of the process by which the teaching of English literature in India was instituted and developed to further British cultural authority and political control provides a general historical and theoretical framework for exploring Wordsworth's influence.[44] While it is beyond the scope of this essay to document the particular complex ways in which Wordsworth's poetry has been "fitted" to the imperial process, there is no question that it has played a part in the bolstering of English cultural authority, both colonial and post-colonial.

Thomas De Quincey, predicting Wordsworth's far-reaching influence "in every clime and in every land," suggests that that influence relies on a mirroring relation between Wordsworth's solitude and the "loneliness" of those places:

> Wordsworth is peculiarly the poet for the solitary and the meditative; and, throughout the countless myriads of future America and future Australia, no less than Polynesia and Southern Africa, there will be situations without end fitted by their loneliness to favour his influence for centuries to come, by the end of which period it may be anticipated that education (of a more enlightened quality and more systematic than yet prevails) may have wrought such changes on the human species, as will uphold the growth of all philosophy, and, therefore, of all poetry which has its foundations laid in the heart of man.[45]

The dissemination of Wordsworth is the dissemination of a civilized solitude that the wilder "loneliness" of remote "situations" may emulate, making Wordsworth and his mountain solitudes a center of the empire in ways that he cannot have foreseen, for all his negotiating and renegotiating of margins and centers.[46] De Quincey's vision of Wordsworth's influence, replicated in situations "without end," recalls the Wanderer's dream of the great changes to arise from the "foundations" of universal education in Book 9 of *The Excursion* (whose language De Quincey echoes). Now, though, Wordsworth himself has become part of the foundation, spirit, and substance of that education—and paradoxically, it is precisely his solitude that "fits" him for this purpose.

Without acceding to De Quincey's myth that distant lands and climes are "wild," we may observe that the idea of solitude is perhaps the ideal commodity for imperial exchange because it can be used to foster the claim that people are the same in their otherness. I think of Elizabeth Bishop's "Crusoe in England," in which Crusoe imperfectly recalls the line from "I Wandered Lonely As a Cloud": " 'They flash upon that inward eye, / which is the bliss . . . ' The bliss of what?"[47] English culture frames Crusoe's "solitude" even when he blanks on the very word that would clinch his connection to the culture by giving that solitude a name.

The question of Wordsworth's imperial influence is inextricably linked to the larger question of the extension of the English language, as De Quincey recognizes:

> for the language in which he writes, thanks be to Providence, which
> has beneficently opened the widest channels for the purest and most ele-
> vating literature, is now ineradicably planted in all quarters of the
> earth; the echoes under every latitude of every longitude now reverber-
> ate English words; and all things seem tending to this result—that the
> English and the Spanish languages will finally share the earth between
> them.[48]

Such hopes may be compared to C. K. Ogden's and I. A. Richards's aspirations for Basic English,[49] and the controversy that surrounded Basic can help us to read the political implications of the joint dissemination of English and Wordsworth. Basic was to be at once simple and pervasive: the language, reduced to its essential building blocks of 850 words, was supposed to be able to go anywhere and say anything. Even Richards, the most dedicated believer in the system's democratic core, cautioned against possible imperialist abuses:

> However desirable a common language for all the world may be, . . . it
> neither can nor should be imposed by one nation or group of nations
> upon others. . . . [I]t must be clear from any threat to the economic,
> moral, cultural, social, or political status or independence of any per-
> son or any people. It must carry no implications of intellectual, techno-
> logical, or other domination. No one in learning the world language
> must have excuse for even the least shadow of a feeling that he is sub-
> mitting to an alien influence or being brought under the power of
> other groups. Most extensions of communications carry this political
> threat.[50]

Under "extensions of communications" we may include the numerous projects of integration with which Wordsworth associated himself and with which he was subsequently associated by others: his idealization of a common language in the Preface to *Lyrical Ballads* (which John

Guillory has analyzed as an important moment in the spread of "the bourgeois sociolect" and the formation of a vernacular canon);[51] his support of the Bell system; and the dissemination of his poetry throughout the empire. All of these pose the "political threat" described by Richards.

When is an extension of English language and culture an extension of one power beyond its "proper" boundaries? The dissemination of Wordsworth in the British Empire suggests that this larger question incorporates a more particular one: When is an extension of Wordsworth an extension of one power beyond its proper boundaries? Such questions cannot be answered generally. It is easy—probably too easy— to read De Quincey's assertion of Wordsworth's "peculiar" appeal to readers in lonely situations as nothing more than a mask for the universal imposition of a "peculiarly" English way of feeling. The missing factor in such a reading is the "peculiarity" of the "meditative" reader. Readers reflect what they read; they also reflect upon it. In many ways, the two kinds of reflection are opposed: "reflection upon" implies a relation of difference between reader and text, and indeed an inversion that places the reader on top. Of course it remains possible to claim that "reflection upon" is ultimately contained within "reflection" (as in the prefigured reading of the ram image outlined above), but such a claim does not negate the fact that, just as texts exist in a twofold relation of difference and similitude to the social and political projects that (problematically) incorporate them, so the reflecting reader is never simply "the same." This neither precludes the use of texts to consolidate cultural authority, nor exonerates those who would seek to limit "reflection upon" to mere reflection. But it ensures that the transmission of texts will not be a simple matter of static reflections infinitely repeated.

NOTES

My thanks to Jess Jackson and Bill Jewett for their help with this essay.

1. John Barrell, *The Infection of Thomas De Quincey* (New Haven: Yale University Press, 1991).

2. Nigel Leask, *British Romantic Writers and the East: Anxieties of Empire* (Cambridge: Cambridge University Press, 1992).

3. Sara Suleri, *The Rhetoric of English India* (Chicago: University of Chicago Press, 1992), 24–74.

4. Edward W. Said, *Orientalism* (1978; New York: Vintage, 1979), 222.

5. Suleri, 26–27, 31.

6. Barron Field wrote to Wordsworth in an 1828 letter, "[A]ll your travellers 'step westward.' You have no oriental poem" (qtd. in *The Letters of William and Dorothy Wordsworth*, 2nd ed., *The Later Years*, ed. Alan G. Hill [Oxford: Clarendon Press, 1978], 1:695, n. 2).

7. On the limits of European knowledge of Asia, North America, Af-

rica, and the Pacific in the eighteenth century, see P. J. Marshall and Glyndwr Williams, *The Great Map of Mankind: Perceptions of New Worlds in the Age of Enlightenment* (Cambridge: Harvard University Press, 1982). On the blurring of racial and ethnic stereotypes in the eighteenth and nineteenth centuries, see C. A. Bayly, *Imperial Meridian: The British Empire and the World 1780–1830* (London: Longman, 1989), 153. As Barrell remarks, most Europeans "conceived of Asia beyond the Tigris as a place where people seemed to run into each other, to replicate each other, to compose one mass without divisions or features" (5).

8. On the development of modern notions of "empire" out of the classical concept of *imperium,* see Richard Koebner, *Empire* (Cambridge: Cambridge University Press, 1961), 18–60; Raymond Williams, *Keywords: A Vocabulary of Culture and Society,* rev. ed. (New York: Oxford University Press, 1983), 159–60; and Bayly, 103, 160–61.

9. The most notable recent analyses of the Wordsworthian imagination as "imperial" are Alan Liu's. See *Wordsworth: The Sense of History* (Stanford: Stanford University Press, 1989), esp. 445–52 on imagination and Napoleonic imperialism; and "Wordsworth and Subversion, 1793–1804: Trying Cultural Criticism," *Yale Journal of Criticism* 2 (1989): 55–100, which details the function of Wales as an "internal colony" and a locus of "subversion" that ultimately serves "the vision . . . of English imperialism" (69).

10. Geoffrey Hartman, preface to *Wordsworth's Poetry, 1787–1814* (1964; Cambridge: Harvard University Press, 1987), xxiii.

11. The relevant manuscripts are MSS. X and Y. See Mark Reed, *Wordsworth: The Chronology of the Middle Years, 1800–1815* (Cambridge: Harvard University Press, 1975), 13, 272, 645–47 (Reed also considers the possibility that most of Book 7 dates from late March–June 13, 1804); Ernest de Selincourt, ed. *The Prelude or Growth of a Poet's Mind,* by Wordsworth, 2nd ed., rev. Helen Darbishire (Oxford: Clarendon Press, 1959), lii-liii, 581; de Selincourt and Darbishire, eds., *The Poetical Works of William Wordsworth* (1949; reprint from corrected sheets, Oxford: Clarendon Press, 1959), 5:370; Jonathan Wordsworth, M. H. Abrams, Stephen Gill, eds., *The Prelude, 1799, 1805, 1850,* by Wordsworth (New York: Norton, 1979), 515–20 (the Norton editors date Book 7 "almost certainly to November 1804"). Subsequent parenthetical references to *The Prelude* are to the Norton edition (1805 version, unless otherwise indicated); references to *The Excursion* are to *Poetical Works.*

12. The echo of Milton's description of the infernal palace in *Paradise Lost* (1.717–18) suggests that delight may represent a false surmise.

13. Contrast the episode of the drowned man in Book 5, whose appearance, Wordsworth tells us, was anticipated and mediated by the "hallowing" spirit of romance (450–81).

14. This is implicit in accounts of European "orientalism" such as Raymond Schwab's early landmark study, *The Oriental Renaissance: Europe's Rediscovery of India and the East, 1680–1880,* trans. Gene Patterson-Black and Victor Reinking, forw. Edward W. Said (1950; New York: Columbia University Press, 1984) and in Said's *Orientalism.* See also Martin Green, *Dreams of Adventure, Deeds of Empire* (New York: Basic, 1979).

15. Nowhere else in Wordsworth does Johnson's voice emerge more distinctly: "At leisure let us view from day to day, / As they present themselves, the spectacles . . . " (*Prelude* 7.244–45).

16. Samuel Johnson, "London" (line 161), "The Vanity of Human Wishes" (line 4), in *Samuel Johnson: Selected Poetry and Prose*, ed. Frank Brady and W. K. Wimsatt (Berkeley: University of California Press, 1977), 51, 57. On the "Juvenalian spirit" in Book 7, see Herbert Lindenberger, *On Wordsworth's "Prelude"* (Princeton: Princeton University Press, 1963), 233–43. See also Mary Jacobus, *Romanticism, Writing, and Sexual Difference: Essays on "The Prelude"* (Oxford: Clarendon Press, 1989), 113.

17. The 1850 edition betrays more strain: "Enough," the poet exclaims in the midst of his inventory, even as he insists that he has been "well pleased" as he "surveyed" the scene "with no unthinking mind" (7.219–20). Even the editors of the Norton *Prelude* are infected with a drive toward classification that coexists with a sense of its futility, as this note on the word "Lascars" suggests: "East Indian sailors (*NED*), but it is doubtful whether Wordsworth had anything so specific in mind" (238, n. 1).

18. See M. Dorothy George, *London Life in the Eighteenth Century* (New York: Capricorn, 1965), 109–53, for a useful survey of immigrants in London in the eighteenth century.

19. *A Guide through the District of the Lakes*, in *The Prose Works of William Wordsworth*, ed. W. J. B. Owen and Jane Worthington Smyser, 3 vols. (Oxford: Clarendon Press, 1974), 2:206. For Wordsworth's sketchy account of the traces left earlier by the Celts, Romans, Saxons, Danes, and Normans who occupied the Lake District, however, see pp. 194–96, 198. Subsequent references to *Prose Works* appear within the text.

20. See Steven Knapp's argument that personification, closely related to the sublime, involves an ambivalent encounter in which the subject is simultaneously identified with and dissociated from power (*Personification and the Sublime: Milton to Coleridge* [Cambridge: Harvard University Press, 1985]). See also Neil Hertz's and Cynthia Chase's brilliant readings of figuration and its opacities in Book 7: Hertz, "The Notion of Blockage in the Literature of the Sublime," *The End of the Line: Essays on Psychoanalysis and the Sublime* (New York: Columbia University Press, 1985), 40–60; Chase, *Decomposing Figures: Rhetorical Readings in the Romantic Tradition* (Baltimore: Johns Hopkins University Press, 1986), 32–64. For two recent considerations of signification in Book 7 and its political and historical contexts, see Geraldine Friedman, "History in the Background of Wordsworth's 'Blind Beggar,' " *ELH* 56 (1989): 125–48; and Ross King, "Wordsworth, Panoramas, and the Prospect of London," *Studies in Romanticism* 32 (1993): 57–73.

21. Sharon H. Laudermilk and Teresa L. Hamlin, *The Regency Companion* (New York: Garland Publishing, 1989), 30–32. "The most outrageous fashions came from Paris," of course: France's implication in outrageous modes, often in ways that link it with the infection of imperialism, is virtually a given. One reason for the choice of white was Napoleon's preference for it. I take "white muslin gowns" to refer to European dresses, but if it were read as referring to non-European gowns, the unexpected resemblance of supposedly distinct native garbs would have many of the same connotations.

22. Alternatively, mirroring the fashions of the other could be seen as a form of inoculation against infection—another strategy that is equally vulnerable to exposure. See Leask, 7–8; Barrell, 15–18; Roland Barthes, *Mythologies*, trans. Annette Lavers (New York: Hill and Wang, 1972), 150–51.

23. S. T. Coleridge, *Biographia Literaria*, vol. 7, *The Collected Works of Samuel Taylor Coleridge*, ed. James Engell and W. Jackson Bate (Princeton: Princeton University Press, 1983), 2:120. Subsequent references to the *Biographia (BL)* appear within the text.

24. This is suggested by the tale of the Maid of Buttermere—a "story drawn / From our own ground" (7.321–22), but then corrupted by its performance on the stage of "half-rural Sadler's Wells" (289), whence it no doubt induced a savage torpor. The tainting of Mary (as much, Wordsworth suggests, through the stage representation as through the misrepresentations of her seducer) casts doubt on the poet's conception of his native district as a "spot . . . / Without contamination" (352–53). Raising the possibility that no clear line of distinction divides local memory from metropolitan culture, the stage representation challenges the comforting notion of "native ground" as a place of grounded reading.

25. Raymond Williams, *The Country and the City* (New York: Oxford University Press, 1973), 142–52. London's population increases were largely due to influxes of former country dwellers, many of whom came to London to escape village conditions (146). Seeking work in London, and often failing to find it, they frequently ended up emigrating from the city to the army or to plantations (George, 109–10). See also George Rudé, *Hanoverian London, 1714–1808* (Berkeley: University of California Press, 1971), 1–19. Williams points out that the frequent depiction of London as a "wen" was usually part of an attempt to isolate poor conditions in order to go on idealizing the country as a whole. He cites Cobbett's famous description as one notable exception (146). An earlier exception is Southey in 1807: "Wealth flows into the country, but how does it circulate there? Not equally and healthfully through the whole system; it sprouts into wens and tumours, and collects in aneurisms which starve and palsy the extremities" (*Letters from England* [London: Cresset Press, 1951], 210).

26. See the Norton *Prelude*, 519.

27. "Metropolis" can denote either the imperial nation-state or the urban center around which its activities are organized; see Fredric Jameson, "Modernism and Imperialism," in *Nationalism, Colonialism, and Literature*, by Terry Eagleton, Fredric Jameson, and Edward W. Said (Minneapolis: University of Minnesota Press, 1990), 65, n. 2.

28. As Marilyn Butler points out, Wordsworth, along with such poets as Thomson, Gray, and Blake, participates in a broader reconception of "country" as an oppositional term that challenged the metropolitan centers' claims to exclusive legitimacy ("Romanticism in England," *Romanticism in National Context*, ed. Roy Porter and Mikuláš Teich [Cambridge: Cambridge University Press, 1988], 41–42).

29. Coleridge, *Lay Sermons*, vol. 6, *The Collected Works of Samuel Taylor Coleridge*, ed. R. J. White (Princeton: Princeton University Press, 1983), 29.

30. Liu traces the intricate process by which Wordsworth appropriates the "imagination" of Napoleon to his own empire of the mind in *The Prelude (Wordsworth, 23–31); The Excursion* reconceives of this imagination of

the imperial self as a collective imagination that would counter Napoleonic modes in the name of England and freedom.

31. Coleridge is criticizing the "modern Jacobinical drama (which, and not the German, is its appropriate designation)"; this hybrid form, he claims, results from a French "*Olla Podrida*" that falsely combines Shakespeare with the "bloated" and "sickly" styles of lesser English writers (*BL*, 2: 209–11, 221). The passage itself is an *Olla Podrida* of anxieties about hybridity.

32. Alan Richardson, *Literature, Education, and Romanticism: Reading as Social Practice, 1780–1832* (Cambridge: Cambridge University Press, 1994), 100.

33. The plan receives its most thorough elaboration in *The Madras School, or Elements of Tuition: Comprising the Analysis of an Experiment in Education, Made at the Male Asylum, Madras, etc.* (London: Bensley, 1808). Subsequent references appear within the text. This edition comprises Bell's earlier publications on the subject; *An Analysis* was first published in 1797. Bell's original pupils were thought to constitute the "most unpromising materials. It was an established opinion, that the half-cast children were an inferior race, both in moral and intellectual faculties, as if a certain mulish obliquity of nature had been produced by crossing colours in the human species" ([Robert Southey], *Quarterly Review* 6 [1811], 2nd ed. [London: Murray, 1820], 265).

34. Richardson, 95. Kenneth Johnson, too, notes Wordsworth's linking of national education and colonialism in *Wordsworth and "The Recluse"* (New Haven: Yale University Press, 1984), 323. See also R. A. Foakes, " 'Thriving Prisoners': Coleridge, Wordsworth and the Child at School," *Studies in Romanticism* 28 (1989): 187–206.

35. Wordsworth, *The Prelude*, ed. de Selincourt, p. 581.

36. As Richardson points out (101), Southey's "Inquiry into the Poor Laws, &c.," *Quarterly Review* 8 (1812), is the source of much of this Virgilian language. The simile is indebted both to the *Georgics* and to the *Aeneid*. If the precedent of the *Georgics* suggests a comparison of bees to the builders of Rome and to the future addition of "new communities," the precedent of the *Aeneid* is more complicated, for there the busy workers in the bee simile are engaged in the building of Carthage, a task that turns out to be abortive. Wordsworth's *Aeneid* translation (1819–23) includes the bee simile (*PW* 4:299, lines 582–92). Subsequent references to Virgil are to the *Aeneid*, trans. Robert Fitzgerald (New York: Vintage, 1983).

37. Helenus had prophesied to Aeneas that a white sow would mark the site of the Trojans' first city, Alba Longa; that scene, in turn, recalls the moment in the *Odyssey* in which the shade of Tiresias tells Odysseus that his travels will end when he meets a traveler who mistakes his oar for a winnowing fan. See David Quint, *Epic and Empire: Politics and Generic Form from Virgil to Milton* (Princeton: Princeton University Press, 1993), 59.

38. See Robert Arnold Aubin, *Topographical Poetry in Eighteenth-Century England* (New York: MLA, 1936), 4–6.

39. Liu, *Wordsworth*, 11, 23.

40. Cf. Liu, *Wordsworth*, 491.

41. Liu, "The Power of Formalism: The New Historicism," *ELH* 56 (1989): 723.

42. A muted version of the irruption of the "Ladies" in Book 7 of *The Prelude.*

43. *William Wordsworth,* ed. Stephen Gill, Oxford Authors Series (1984; reprint with corrections, Oxford: Clarendon, 1990), 264.

44. *Masks of Conquest: Literary Study and British Rule in India* (New York: Columbia University Press, 1989). Pages 55–56 allude to the role of Wordsworth, particularly in Christian schools (as opposed to secular government schools). Indications of Wordsworth's dissemination throughout the Empire are abundant. For example, sales of Wordsworth editions (including school texts) were evidently considerable. The editions were often printed from the plates obtained from publishers in Great Britain; some were sheets from Great Britain with cancelled local title pages; some were export copies. I am grateful to Mark Reed for providing me with a summary of these findings in advance of the publication of his Wordsworth bibliography (personal communication, June 29, 1994).

45. Thomas De Quincey, *Recollections of the Lakes and the Lake Poets,* ed. David Wright (New York: Penguin, 1970), 144. Carlyle in 1840 makes even greater claims for Shakespeare: "England, before long, this Island of ours, will hold but a small fraction of the English: in America, in New Holland, east and west to the very Antipodes, there will be a Saxondom covering great spaces of the Globe. And now, what is it that can keep all these together into virtually one Nation . . . ? This King Shakspeare, does not he shine, in crowned sovereignty, over us all, as the noblest, gentlest, yet strongest of rally-signs . . . ? We can fancy him as radiant aloft over all the Nations of Englishmen, a thousand years hence" (*On Heroes, Hero-Worship and the Heroic in History* [1897; New York: AMS Press, 1969], 113–14).

46. See *A Guide,* in which Wordsworth imagines the vales as a "pure Commonwealth," an "almost visionary mountain republic" in the midst of a "mighty empire" (*Prose Works,* 2:206–207).

47. Elizabeth Bishop, *Collected Poems, 1927–1979* (New York: Farrar Straus Giroux, 1983), 164.

48. De Quincey, 144.

49. The system is elaborated in many places, including C. K. Ogden, *The System of Basic English* (New York: Harcourt, Brace, 1934); and I. A. Richards, *Interpretation in Teaching* (New York: Harcourt, Brace, 1938), 196–211, and *Basic English and Its Uses* (New York: Norton, 1943). Also of interest is William Empson's "Basic English and Wordsworth," a radio talk originally published in *Kenyon Review,* 2 (Autumn 1940), reprinted in Empson, *Argufying: Essays on Literature and Culture,* ed. John Haffenden (Iowa City: University of Iowa Press, 1987), 228–38.

50. Richards, *Basic English and Its Uses,* 11.

51. John Guillory, *Cultural Capital: The Problem of Literary Canon Formation* (Chicago: University of Chicago Press, 1993), 124–33.

Twelve

ANNE K. MELLOR

"Am I Not a Woman, and a Sister?": Slavery, Romanticism, and Gender

THE ATTEMPT TO end the British involvement in the slave trade and to emancipate the slaves in the British crown colonies in the West Indies was perhaps second only to the French Revolution in its impact on the social consciousness of writers, especially women, in England between 1780 and 1830. On May 14, 1772, the famous judgment of William Murray, Lord Mansfield, presiding on the King's Bench, had ruled in the case of James Somerset, a black slave who had been brought to England, versus his master, Mr. Stewart of Virginia, that slavery was not lawful in England; Lord Mansfield maintained that England was by nature "a soil whose air is deemed too pure for slaves to breathe in."[1] Somerset thereby gained his freedom, making England a mecca for slaves in the British West Indies. Significantly, in that case, Mr. Dunning, the lawyer defending the slave owner, Mr. Stewart, argued that slavery, *like marriage*, was a "municipal" rather than a "natural" relationship. Both slavery and marriage were therefore constructed by legal custom, were similar to the feudal villenage still recognized in British common-law, and were thus not subject to "natural" law. The implied parallel between wives and slaves in this argument—and Lord Mansfield's refusal to rule against the "municipal" servitude of wives—did not escape the attention of the women writers of the period.

The legal abolition of slavery in England itself in 1772 ended neither the slave trade nor the institution of slavery in the colonies. By 1775 the triangular slave trade had reached its peak: typically, British merchants sent "trappers" and ships to the Gold Coast of Africa where they kidnapped or bought 38,000 to 42,000 Africans annually, at a maximum of 15 pounds per head. These Africans were then shipped under appalling conditions on "the Middle Passage." During this sea-passage 13 percent typically died; another 33 percent died later during the "seasoning" or breaking-in period at the other end. They were shipped to the West Indies to work in the tobacco and sugar-cane fields, where they were sold at an average of 35 pounds each. The profits from this sale were then used to buy sugar and tobacco that was sold again, at much higher prices, in England and Europe; total profits ranged from 600,000 to over one million pounds annually. Bristol and Liverpool were the center of the British slave-trade; their merchants argued persuasively in the Houses of Parliament that the British economy, and the ability to gratify the national addiction to refined sugar and its products, depended on the continuance of the slave trade. In addition, the lobby of the extremely wealthy West Indian planters, the British owners of the slave plantations who lived either in England (as does Sir Thomas Bertram in Jane Austen's *Mansfield Park*)[2] or abroad, on their plantations (as does Mr. Vincent in Maria Edgeworth's *Belinda*), exerted an enormous influence on British politics.

Between 1778, when Prime Minister William Pitt introduced the first bill attempting to regulate the slave trade, and 1807, when the slave trade was legally abolished, debate raged in England concerning the slave trade. The powerful Standing Committee of Planters and Merchants argued that both the slave trade and the institution of slavery in the West Indian colonies were necessary to Britain's economic survival (especially since France and Holland had recently begun to make serious inroads into the slave trade). Moreover, both were morally justified on the grounds that many of the Africans had been slaves in their own countries and, further, were savages or heathen incapable of rational thought or moral feeling and hence unfit for freedom. African slaves should be regarded as "children" who required a "benevolent" master to teach them the civilizing benefits of Christian doctrine and the Protestant work ethic. Thomas Bellamy's influential play *The Benevolent Planters*, which was first performed at the Theatre Royal, Haymarket, in 1789, makes this pro-West Indian lobby argument in a particularly compelling form, even though Bellamy's planters acknowledge that slave masters who abuse their slaves do not deserve their loyalty. In the final scene of Bellamy's play, the slave Oran, having been reunited with his beloved Selima by his generous owner, Goodwin, who has purchased her for Oran, fervently concludes:

> Lost in admiration, gratitude, and love, Oran has no words, but can only in silence own the hand of Heaven . . . O my masters! . . . let my re-

stored partner and myself bend to such exalted worth; while for ourselves, and for our surrounding brethren, we declare, that you have
proved yourselves *The Benevolent Planters*, and that under subjection like
yours, SLAVERY IS BUT A NAME.[3]

In direct rebuttal, the abolitionists who wished to end not only the
slave trade but the very institution of slavery in the colonies argued
first, that the institution of slavery itself was immoral and violated both
the natural rights of man and Christian doctrine; and second, that the
actual conditions imposed on Africans both during the middle passage
and on the slave plantations were far more barbaric and uncivilized
than anything they had experienced in Africa, and called into question
the morality of England itself as a Christian nation. The infamous legal
case of the *Zong*—a slave ship whose captain, Luke Collingwood, in
1781 threw 132 plague-infected Africans to the sharks in order to collect insurance on this jettisoned "cargo"—raised widespread horror
at the cruelty of the slave trade. This event was so shocking and memo-
rable to the British public that even fifty years later it inspired both
J. M. W. Turner's brilliant painting "The Slave Ship" and John Ruskin's
passionate moral denunciation of British imperialism in his essay "Of
Water, as Painted by Turner."

The leading voices in the attempt to end the slave-trade were Granville Sharp, who brought the Somerset case to trial, and Thomas Clarkson, the son of an Anglican head-master and an outstanding student
at Cambridge University, who found his life's work when in 1785 he
wrote a prize Latin essay on the assigned topic: "is it right to make men
slaves against their wills?" Arguing in abstract terms that slavery is immoral and drawing his examples from the Quaker Anthony Benezet's
powerful descriptions of the inhumane conditions of slavery in the
West Indies, Clarkson became obsessed with the evil he had discovered.
On his return from collecting his prize in London, he recalls, " . . . all
my pleasure was damped by the facts which were now continually before me. It was but one gloomy subject from morning to night. In the
daytime, I was uneasy. In the night I had little rest. I sometimes never
closed my eye-lids for grief . . . I frequently tried to persuade myself in
these intervals that the contents of my essay could not be true. . . . Coming in sight of Wades Mill in Hertfordshire, I sat down disconsolate on
the turf. . . . Here a thought came into my mind, that if the contents of
the Essay were true, it was time some person should see these calamities
to their end."[4]

Pedantic, thorough, and absolutely convinced of the rectitude of his
cause, Clarkson never wavered in his commitment to end slavery. In
1786 he published his prize essay *On the Slavery and Commerce of the Hu-*

man Species, Particularly the African and in 1787 joined the Quaker committee founded by Granville Sharp to abolish the slave trade. He was
sent to Bristol and Liverpool by the Committee to determine the actual conditions aboard the slave ships; his indefatigable research, based
on numerous interviews with captains, sailors, ships' surgeons, and escaped slaves formed the backbone of the abolitionists' attacks for years
to come. Armed only with pencil and paper, Clarkson crawled through
the holds of ships, haunted the waterfront pubs where drunken, rowdy
sailors talked most freely, and risked his life to gain access to crewmen
forbidden to speak with him. He uncovered not only the appalling
treatment of the Africans aboard the slave ships and the difference
between "loose" and "tight" packing (allowing chained men, women,
and children room to turn over or not), but also the brutal floggings,
starvings, and even murder of the British sailors unlucky enough to
sign up for these voyages.

After he presented this documentary evidence to the Parliamentary
Privy Council Committee assigned to investigate the slave trade in
1789, Clarkson spent six months in France in an unsuccessful effort to
persuade the leaders of the French Revolution to abolish their slave
trade and slavery in the French colonies. For the next five years, Clarkson rode thousands of miles, scouring the ports and seagoing vessels
of England for witnesses willing to testify to Parliament about the actual practices in the slave trade (so vehemently denied by the shipown-
ers and planters); in 1794, his health completely gave way and he was
forced to retire from this work.

Clarkson's authoritative *History of the Rise, Progress and Accomplishment of the Abolition of the African Slave-Trade, by the British Parliament* was
not published until 1808, but he had made the results of his research
available to the Privy Council Committee assigned to investigate the
slave trade in 1789. This committee was chaired by William Wilberforce, the member of Parliament from Hull who headed the efforts to
introduce bills abolishing the slave trade and slavery in Parliament between 1788 and 1807. The largest and most sustained outcry against
both the slave trade and the institution of slavery was organized by the
Quakers, who established antislavery societies throughout England between 1780 and 1830.

Women were major participants in these societies—the Ladies Anti-
Slavery Society in 1832 submitted a petition with 187,000 names demanding immediate emancipation of all slaves—and they became the
leading figures in the social protests against the slave trade between
1788 and 1792.[5] They organized boycotts of sugar (advocating the use
of honey or "free" grown East Indian sugar instead) and wrote numerous poems, novels, and tracts condemning the slave trade. Hannah

More's fierce attack on the slave trade in her poem "Slavery," first published in 1787, is representative of similar work by Ann Yearsley, Helen Maria Williams, and Anna Barbauld, and was widely circulated. Hannah More insisted on the common humanity that Africans shared with Europeans—"Respect His sacred image which they bear. / . . . Let malice strip them of each other plea, / They still are men, and men should still be free."[6] At the same time she denounced the "white savage" who, ruled by "lust of gold / Or lust of conquest," forfeited any legitimate claim Europe might make to being either civilized or Christian.

Gender played a significant role in the arguments for the abolition of slavery. The most prominent male abolitionist writers, such as Clarkson, Wilberforce, Thomas Day, and William Cowper, tended to attack slavery as a violation of "natural law," the argument that all men are born equal and have certain inalienable "rights." As a man, the black African belongs to the same species as the white European, and is entitled to the same "liberty, equality and fraternity." This is the doctrine that underlay the revolutionary movements in America and France and that produced the widely copied Wedgewood medallion. As the black speaker in William Cowper's widely reprinted poem "The Negro's Complaint" (1788) asserts, "Still in thought as free as ever, / What are England's rights, I ask, / Me from my delights to sever, / Me to torture, me to task? // Fleecy locks and black complexion / Cannot forfeit Nature's claim."[7] And this is the position asserted by the recaptured West Indian slave in Thomas Day's famous poem *The Dying Negro* (1773) who, bidding farewell to his white fiancée, prefers to commit suicide rather than return to the slave plantations of the West Indies. As he denounces his white master,

> And thou, whose impious avarice and pride
> Thy God's blest symbol to my brows denied,
> Forbade me or the rights of man to claim.
> Or share with thee a Christian's hallowed name,
> Thou too farewell!—for not beyond the grave,
> Thy power extends, nor is my dust thy slave.
> Go bribe thy kindred ruffians with thy gold,
> But dream not nature's rights are bought and sold.[8]

Women writers such as Hannah More, Ann Yearsley, Helen Maria Williams, and Anna Barbauld, on the other hand, tended to condemn slavery because it violated the domestic affections, separating mothers from their children, husbands from their wives, and subjecting black women to sexual abuse from their white masters. In Hannah More's words, again from her poem "Slavery,"

Figure 1
The Wedgewood Medallion: "Am I not a man
and a brother?" (Wedgewood & Sons, Ltd.)

> Whene'er to Afric's shores I turn my eyes,
> Horrors of deepest, deadliest guilt arise;
> I see, by more than fancy's mirror shown,
> The burning village and the blazing town:
> See the dire victim torn from social life,
> The shrieking babe, the agonizing wife;
> She, wretch forlorn! is dragg'd by hostile hands,
> To distant tyrants sold, in distant lands!
> Transmitted miseries, and successive chains,
> The sole sad heritage her child obtains!
> E'en this last wretched boon their foes deny,
> To weep together, or together die.
> By felon hands, by one relentless stroke,
> See the fond links of feeling nature broke!
> The fibres twisting round a parent's heart,
> Torn from their grasp, and bleeding as they part.[9]

By focusing on the violation of familial relationships as the fundamental evil of slavery and the slave trade, these women writers implicitly
appealed to a different system of morality. The male writers grounded
their condemnation of slavery on an ethic of justice, on the argument
that under a just system of law, all individuals should be treated the
same. The female writers appealed instead to what Carol Gilligan has

taught us to call an ethic of care,[10] the argument that under a moral government, all legal and social institutions should function so as to ensure that, in the resolution of social conflict, no one is irreparably hurt and the needs of all are taken into account.

By focusing on the ways in which slavery and the slave trade violated domestic relationships, women writers implicitly and often explicitly drew parallels between the female African slave subjected to the sexual abuse of her white master and the white British wife subjected to the same abuse. In her *Vindication of the Rights of Woman*, for example, Mary Wollstonecraft had argued that British wives were no different from slaves: "When, therefore, I call women slaves, I mean in a political and civil sense."[11] She based her argument on both legal and psychological grounds. Lord Mansfield's 1772 antislavery judgment had left intact the legal definition of marriage as a "municipal" relationship, a legal institution derived from feudal villeinage, in which the wife exists under the "coverture" of the husband. In other words, a wife is not a "person" in law: she cannot own property, have custody of children, bring legal suits—although she is held individually responsible for any crimes she might commit. Psychologically, this legal construction of the wife as "covered" by her husband produces an economic and emotional dependence, what Wollstonecraft calls a "slavish dependence,"[12] of the wife upon her husband or male relatives. Such dependence corrupts both partners, Wollstonecraft insists, for women "may be convenient slaves, but slavery will have its constant effect, degrading the master and the abject dependent."[13]

It is important to recognize that Wollstonecraft uses the term "slavery" in both a literal and a metaphorical sense. She believes that the institution of marriage in England in 1792 is legal slavery, no different in kind from that imposed on Africans in the British West Indies. Commenting on the arguments of the male conduct-book writers that British women must be subjected to the "severe restraint" of propriety or social morality, she asks,

> Why subject her to propriety—blind propriety, if she be capable of acting from a nobler spring, if she be an heir of immortality? Is sugar always to be produced by vital blood? Is one half of the human species, like the poor African slaves, to be subject to prejudices that brutalize them, when principles would be a surer guard, only to sweeten the cup of man?[14]

At the same time, Wollstonecraft frequently uses the terms "slave" or "slavery" figuratively, to underline her attack on female psychological dependence, either on men or on social mores. In the very next paragraph she condemns women for becoming "slaves to their persons," for setting too high a value on personal appearance. And a few pages later she attacks "a slavish bondage to parents," for those daughters "taught slavishly to submit to their parents . . . are prepared for the slavery of marriage." But she is careful immediately to qualify this rhetorical usage, "I do not dream of insinuating that boys or girls are always slaves, I only insist that when they are obliged to submit to authority blindly, their faculties are weakened, and their tempers rendered imperious or abject."[15]

Even though Wollstonecraft distinguishes between the literal and figurative construction of slavery in her text, she nonetheless insists that if British women are kept in a state of ignorance or "perpetual childhood," uneducated, and trained only to be pleasing to their masters and "cunning, mean and selfish" to everyone else, they are no different in *character* or *nature* from a sycophantic slave. Her program for the emancipation of women is equally clear: a rational education that teaches women the value and practice of honesty, compassion, affection, modesty, and useful work, an education that leads to what she would call *rational love* and an egalitarian marriage based on "companionship" rather than sexual desire.

The recognition of the female abolitionist writers that the female African slave and the European wife are both confined to legal slavery produced in the early 1830's an alternative, and equally widely distributed, medallion: "Am I not a Woman and a Sister?" By including the figure of the white woman as well as the black woman on a single roundel, this medallion implicitly asserted both their common humanity and their common sexual slavery, since the question is addressed both to white women and to white men.

At the same time, this roundel points to the implicit religious and class biases that everywhere informed the abolitionist debates. As Moira Ferguson has reminded us, both male and female abolitionist writers, however much they advocated an end to the slave trade and the institution of slavery, participated in a colonial discourse we now call Christian "Anglo-Africanism." They shared the assumption, in Winthrop Jordan's summary, that "to be Christian was to be civilized rather than barbarous, English rather than African, white rather than black."[16]

In Hannah More's revealing lines, which I omitted earlier, "Barbarians, hold! th'opprobrious commerce spare, / Respect His sacred image which they bear, / *Though dark and savage, ignorant and blind,* / They claim the common privilege of kind; / Let malice strip them of each other plea, / They still are men, and men should still be free"[17] (my italics). As the women's abolitionist medallion illustrates, the black slave woman *kneels to* the white European woman. Within their common slavery, the European woman assumes a superior position, standing rather

Figure 2
Abolitionist Roundel: "Am I not a woman and a sister?"
(Wilberforce House, Hull City Museums and Art Gallery)

than kneeling. She is implicitly equated with the power of both Justice (she carries the scales of Justizia) and Christian scripture: "Let *us* break *their* bands asunder and cast away *their* cords" (my italics). In dramatic tension with Wollstonecraft's argument that European women are slaves, as Barbara Bush and Deirdre Coleman have recently reminded us, female abolitionists wished to affirm their *difference from* and *superiority to* the black slave woman.[18] The roundel clearly suggests that slave women are dependent on European women for their freedom; European women are here portrayed as having both the political ability and the moral reponsibility to help their less fortunate sisters; white female Justice thus extends her helping hand to the grateful black female slave.

Although the British female abolitionist writers did not contest the assumption that a white, Christian, European woman is superior in degree if not in kind to a black, non-Christian, African woman, these writers on many occasions gave a voice of moral authority to the black slave that does not occur in the writings of the canonical male Romantic writers. This may have been caused, as Mary Jacobus has suggested, by the commitment of "masculine Romanticism" or male Romantic humanism to the construction of a potentially transcendent mind or subjectivity, an enduring self-consciousness that necessarily involves the erasure of the body and the material limitations of history.[19] Black characters occur far more frequently in literary texts by female than by male writers in this period. Moreover, they typically demonstrate a moral integrity that functions to reveal and implicitly denounce the hypocrisy and corruption of male-dominated European society. At the same time, their morality is explicitly defined as a naive innocence that remains dependent on wiser European men and women for its proper development. Examples from the writings of Joanna Baillie, Maria Edgeworth, and Amelia Opie will illustrate this pattern.

In two plays by Joanna Baillie, black males play pivotal roles in the moral resolution of the action. In *Rayner* (1804), the unjustly imprisoned Rayner is guarded by Ohio, a freed American slave, who is initially presented to the viewer as a skulking, foul-mouthed figure, a man degraded by "many hardships" to "the base thing that he is," a "curs'd, spite-envenomed toad," in the words of the prison-master, Hardibrand. Yet even the hardened, cruel, prison-master is able to feel some sympathy for Ohio, and his reluctant sympathy uncovers Baillie's own condemnation of the slave trade. As Hardibrand describes Ohio, he is

> Of royal line; born to command, and dignified
> By sufferings and angers past, which makes
> The meanest man ennobled: yet behold him;
> How by the way he sidelong straddles on
> With his base tankard! — O, the sneaking varlet!
> It makes me weep to hear his piteous tale,
> Yet my blood boils to run and cudgel him.[20]

At the moment when the executioner lifts his axe to decapitate the unjustly condemned Rayner, the gallows stand collapses, its wooden supports having been sawed through, wounding the executioner and delaying the execution just long enough for Rayner's pardon to arrive. Ohio, whom Rayner has befriended and to whom he has given his coat, then exults: "I did it! / He offer'd me his cloak: he pitied me; / And I have paid him back."[21] Ohio here functions as the "deus ex machina," the blessed savior of the wrongly accused hero and the voice of moral justice in the play. But even as Baillie grants to the freed black slave this position of moral authority, she reinscribes him within an Anglo-African discourse of dependency. Moved by Ohio's loyalty to Rayner, Hardibrand promises Ohio, "I'll take thee home, and make a man of thee. / . . . Thou has a gen'rous mind, altho' debased / With vile oppression and unmanly scorn."[22] "*Make a man of thee*": is Hardibrand offering to make Ohio into a gentleman, a man of a higher class or status than he currently enjoys? Or is he offering to make Ohio "human," as opposed to the "toad" he has been? Both readings are possible, and Baillie's text does not allow us to dismiss the latter, more uncomfortable suggestion that she too subscribes to Hardibrand's explicit assumption of European superiority over the "royal" African.

This same tension between black moral authority and black cultural inferiority recurs in Baillie's comedy, *The Alienated Manor* (1836). The young freed slave Sancho, whose mentally retarded master has been cheated out of his life savings in a game of dice by Charleville and then thrown in jail for debt, passionately and persuasively attacks this miscarriage of justice to Charleville's servant:

> Ay, my massa be poor, and everybody be angry wit him. — Your massa not angry, your massa very fond of him when he shake a te dice, and tak all te money from him. Te tevil will shake him over te great fire for tat.[23]

The dramatic authority of Sancho's moral outrage is undermined in this play, however, by his use of West African Pidgin English, a language which in the early nineteenth century was viewed as a simplified, "baby-talk" form of Standard English spoken by people with inferior linguistic or cognitive abilities.[24] Sancho's moral authority is further undercut by his eagerness to kill the man who cheated his master and by his excessive gratitude to Crafton, the man who promises to free his master: "O good Massa Crafton! me tank you, me embrace you, me kneel to you." Nonetheless, Baillie gives Sancho the last word, a final reaffirmation of his natural and legal rights. When Crafton raises him from his knees, saying, "Let no man be upon his knees but when he is at his prayers. Come with us and fear nothing; though this was a desperate attempt, a very wicked attempt against the laws of the land," Sancho defiantly asserts, "Me care for te laws when te laws care for me."[25]

Maria Edgeworth engages in a similarly contradictory effort both to grant the black voice absolute moral authority and at the same time to contain it within a social discourse of racial inferiority. In her play *The Two Guardians* (1817), St. Albans, a wealthy young West Indian planter, comes to England with his black slave, Quaco. As soon as he arrives in London, St. Albans informs Quaco that he is "free": "From the moment that you touched English ground, Quaco, you ceased to be a slave." St. Albans then pays him for all his previous labor. Quaco, however, insists that he will never leave: "me will be Massa's slave alway" or if not his slave, then his servant who will "do / Twice the work of slave for you; / Fight for Massa twice as long; / Love for Massa twice as strong."[26]

As St. Albans is exposed to the hypocrisies, cruelties, and deceitfulness of fashionable English society, Quaco becomes the voice of moral honesty and sincere love: he gives his earnings to the starving widow cheated of her pay by St. Albans's selfish hostess; he sees through the duplicities of the lovely Juliana, whom St. Albans is courting, a girl whom Quaco "can't love";[27] and he is on hand to rescue St. Albans when he is almost killed by a fall from a bad horse sold to him by a false friend. By constantly contrasting Quaco's loyalty, compassion, and rectitude to the cruel duplicities of the young lords and ladies "of fashion," Edgeworth insists on the moral superiority of the "childlike" black to the self-indulgent cruelties of the spoiled European youths, Juliana and Beauchamp Courtington. At the same time, she defines Quaco as *only* a child, one who eagerly seeks to sustain his dependence upon his superior white master.

The most radical attempt to construct the black woman as the moral superior of the British white woman occurs in Amelia Opie's first novel *Adeline Mowbray* (1804), significantly subtitled "The Mother and Daughter." Here Opie suggests that her heroine's true mother is not the Mrs. Mowbray who cruelly vows never to see her daughter again until she has suffered as much as her mother (Adeline has innocently attracted and then violently repulsed the sexual attentions of her mother's new husband, the libertine Sir Patrick O'Carroll). Even after Adeline's devoted lover and Godwinian disciple Glenmurray has died, reducing her to insanity for six months, even after she has been deserted by her husband, Berrendale, Mrs. Mowbray refuses to see her daughter and granddaughter Editha.

Only the escaped black slave woman and domestic servant, Savanna, whose husband, William, has been saved from imprisonment for debt by Adeline, remains loyal to Adeline through all her trials and sufferings, nursing her through her insanity and grief, declaring "war" on the unfaithful Berrendale and exposing his lies both at home in England and abroad in Jamaica, and using her own meager wages to buy food and medicine for Adeline when her husband refuses to let her share his meals and then abandons her. Despite Adeline's deathbed reconciliation with her biological mother, it is in the arms of this "true" mother Savanna that Adeline dies. Throughout this novel, Savanna represents the virtue of an enduring and passionate maternal love, caring as much for Adeline as she does for her own child, the Tawny Boy. She is "the only person now in the world, perhaps, who loves me with sincere and faithful affection" (189), Adeline tells her faithless husband, and on her deathbed she proclaims to her doctor, "She is my nurse, my consoler, and my friend" (272).[28]

Even as Opie makes this radical claim for the superior maternal love and faithful care of the black woman, she locates Savanna within an economic and social condition of dependency. The dying Adeline continues to regard Savanna as one of her possessions: as she writes to her mother, "I owe [Savanna], my mother, a world of obligation! She will make my last moments easy, and you must reward her. From her you will receive this letter when I am no more, and to your care and protection I bequeath her" (266). The text further emphasizes Savanna's limited economic resources. As food and medicine are brought to the dying Adeline, " 'This it be to have money,' said Savanna, as she saw the various things prepared and made to tempt Adeline's weak appetite:—'poor Savanna mean as well—her heart make all these, but her hand want power' " (272). The novel ends with Adeline's return to her mother's house, where Savanna will once again be a paid servant, assigned to the "care" of Mrs. Mowbray. "I will love her as my child" (270), pledges Mrs. Mowbray; "Savanna shall be our joint care" (274), she further affirms, assigning the responsibility for Savanna's well-being to herself and the Quaker Rachel Pemberton.

Despite such markers of economic and social inferiority—Savanna consistently speaks Black English while her educated son speaks Standard English, and she is prone to extreme and violent outbursts of emotion deemed "improper" by the Quaker Rachel Pemberton—Opie establishes Savanna as the embodiment of moral virtue and domestic affection. Only when Adeline is alone with Savanna and their two children does she experience complete happiness. Watching Tawny Boy building card-houses for the infant Editha, listening to Savanna's "rapturous praises," Adeline, "alive only to the maternal feeling, at this moment had forgotten all her cares; she saw nothing but the happy group around her, and her countenance wore the expression of recovered serenity" (192). While this idyll is immediately interrupted, it opens up the utopian possibility with which the novel closes, the possibility that Editha might be raised by a female-dominated community which includes a woman of color. As Roxanne Eberle has observed, Adeline's dying letter "elaborates a complex system of duty and debt which will ensure that Savanna remains free; she will be protected by other women" who have the economic power to do so.[29] Moreover, Savanna will be a recognized and fully accepted member of this family of choice constructed by the dying Adeline for her daughter Editha, a family that includes Adeline's mother, the Quaker Mrs. Pemberton, and Savanna. In this all-female community, a feminotopia that includes a woman of the landed gentry, a middle-class white woman and a black working-class woman residing in the fortified pastoral arcadia of Rosevalley, Savanna functions simultaneously if contradictorily as both servant and co-mother, indeed as the only mother who yet deserves that title, of the infant Editha. The last line of the novel further identifies Savanna with the bosom of the lord within which the troubled Adeline Mowbray finally comes to rest: "in imperfect accents exclaiming 'I thank thee, blessed Lord!' she [Adeline] laid her head on Savanna's bosom and expired" (275).

Again, in her powerful antislavery poem for children, "The Black Man's Lament" (1826), Amelia Opie grants both social equality and moral authority to the black slave. She allows him to speak in his own voice without narrative framing; she represents his speech in Standard, if grammatically incorrect, English; and she permits him to refute with cogency the argument that Negro slaves are better off than the English peasant:

> Who dares an English peasant flog,
> Or buy, or sell, or steal away?
> Who sheds his blood? treats him like dog,
> Or fetters him like beasts of prey?
>
> He has a cottage, he a wife;
> If child he has, that child is free.
> I am depriv'd of married life,
> And my poor child were *slave* like *me.*[30]

Opie authorizes the black man's claim to social and legal equality with the free Englishman and undercuts the pro-planter argument for the improvement of slavery under more benevolent masters ("There are, I'm told, upon some isles, / Masters who gentle deign to be; / And there, perhaps, the Negro *smiles*, / But *smiling* Negroes *few* can see."). But now, following her conversion to the Society of Friends in 1825, Amelia Opie insists that Christianity offers the African slave a lasting comfort he cannot gain at home in Africa:

> Well, I must learn to bear my pain;
> And, lately, I am grown more calm;
> For Christian men come o'er the main,
> To pour in Negro souls a balm.

The Christianity that the Quaker Opie invokes demands that the slave both repress his anger at the injustice he experiences and reaffirm a position of inferiority to the more "civilized" white man:

> They tell us there is one above
> Who died to save both bond and free;
> And who, with eyes of equal love,
> Beholds White man, and *humble me.*
>
> They tell me if, with patient heart,
> I bear my wrongs from day to day,
> I shall, at death, to realms depart,
> Where God wipes every tear away!

> Yet still, at times, with fear I shrink;
> For, when with sense of injury prest,
> I burn with rage! and *then* I think
> I ne'er can *gain* that place of rest.[31]

Opie's rendering of the black slave's language in ungrammatical Standard English rather than Pidgin or Black English implicitly endorses the Anglo-African view that Standard English is a superior language.[32] Nonetheless, Opie ends her poem by giving authorial vindication to her black narrator, with whom she also expresses sympathetic identification: "it rends my heart to know / He only told a *tale of truth.*"

Even those female writers, such as Mary Wollstonecraft and Mary Robinson, who resist the Anglo-African construction of the Christianized slave as superior in kind to the free non-Christian African, slip into the assumption that the literacy and rationality of European culture render it superior to an oral, superstitious African culture. As Zelma, Mary Robinson's protagonist in "The Negroe Girl" (1800), proclaims,

> The tyrant white man taught my mind
> The letter'd page to trace;
> He taught me in the soul to find
> No tint, as in the face:
> He bade my reason blossom like the tree—
> But fond affection gave the ripen'd fruits to thee.

Here Robinson implies that the enlightened Zelma will have "fruits" to give her black lover Draco superior to those she would have borne without the benefit of a European education; and the foremost among these "fruits" is the conviction that her soul is *without color,* as pure or white as that of an Englishman.

By allowing black men and women to speak for themselves, by giving their voices moral authority, and by insisting on the sympathetic identification with them felt both by other characters in the text and by the author herself, British women writers in this period introduced a new dimension into the discourse of abolition. Moving away from the abstract rhetoric of the rights of man engaged in by Clarkson, Wilberforce, Cowper, Day, Coleridge, and Wordsworth, they developed a rhetoric of sympathy grounded in the celebration and preservation of the domestic affections, a sympathy that incorporated the black man and woman into their own political family.

From our current perspective, however, we can see that the abolitionist discourse employed by both male and female writers in the Romantic period only translated one form of slavery, legal slavery, into another form, the "slavery" of assimilation. Black men and women could be welcomed into the European "family of man" only insofar as they could be seen as participating in the same domestic affections, the same familial relationships and loyalties, as those which governed European emotions, however much the specter of miscegenation and interracial marriage haunted this utopian discourse. "Am I not a Brother?" "Am I not a Sister?" The suggestion that the black man or woman might not feel kinship with the white European colonizer is one that none of the abolitionist writers could directly confront. Such arguments were left to the pro-slavery lobby, who insisted on the essential racial difference of Africans, on their innate "savagery," as the basis of their enslavement. This is the pernicious legacy of the Enlightenment discourse of emancipation with which we are still wrestling: how can we develop a discourse of racial—and sexual—difference that *values* difference for its own sake without granting political, legal, or cultural priority to one of these differences?

NOTES

1. *The English Reports* 98 (King's Bench Division 27): "Somerset against Stewart, May 14, 1772, Lord Mansfield Presiding," Lofft 1 (London: Stevens and Sons; Edinburgh: William Green & Sons, 1909), 500.

2. For the most insightful discussion of the function of slavery in Austen's *Mansfield Park* to date, and of Fanny Price as the stereotypical "grateful Negro," see Moira Ferguson, "*Mansfield Park*: Slavery, Colonialism and Gender," *The Oxford Literary Review* 13 (1991), 118–39. Also see Margaret Kirkham, *Jane Austen: Feminism and Fiction* (New York: Barnes and Noble, 1983), 116–19; Edward Said, *Culture and Imperialism* (New York: Knopf, 1993), 80–96; Frank Gibbon, "The Antiguan Connection: Some New Light on Mansfield Park," *Cambridge Quarterly* 11 (1982), 298–305; and Meenakshe Mukharjee, "To Hear My Uncle Talk of the West Indies," in *Women Writers: Jane Austen* (New York, 1991), 49–69.

3. Thomas Bellamy, *The Benevolent Planters* (London, 1789), 13.

4. Thomas Clarkson, *History of the Rise, Progress and Accomplishment of the Abolition of the African Slave-Trade, by the British Parliament* (London, 1808), vol. I, 170–71.

5. On the involvement of British women in the abolitionist and other social movements between 1775 and 1825, see Clare Midgley, *Women against Slavery—The British Campaigns, 1780–1870* (London and New York: Routledge, 1992), 1–120, and Linda Colley, *Britons—Forging the Nation 1707–1837* (New Haven: Yale University Press, 1992), 273–81.

6. Hannah More, *Slavery: A Poem* (London, 1788), 10, lines 136–40.

7. William Cowper, *The Negro's Complaint* (London, 1788; repr. 1826), 4–5.

8. Thomas Day, *The Dying Negro* (London, 1773), 6.

9. Hannah More, *Slavery*, 7–8, lines 95–110.

10. Carol Gilligan, *In A Different Voice—Psychological Theory and Women's Development* (Cambridge: Harvard University Press, 1982). For an analysis of the ethic of care as fundamental to women's writing in the Romantic period, see my *Romanticism and Gender* (New York and London: Routledge, 1993). Gary Kelly further argues that this ethic, an ideology of sympathy and domesticity or of "reason" and "virtue," was fundamental to the emergence of a middle or professional class identity in this period in his *Women, Writing, and Revolution 1790–1827* (Oxford: Clarendon Press, 1993), chap. 1.

11. Mary Wollstonecraft, *Vindication of the Rights of Woman* (London, 1792), ed. Carol Poston (New York: Norton, 1975), 167.

12. Ibid.

13. Ibid., 5.

14. Ibid., 144–45.

15. Ibid., 155.

16. Winthrop D. Jordan, *White over Black: American Attitudes toward the Negro, 1500–1812* (Chapel Hill: University of North Carolina Press, 1968), 94. For an extended discussion of the role played by Anglo-African attitudes in the writing of female British writers in this period, see Moira Ferguson, *Subject to Others—British Women Writers and Colonial Slavery, 1670–1834* (New York: Routledge, 1992).

17. Hannah More, *Slavery*, 10.

18. See Barbara Bush, *Slave Women in Caribbean Society 1650–1838* (Kingston: Heinemann; Bloomington: Indiana University Press; London: James Currey, 1990), chap. 2; and Dierdre Coleman, "Conspicuous Consumption: White Abolitionism and English Women's Protest Writing in the 1790s," *ELH* 61 (1994), 341–62.

I wish to correct the ahistorical and partial account of the rhetorical relationship of British marriage to African slavery presented by Coleman in this essay. Focusing on Coleridge's evasive essay on the slave-trade and Benjamin Flower's *The French Constitution* (1792), both of which construct the white Lady as the worst abuser of slaves, and relying on an inadequate reading of John Gabriel Stedman's *Narrative of a Five Years Expedition against the Revolted Negroes of Surinam* (1796/1988), Coleman rhetorically identifies the British female abolitionist or wife with the (totalized) West Indian planter's wife. She portrays them both as insensitive to the literal sufferings of African slaves and, worse, as sexual rivals for the attentions of the white man who in their jealousy tortured, killed, and even figuratively drank the blood of their black female competitors.

Coleman rightly wishes to contest the too-easy analogy Wollstonecraft and other feminist writers drew between marriage and slavery, an analogy she calls "obscene" (354), but in so doing she goes too far in the other direction, suggesting that all white English women were racists incapable of understanding the African slave's suffering as anything more than an occasion for either the display of sensibility or a reflection upon the brutality of their own marriages. Coleman significantly eliminates from her account of Stedman's *Narrative* the generosity of Elizabeth Godefrooy, who bought Stedman's beloved house-slave Joanna and gave her to Stedman so that she might, if she chose, accompany him to England (Stedman, *Narrative*, 1796, vol. 2, 82–83).

19. Mary Jacobus has analyzed Wordsworth's necessary erasure of the slave trade from *The Prelude* in her *Romanticism Writing and Sexual Difference— Essays on The Prelude* (Oxford: Clarendon Press, 1989), chap. 3. Also see my discussion of the erasure of the body from Romantic male autobiography more generally, in my *Romanticism and Gender* (New York and London: Routledge, 1993), chap. 7.

20. Joanna Baillie, *Rayner*, in *Miscellaneous Plays* (London, 1804), 68.

21. Ibid., 135.

22. Ibid.

23. Joanna Baillie, *The Alienated Manor*, in *Dramas*, 3 vols. (London, 1836), vol. I, Act IV, scene i, 206.

24. West African Pidgin English was constructed by African slaves and traders to communicate with British slave traders, sailors, and merchants along the West Coast of Africa during the 17th and 18th centuries, and combines a largely English vocabulary with African phonological and syntactical structures. It then became "creolized" (a mother-tongue) in the West Indies, where it developed a richer vocabulary and more complex grammatical forms. On the structure of West African Pidgin English, a language here accurately represented by Joanna Baillie, Maria Edgeworth, and Amelia Opie, and the transformation (or "decreolization") of West African Pidgin English into what is now known as Black English, see *inter alia* the following: Elizabeth Closs Traugott, "Pidgins, Creoles, and the Origins of Vernacular Black English," in *Black English—A Seminar*, ed. Deborah Sears Harrison and Tom Trabasso (Hillsdale, N.J.: Lawrence Erlbaum, 1976), 57–94; J. L. Dillard, *Black English—Its History and Usage in the United States* (New York: Random House, 1972), 39–138; David Dalby, *Black through White: Patterns of Communication* (Bloomington: Indiana University African Studies Program, 1969); and Peter Muhlhauser, *Pidgin & Creole Linguistics* (Oxford: Basil Blackwell, 1986).

On the erroneous nineteenth-century and early twentieth-century assumption that Pidgin and Creole languages were simplified versions of complex European languages (or "baby-talk") spoken by people with inferior cognitive or linguistic abilities, rather than independent contact-zone languages with unique and ascertainable historical developments, see Dell Hymes, ed., *Pidginization and Creolization of Languages* (Cambridge: Cambridge University Press, 1971), 3–11. Those wishing to pursue these issues further should consult *A Comprehensive Annotated Bibliography of American Black English*, compiled by Ila Wales Brasch and Walter Milton Brasch (Baton Rouge: Louisiana State University Press, 1974).

25. Baillie, *Alienated Manor*, Act V, scene ii, 238.

26. Maria Edgeworth, *The Two Guardians*, in *Comic Dramas, in Three Acts* (London, 1817), 160, 163.

27. Ibid., 183.

28. Amelia Opie, *Adeline Mowbray—The Mother and Daughter* (London, 1804; Pandora Press, 1986). All further references to this edition will be cited in the text.

29. Roxanne Eberle, "Amelia Opie's *Adeline Mowbray*: Diverting the Libertine Gaze; or, The Vindication of a Fallen Woman," *Studies in the Novel* 26 (1994) 145.

30. Amelia Opie, *The Black Man's Lament* (London, 1826), 22.

31. Ibid., 24–25.

32. For a Marxist analysis of the politics of vulgar (non-grammatical) versus refined (grammatical) English in the Romantic period, see Olivia Smith, *The Politics of Language 1791–1819* (Oxford: Clarendon Press, 1984), chap. 1, 2, 6.

Thirteen

SONIA HOFKOSH

Tradition and The Interesting Narrative: *Capitalism, Abolition, and the Romantic Individual*

> The existing order is complete before the new work arrives;
> for order to persist after the supervention of novelty, the *whole*
> existing order must be, if ever so slightly, altered; and so the
> relations, proportions, values of each work of art toward the whole
> are readjusted; and this is conformity between the old and the new.
> —T. S. Eliot (1919)[1]

> The recognition that tradition bestows is a partial form of
> identification. In restaging the past it introduces other,
> incommensurable cultural temporalities into the invention of tradition.
> —Homi K. Bhabha (1994)[2]

IN "Out of Africa: Topologies of Nativism," Kwame Anthony Appiah outlines a set of directives for teaching modern African literature to students in Africa, as distinct from teaching that literature in the American academy. African students should read specifically "to connect . . . with their geographical situations," to "value and incorporate the African past," whereas the function and effect of reading African writing in the West should be "to extend the American imagination . . . beyond the narrow scope of the United States" and its determining systems of value—economic and political as well as aesthetic.[3] Positing such "different conceptions of reading" (159) aimed alternately at the consolidation of African national identity and tradition and at the translocation of Western self-consciousness and its history of dominance, Appiah's pedagogical correlatives also recognize the dialectical nature of the cultural encounter at issue in African writing. If "the language of empire, of center and periphery, identity and difference, the sovereign subject and her colonies, continues to structure the criticism and reception of African literature *in* Africa as elsewhere," that literature nonetheless can and should be read to challenge such a "rhetoric of alterity"—itself a "Western thematic"—which assumes the polarity of self (indigene) and other (alien) as an "organic" formulation rather than as a set of conventionally (and often violently) occupied positions (163). Thus the mode of reading which Appiah proposes for African students that would "expose the ways in which the systematic character of literary (and, more broadly, aesthetic) judgments of value is the product of certain institutional practices" might constructively motivate readers in the United States as well. Reading African writing here, we too can learn to readjust the "relations, proportions, and values" of our own cultural conformity.

Appiah's critique of the oppositional topos implicit in nativist discourse is elaborated in the context of modern African literature and criticism, particularly as it is exemplified in the writing of Chinua Achebe and Wole Soyinka. With other African writers in the European languages, according to Abiola Irele, these Nigerian authors constitute the main focus of African letters "as a cultural phenomenon and also as an object of academic study," as a discrete and significant body of works, a tradition.[4] For Irele, modern African writing characteristically and fundamentally engages questions of identity—of "presence" (82) or "integrity of being and consciousness" (83)—primarily *as* a question of tradition. Tradition is "felt as the anchor of consciousness, of a presence in the world" (71), and figures as "both theme and determining factor of the very form" of modern African expression (96). But while tradition in this way defines at once the substance and the shape of African writing, it is also associated at the moment of invention with "historical grievance" (76), with the brutal dislocations, the unworlding, compelled by the slave trade and colonialism. Irele traces the tension thus built into the making of an African tradition back to the eighteenth century, specifically to *The Interesting Narrative of the Life of Olaudah Equiano, or Gustavus Vassa, the African,* published in London in 1789. In its introspective mode, Equiano's autobiographical *Interesting Narrative* inaugurates the tradition of African letters, anticipating the emphasis on "self-representation" and "self-reflection" (76) that will become a central feature in the discursive project of modern writers in Africa.

Irele's discussion should remind us once again that tradition is transitional, not a static or always already established structure or syllabus, but on-going, in the process of coming into being through struggle and revision: "It cannot be inherited, and if you want it you must obtain it

by great labour."[5] Without denying the central, even originary, place of
Equiano's text in the making of a tradition of African letters, nor, alternatively, diffusing the importance of its status as "the prototype of
the nineteenth-century slave narrative" and therefore "the very foundation upon which most subsequent Afro-American fictional and non-
fictional forms are based,"[6] I want to look at this African writer's participation in, contribution to, and revisionary potential for another
history, a romantic history, a history of the individual ("presence" or
"consciousness") that has a political as well as an aesthetic unfolding. I
want to emphasize that this is not to read Equiano in order to measure
the value of his work by trying whether it can be inserted into what
Appiah calls "a Great White Tradition of masterpieces."[7] "Fitting in" is
not really the issue here.[8] Rather, to read Equiano in reference to this
other history is to restage the past, to reread that history *as* other, to
defamiliarize the terms and tendencies of its elaboration into such an
exclusive, capitalized canon. *The Interesting Narrative* is not a "new work"
in the sense that T. S. Eliot means when he refers in "Tradition and the
Individual Talent" to the supervention of novelty which necessarily al-
ters the existing order of the past. But the relatively recent rediscovery
of Equiano's work *in the academy*[9] nonetheless "calls for a reinvention of
the radical difference of *our own* cultural past."[10]

One point of examining Equiano's link to the tradition of British
romanticism is to suggest the plural and transformative position his
text occupies in the very construction of tradition and in the cultural demarcations tradition inscribes. At once spiritual autobiography
and abolitionist polemic (among other things), Equiano's text cannot
be fully appropriated to conventional categories of literary history. It
introduces Homi Bhabha's "incommensurable cultural temporalities"
into the narrative of a coherent past. Yet even as it resists the fixity of
categorical definitions, such as the difference between an aesthetic of
the personal and a political intervention—or between an African text
and a British one—*The Interesting Narrative* reveals the investments at
stake in establishing principles of difference, investments that both inform and unsettle the account of (generic, national, racial) identity
such conventional categories subtend. To say that Equiano's text cannot
be fully appropriated to conventional categories is not to suggest that
it transcends the definitional rigors of tradition. Rather, it is to suggest
that the text casts those rigors into relief; it highlights the way tradition is never simply the same, never simply or consistently itself, that it
works through and to contain (include, regulate, subsume) difference.
This essay explores the mutual purchase that obtains between tradition
and *The Interesting Narrative* through the converging discourses of capitalism, abolition, and individualism that Equiano's text puts into play:
that commerce consolidates the force of tradition even while operating

within tradition to shift ("if ever so slightly") its terms, its values, and its effects.

*   *   *

I, who had been a slave in the morning, trembling at the will
of another, was become my own master, and completely free.
                                        —Olaudah Equiano (1789)

Can he who the day before was a trampled slave suddenly
become liberal-minded, forebearing, and independent?
                                        —Percy Shelley (1818)[11]

To consider *The Interesting Narrative of the Life of Olaudah Equiano* in the context of the specific conditions of its production ("never singular but always several")[12] is to locate it in the political history of the British abolitionist movement, as a critical contribution to the agitation against the slave trade gathering force in the late eighteenth century. Equiano occupied a significant position in that history. He was a public figure, a "recognized leader of the black community in Britain."[13] He was one among a number of politically visible Africans in London of the 1780s and 1790s, including Ottobah Cugoano, whose polemical *Thoughts and Sentiments on the Evil and Wicked Traffic of the Slavery and Commerce of the Human Species* (1787) Equiano may have helped draft. He served on the London Committee for the Black Poor, had been a government employee, and was a frequent writer of letters to newspapers such as the *Public Advertiser*, to prominent legislators and abolition committees, and even to the queen. He collaborated with a range of influential activists from the reformer Granville Sharp to the republican Thomas Hardy. With the appearance of *The Interesting Narrative*, Equiano traveled to cities throughout England, Scotland, and Ireland to sell copies of his book and to lecture on the cause of antislavery.[14]

The Interesting Narrative is thus a document generated in the context of a political career. Equiano explicitly situates it as public performance, deflecting the personal implications of writing his life in order to identify that utterance as functional social discourse:

> I am not so foolishly vain as to expect from it either immortality or literary reputation. If it affords any satisfaction to my numerous friends, at whose request it has been written, or in the smallest degree promotes the interests of humanity, the ends for which it was undertaken will be fully attained, and every wish of my heart gratified. (I, 3)

Personal gratification, the author suggests, is motivated by others' pleasure, the "satisfaction of numerous friends." In lieu of vanity and reputation—characteristics of self-interest—Equiano invokes the more universally construed "interests of humanity." What Fredric Jameson calls the "libidinal investment" of this Third World text "is to be read in primarily political and social terms."[15] Addressed in particular to the Lords and Gentlemen of Parliament, Equiano's *Interesting Narrative* claims its place in the public sphere, as a political intervention in a vital national debate, as an "instrument" (I, iv) in the formation of public opinion and legislative policy.

Yet, if the "interest" in *The Interesting Narrative* is public rather than private, national rather than individual, the force of adding his own experience to the academic abolitionist arguments of Anthony Benezet's *Some Historical Account of Guinea* (1771) and Thomas Clarkson's *An Essay on the Slavery and Commerce of the Human Species* (1786), for example, suggests precisely that the instrumentality of Equiano's book *is* the personal:

> Permit me, with the greatest deference and respect, to lay at your feet
> the following genuine narrative; the chief design of which is to excite
> in your august assemblies a sense of compassion for the miseries which
> the Slave-Trade has entailed on my unfortunate countrymen. By the
> horrors of that trade was I first torn away from all the tender connec-
> tions that were naturally dear to my heart. . . . (I, iii)

Equiano enters the political debate through personal experience. As the work of "an unlettered African," his "genuine narrative" provides for the abolitionist argument that "something else" Cugoano had called for in *Thoughts and Sentiments* to supplement the efforts of the "learned gentlemen" who write against the slave trade.[16] Equiano speaks in that authentic voice from Africa that Clarkson can only imagine or suppose.[17]

Further, *The Interesting Narrative* seeks to influence ("excite") the collective, political body of Parliament ("august assemblies") through the vocabulary of sentiment and feeling, appealing directly to the very hearts of its individual members: "May the God of Heaven inspire your hearts with peculiar benevolence on that important day when the question of Abolition is to be discussed" (I, v). The preface to the 1814 edition (the twelfth edition of the book printed in Britain) underscores the efficacy of such a personal appeal:

> Being a true relation of occurences which had taken place, and of suf-
> ferings which he had endured, it produced a degree of humane feel-
> ings in men's minds, to excite which the most animated addresses and
> the most convincing reasoning would have laboured in vain.[18]

The book is directed not to the reason, an abstract quantity, but seeks rather to register its effect in the very bodies of its readers—at their feet, in their hearts, and in their minds. It represents individual experience to them—both the author's and their own—creating for them an isolate, intimate space through which they can respond sympathetically to its argument. It operates from inside out, self-referentially, narrowing its focus in order to universalize its appeal, claiming its authority on an internal logic ("that *such a man*, pleading in *such a cause* will be acquitted of boldness and presumption," I, iv). The political dimension of the text is thus itself articulated in libidinal language; in Equiano's abolitionist intervention, his life story, the political is the personal.

But if such a complex embeddedness of public and private might be understood in Jameson's terms as the distinguishing feature of the minority text in an era of (emergent) capitalism, it might also be seen as a crucial factor in the very history of that emergence. Recent debate among economic and political historians about how to explain the progress of the abolitionist movement in late eighteenth-century Britain interrogates the "convergence of humanitarian ideals and capitalist ideology."[19] The ground of that interrogation may shift, "from the direct clash of imperial economic forces [as in C. L. R. James or Eric Williams] to battles for the minds and hearts of metropolitans [as in Roger Anstey or David Brion Davis],"[20] but the question remains largely about "the relation of society to consciousness"[21]—or, to adapt Jameson's terminology, the relation of the public world of classes, economics, and political power to the private domain of subjectivity, sexuality, and the literary.[22] One of the central premises informing much of the current discussion about the history of antislavery is "that the abolition of slavery cannot be explained by direct extrapolation from pure economic motives or mechanisms any more than from pure moral consciousness."[23] Rather, with their various disciplinary emphases and their differing theoretical assumptions, historians tracing the causes and consolidation of the British abolitionist movement uncover the intersection of these opposing categories in early antislavery activity, disclosing the operation of a conceptual framework which links rather than separates public and private, economics and ethics, tradition and the individual talent.[24]

Transcribing his own past, Equiano enacts the fundamental and inseparable intersections implicit in the history his text helps mobilize. When he purchases his manumission for forty pounds sterling ("I, who had been a slave in the morning, trembling at the will of another, was become my own master, and completely free"), he demonstrates not only that economic values translate into personal ones, but more precisely that the economic structure of property and power underwrites the very possibility of individual freedom even as that structure is itself girded by an individualist paradigm, the rights of man. Buying his freedom, possessing by that purchase a self "liberal-minded, forbearing, and independent," Equiano dramatizes that in the age of democratic revolution—in America, France, and San Domingo—the rhetoric of rights involves a model of individual agency that relies on the concept of absolute property ("in one's own person") and thus imbricates the economic and the psychological dimensions of self-mastery.[25]

*   *   *

The only security of property that nature authorizes and reason sanctions is, the right a man has to enjoy the acquisitions which his talents and industry have acquired.
—M. Wollstonecraft (1790)

Here and there a Napoleon of finance, by luck and industry, could make enough to purchase his freedom.
—C. L. R. James (1938)[26]

The institution of slavery by which one man could be said to own another as private property fostered the emerging economics of capitalism in specific and measurable ways, both in terms of modes of production and patterns of consumption—of sugar or of cotton textiles, for example.[27] But so too did capitalism as it developed into the dominant economic system in Europe depend on the Enlightenment notion of individualism theorized in John Locke's political philosophy, advanced in the interest-driven economics of Adam Smith's *The Wealth of Nations* (1776), and put so profitably into practice by many among the entrepreneurial bourgeois who were active in the agitation to abolish chattel slavery in the British West Indies: "The human essence is freedom from dependence on the will of others, and freedom is a function of possession."[28] Capitalism derives its operative logic from the same basic assumption as the liberatory project of abolition, which posits self-ownership as one of the fundamental, defining features of human morality.[29] This is the "paradox" that Equiano's *Interesting Narrative* performs.[30] Individualism is two-faced, double-edged; capitalism (the means of exploitation) and abolition (the way to freedom) two sides of the same cognitive coin.[31] Equiano's manumission turns on just such a coin (forty pounds sterling), turns a slave into a master, the trampled and abject into the prototype of independent and creative consciousness.

It is a primary aim of *The Interesting Narrative* to detail the brutalities of chattel slavery and of the racist violence sanctioned by colonial policy. But in the moment that he buys his freedom, Equiano's history might also be seen to literalize the ethos of possessive individualism, exposing even as it does so the double edge that defines the paradigm of the entrepreneurial subject: the self as owner depends on the prin-

ciple that selves can be owned, freedom on the possibility of alienation, identity on difference. For Houston Baker, the manumission exemplifies Equiano's "adept mercantilism": mastering the economic system empowers a unified subjectivity, "a man who has repossessed
himself," an individual.[32] "Having achieved his individuality as a freeman," Joseph Fichtelberg conversely argues, "Equiano can exercise it
only in an economic system where humans are commodities, empty
markers, ciphers."[33] Two sides of one economy. Taken together, these
opposing readings of the economic relations manifest in the moment
of liberation suggest that at such a moment Equiano might be at once
master and slave, empowered and alienated, subject and object, his own
uncanny double: the same and different.

Identity in *The Interesting Narrative* is elaborated in the dynamic of
these oppositions, a complex of competing and mutually constitutive
positions and values. Identity circulates, changes character, but without
wholly occupying or abandoning one position or the other.[34] Instead,
at the moment he becomes his own master, or, even from the moment
when, as "a Napoleon of finance," he makes enough to purchase his
freedom, Equiano enacts both the imperial gesture of accumulation
and its contrary, the impossibility of such a totalizing, appropriative
posture.

> Heavens! who could do justice to my feelings at this moment! Not con-
> quering heroes themselves, in the midst of a triumph—Not the tender
> mother who has just regained her long-lost infant, and presses it to her
> heart—Not the weary hungry mariner, at the sight of a desired friendly
> port—not the lover, when he once more embraces his beloved mistress,
> after she has been ravished from his arms!—All within my breast was
> tumult, wildness, and delirium! (II, 15–16)

This moment offers a dynamic at once of affiliation and disavowal. Mar-
shalling multiple figures, none of which can "do justice to [his] feelings," Equiano represents his experience in an excess of contradiction.
Not this, not that, nor even the other, his powerful feeling ("tumult,
wildness, and delirium") overflows as a series of images of conquest and
reunion, loss and gain, images at once conventionally construed and
inappropriate, familiar and yet strange. The excess signals the way traditional figures may indeed constitute the very substance of self-expres-
sion—what he has "all within," his own discursive property—at the
same time that such formulated phrases can never be fully appropriate
to individual desire ("my imagination was all rapture . . . ") which will
always want something else.[35] Extending the boundary of identity ("all
within") out to its descriptive limits, Equiano represents individuality
as delimited by the sheer force of accumulation—accumulated figures,

signs of possession—a movement outward that takes in and trades on other('s) desires (the hero, the mother . . .), an internalization of capitalist romance.

Such a scene of internalization aligns the model of identity exemplified at this crucial moment in Equiano's narrative to the romantic tradition as it is articulated in late eighteenth-century culture as a discourse of freedom and individual rights, for instance in the Ur-romanticism of William Godwin's political economy ("The rules by which my actions shall be directed are matters of a consideration entirely personal"), Mary Wollstonecraft's two vindications ("The only security of property that nature authorizes and reason sanctions is, the right a man has to enjoy the acquisitions which his talents and industry have acquired"), or William Blake's allegory of individual man recreating the nation ("I must Create a System or be enslaved by another Man's").[36] While Equiano shares with these writers notions of the foundational value of the personal, in *The Interesting Narrative*, the discourse of freedom does not simply function in opposition to the coercive rules or directives externally imposed, another man's system over against my own. Equiano's text also works within those structures or, more precisely, it shows how those structures work within. The "inhuman custom"[37] of slavery is clearly the explicit target of Equiano's political polemic, but the narrative simultaneously traces the way humans become accustomed to the terms and values of the dominant system and reproduce them ("mind-forg'd manacles")[38] in their own persons.[39]

For many readers, the central problematic of *The Interesting Narrative* involves exactly this "process of acculturation,"[40] Equiano's internalization of the dominant economy, "mental colonization."[41] But the trajectory that the narrative of Equiano's individual "talents and industry" accomplishes—from slave to master, African to Anglophile, margin to metropole—suggests not only that he adopts forms of culture—"fashions, manners, customs, &c." (II, 250)—that are not natural to him and that therefore go against the indigenous grain, but also that his progress toward freedom, even toward a more perfect grace, discloses the contradictions within the notion of the individual that can be subsumed into "the whole existing order" only through a transformative process of displacement. If one of Romanticism's defining characteristics is the will toward "self-possession,"[42] then, Equiano's narrative should remind us to consider such a desire neither as a universal value nor as the exclusive territory of a few (white, male) writers undertaking the elaboration and consolidation of a national tradition. Rather, such a model of mastery is deployed within the history of individualism, itself embedded in an economic system that operates at the level of cognition, not just commerce, to produce "relations, proportions, values," not just commodities. Historicized through Equiano's diasporic imagination, the romantic tradition can in this sense hardly be called "anti-capitalist,"[43] for all its theoretical disdain of "getting and spending."[44] It might instead be seen as complicitous in the development of capitalism even as its emancipatory rhetoric struggles toward reinvention.

NOTES

1. "Tradition and the Individual Talent," *Selected Prose of T. S. Eliot,* ed. Frank Kermode (New York: Harcourt Brace Jovanovich, 1975), 37–44; 38–39.

2. Homi K. Bhabha, *The Location of Culture* (London: Routledge, 1994), 2.

3. Kwame Anthony Appiah, "Out of Africa: Topologies of Nativism" in *The Bounds of Race: Perspectives on Hegemony and Resistance,* ed. Dominick LaCapra (Ithaca: Cornell University Press, 1991), 134–63.

4. Abiola Irele, "African Letters: The Making of a Tradition," *The Yale Journal of Criticism,* 5 (Fall 1991), 69–100; 74.

5. T. S. Eliot. "Tradition and the Individual Talent," 38.

6. Henry Louis Gates, Jr., "Introduction," *The Classic Slave Narratives,* ed. Henry Louis Gates (New York: New American Library, 1987), xii, xiv. Cf. Gates's discussion of *The Interesting Narrative* in *The Signifying Monkey: A Theory of African-American Literary Criticism* (New York: Oxford University Press, 1988), 152–58; and Angelo Constanzo, *Surprising Narrative: Olaudah Equiano and the Beginnings of Black Autobiography* (New York: Greenwood, 1987).

7. "Out Of Africa," 142.

8. "Tradition and the Individual Talent," 39. Here it should be clear that my use of T. S. Eliot does not simply ratify his position in "Tradition and the Individual Talent" or in literary history, so much as it invokes his terms to adapt them toward another purpose. Irele also employs Eliot's critical terminology (81), as do the authors of the nativist polemic Appiah cites in his essay (Chinweizu, Onwuchekwa Jemie, and Ihechukwu Madubuike, *Toward the Decolonization of African Literature* [Enugu, Nigeria, 1980], 106).

9. By Paul Edwards in his edition of 1968.

10. Fredric Jameson, "Third-World Literature in the Era of Multinational Capitalism," in *Social Text* 15 (Fall 1986), 65–88; 66.

11. Olaudah Equiano, *The Interesting Narrative of the Life of Olaudah Equiano, or Gustavus Vassa, the African,* 2 vols. (London, 1789; rpt. London: Dawsons of Pall Mall, 1969), II, 16–17. All references to the text will be to this facsimile edition except where noted. Percy Shelley, "Preface" to "The Revolt of Islam," *Shelley:Poetical Works,* ed. Thomas Hutchinson (Oxford: Oxford University Press, 1970).

12. Aijaz Ahmad, "Jameson's Rhetoric of Otherness and the 'National Allegory' " in *In Theory: Classes, Nations, Literature* (Verso, 1992), 122.

13. Victor C. D. Mtubani, "The Black Voice in Eighteenth-Century Britain: African Writers against Slavery and the Slave Trade" in *Pylon: The Atlanta University Review of Race and Culture,* 45 (June 1984), 85–97; 91.

14. On the contribution of Equiano and other African writers and activists to British abolition, see Wylie Sypher, *Guinea's Captive Kings: British Anti-*

Slavery Literature of the Eighteenth Century (Chapel Hill: University of North Carolina Press, 1942); Folarin O. Shyllon, *Black People in Britain 1553–1833* (London: Oxford University Press, 1977) and "Olaudah Equiano: Nigerian Abolitionist and First National Leader of Africans in Britain," in *Journal of African Studies* 4 (1977), 433–51; Peter Fryer, *Staying Power: The History of Black People in Britain* (London: Pluto Press, 1984); Paul Edwards, "Three West African Writers of the 1780s," in *The Slave's Narrative*, ed. Charles T. Davis and Henry Louis Gates, Jr. (Oxford: Oxford University Press, 1985), 175–98; Keith A. Sandiford, *Measuring the Moment: Strategies of Protest in Eighteenth-Century Afro-English Writing* (London and Toronto: Associated University Presses, 1988). On Equiano's reform activism and the making of the working class, see also Peter Linebaugh, *The London Hanged: Crime and Civil Society in the Eighteenth Century* (London: Penguin Press, 1991), esp. 415.

15. Jameson, "Third-World Literature," 72.

16. "The kind exertions of many benevolent and humane gentlemen against the iniquitous traffic of slavery and oppression, has been attended with much good to many. . . . However, notwithstanding all that has been done and written against it, that brutish barbarity, and unparalleled injustice, is still carried on to a very great extent in the colonies. . . . It is therefore manifest, that something else ought yet to be done." Ottobah Cugoano, *Thoughts and Sentiments on the Evil and Wicked Traffic of the Slavery and Commerce of the Human Species, Humbly Submitted to the Inhabitants of Great Britain* (London, 1787), 1–3.

17. See the imaginary conversation with an African in *An Essay on the Slavery and Commerce of the Human Species, Particularly the African* (Miami, Florida: Mnemosyne, 1969), 81–86. For early controversy about the issue of authenticity in Equiano's account of himself and his African homeland see *The Interesting Narrative*, appendix A: "To the Reader," and the letters on the *Oracle* article which appeared in the 5th edition of *The Interesting Narrative* in 1792. The controversy continues in S. E. Ogude, "Facts into Fiction: Equiano's Narrative Revisited," *Okike: An African Journal of New Writing*, 22 (Sept. 1982), 57–66.

18. *The Interesting Narrative* (Leeds: James Nichols, 1814) in *The Classic Slave Narratives*, ed. Henry Louis Gates, Jr. (New York: New American Library, 1987), 5.

19. *British Capitalism and Caribbean Slavery: The Legacy of Eric Williams*, ed. Barbara L. Solow and Stanley L. Engerman (Cambridge: Cambridge University Press, 1987), 18.

20. Seymour Drescher, "Paradigms Tossed: Capitalism and the Political Sources of Abolition," in *British Capitalism and Caribbean Slavery*, 191–208; 196. See C. L. R. James, *The Black Jacobins: Toussaint L'Ouverture and the San Domingo Revolution* (1938; rev. ed. New York: Vintage, 1963); Eric Williams, *Capitalism and Slavery* (Chapel Hill: University of North Carolina Press, 1944); Roger Anstey, *The Atlantic Slave Trade and British Abolition, 1760–1810* (Atlantic Highlands, N.J.: Humanities Press, 1975); Howard Temperley, "Anti-Slavery as a Form of Cultural Imperialism," in *Anti-Slavery, Religion, and Reform: Essays in Memory of Roger Anstey*, ed. Christine Bolt and Seymour Drescher (Folkestone, Eng. and Camden, Conn.: Archon, 1980), 335–50; David Brion Davis, *The Problem of Slavery in the Age of Revolution, 1770–1823* (Ithaca: Cornell University Press, 1975).

21. Thomas Bender, "Introduction," in *The Antislavery Debate: Capitalism and Abolitionism as a Problem in Historical Interpretation*, ed. Bender (Berkeley: University of California Press, 1992), 1–13; 2.

22. Jameson, "Third-World Literature," 69.

23. Drescher, "Paradigms Tossed," 194–95.

24. Seymour Drescher's recent work exemplifies the imbrication. Drescher argues against Davis's hegemony of "humanitarian ideals" (or bourgeois ideology) account and for the efficacy of popular, collective agitation. In "Paradigms Tossed," however, he details the way that agitation operates through the "everyday practices of commercial capitalism" (202) and thus through the private sphere, where Wedgewood's medallion and the popular print of a loaded slave ship would have been decoratively displayed, and where the boycott of West Indian sugar by women whose political agency was limited to the domestic realm of consumption would have been implemented. See also Davis's response to Drescher in "Capitalism, Abolitionism, and Hegemony" in Solow and Engerman, *British Capitalism and Caribbean Slavery*, 209–27. For a recent discussion of the role the conception of a privatized domestic virtue played in the politics of Britain's involvement with Carribbean slavery, see Charlotte Sussman, "Women and the Politics of Sugar, 1792," *Representations* 48 (Fall 1994), 48–69.

25. I draw here on the account of property and individualism in Elizabeth Fox-Genovese and Eugene D. Genovese, *Fruits of Merchant Capital: Slavery and Bourgeois Property in the Rise and Expansion of Capitalism* (New York: Oxford University Press, 1983), esp. 272–98; 298. My discussion is also generally indebted to Elizabeth Fox-Genovese's reminder in *Feminism without Illusions: A Critique of Individualism* (Chapel Hill: University of North Carolina Press, 1991), that individualism and its attendant discourse of rights is the product of a particular historical period—the age of democratic revolution; see esp. 113–38.

26. *The Black Jacobins*, 11.

27. See the specific histories of production and consumption detailed in Part II of *The Atlantic Slave Trade: Effects on Economies, Societies, and Peoples in Africa, the Americas, and Europe*, ed. Joseph E. Inikori and Stanley L. Engerman (Durham: Duke University Press, 1992).

28. On the concept of possessive individualism as a moral basis for capitalist ideology see C. B. Macpherson, *The Political Theory of Possessive Individualism: Hobbes to Locke* (Oxford: Oxford University Press, 1962); 3.

29. In *An Essay on the Slavery and Commerce of the Human Species*, for example, Clarkson distinguishes slavery as a punishment for crimes from slavery which involves the idea of ownership: "Thus then may that slavery, in which only the idea of *labour* is included, be perfectly equitable, and the delinquent will always receive his punishment as a *man*; whereas in that, which additionally includes the idea of *property*, and to undergo which, the delinquent must previously change his nature, and become a *brute*, there is an inconsistency, which no arguments can reconcile, and a contradiction to every principle of nature, which a man need only appeal to his own feelings immediately to evince" (Miami, Fla.: Mnemosyne, 1969, [76]).

30. For an attempt to "resolve the paradox" of how capitalism at once promoted the development of slave systems and yet introduced ideology

which challenged those systems, see Robin Blackburn, *The Overthrow of Colonial Slavery, 1776–1848* (London: Verso, 1988), which is concerned primarily to integrate movements of resistance and accommodation among the slaves in "the plantation zone" into the analysis of the metropolitan abolitionist movement. On slave resistance in the colonies, also see Michael Craton, *Testing the Chains: Resistance to Slavery in the British West Indies* (Ithaca: Cornell University Press, 1982).

31. See Homi K. Bhabha's characterization of the "Janus-faced discourse of the nation": "meanings may be partial because they are *in media res*; and history may be half-made because it is in the process of being made; and the image of cultural authority may be ambivalent because it is caught, uncertainly, in the act of 'composing' its powerful image." "Introduction," *Nation and Narration*, ed. Homi K. Bhabha (London: Routledge, 1990), 1–7; 3.

32. Houston A. Baker, *Blues, Ideology, and Afro-American Literature: A Vernacular Theory* (Chicago: University of Chicago Press, 1984), 33; 38–39.

33. "Word Between Worlds: The Economy of Equiano's *Narrative*," *American Literary History*, 5 (Fall 1993), 459–80; 471.

34. In her discussion of *The Interesting Narrative*, Susan M. Marren calls this identity "transgressive" and explains it as "a fluid positioning, a mode of articulation of newly imagined, radically nonbinary subjectivities" in "Between Slavery and Freedom: The Transgressive Self in Olaudah Equiano's Autobiography," *PMLA* 108 (Jan. 1993), 94–105; 95. Marren concludes that this transgressive self *transcends* the dynamic of alterity, whereas I suggest an *internalization* that highlights the limits of identity. See Geraldine Murphy's reading of Equiano's "dissident colonialism" as a stance that exposes "the positionality of European—and African—identity" in "Olaudah Equiano, Accidental Tourist," *Eighteenth-Century Studies*, 27 (Summer 1994), 551–68; 557.

35. His libido liberated with his manumission, Equiano remarks that "some of the sable females, who formerly stood aloof, now began to relax and appear less coy." But he directs his desire elsewhere: "my heart was still fixed on London" (II, 19).

36. William Godwin, *An Inquiry Concerning Political Justice, and Its Influence on General Virtue and Happiness* (London: William Pickering, 1993), 86; Mary Wollstonecraft, *A Vindication of the Rights of Men* (New York: New York University Press, 1989), 24; William Blake, "Jerusalem," I, plate 10 in *The Poetry and Prose of William Blake*, ed. David V. Erdman (Garden City, New York: Doubleday, 1970).

37. Mary Wollstonecraft, *A Vindication of the Rights of Men*, 14.

38. William Blake, "London," *The Poetry and Prose of William Blake*, 26.

39. Orlando Patterson's account of manumission as initiating a new obligation to the master in the form of gratitude can be considered also in terms of the ideology of individualism, which, functioning to internalize constraint, effects a shift from domination by physical force or material conditions (such as in slavery) to the embedded coercion of conscience and responsibility, what Equiano calls "the generous mind . . . struggling between inclination and duty" (II, 20). See *Slavery and Social Death: A Comparative Study* (Cambridge: Harvard University Press, 1982) and Susan M. Marren's application of Patterson's model to Equiano in "Between Slavery and Free-

dom: The Transgressive Self in Olaudah Equiano's Autobiography," esp. 96, 101.

40. William L. Andrews, "The First Fifty Years of the Slave Narrative, 1760–1810" in *The Art of the Slave Narrative: Original Essays in Criticism and Theory*, ed. John Sekora and Darwin T. Turner (Western Illinois University, 1982), 6–24; 20.

41. Chinsole, "Tryin' to Get Over: Narrative Posture in Equiano's Autobiography" in *The Art of the Slave Narrative*, 45–54; 50. Also see M. van Wyk Smith's argument that Equiano "deliberately exploit[s]" orthodoxy to articulate an "antidiscourse of black consciousness" in "Writing the African Diaspora in the Eighteenth Century," *Diaspora* 1:2 (Fall 1991), 127–42; 129; 139.

42. For an analysis of "self-possession" as "a crucial element of the larger ideology of romanticism itself," see Marlon B. Ross, *The Contours of Masculine Desire: Romanticism and the Rise of Women's Poetry* (New York: Oxford University Press, 1989), 10.

43. See Robert Sayre and Michael Lowy, "Figures of Romantic Anticapitalism," in *Spirits of Fire: English Romantic Writers and Contemporary Historical Methods*, ed. G. A. Russo & Daniel P. Watkins (Rutherford, N.J.: Fairleigh Dickinson University Press, 1990), 23–68.

44. William Wordsworth, "The world is too much with us," *Poetical Works*, ed. Ernest de Selincourt (Oxford: Clarendon Press, 1935).

CONTRIBUTORS

LAURA DOYLE is Assistant Professor of English at the University of Massachusetts, Amherst. She is the author of *Bordering on the Body: The Racial Matrix of Modern Fiction and Culture.* She is currently editing a volume entitled *Political Phenomenologies* and is writing a book on race and sentimental narrative.

MOIRA FERGUSON is the James E. Ryan Chair in English and Women's Literature at the University of Nebraska–Lincoln. Her recent publications include *Subject to Others: British Women Writers and Colonial Slavery 1678–1834, Colonial and Gender Relations from Mary Wollstonecraft to Jamaica Kincaid,* and *Jamaica Kincaid: Where the Land Meets the Body.*

NANCY MOORE GOSLEE is an Alumni Distinguished Service Professor of English and Chair of the Women's Studies Program at the University of Tennessee. She has published two books on Romantic Poetry: *Uriel's Eye: Miltonic Stationing and Statuary in Blake, Keats, and Shelley* and *Scott the Rhymer.* In addition to completing a facsimile edition of one of Shelley's notebooks, she is also completing a critical study of how Shelley drafts and revises figures of allegorical personification. Her essay on Hemans in this volume emerged from her teaching of Romantic women writers to sometimes skeptical, sometimes enthusiastic students.

ALISON HICKEY is Assistant Professor of English at Wellesley College. Her contribution to *Romanticism, Race, and Imperial Culture, 1780–1834* emerges from her manuscript on Wordsworth and figuration. She is now at work on a study of literary collaboration and English Romanticism.

SONIA HOFKOSH is Associate Professor at Tufts University where she teaches English and Women's Studies. Her book on Romantic authorship and the culture of difference is forthcoming from Cambridge University Press.

JOSEPH LEW is Associate Professor in the English Department at University of Hawaii at Manoa. He has recently published articles on several Romantic novelists and is currently working on a large study of British Orientalisms in the eighteenth century and the Romantic period.

DEIDRE LYNCH is Assistant Professor of English at the State University of New York at Buffalo. She is currently completing a manuscript on the British novel, the eighteenth-century consumer revolution, and the invention of psychological meaning, titled *Face Value: The Economy of Character.* Questions about genre, gender, and national literatures focus her recent projects, which include the anthology *Cultural Institutions of the Novel*, which she co-edited with William B. Warner, and an essay on Jane Austen and home.

SAREE MAKDISI is Assistant Professor of English at the University of Chicago. He is currently completing a book-length study of the emergence of modern imperial culture and representations of Nature and colonialism in the British Romantic period. In addition to his publications in the field of British literature, he is also working on a series of essays concerning contemporary Arab culture, some of which have appeared in the journals *Boundary 2* and *Critical Inquiry*.

ANNE K. MELLOR is Professor of English at the University of California, Los Angeles, and author of *Blake's Human Form Divine, English Romantic Irony, Mary Shelley: Her Life, Her Fiction, Her Monsters,* and *Romanticism and Gender*. She edited *Romanticism and Feminism* and, with Audrey Fisch and Esther Schor, *The Other Mary Shelley: Beyond Frankenstein*. She is currently completing, with Richard Matlak, a new historicist teaching anthology entitled *British Literature, 1780–1830,* and is beginning a series of essays on the intersections of gender with race and class in the Romantic period.

ASHTON NICHOLS is Associate Professor of English at Dickinson College. He is author of *The Poetics of Epiphany* as well as essays on Wordsworth, Walcott, Achebe, and African exploration narratives. He recently completed a volume entitled *The Revolutionary "I": Wordsworth and the Politics of Self Presentation*.

BALACHANDRA RAJAN is founder and editor of *Focus*, and author of numerous works, including *Paradise Lost and the Seventeenth Century Reader, W. B. Yeats: A Critical Introduction, The Lofty Rhyme: A Study of Milton's Major Poetry, The Overwhelming Question: A Study of the Poetry of T. S. Eliot,* and *The Form of the Unfinished: English Poetics from Spenser to Pound*.

ALAN RICHARDSON is Professor of English at Boston College. He is author of *Literature, Education, and Romanticism: Reading as Social Practice, 1780–1832* and of numerous essays on Romantic-era literature and culture, particularly in relation to gender, colonialism, and the social construction of childhood.

RAJANI SUDAN teaches in the English Department at the University of Texas at Arlington. She has published articles on Johnson and De Quincey, and in film, and is currently completing a book entitled *Fair Exotics: Xenophobia in the Age of Romanticism*.

INDEX